Property of

Dr. Ethel Closson Smith

not to removed from

Voice Studio

Training the Singing Voice

Da Capo Press Music Reprint Series

MUSIC EDITOR
BEA FRIEDLAND
Ph.D., City University of New York

Training the Singing Voice

AN ANALYSIS OF THE WORKING CONCEPTS
CONTAINED IN RECENT CONTRIBUTIONS
TO VOCAL PEDAGOGY

VICTOR ALEXANDER FIELDS

DA CAPO PRESS • NEW YORK • 1979

Library of Congress Cataloging in Publication Data

Fields, Victor Alexander, 1901-
    Training the singing voice.

    (Da Capo Press music reprint series)
    Reprint of the 1947 ed. published by King's Crown
Press, New York.
    Bibliography: p.
    Includes index.
    1. Singing–Instruction and study. I. Title.
MT820.F43   1979   784.9'32   79-9865
ISBN 0-306-79510-8

This Da Capo Press edition of *Training the Singing
Voice: An Analysis of the Working Concepts Contained
in Recent Contributions to Vocal Pedagogy* is an
unabridged republication of the first edition
published in New York and London in 1947 by King's
Crown Press, a subsidiary of Columbia University Press.

Published by Da Capo Press, Inc.
A Subsidiary of Plenum Publishing Corporation
227 West 17th Street, New York, N.Y. 10011

Training the Singing Voice

Training the Singing Voice

AN ANALYSIS OF THE WORKING CONCEPTS
CONTAINED IN RECENT CONTRIBUTIONS
TO VOCAL PEDAGOGY

VICTOR ALEXANDER FIELDS

KING'S CROWN PRESS
New York and London

King's Crown Press is a subsidiary imprint of Columbia University Press established for the purpose of making certain scholarly material available at minimum cost. Toward that end, the publishers have adopted every reasonable economy except such as would interfere with a legible format. The work is presented substantially as submitted by the author, without the usual editorial and typographical attention of Columbia University Press.

Printed in the United States of America

To MARY ELIZABETH,

whose faith has never faltered
and whose love
has never failed

ACKNOWLEDGMENT

I am indebted to many earnest advocates of the cause of vocal education; fine friends all, whose generous encouragement and advice were of inestimable value to me during the years of preparation for this study and while gathering the materials that were essential for its completion. I feel especially grateful for the steadfast guidance of Professors James L. Mursell, Helen Walker, Carter Alexander, Norval Church, and Harry R. Wilson, and for the loyalty and heartening friendship of Dr. James F. Bender. I trust this treatise will vindicate their faith.

CONTENTS

LIST OF TABLES

Training the Singing Voice

CHAPTER I

ORIENTATIONS FOR THIS STUDY

AIMS AND PURPOSES

There is certainly no lack of printed material on the subjects of singing and voice culture. But it is inaccessible to teachers because it is extremely diversified and fragmentary and rather diffusely distributed throughout a variety of books, periodicals, scientific papers, reports of experiments and published interviews that have never been correlated from the standpoint of a definite vocal pedagogy. Furthermore, what is written about the singing voice is so often overlaid and interwoven with conflicting theories and extravagent conjectures that misinterpretations are inevitable. Where there is abundant verbal testimony to support a given procedure there is not one shred of documentary or experimental evidence. Teachers of singing fall an easy prey to unscientific writings on voice for want of orientation in the foundational principles of their subject and much inherited misinformation is thus perpetuated. The resultant confusion has been costly to education. It has discouraged research workers from making much needed investigations in the field of vocal education. Obviously, the work of classifying the known theories and teaching concepts must precede any further research in this area if serious blundering and repetitious effort are to be avoided.

An analytical study and comparison of the many recent contributions to vocal pedagogy would facilitate the appraisal of teaching methods, old and new. Both pedagogy and research would be benefited by the juxtaposition and classification of the principal ideologies and methodologies pursued by the singing profession. The findings of such a study would provide the vocal scientist with a background of useful knowledge against which to formulate and test his own theories. The teacher would enjoy the counsel and caution of his contemporaries through an exchange of ideas gathered from a range of knowledge and experience wider than his own. Needless trial and error experience might thus be obviated and the teaching profession as a whole provided with a purposive viewpoint, definite objectives and a sounder educational procedure for future use. These aims are all encompassed in the three general purposes that motivate this study:

1. To survey and correlate available sources of bibliographic information on methods of training the singing voice.

2. To provide a core of organized information for the use of all teachers of singing.

3. To provide an orientation and background for research in this and related fields.

Teachers of singing will therefore find this study useful as an orientation in the hitherto tangled areas of vocal pedagogy and vocal science; as a means of comparing their own teaching methods with the prevalent methodologies in the profession; as a source of useful information on certain unfamiliar aspects of vocal theory and practice; as a direction finder in selecting suitable topics of research where investigations are now most needed; and as a stimulus and incentive for the freer expression and exchange of ideas along the lines suggested in this treatise. This study should also prove useful as a teacher-training text for newcomers in the vocal teaching profession.

Plan of Attack

To achieve the foregoing purposes, the initial procedure indicated is to extract from a widely scattered bibliography, all data concerning the fundamental concepts currently used in training the singing voice and to present an analysis and interpretation of these working concepts in unified form. But the charting of unexplored regions of vocal pedagogy calls for more than a survey of vocal literature. It will also be necessary to bring to light some of the primary principles and dominant schools of thought that govern the art of the singer; to dispel the mystery that enshrouds the teaching of singing; to simplify the vocal terminology; to bring a semblance of system and order into the verbal chaos that now envelops a profuse and complex vocal literature. A suitable bibliography would afford a much needed orientation in available sources of current bibliographic information on this subject. A working vocabulary of defined terms might be helpful in interpreting all these findings. Finally, a compilation of problems and controversial questions derived from this study would provide useful suggestions for research workers in this and related fields.

The process of gathering and refining all this information calls for detailed planning inasmuch as there is no work at present which describes in accurate scientific language, the present state of our knowledge concerning the training of the singing voice. A preliminary consideration of the causes of confusion in the vocal teaching profession and an appreciation of the purposes, procedures and values of this research might be helpful to an understanding of its findings. To this end, Chapter I presents an introductory discussion. Chapters II through X report the detailed findings of this study with interpretational summaries arranged in appropriate categories, and Chapter XI gives a final summation of outcomes.

Causes of Confusion in the Vocal Profession

The specific causes of confusion in the vocal teaching profession are many and varied. Even a cursory survey of literature on the subject reveals astonishing inconsistencies and conflicts of pedagogical opinion. From a general viewpoint, this diversity of opinion apparently arises from the fact that a multiplicity of specific teaching procedures is being developed by individual teachers without reference to the broader pedagogical principles underlying them. Most singing teachers readily admit that the field of vocal pedagogy stands badly in need of clarification; that sooner or later a pioneering effort must be launched that will help set up frontiers of rational thinking in this all too neglected educational area.

The following mass of critical comment, outlining twenty-one different categories of complaint voiced by authors, was compiled to illustrate some of the prevalent instabilities in the vocal teaching profession that led to the formulation of this study. All bibliographical citations are enclosed in brackets and are numbered so as to correspond to the numbered items in the complete annotated bibliography given at the end of this treatise.

INHERENT DIFFICULTIES IN THE SUBJECT

1. *Singing as an art suffers from its complexity.* Many sciences are involved, such as psychology, physiology, acoustics, etc. [Drew 147, p. 160; Pressman 452]

2. *The vocal function is not open to direct observation in life.* "Observations made by reflected light [laryngoscope] tell only part of the story." [Evetts and Worthington 167, p. 411] The singing teacher, unlike the instrumental teacher, deals with unseen things and is therefore given to speculation and charlatanry, which not only places his profession in ill-repute, but frequently ruins careers as well. [Witherspoon 677, p. 11] A singer cannot sing a normal tone with a laryngoscopic mirror in the back of his mouth. [Aikin 4] Cadaveric dissections do not function like living larynxes. [Curry 124, p. 50] Most pictures or charts of the throat

are deceiving in that they show the throat and vocal apparatus only in a state of relaxation. [La Forest 326, p. 97.]

3. *The subjective nature of singing makes accurate self-analysis difficult.* Aesthetic self-judgment, because of its psychological nature, varies with the individual. Applied to the singing performance, such judgments defy standardization and lead to considerable confusion in vocal training. [Newport 419; Wilcox 669, p. 1] "The mechanism involved is complex, variable and never under conscious control." [Bartholomew 37]

4. *The subjective nature of listening.* Vocal observations by a listener (teacher) are bound up in aesthetic, emotional and auditory reactions to sound. The average listener does not accurately hear what the singer actually performs. Hence, listening judgments of a singing performance are largely based on psychological, rather than physiological impressions of the tones heard. [Seashore 506, p. 7] "No two ears hear exactly the same." [Stanley 575]

5. *Individuality of voices.* No two voices are exactly alike, making standardization and comparisons difficult. [Votaw 625; Haywood 234]

6. *Confusing similarities exist between the singing voice and the speaking voice.* "Speech has singing aspects and song has speech characteristics." [De Bruyn 131] "Singing is really speaking set to music." [Skiles 563; Landt 332] "Singing may be considered a slow-moving picture of speaking." [Harper 228, p. 107] See also Chapter IX.

NEED FOR SCIENTIFIC ORGANIZATION OF THE SUBJECT

7. *Authentic bibliographies are lacking.* Many of the published works on voice contain vague or misleading material. [Kuester 324] The lack of bibliographical information about the voice is amazing. [Redfield 462, p. 264] "Many books on singing . . . pass on erroneous ideas as truth." The power of the printed page is thus exploited. [Witherspoon 677, p. 11] On the whole, books on vocal technique are unreliable since they abound in unscientific statements. [Stanley 578]

8. *Vocal literature is largely unscientific and fragmentary.* Biased opinions prevail throughout the literature on voice. "The criticism that music [voice] lags behind the other subjects of the curriculum in adapting the scientific method, is a just one." [Kittle 318] In the teaching of singing, "the word 'science' has been misapplied to theories and beliefs." [Shaw 518, p. 7] "One could easily build a comedy of errors by citations from standard music books." [Seashore, 507] There is at present no accurate, scientific, single work that reviews all our knowledge of the human voice. [Curry 124, Foreword]

9. *Vocal authorities disagree on many fundamental issues.* "Reputable

dissenters are sufficiently strong to leave the 'vocal science' of today in a most unscientific position." [Thompson 610] "The judgments of experts on points connected with vocal performance are most extraordinarily varied." [Mursell and Glenn 413, p. 278] Vocal authorities disagree on even "the most elementary and fundamental points." [Redfield 462, p. 280] There is a total lack of "doctrinal unity" and a lack of "uniform professional language" among vocal technicians. [Roach 472] Vocal literature "reveals a surprising lack of unanimity of opinion." [Henley 261]

10. *Basic teaching concepts are not clearly defined.* Teaching theories are largely empirical, vague and without scientific explanation. [James 300, p. 7] The cause of confusion in teaching singing is the lack of "a sound theoretical basis." [Kwartin 325, p. 15] Very few teachers agree on basic vocal principles. [Campajani 91]

11. *Conflicting and ambiguous terminologies exist.* More than anything else, misleading terminology has served to confuse the vocal teaching profession. [Shaw 518, p. 11] "There is a vast verbiage of synonyms for tone quality in vogue, none of them satisfactorily differentiated or defined." [Seashore 507] So-called differences of opinion are usually differences in terminology. [De Young 137; Hill 272, p. 53] "The terminology of the art is more than half figurative." [Henderson 243, p. 54] One group literally "does not speak the other's language." [Bartholomew 37] "One has but to look at the conglomeration of terminology. . . ." [Muyskens 415]

12. *Prevalent use of imagery in place of explicit instructions.* (E.g., "singing on the breath," "the voice always flows from diaphragm to head," "The voice is like a flower. Its roots are imbedded in the breathing organs, its stem is the flowing breath stream, its blossom is the resonance in the head cavities.") The Italians used "drink the tone" and "inhale the voice" as a means of freeing the throat. [Henley 256] In teaching voice, circumlocution is often necessary, even to the extent of using "what the scientist sometimes denounces as fantastic, false imagery." [Bartholomew 38] Imagery is very useful in vocal pedagogy. [Ortmann 437] The use of metaphorical terms by singing teachers often causes misunderstandings. [Scholes 496]

13. *Fancy holds sway over fact.* Nonsensical generalizations about unknown factors often take the place of reasoned investigations. Teachers are often guilty of arbitrary generalizations which attribute all good tone-production to the influence of the nose, diaphragm, uvula or other individual parts. [Drew 147, p. 113] "One could make a museum of freak ideas" pertaining to the teaching of voice. [Amelita Galli-Curci 197] The following mystifying statements are vague generalizations made by authors, pertaining to several unknown factors of voice production. To avoid offense, they are quoted here anonymously:

a) "Although the air is directed through the nose the tone is never in the nose, nor is it nasal. It is above the nose, coming through the nose."

b) "Walk about the room with arms upstretched to take the weight off the chest."

c) "Singing the tone softly with hand on head is sometimes useful to prevent the thin register from being forced upwards."

d) "We use 'squeals' first of all, to awaken the interosseus spaces."

e) "It is also necessary to imagine you are singing from above downward in order that you may be 'on top of the tone.'"

f) "'Pushing' may be avoided, if the chest is kept open to quiet the flow of air before it acts on the vibrator."

g) "To keep loose breath from entering the lungs, all muscles must be in a continual state of tonicity (elastic tension) and lungs must fill from the bottom up."

h) "He who breathes with the upper and forgets that he has a lower part to his trunk is sure to fail as a singer."

i) "The vowels must be started on the underlip and held in the space between the underlip and the teeth and never allowed to slip back behind the teeth into the buccal cavity."

j) "Be able to hold your structure—body, throat, and head—open thirty seconds at a time, releasing easily from the foundation upward, ten consecutive times."

k) "To sing well you must continually feel 'hollow-headed,' 'full-throated,' 'broad-chested' and 'tight-waisted.'"

l) "Before starting to phonate, inspire the breath, with the minimum possible tension, by expanding the lower ribs and diaphragm. Then, at the moment of attack, continue this 'out' (inspiratory) gesture and take the tension smoothly, without jerking. As the tone is established, hold this tension which must be 'timed' to occur at the moment of attack—not too soon and not too late. By attacking the tone on the inspiratory gesture, you have established the necessary inspiratory tension."

m) "In order to bring out the color of the tone, the whirling currents must vivify all the vocal sounds that enter into it and draw them into their circles with an ever-increasing, soaring tide of sound."

n) "Exalt the mighty diaphragm! It is the key to true vocal technique."

14. *Empirical knowledge predominates.* Effects are often treated as causes and reasoning starts from different fundamental assumptions re-

garding identical facts. [Shaw 543] The teacher's lack of information is usually camouflaged by high-sounding phrases that "almost never mean anything to the student." [Redfield 462, p. 265 and p. 280; Scott 501, Foreword] "The ground is overrun by empiric theories . . . tone is worshipped as a fetish and confusion of doctrine prevails." [Davies 127, p. 75]

NEED FOR SYSTEMATIC TEACHER TRAINING

15. *Many teachers of singing lack scientific or scholastic training.* There is a dearth of thoroughly trained teachers. [Fellows 176] Teachers who are content with empirical knowledge often object to the scientific reports of others when they receive them. [Smith 567] "Specialists [in voice] too often remain ignorant of relevant facts in closely related fields." [Bartholomew 37] Authors of so-called singing methods are woefully ignorant regarding modern acoustical research. [Drew 147, p. 134]

16. *Good singers often lack ability as teachers.* "Many who are themselves good singers . . . make poor teachers of singing." [Wodell 681] Even the distinguished artists often "do not know how to explain themselves lucidly." [Herbert-Caesari 268] Great artists are seldom great teachers because they seldom know why they sing perfectly and why certain vocal deviations are disastrous. [Dossert 140, p. 16] This is especially true of so-called "natural" singers. [Henley 261] The great singer, preeminent in his art, but woefully lacking in scientific background, often presumes to offer instructions in the most scientific aspects of vocal anatomy, physiology, psychology and physics. Would that he were better equipped to express himself in accurate scientific language. [Drew 147]

17. *Good teachers often lack ability as singers.* "Out of every hundred persons who teach singing today . . . [there are] two who really know how to sing." [Frances Alda 6, p. 294]

PROFESSIONAL INSTABILITY

18. *Lack of teaching standards.* Vocal teaching methods and procedures are often haphazard, perfunctory, unscientific and even cabalistic. "Such teaching is apt to spell the ruin of a good voice." [Capell 92] If there are nearly as many methods as teachers it is because there is hardly any agreement among singers or teachers as to a standard, trustworthy method of singing. [Samoiloff 484, p. 5] "Every teacher has his own method." [Dunkley 151, Preface] Conflicting methods and theories abound in the teaching of singing. [Hill 272, p. 53] Vocal teaching is less exact than any other branch of musical education. [Dossert 140, p. 11]

19. *Lack of regulation of teacher qualifications.* Charlatanry is quite

common among vocal teachers in this country. Anyone who wishes to, can begin to teach voice. [Frances Alda 5] "There are thousands of dishonest teachers . . . [who] know nothing of the fundamental principles of voice production." [Lombardi 356] "In no other profession does the crank and charlatan flourish more blatantly." [Allen 7, p. 21]

20. *Strong traditions prevail in the vocal teaching profession,* preventing the infusion of new ideas. The prevailing confusion in this subject is partly caused by the fact that vocal musicians are slow to accept scientific terminologies and points of view; so that well established facts of physics, physiology and psychology are practically inaccessible to them. [Seashore 511, p. 9] "Famous old traditions of the art of singing are . . . nothing more than guess-work made respectable by age." Most modern ideas on voice production have their origin in this doubtful source. [Zerffi 701] "Traditional lore rather than the basic principles of science" have guided the singing teacher for more than a century. [Wharton 655, p. 90] "A change of methods is not as necessary as a change of attitude or viewpoint." Some teachers still resist change and refuse to admit the possibility of improvement in methods that were acquired thirty or forty years ago. [Bartholomew 39]

21. *Hurried and careless teaching practices exist,* sometimes prompted by unethical and mercenary motives. [Frances Alda 5] "The stage and the concert platform are overloaded with singers who, in plain English, do not know how to sing." [Henderson 244] High pressure teaching is used to bring about short cuts. [Henley 252] "Avoid teachers who make extravagant promises and beguile by flattery . . . who claim the discovery of new and wonderful methods . . . who promise results in a short or specified time . . . who claim to teach the method of some well known artist with whom they never studied or only studied for a short period . . . who offer a few tricks as a 'cure-all' for all vocal ills . . . who teach voice by correspondence courses." [Quoted from a bulletin issued by the American Academy of Teachers of Singing. 13]

HISTORICAL ASPECTS

Modern scientific research is increasingly affecting educational procedures. Such subjects as mathematics, reading, geography and history, for example, are continually being sifted and analyzed for criteria by which teaching procedures in these subjects may be tested, standardized and improved. It is now generally agreed that the teaching of all art is based upon science. The sculptor must have a knowledge of anatomy, the painter must know color and light, the architect must know mathematics and physics. The art of the singer likewise depends upon a knowledge of certain fundamental principles whose formulation is the work of the vocal scientist.

Prior to 1800, the belief was widely held that there was no objective way of studying the voice, just as it was thought that the mind would not yield to investigation. Modern medical science was still in its infancy and psychological research had not yet begun as a science. [Hale 709, p. 12] Klingstedt writes that the teachers of the golden age of *bel canto* (ca. 1700-1775) taught a natural method of singing that was based on the strict obedience of the singer's voice to a well-trained ear. [320, p. 4] There was little or no technical or scientific knowledge of the vocal organs at that time and most of the teaching was done by precept and example. [Herbert-Caesari 269, p. 1] According to Lang, the bel cantists were able to achieve a "sovereign command over the human voice . . . Their incomparable vocal art—never even remotely reached in modern times—was employed for high artistic aims." [333, p. 448 ff.] Manuel Garcia (1805-1906) came to be regarded as the father of vocal science. Prior to his invention of the laryngoscope in 1855 all so-called scientific observations were largely conjectural since there was no satisfactory method of observing the vocal cords in action. [Thompson 610]

What was then known about the singing voice is in no way comparable to what is now known. Since the turn of the twentieth century, hundreds of writers have attempted to bombard the unknown areas of this subject with rational methods of inquiry and discussion in an effort to overcome the ignorance and confusion that still prevail in an art that is as old as mankind. A survey and analysis of the numerous recent contributions to vocal pedagogy may well be considered prerequisite to further research or study in this field.

THE PROBLEM AREA DEFINED

Because of its considerable scope, the problem underlying this study was narrowed down to workable proportions by eliminating thirty adjacent vocal areas, and by including only those publications that are written in the English language. The adjacent areas not included in this study are:

1. song literature
2. technical vocal exercises and drills
3. song programs and repertoire building
4. general musicianship for singers
5. music theory for singers

6. children's singing voice
7. adolescent or changing voice
8. community singing
9. speaking voice and phonetics
10. vocal anatomy and physiology (medical)

11. vocal pathology (medical)
12. history of singing and voice culture
13. physical health and hygiene of the vocal organs
14. phonographic recordings of singers
15. singing for the radio and crooning

16. singing as a professional career
17. operatic singing and grand opera
18. biographies of famous singers
19. technical training of singing teachers
20. teaching singing in the elementary schools

21. vocal satire, humor and fiction
22. preparing for auditions
23. how to choose a vocal teacher
24. the study of foreign languages for singing
25. qualifications of singing teachers

26. recreational and school assembly singing
27. news items on voice and singing
28. vocal acoustics
29. group training of the singing voice
30. song writing

For purposes of this study, a fifteen year bibliographical period was chosen as representing the period of recency immediately preceding the commencement of this study.

Nine main areas of investigation were set up and defined as follows:

    I. Pedagogy—general and specific information concerning the teaching of singing and voice culture.

   II. Breathing—the activation and control of the respiratory organs in singing.

  III. Phonation—the inception of vibratory activity in the glottis to produce voice.

  IV. Resonance—an accessory vibratory factor that operates to amplify and enrich the voice.

V. Range—extent of the musical scale covered between the lowest and highest pitches of the voice.

VI. Dynamics—the variation and control of loudness and carrying power of tone.

VII. Ear training—developing hearing acuity for vocal sounds.

VIII. Diction—enunciation and verbal intelligibility in vocal expression.

IX. Interpretation—the communication of mood and thought values in singing.

The first of these nine divisions provides a general approach to the subject, the other eight may be considered components of the act of singing. Together they constitute an organic configuration that encompasses all the primary pedagogical aspects of the singer's art.

Concerning the definition of the term *concept*, William James has this to say: "The function by which we identify a numerically distinct and permanent subject of discourse is called conception; and the thoughts which are its vehicles are called concepts." [711, p. 461] This definition of *concept* is employed in this study.

Finally, the pedagogical procedures discussed throughout this study are primarily intended for the basic training of the post-adolescent singing voice, although a wider application is possible.

RATIONALE OF PROCEDURES USED

This research calls for a study of ideas or concepts rather than authors. The sources of information, ostensibly representing bona fide publications of carefully edited subject matter, play an impersonal and subordinate role in the findings. Publishing a book is not a haphazard or careless procedure but an act of deliberate planning, often requiring months of preparation. Likewise, an article appearing in a periodical or scientific journal is the result of a critical selection and evaluation of subject matter. In either case, the final copy appearing in published form usually represents a carefully prepared and edited statement by the author. It is presumed, therefore, that a printed article or text on any subject is information consciously transmitted by the author for a specific purpose and that the information contained therein represents his carefully reasoned judgments on the subjects discussed.

It may be questionable whether most of the texts and articles on the singing voice bespeak the viewpoint of the vocal specialist whose knowledge and experience in handling beginners is beyond challenge, but no attempt will be made to validate either the opinions expressed or the methodologies proposed. The very absence of documentary proof or experimental evidence might provide an incentive to further research in this subject, if the need were clearly enough indicated by the evidence at hand. To this end, the correlations of concepts in each area of this study are based on their relevancy to certain categories of basic information on the training of the singing voice rather than on the integrity of their authors' thinking processes or the reputations the authors hold, as individuals, for successful teaching. An obscure practitioner may make suggestions that are as valuable to the teaching profession as the individual contributions of some of the most distinguished professional singers, especially if the latter lack the education, scientific training or teaching insights and abilities that are required for pedagogical research. In the exploration of subject matter, as patterns emerge that turn up new problems, questions may sometimes be asked rather than answered. Such questions will be listed among the outcomes of this study.

THE BIBLIOGRAPHIC CARD

The bibliographic card becomes an important tool in this type of research since, like the questionnaire, it is an instrument of inquiry used for gathering and recording needed information. By documentary perusal, rather than by personal contact, the "interviewer" receives and records his data on the bibliographic card. In this study, the following three types of information will be needed: a) bibliographic information or publication data; b) subject notes or excerpts from the works read; and c) method notes, including comments, annotations and other interpretative data. Essential information taken out of literature from widely scattered sources will be brought together by this means, assessed and classified, and made available to the teaching profession.

To meet these requirements, a card was devised that provided a method of recording fourteen different types of information, as follows:

Information on front of card:

1. number of card
2. general area of application of subject note
3. library building where book or document is located
4. call number of book or document
5. name of author, title of work, other publication data
6. author's credentials
7. comment, footnote or documentary reference pertaining to subject note

8. annotation (critical, historical or descriptive appraisal of entire book or document)

9. terminology in subject note that needs definition

Information on back of card:

10. a series of 14 lettered (A to N) and 38 numbered (1 to 38) squares printed on the margin of each card to be used for checking the category in which each subject note belongs

11. the subject note or excerpt copied from the work read (in literal or condensed form)

12. a space for reduction of the subject note to a basic idea or concept (when necessary)

13. the page number of the subject note

14. a bottom margin for inserting a line marker bracket that indicates the original location of the copied excerpt on the printed page

Only statements of a pedagogical nature will be culled out of the literature on *singing* and *voice culture*. These will be recorded, one on each card. The cards will then be sorted out and classified according to content and derivation of materials. By checking a combination of the 14 lettered and 38 numbered marginal squares provided on each card it will be possible to identify and classify a maximum of 14 main content groupings and 14 x 38 or 532 subordinate categories of subject notes, should the need arise. It will also be possible to determine which were documented statements and which were statements made by professional singers; and to identify and classify various other types of subject notes, such as historical information, background data, scientific experiments, notes on the causes of confusion in vocal teaching, etc.

The homogeneity of concepts in each category will be indicated by their frequency of recurrence within the orders of classification used. These frequencies will be numerically summarized in *Tables One* through *Ten*.

Controversial questions will be italicized in each of these tables and summarized in *Table Eleven*.

Each category of concepts will be separately reviewed and discussed in its appropriate chapter. The sequence to be followed in these discussions will correspond to the plan that appears in each of the summarizing outlines (Tables I-IX) at the beginning of each chapter.

The study will be implemented throughout with working definitions of vocal and nonvocal terms. The first use of each defined term will be italicized. These definitions will be provided to facilitate comprehension of the text. Definitions derived from Webster's *New International Dictionary* will be indicated by a (W).

Bibliographical references will be indicated throughout the text within brackets, by giving the author's name followed by the number of the item as it is listed in the final bibliography.

The bibliography will be annotated to facilitate the future selection of books and articles by those who might wish to re-explore some of the areas described therein.

THEORETICAL AND INTERPRETATIONAL ASPECTS

A separate division of each chapter will discuss the most significant theories expressed in the writings and findings of experimenters, vocal scientists and teachers of singing. A theory can be likened to a scaffolding on an incomplete building whereby workmen are being supported while they continue to build greater and more permanent structures. So it is in this subject. The theoretical nature of some of the information available on the singing voice does not preclude the derivation therefrom of certain guiding principles with which to conduct more reliable investigations.

It is conceded that the opinions of recognized authorities in a given field carry considerable weight. However, since even authorities are known to disagree on many aspects of vocal training it is often necessary to arrive at basic principles according to the opinion of the majority. Such formulations will serve to supplement whatever objective evidence is presented and may provide important clues to the discovery of new areas of research.

A *summary and interpretation* section at the end of each chapter will include condensations and summaries of authors' opinions and a discussion of dominant schools of thought. The primary purpose of the interpretative discussions will be to provide a logical continuity of thinking for the teacher, with reference to an organismic or whole concept of singing. Through this synthesis of conceptuality, many ideational fragments will be welded together within a suitable frame of reference. Specialization in the study of the human body necessarily tends to divert attention from the whole organism to the activity of its separate parts. In vocal work, the danger of specialization lies in over-stressing technical analysis, rather than coordination. [Witherspoon 677, p. 1.] Therefore, the point of view to be presented in the interpretation of each chapter is that wholes take precedence over parts in training the vocal mechanism, and that the application of the specific teaching procedures recommended must not do violence to the broader pedagogical principles underlying them.

In conclusion, it is pointed out that scientific discoveries about the singing voice may not seem important to the teaching profession until they are given a pedagogical interpretation. The laboratory research worker is often far removed in his thinking from the teaching practices of the class room or studio. Conversely, the singing teacher often must handle unpredictable personality problems with intuitive insight and improvised instructional techniques that are not readily amenable to experimental analysis. [Muyskens 415] The interpretational treatment of this study will attempt to harmonize these two unfriendly but not irreconcilable points of view; that of the teacher and that of the vocal scientist.

CHAPTER II

CONCEPTS OF VOCAL PEDAGOGY

Definition: In a general sense, *pedagogy* refers to the principles and methods employed in practicing the art or profession of teaching. Specifically it is a system of imparting knowledge by formulating, regulating and applying the principles and rules that pertain to the acquisition of a particular type of knowledge or skill. Since the subject herein treated is the training of the singing voice, the term *vocal pedagogy*, as used in this treatise, may be interpreted to mean: the aggregate of principles, rules and procedures pertaining to the development, exercise and practice of the art of singing; and the process of training, by a prescribed course of study or technical discipline, the individual's innate capacity for vocal utterance in song. These general concepts are derived from definitions in *The Dictionary of Education* [706] and Webster's *New International Dictionary* (second edition). Other definitions pertaining to concepts of vocal pedagogy are provided, when needed, throughout this text. *Table One*, at the beginning of this chapter, presents a tabulation of all the concepts reviewed herein, as well as the outline or working plan followed in the chapter.

THEORIES OF VOCAL PEDAGOGY

INTRODUCTORY CONCEPTS

The singing voice. The word *voice* (from *vocare*: to call) has several different meanings in its applications to the pedagogy of singing. The most common one is given by Webster: *voice* is sound uttered by the mouth of human beings "in speech or song, crying, shouting, etc." Since the term has many facets, each presenting either functional or theoretical aspects of a parent concept, multiple definitions are necessary. The following are typical:

1. *voice as sound:* the *singing voice* is the tonal output of the singer;

the final acoustical or audible effect of the vibratory action of the larynx, enhanced by resonance, pitch, dynamics, rhythmic and other aesthetic effects. [Mackenzie 364, p. 25]

2. *voice as an acoustical instrument:* the human *voice* is a device for producing successive pulsations in the atmosphere. [Redfield 462, p. 267]

3. *voice related to breath:* "*voice* is vocalized breath. When the breath is exhausted, the tone ceases." [Clippinger 104, p. 5]

4. *voice as resonance:* "*voice* is resonance and nothing more." [La Forge 328]

5. *voice as purposive communication:* voice may be defined as acquired utterance for purposes of communication relative to the practical and aesthetic exigencies of life. [Garnetti-Forbes 198, p. 105; Negus 418, p. 288]

6. *voice in relation to nervous energy:* "*voice* is an electro-magnetic force dependent upon the sympathetic nervous system." [Gescheidt 200, p. 7] "the localization of motor functions of *voice* in given cortical areas can be deduced from the pathological state of these areas." [Curry 124, p. 159]

7. *voice related to singing:* "singing is the interpretation of text by means of musical tones produced by the human *voice*." [Henderson 243, p. 3; also Hall and Brown 227, p. 15]

Drew calls attention to the fact that *voice* has at least two distinct meanings for the singing teacher; one for the mechanism and the other for its tonal product. Each individual has one voice only in the former sense, but several voices in the latter. "This difference introduces factors that make arguments about the voice by analogy with other instruments particularly dangerous." [147, p. 163; 148] *Voice* also has other implicit musical, psychological, phonetic and physiological connotations that are used to define, crystalize or enrich some of the vagrant concepts associated with the pedagogy of singing. These are discussed under various headings throughout this treatise. (e.g., *phonation, diction, interpretation,* etc.) Inasmuch as *voice* and *singing* are often used synonymously by authors and teachers (e.g., "singing [voice] is the transmutation of energy into tone" [Jones 307, p. 11]) the term *singing voice* is usually employed throughout this study as a preferable designation for that type of vocal activity that enters exclusively into the teaching of singing.

The concepts of singing commonly employed by vocal teachers are represented in the following typical definitions: *singing* is the utterance

TABLE ONE

SUMMARY OF CONCEPTS OF VOCAL PEDAGOGY USED IN TRAINING THE SINGING VOICE

	total number of statements	sub-total	grand total	statements by prof. singers	documented statements	undocumented statements
I. *Theories of vocal pedagogy*			145			
A. Introductory concepts	34	34		1		34
B. Preliminary considerations		43				
1. benefits of vocal study	10			1		10
2. prerequisites of vocal study	20			4		20
3. the vocal training period	13			3		13
C. Objectives of vocal training	23	23		2		23
D. Coordination as a physiological factor	14	14			5	9
E. Standardization of vocal training		31				
1. *vocal training can be standardized*	13			1	1	12
2. *vocal training cannot be standardized*	18			8		18
II. *Methods of vocal pedagogy*			545			
A. Psychological approach		374				
1. importance of the psychological approach	63			5	5	58
2. voice training as habit formation	14			2		14
3. singing as a natural function						
a) the vocal act is unconscious and involuntary	58			2	6	52
b) spontaneity and naturalness are characteristics	19			5		19
4. freeing the vocal mechanism						
a) relaxation a factor in vocal training	43			4	6	37
b) economy of effort principle	51			7	2	49
c) overcoming inhibitions and fears	21				1	20

TABLE ONE (continued)

	total number of statements	sub-total	grand total	statements by prof. singers	documented statements	undocumented statements
5. expressional factors in singing						
a) singing as a form of self expression	36			5	1	35
b) singing as joyous release	16				1	15
c) singing as compared to speaking	53			2	9	44
B. Technical approach		171				
1. technical principles and objectives	19			3		19
2. removing muscular interferences	23			2	4	19
3. handling beginners						
a) classifying voices	30			6	2	28
b) first lessons	15			1		15
4. the song approach						
a) *songs are useful as technical exercises*	24			2		24
b) *songs are not useful as technical exercises*	10			2		10
5. principles and procedures used in practicing						
a) principles of vocal practice	10			1		10
b) supervision of practice	9					9
c) silent practicing as a device	5					5
d) piano accompaniments	8			1	1	7
e) various factors in practicing	18			3	4	14
TOTALS	690	690	690	73	48	642

of sounds "with musical inflections or melodious modulations of voice, according to fancy or the notes of a song or tune" (W); "singing is the musical expression of the voice" [Grove's *Dictionary of Music* 708]; "*singing* is the message that is sent by sound [voice] as emotion and thought qualify and impart [musical] pitch and word forms to it" [Savage 490, p. 85]; *singing* is a musical-vocal interpretation of a text. [Henderson op. cit.]

Training the singing voice. Training the singing voice may be defined as a process of administering systematic instruction and exercise to the individual student for the purpose of developing those mental and physical abilities that enter into the artistic performance of vocal expression in song. (W) The course of vocal training designed and administered by the teacher of singing has a usual five-fold purpose:

   a) to develop the mental faculties that control singing;

   b) to accustom the vocal organs to regular, systematic and sustained action in singing;

   c) to bring under control all the musical-vocal resources of the student;

   d) to regulate, train and improve the student's vocal expression and interpretative singing abilities, by means of corrective methods of exercise and study;

   e) to impart knowledge of and expertness in the execution or performance of vocal music.

The singer's vocal apparatus is unique in that it is the only musical instrument that is complete in itself, being player and instrument combined. [Hill 272, p. 14] Therefore, the singer must regard himself as both performer and instrument [Dunkley 151, p. 4] but, unlike an instrumentalist, he develops his own performing device while he is learning to master it. [Samoiloff 484, p. 14] This development calls for training under expert guidance, a process otherwise known as *voice placement* or *voice culture*. [Lombardi 355]

According to Samoiloff, the foundation of all good singing is correct placement of the voice, a product of perfect mental and physical coordination, the source of all purity, brilliance and beauty of tone. [484, p. 16] The terms *voice placement* and *voice culture* are variously defined as follows:

   1. *Placing* the voice means "unerring tuning" or learning to sound each tone in the vocal range so that it corresponds exactly with the pitch sounded on a reliably tuned instrument. [Henley 264]

2. *Placing* is the directing of each vocal sound so that it can be properly reinforced. [Hill 272, p. 27]

3. *Voice finding* is a more appropriate term than *voice placing*. The three factors involved are: tone production, word formation and dynamics or projection. [Brown 78, p. 74; 68]

4. The voice is not *placed*. What really happens is that tones are placed with maximum quality, resonance and ease of production, regardless of range. [Martinelli 373]

5. The voice is properly *placed* only when the "proper shaping of the upper air passages becomes quite automatic." [Redfield 462, p. 268]

6. The foundation of all *voice culture* is "the proper functioning of the vocal instrument as an organ of the body." [New York Voice Educators Committee 423; Marafioti 368, p. 16]

7. *Voice culture* means "correct manipulation of the vocal muscular system." [Ruff. 476]

In conclusion, vocal pedagogy as a science subsumes many theoretical and methodological aspects of all the intricate acoustical, physiological, psychological and technical details of a teacher's system of training the singing voice. [Herbert-Caesari 269, p. xi] These introductory comments, and those which follow in this chapter, represent the substance of 690 concepts of vocal pedagogy, gathered from 702 books and articles on the singing voice. These concepts are all categorically summarized in *Table One*.

PRELIMINARY CONSIDERATIONS

Benefits of vocal study. In a pamphlet issued in 1933, the American Academy of Teachers of Singing lists the following twelve reasons for studying singing nonprofessionally:

1. *Singing is healthful.* It promotes deep breathing and therefore develops the lungs and purifies the blood.

2. *Singing promotes good posture* and graceful carriage of the body.

3. *Singing lends expressiveness* to the countenance and animation to the mind.

4. *Singing increases poise* and self-confidence and develops character through difficulties overcome.

5. *Singing improves the speaking personality.* It enriches the speaking voice and improves diction.

6. *Singing strengthens memory* and the power of concentration.

7. *Singing improves the interpretative sense* by stimulating a deeper understanding of poetry and prose texts.

8. *Singing develops appreciation* of the art of great singers.

9. *Singing promotes interest in music* generally and especially in the literature of song.

10. *Singing is uplifting* to the individual through the absorbing pursuit of an ideal.

11. *Singing provides emotional catharsis* and is an important medium of self expression to the individual.

12. *Singing is self satisfying* as a means of entertainment.

These are typical evaluations endorsed by the teaching profession. [11] The health factor is especially stressed. "Singing is . . . energetic exercise," says Scott. "Limp, listless people cannot sing." [501, p. 41; also MacCrate 362] Doubleday reports that only 3 out of 3000 members of choirs and singing societies in London, England became ill with influenza during a great epidemic of that disease. [141] Sir Morell MacKenzie, a prominent British physician and voice specialist makes a similar observation regarding the health-promoting value of singing. "The rare occurrence of pulmonary disease among singers is well known," he says. [364, p. 133] Podolsky, another physician, declares that, even when illness is prevalent, singing is one of the best of health-promoting hobbies. [449]

Barnard writes, in the Idaho Journal of Education, that singing is the "natural basis for complete musical education." [35] It also develops poise, improves health and removes inhibitions. [16] Edward Johnson, of the Metropolitan Opera Company, advocates "voice study for everybody." In his opinion, it has great monetary value if followed professionally but, for even the average individual, it promotes happiness, is a mark of culture and refinement and, above all, it develops courage and stamina. [305]

PREREQUISITES OF VOCAL STUDY

Can everyone sing? Shaw maintains that the ability to sing is latent within each individual. "The physiological functioning of the vocal organ is practically the same in song and speech." Hence, anyone who can speak can also learn to sing. [533] "The voice is a birthday present when a child enters the world." It merely requires development. [Votaw 625] "If you are a normal, healthy person with a speaking voice, you also have a singing voice," says La Forge. [329] In this opinion he is supported by Novello-Davies [430, p. 24] and Zerffi. The latter adds, however, that the ability to carry a tune is a prerequisite to vocal study. "This does not mean that everyone can become a prominent singer. There are wide differences in voice boxes." [699] Mowe maintains that the old misconception that a good singing voice is limited to a very few who possess special endowments should be corrected by promulgating an "everybody can sing" policy in the vocal teaching profession. "Good singing depends on the proper *use* of the voice rather than on some 'extra part' in the throat of the singer that the non-singer does not possess." [406; 403] Therefore, he adds, "we know and can say with authority that any normal person can develop a good [singing] voice." [404] The New York Singing Teachers Association also endorses this viewpoint. [422]

Kirsten Flagstad insists that "voice alone has never made an artist." There must also be "a musical character" behind the voice, vitality, self-discipline, quick thinking and "a complete independence of spirit." [182] "Talent is not enough," says Nelson Eddy, in an interview. One must also possess a tremendous love of music, irresistible drive to succeed, an aesthetic sense, business sense and common sense. [155] Good health, a passion for singing, and a musical ear must be added to good voice as "absolute requisites for vocal success," according to Lombardi. [354] Finally, Miller presents as his twelve "foundation stones of good singing": 1) intelligence; 2) concentration; 3) ambition; 4) sense of joy and buoyancy of spirit; 5) ability to relax mentally and physically (freedom from ·inhibitions); 6) general musicianship, including innate sense of rhythm; 7) fine memory; 8) personality and showmanship; 9) capacity for learning music and languages; 10) interpretational skill; 11) sensitive ear for music; 12) strong and healthy vocal apparatus. [399]

THE VOCAL TRAINING PERIOD

When to begin vocal study. The opinions of three professional singers agree that a vocal career, especially for girls, should not be started too early in life; not until the vocal apparatus has matured; perhaps not before the age of sixteen or seventeen. They advise using the early years for musical and general education and culture because such a background will immeasurably facilitate the vocal training program when it is started later. [Frances Alda 5; Gladys Swarthout 600; Lily Pons 451] Allen believes that the male voice generally is not ready for solo singing until the age of nineteen is reached. [7, p. 13] Ruff chooses sixteen as the age for girls' voices and eighteen for boys' voices. [476] Woods would begin voice culture in high school. [687] Mursell and Glenn believe that singing "must nearly always be the core of the school music work" at all age levels. It is therefore presumed that teaching singing (and its correlative voice training) would begin in early childhood at the elementary school age. [413, p. 278] Novello-Davies would have voice culture taught "as soon as one commences to think." [430, p. 31]

How long to study? Opinions vary as to the length of time it takes to train the singing voice. La Forest believes that building a voice is largely a matter of muscle training. Therefore voice building should not take any longer than any other type of muscle training program. [326, p. 134] Shaw claims that some type of persistent and continuous vocal training is always necessary, even in the case of the "natural singer." [537] "To sing well . . . requires a great deal more than mere voice," says Chaliapin. [95] "Innate talent" is called for, rather than "natural vocal equipment." [Stanley. 573; 578] In short, singing requires years of hard work and patient study. Obviously, there is no short cut, even "when nature is lavish with her gifts." [Allen 7, p. 10]

"Do you know why singing is a lost art?" asks Bergére. It is because, nowadays, voice students refuse to study long enough. Hurry and impatience are the besetting sins of the vocal teaching profession. [45] Samoiloff also blames "the commercial attitude" and the lack of patience of so many pupils for the dearth of good singers today. [483] Byers believes that it takes at least three years to train a voice properly, the criterion of accomplishment being a so-called "artistic level" of performance. (See Chapter X.) [89] Henley would stretch the period of vocal training to five years. [252] He adds that the old Italian masters could impart their entire singing method in a half hour of instruction, but it might take a pupil five or six years to learn to apply it properly. [253] Lauritz Melchior advises staying with one teacher as long as possible since much time is wasted in the voice building program by having each new teacher "begin by tearing down some of the structure you already have built." [388]

GENERAL OBJECTIVES IN TRAINING THE SINGING VOICE

Educational *objectives* are the purposes, standards or goals to be realized through the application of systematic teaching procedures. *General objectives* are the desired ultimate results of a system of training, as broadly viewed. *Specific objectives* are the results to be expected from the various techniques and intermediate processes of instruction employed to achieve a general objective. [Dictionary of Education 706] The opinions of 23 authors are summarized in this area.

Frances Alda holds that the teacher must not only train the voice of the singer but he must also teach the singer how to preserve his voice for years to come. This is stated as one of the main objectives of vocal teaching. [6, p. 296] The muscular mechanism must be coordinated and strengthened, throughout its range, to sustain the full power of the voice and to render the vocal instrument "automatically responsive to the will of the singer." [Wilcox 668; also Lewis 343, p. 2] According to Haywood, singing instruction must rest on a triple foundation which includes technical voice development, the cultivation of style and skill in interpretation. [234] Wodell maintains that the first duty of the singing teacher is "to conserve the natural beauty of the young voice." [679] Other general objectives mentioned by authors include the following:

1. The appreciation of a tonal ideal through ear training. [Hall and Brown 227, p. 5]

2. Achieving a state of conscious, comfortable physical reaction to tone production. [Ibid.]

3. The complete subordination of technique to artistic expression in song. [Ibid.]

4. Developing "a musical mentality." [Mursell 411, p. 225; Clippinger 114; 104, p. 1]

5. Developing "automatic control of the vocal instrument." [Wharton 655, p. 59]

6. Building a song repertoire. [Henley 263]

7. Discovering the "natural voice through speech"; learning "to hold it in its natural position through breath control." [Stella Roman 475]

According to Fory, simplicity is the keynote of all vocal teaching. The early masters developed "a free vocal apparatus . . . , a good ear and artistic discretion." These lead to vocal success. [190] Austin-Ball claims that the main objectives of vocal training are "to develop in the mind of the student the right idea or concept of a beautiful tone" and also to cultivate, through exercise, optimum conditions in the instrument "through which the idea must be expressed." The old Italian method fostered this ideal. [31, p. 66] Barbareux-Parry believes that the achievement of all vocal teaching objectives are encompassed in a two-fold approach: a) the psychological approach, which deals with the mentality of the singer, his musicianship and artistic imagination; b) the technical approach, which deals with the physical preparation and "tuning" of the vocal instrument.

In short, vocal training simultaneously develops the vocal instrument and the artist who will play upon it. [34, p. 76] Waller sums up the process and purpose of voice building in three steps: "You liberate the voice; you strengthen it; you beautify it. Each one of these processes helps the other two." [630] Finally, Stanley stresses the importance of developing the musical and artistic abilities of the singer. Sometimes singers are successful in spite of poor vocal equipment, because they possess exceptional musical, dramatic and artistic abilities. He adds, however, that the importance of the voice itself is not to be ignored. "Such singers would have attained greater success with better vocal equipment." [577, p. 364] Herbert-Caesari claims that a good teaching method is one that develops a uniformly good quality throughout the vocal range, preserves the health of the vocal mechanism and develops the expression of the whole personality in song. [269, p. 175] Wilcox lists correct posture, deep breathing, flexible tongue and jaw, purity of vowels, and "an emotional attitude of buoyancy and interest" as multiple objectives in voice teaching. [666] According to the New York Singing Teachers Association, the main purposes of training the singing voice are to develop "quality, range, power, agility and flexibility" in the coordination and control of all those vocal elements that enter into the art of singing. (e.g., breathing, tone production, diction and interpretation) [421, p. 35]

COORDINATION AS A PRIMARY PHYSIOLOGICAL FACTOR

Physiology is the study of the animate functions of the organs and parts of the human body. (W) Since voice is a product of the functioning of the vocal tract, the science of voice training may be considered a specialized outgrowth of its parent science, physiology. [Aikin 4; Passe 443, p. 45] It is not unusual to find, therefore, that discussions of vocal pedagogy are often related to concepts of vocal physiology. It is the concensus of 14 statements that intelligent voice teaching should be based upon a sound knowledge and understanding of vocal physiology. Owsley would have the vocalist make a careful study of such branches of physiology as the skeletal, muscular, nervous, circulatory and respiratory systems of the body. [441, p. 10] Muyskens outlines a physiological approach to voice culture through a system that first trains the larger postural and respiratory muscles of the body and then gradually trains the smaller "valving" muscles in the larynx, throat and mouth. [415] Shaw finds that to teach an understanding of the general nature of the vocal mechanism will help "to establish confidence in the mind of the singer."[537]

In studying the basic physiology of the vocal instrument, the teacher of singing is reminded that voice is a product of many coordinating muscular movements or synergies, each one governed by a time factor and a dynamic factor. "Not only must the proper degree of muscular contraction be present, but it must be present at the proper moment." Experimental measurements indicate "the remarkable fineness" with which these muscular coordinations take place. [Ortmann 437] Another principle of vocal action is reported by Stevens and Miles: "The contributing sets of muscles [e.g., in respiration and phonation] act synchronously rather than consecutively." [583] Furthermore, muscles in the body always act in antagonistic interrelationships; that is, "no muscle acts by itself, it is always acting against an opponent." [Shakespeare 517, p. xiv] Thus, the contraction of one muscle always involves the corresponding stretching of another muscle and vice versa. [Orton 439, p. 34]

The term *coordination* is used to describe "the action of the controlling principle in the brain whereby the different parts [muscles] of the body are made to work harmoniously" and in constant equilibrium. [Mackenzie 364] Vocal muscular coordinations cannot yet be measured accurately. But their contributing or component muscular actions can be minutely described and thus group coordinations can be approximately and synthetically inferred from separate investigations of subordinate parts. [Stanley 577, p. 304] According to Swain, "balanced coordinative cooperation" of all the vocal muscles and their related parts should be the foundational objective of any system of training the singing voice. [598] (See also Chapter III.) Finally, Herbert-Caesari finds that singing involves the coordination of many variables, such as vowel shape, attack, pitch, volume, breath control, resonance and relaxation. He therefore maintains that coordination is the keynote of all systems of vocal training. [269, p. xiv]

IS STANDARDIZATION OF VOCAL TRAINING POSSIBLE?

The term *standardization* refers to the common acceptance of certain general teaching objectives by all teachers of singing, and also the adoption and use of commonly accepted teaching methods and procedures. *Method* is defined as a definite system or procedure followed by a teacher in pursuing a given objective; it is a means to an end. (W) Out of 31 opinions gathered on this controversial topic, 13 support the belief that certain basic vocal training procedures and techniques can be standardized and 18 are opposed to standardization.

Supporting standardization. Shaw claims that "the only thing that can be standardized in voice production is that part which can be measured." Insofar as voice training involves laws that govern the exact sciences (e.g., anatomy, physiology, physics, acoustics) standard teaching procedures can be formulated. However, insofar as voice training does not rely upon the exact sciences (e.g., in psychology, philosophy, aesthetics) exact predeterminations of teaching outcomes are not possible. Hence standardizations are impossible. [518, p. 89] "There can be only one set of [teaching] principles," says Mowe. "As long as we are working toward the same goal, it isn't of primary importance which road we take." Therefore, any method is a good method if it does not conflict with the general objectives of vocal teaching.[404]

Ortmann believes that the wide discrepancies among voice methods are "more imaginary than real." [437] "If two differing methods both get results, there must be something common to both of them that is of value." An effective vocal pedagogy should encompass the basic truths of methodology and discard the half-truths, even if they have become "hallowed by hoary tradition." [Bartholomew 38] Kerstin Thorborg believes that the fundamental techniques of voice building are the same for all singers, "regardless of range or quality" of voice. [611; also Novello-Davies 430, p. 139] Gescheidt likewise insists that teaching techniques can be standardized since individual differences are anatomical rather than physiological and vocal coordinations involving muscular training are alike for all singers. [200, p. 7] Wilson feels that basic principles are the same for all, "although different voices have individual problems." The use of a common basic approach makes group teaching possible. [674, Foreword; also Samoiloff 484, p. 6; Allen 7, p. 22] The following nine attributes of correct singing, according to Barbareux-Parry, are developed by techniques that can be standardized. They are: 1) a perfectly tuned pitch throughout the vocal range; 2) a uniformity of resonance on each tone; 3) delicacy of touch, spontaneity and freedom of utterance throughout the voice; 4) well balanced pianissimo to fortissimo controls on separate and connected tones; 5) mastery of legato and staccato techniques; 6) a well poised *mezza voce;* 7) standard diction; 8) sincerity of interpretation; 9) facial expression and posture well disposed. She warns, however, that the danger of all systems of voice culture is the loss of individuality through mechanical over-training. [34, p. 183 and p. 140]

Opposing standardization. The opinions against standardization of teaching methods are epitomized in the argument that each individual must be treated differently because no two voices are exactly alike. [James 300, p. 9; Hill 272, p. 53] According to Caruso, there are as many methods as there are singers and one singer's method might be entirely useless to another who tried it. Only the musical part of a vocal education can be standardized. [Marafioti 368, p. 156 and p. 16] Other representative statements supporting this belief are:

1. Each singer must discover his own technique by himself. "The teacher only holds the light for him." [Conklin 121, p. 9; Brown 68]

2. The best method is always the one that suits the particular needs of the individual using it. [Stock 589]

3. "There is no such thing as standardizing" a vocal method. [Skiles 561]

4. "Every throat is built differently." Every singer must therefore find his own method, the best one being that which feels easiest. [Feodor Chaliapin 95; Stella Roman 475]

5. "I am vigorously opposed to any 'set' method of vocal instruction." [Charles Hackett 219]

6. "No hard and fast rule can apply to everyone." [Paul Althouse 9]

7. Stereotyped vocal methods should be avoided because they limit the singer to only one type of placement. [Witherspoon 676]

8. Even when two voices seem fundamentally alike at first, their development "may work out on quite opposite lines." [Geraldine Farrar 170]

9. "No 'set' method can be given since no two pupils experience the same difficulties." [Elizabeth Schumann 498]

10. "Our voices are just as individual as our features"; each individual therefore has his own distinctive style of expression. [Blatherwick 16; 50]

METHODS OF VOCAL PEDAGOGY

PSYCHOLOGICAL APPROACH

Importance of the psychological approach. In 63 statements that were gathered in this area the importance of some form of mental training is emphasized. "The education of the mind . . . comes first in the exploitation of every art," says Marafioti. This includes the consideration of such factors as intellectual training, inspirational and emotional effects and those intangible aesthetic features of singing "which do not belong to the voice in its simple form of physical sound." [368, pp. 55 and 56] Toren discusses this point as follows: "If we believe that good singing must have a spiritual and mental, as well as a physical basis, then it becomes a part of the teacher's task to help in the development of those aspects" of singing which are purely psychological. [618] Shaw declares that a better understanding of this relationship between spiritual and physical factors in singing will "sound the key note of future progress . . . in vocal art." [531]

According to Mursell and Glenn, "voice building, or better, voice discovery, should not aim at mechanical precision, but flexible control dictated by musical conceptions." [413, p. 299] Singing more directly engages those psychological functions upon which our perception of musical experience depends than is true of any artificial instrument. [Mursell 411, p. 224] "It is not a certain muscular activity that produces a certain tone, . . . it is a certain mental conception of a tone that produces a certain muscular activity." [Smith 567; Sacerdote 481] This is especially true of the perception and control of musical pitch. [Dunkley 151, Preface] (See also Chapters III and V.) Opinions in this area are summarized in the following representative statements:

1. The consideration of musical talent is a primary psychological factor in voice culture. [Shaw 541]

2. Mental discipline is "a vitally important element in training the voice." [Wilcox 666]

3. The best and most successful teachers train the mind rather than the voice; the ear rather than the physical mechanism. [Hill 272, p. 54]

4. Voice production is a neuro-muscular response that is psychologically controlled. [Gescheidt 200, p. 38]

5. "Voices are under orders from headquarters—the human brain." [McLean 386]

6. "Thought is the only power by which to control a vocal organ. . . . What follows should be devoid of all bodily sensation." [Ibid.]

7. The voice does not tire if simply asked to follow the mind. What is called voice-fatigue is really voice-rebellion. Great singers may become exhausted mentally, but never voice-tired. [Hill 272, p. 52]

8. "Singing is as much a matter of psychology as of tone." Lawrence Tibbett [614]

9. "Voice belongs to mind." [Lawrence 335, p. 3]

10. Vocal controls are all mental, not physical. [Henderson 240, p. 79; Earhart 152, p. 8]

11. We can sing as beautiful a tone as we can think. [Nicoll and Dennis 426, p. 8]

12. Sustaining a tone is the result of audibly sustaining the thought underlying it. [Davies 127, p. 129]

13. "The mind sings, not the voice." [Kirkpatrick 317]

14. The brain, the heart, the whole body sings, projecting tones which the singer's mind first conceives. [Frieda Hempel 239; La Forest 326, p. 179]

15. "The voice must be trained with musical rather than mechanical ideas." [Clippinger 104, Foreword] "Mentality and mechanism" are the mainstays of vocal training. But we are primarily developing concepts, not muscles. [112] Therefore, direct control in voice training is pedagogically unsound. [104, p. 1] "Voice does not sing. Musical intelligence sings." [117]

16. The old Italian school was founded on psychological procedures for training the mind and ear; thus indirectly controlling and cultivating the physical vocal organs. [Kelly 312]

17. Voice training is an "inside job." [Hall 223]

18. The art of singing is predominantly mental, not physical, requiring imagination and interpretative skill. [Stephens 582; White 659, p. 39]

19. Imagination and creative effort should enter into even the singing of scales and exercises. [Witherspoon 677, p. 10]

20. Voice is an instrument of emotional expression and its production and control can be approached only through the imagination. [Allen 7, p. 23]

21. Concentration, intense and unwavering, is the greatest mental aid to expression in singing. All progress depends upon this ability. [Wood 686, p. 18]

22. Voice teaching is positive when it promotes mental activity and negative when it enforces conscious physical controls. [Stanley 577, p. 317]

23. The voice pupil must be taught to sing by inspiration and must be protected from the specious doctrines of breath support, registers and diaphragmatic control. [Marafioti 368, p. 220]

24. "Every good thing in the way of adjustment of the vocal instrument can be brought about by indirection . . . and the dangers of local action thus avoided." [Wodell 681; Thomas 606; Hall 222]

25. Correct control of all the vocal muscles can be achieved through "mental pictures." [Queena Mario 371]

In conclusion, Harold G. Seashore's comment that the psychological approach is preeminent in all vocal teaching is interesting. Vocal science, he claims, is indebted to psychology for important factual disclosures in an otherwise obscure pedagogy that hitherto was largely governed by empirical observations. [514] "The science of voice draws upon many fundamental sciences; notably physics, physiology, anatomy, anthropology, neurology and psychology. . . . It has become the function of psychology to integrate these basic scientific approaches into an applied science which we may call the 'psychology of the vocal arts.' " [C. E. Seashore 505]

Voice training as habit formation. Webster defines *habit* as "an aptitude or inclination for some action acquired by frequent repetition and showing itself in increased facility of performance or in decreased power of resistance." The principle of habit formation is of fundamental importance in training the singing voice and practice procedures usually subserve the purposes of habit formation. Through repetitive practice, consciously controlled muscular techniques gradually become unconscious actions. [Stanley 577, p. 310; Shakespeare 517, p. xiv] However, as in walking and talking, singing habits must be acquired gradually and along the lines of natural growth and development. [Witherspoon 677, p. 9] Ultimately, the singer's performance must also be accomplished without conscious thought, hesitancy or concentration. [Dictionary of Education 706]

Habitual ease in singing gives evidence of technical mastery, according to Woodside. That is to say, when a perfect technique becomes habitual, it appears spontaneous and natural. [690, p. 14] "Learn to sing your song until you're hardly conscious of the words or music," says Jeanette MacDonald. "Then it will become spontaneous, alive, and a part of your personality." [363] Vocal techniques must eventually become automatic if the singer is to free his mind from physical distractions and devote himself entirely to interpretative responsibilities. [Henderson 243, p. 125] Such techniques are not truly learned until they have become second nature in the performance. Habit formation is a slow process and the impatient singer often mistakes understanding for assimilation. [Allen 7, p. 12; Obolensky 432] As Greene puts it, "the physical use of his voice must be the unconscious response to the play of the singer's feelings. That is a matter of years, and few singers have the patience to see it through." [209, p. 4] The primary object of all vocal training, then, is to "train the brain so that it becomes capable of directing and controlling the functioning of the vocal apparatus subconsciously." That is the function of *habit formation.* [Philip 446, p. 4]

SINGING AS A NATURAL FUNCTION

The *natural voice* is one that is capable or artistic expression in singing although it has never submitted to formal technical training. Furthermore, such a voice is produced with complete ease and freedom throughout its compass and is entirely free from mechanical or technical limitations or defects. [Herbert-Caesari 269, p. 4] (See also Chapter V.) The natural-voiced singer is a curious phenomenon in the vocal profession and singing teachers often look for so-called "natural results" in measuring the vocal achievements of their pupils. The general characteristics of a natural singing technique are discussed in 77 statements which are summarized in two main categories as follows:

I. *The vocal act is unconscious and involuntary* when it is correctly (naturally) performed. This is the consensus of 58 opinions gathered on this subject. "We have no direct control over the action of the vocal cords," says William Shakespeare in the *Encyclopedia Brittanica*. [516] If the vocal mechanism is faulty, it can be adjusted through corrective exercises. But in its normal functioning the vocal mechanism is entirely automatic and should not be molested. [Gescheidt 199] The following typical summarizing statements further represent this point of view:

1. The singer must be trained to rely largely upon his subconscious faculties and "to give expression through reflexes rather than through conscious direction of every detail." [Speetzen 569]

2. To prevent physical strain and vocal fatigue, lay aside all voluntary muscular controls. Correct vocal action is unconscious and free from tension. [Barbareux-Parry 34, p. 268]

3. "Correct action of the voice mechanism must be induced and not forced." Correct vocal action is always involuntary. [New York Singing Teachers Association 421, p. 35]

4. "The (vocal) chords act automatically. It is therefore worse than useless even to think of them." [James 300, p. 20; Bergère 45]

5. Singing is an automatic process which can be seriously disturbed by giving too much attention to the physiology of its parts. [Shaw 518, p. 188; Warren 637]

6. The physical phenomenon called vocal sound is the combined product of mind and muscle. Yet, because its muscles are largely involuntary in their actions, their activities are indirectly governed by willing an act that involves their automatic functioning. [Wilcox 669, p. 2 and p. 12]

7. "Most voices suffer from over-analysis. . . . The best vocal work is . . . largely automatic." [Amelita Galli-Curci 197]

8. Simplicity is the keynote of good teaching. "As a real teacher grows he discards . . . all attempts at conscious control of the complicated vocal apparatus." [Fory 190]

9. "Direct control . . . has led to . . . fantastic [and misleading] theories." [Clippinger 104, Foreword]

10. Ignore the larynx "as if it did not even exist." [Hill 272, p. 53]

11. When at their best, all vocal actions are involuntary. [Stock 585]

12. The complex vocal mechanism is "never entirely under conscious control." [Bartholomew 38; Shaw 521; Negus 418, p. 436]

13. Conscious control leads to constriction. [Skiles 560]

14. The only thing to do is to let the physical instrument alone. [Savage 490, p. 92 and p. 112; Conrad Thibault 605]

Because of the involuntary nature of vocal action it is not necesary for the singer to have a knowledge of the structure of his vocal organs in order to govern their action properly. Shakespeare believes that muscular awareness, however slight, can inhibit freedom of action. Therefore, even mentioning the names of muscles should be avoided as much as possible. [517, p. 63; Negus, op. cit.] Greene finds that anatomical discussions tend to confuse the vocal student by making him self-conscious about organs that should function automatically. [209, p. 6] Henderson likewise claims that preoccupation with physical factors crowds out the fundamental aim of singing—to sing well. [240, p. 79; Philip 446, p. 26] "We cannot be conscious of the muscles involved in singing," says Ortmann. "We cannot even see them." Vocal physiology is for the teacher, not the student. [437] The best artistic results may be obtained "without the knowledge of the location of a single nerve or muscle." [Austin-Ball 31, p. 15 and p. 28; Whittaker 662, p. 70]

In conclusion, Wilson recommends a modified form of vocal control involving only those muscles "for which the student has conscious control; namely, the jaw, the lips and the tip of the tongue." [674, p. 7] Herbert-Caesari, while admitting that phonation is a subconscious act, also insists that by constant vigilance toward external physical sensations "there must be conscious, intelligent control of every tone emitted." [269, p. 28]

II. *Spontaneity and naturalness are the chief characteristics* of the vocal act in singing. Nineteen statements support this assumption. Among them are those of 5 professional singers who maintain that "obedience to natural law" is the singer's only guide, since violations are always penalized. [Witherspoon 677, p. 3] Paul Althouse believes that "most people have voices that are correctly placed to begin with." [9] Galli-Curci claims that "the old Italian [singing] teachers were the simplest of men. . . . Their idea was to get as close to nature as possible." [197] In Marian Anderson's opinion, the singer's tone must be as spontaneous and natural as a baby's tone. [12] Frances Alda adds an interesting observation: Watch a canary sing. It can outlast a good singer on a single trill. This is a lesson in spontaneous tone production, without effort or strain. [6, p. 298]

The remaining statements in this category are summarized as follows:

1. "Allow the voice to sing spontaneously." Make no effort to control it consciously. [Thomas 609.]

2. Simulated expression can convince no one. "To be effective expression must be spontaneous." [Samuels 487, p. 42]

3. "Spontaneity is the spirit of good singing." [Clippinger 104, p. 2]

4. The action of the vocal organs should be "as instinctive as the functioning of the seeing eye." The vocal tone should always be free and spontaneous. [Brown 67] All admonitions and conscious controls in singing are fruitless. [78, p. 65]

5. "Singers are forever told to sing naturally; and are forever refusing to do so." [Irvine 295]

6. A natural technique is best built upon natural reflexes which originate in vital rather than artistic processes. The vocal instrument is unique in that so much of its technique is a gift of nature. [Drew 147, p. 158 and p. 177]

7. Singing is and should remain a spontaneous, effortless reflex action, devoid of all forms of muscular control. [Gescheidt 200, p. 9; La Forest 326, p. 181]

8. "Voice [singing] should be the spontaneous expression of one's personality." [Jones 307, p. 5]

FREEING THE VOCAL MECHANISM

Freedom is a term often used in singing. It is defined as a condition of natural, unforced and unrestricted operation of the vocal organs. (W) "Freedom is the fundamental pillar of voice production," says Marafioti. With it, the singer enjoys complete and perfect command of all his vocal resources at all times. [368, p. 75] The 115 statements gathered in this area have been summarized in three groupings:

a) relaxation as a factor (43 statements)
b) the economy-of-effort principle (51 statements)
c) overcoming inhibitions and fears (21 statements)

Relaxation as a factor in voice training. Literally, *to relax* (from *laxus:* loose) means to make less firm, rigid or tense; also to slacken and loosen; to release from restraint. (W) From these fundamental concepts is derived the current use of the term *relaxation* in vocal pedagogy; namely, the elimination of unnecessary mental and muscular tensions and strains while singing. There is considerable misunderstanding among singers regarding the meaning of the term *relaxation,* caused, in large measure, by confusing the concepts of *relaxation* with those of *rigidity* and *inertia.* [La Forest 326, p. 153] *Rigidity* or *tightness* implies the absence of flexibility in a muscle and considerable resistance to change of form or movement. On the other hand, during a condition of *inertia,* there is complete muscular inaction; the inert muscle is utterly "destitute of motivating power" and a languid or lifeless condition prevails. *Relaxation* is an intermediate state between these two extremes. In relaxation, neither rigidity nor inertia exists; but a condition of muscular *tonus* in which healthy tension or partial contraction of muscle fibres is present, even while muscles are at rest. (W) During a state of relaxation, "the maintenance of the sustained [involuntary] contraction known as *tonus* is apparently not associated with increased expenditure of energy, . . . consequently no signs of fatigue are manifested." [Starling's *Physiology* 713, p. 195]

According to Mursell and Glenn, "relaxation means the freeing of [any] positive movement from the pull of antagonistic muscle groups." It is not a static condition of muscles, joints or throat, but "it depends entirely on the type and control of movement" employed. [413, p. 244] When intrusive, voluntary controls conflict with an otherwise automatic or spontaneous muscular action, obstructing muscular tensions are generated. Relaxation means the elimination of such conflicts between parts of the vocal tract. [Herbert-Caesari 269, p. 146] In other words, relaxation is a relative condition calling for the absence of abnormal tightness, not looseness of the vocal organs. [Henderson 243, p. 29]

The apparent confusion of terminology in this area has caused some writers to abjure relaxation as a teaching nostrum, while others attempt to clarify the concept of relaxation by using synonymous expressions or explanatory statements like the following:

1. Avoid rigidity, but never relax. [Brown 78, p. 116]

2. The ideal condition for singing is "controlled relaxation." [Allen 7, p. 36]

3. Relaxation is always "a relative condition," never absolute. [Eley 160; Austin-Ball 31, p. 9]

4. It (relaxation) is not "the slumping together, non-control" that is present in sleep; but rather, "an expansive . . . vitalized . . . tension in the muscles doing the work." [Gladys Swarthout 599]

5. "A better word [for relaxtion] is coordination, which means that particular degree of relaxation or non-relaxation enabling us to get the desired tonal result with the least waste of energy." [Ortmann 437]

6. "Poise" should be used in place of relaxation. The former suggests strength while the latter suggests weakness. [Clark 100]

7. Singing involves correct physical action, not complete relaxation. Hence instructions to relax completely, which is impossible, are misleading. [Witherspoon 677, p. 16; also 675]

8. "The great vice of singing is looseness, not tightness. . . . A fine tone cannot come through a loose voice. . . . Feeling implies tensity." [Scott 501, p. 49 and 126]

9. "Absolute relaxation is impossible. . . . One of the teacher's greatest problems is to develop in the pupil the ability to maintain the correct degree of muscle tone." [Stanley 578; also 575]

10. "In singing one must retain a certain degree of muscle tone." [Felderman 174]

11. Good tone results from the vibration of "surfaces that are tense," not relaxed. [Louis Graveure 208]

12. "Relaxation is the exclusive privilege of the audience. . . . Let us forget relaxation as far as the singer is concerned." [Robinson 474]

To render the vocal instrument completely responsive to the mind and imagination of the singer, it is first necessary to remove all extraneous and unnatural tensions in the body. "When that is done everything is possible to the singer," says Clippinger. [113] The teacher's responsibilities in freeing the singer's body and the vocal mechanism are clearly indicated since relaxation always favors optimal vocal action. [Rimmer 471] Dan Beddoe makes the assertion that "probably more voices are ruined by strain than through any other cause." [42] Such strains impair phonation, breathing, resonance and posture. "Tenseness to any appreciable degree in the body of the singer is immediately communicated to the vocal muscles." [Thomas 609] Bodily tensions invariably spread into the diaphragm muscle and prevent its free movement. [Garnetti-Forbes 198, p. 85] Sound vibrations generated in the larynx are dampened by abnormal rigidity of the muscles. "If all strain in singing be removed, the vocal apparatus will be predisposed to correct resonance." [Samuels 487, p. 26] Therefore, "relaxity . . . is the great secret of voice production." [White 658, p. 77]

Although the importance of relaxation in singing is freely acknowledged by authors, specific methods for inducing relaxation are seldom given. General therapies are sometimes referred to, but these are not peculiar to singers' needs. The *Dictionary of Education* lists such techniques as the light manipulation of muscles, alternate tensing and relaxing of muscles, and concentration on peaceful thoughts and images of ideal tones (listening) as methods most often used in general relaxation therapy. [706] Mursell and Glenn would emphasize economy of effort throughout the vocal training period, induced by the proper "infusion of musical intelligence . . . into the movement complex required to actuate the [vocal] instrument. . . . The way to work for relaxation . . . is to work for economical coordination" and efficiency in actions and movements. [413, p. 244] Davies believes that relaxation is entirely controlled by the mind. [127, p. 104] Tension of body brings with it tension of mind and vice versa. Hence, the mental approach is favored. [Orton 439, p. 86] "The moment the thought is removed from a muscle it relaxes," says Clippinger. [104, p. 14] Mackenzie recommends energetic exercise for a short time at full tension in order to induce smooth coordination and ultimate relaxation of the larger body muscles. [364, p. 120] Novello-Davies suggests that complete relaxation be accomplished by lying flat on a couch. "Feel that the couch surface is bearing you up, and not that you are bearing down on it." [430, p. 38]

Economy of effort as a principle; letting versus striving. In correct singing, as in all forms of spontaneous vocal expression, "the body coordinates automatically to the thought." Employing this principle, the singer will manage his vocal organs without loss or waste of energy, strictly eliminating all superfluous effort and husbanding all his mental and physical resources so as to produce the best possible results with the minimum expenditure of energy. Thus, the natural efficiency of the correctly functioning vocal instrument spells *economy of effort* for the singer. [*Harvard Dictionary of Music* 704, article on "Voice."] In other words, do not *strive* to sing; *let* yourself sing. [Klingstedt 320, p. 48] Paul Althouse declares that "singing should be as natural as speech." If any instructional method involves vocal tension or excessive effort, it is safe to assume that it is an improper method "and probably detrimental to the voice." [9] This opinion is corroborated by six other professional singers. "The very fact that the voice becomes tired is an indication of incorrect singing methods," says Frieda Hempel. [239] "The well used voice does not tire." [Marian Anderson 12] Singing is an easy, effortless action. "If it feels like hard physical work, your method is probably wrong." [Beniamino Gigli 203] "Never force the voice" is Feodor Chaliapin's advice. [95] Elizabeth Rethberg adds: "Keep relaxed." Don't work to sing. "Imagine yourself simply a channel through which the tone pours." [463] Giovanni Martinelli writes that his singing teacher used no fixed, rigorous method at all. "He taught me to relax and release my voice naturally." [373] The economy of effort principle is further described in the following typical summarizing statements:

1. Correct singing requires mental rather than physical effort and is

therefore untiring, even after hours of performance. When strain is felt, the method is wrong. [Samoiloff 484, p. 31; Wharton 655, p. 92]

2. " 'Unconscious effort' is the *sine qua non* of fine singing." [Warren 636] "Unnecessary tension and rigidity can spoil everything." [Ibid. 637]

3. "The supreme vocal virtue is 'effortless artistry.' " [McLean 386]

4. "The singer should always give the impression of being perfectly at ease." [Christy 97; Hemery 238, p. 118]

5. Exercises for attack should also develop economy of effort. [Judd 309, p. 14]

6. Technique without ease is an unfinished product. Public performance must therefore wait on its acquirement. [Allen 7, p. 12]

7. "Purity of tone and ease in production are inseparable." [Glenn 204]

8. A voice produced with ease has a greater carrying power. [Howe 284, Introduction]

9. The right way is always the easy way. [Orton 439, p. 106]

10. Don't try to do anything. Merely *allow* the tone to come. [Jeffries 302; Butler 86]

11. "One fails to sing well when he tries [strives] to sing well." [Mac-Burney 361]

12. "Allow the voice to sing. Do not make it sing." [Haywood 237, vol. II, p. 8]

13. Faith and freedom are all you need for voice placement. Quit trying to help your vocal cords. "They will perform if you believe they can." [Efnor 159, lesson 3]

14. Correct vocal action must be induced. It cannot be forced. [Dunkley 151, p. 2]

Overcoming inhibitions and fears. The *Dictionary of Education* defines *inhibition* as the "restraint of an impulse or function by an opposite force from within." [706] A common cause of vocal inhibition in singing is fear. *Fear* is an emotional response characterized by apprehension, uncertainty or alarm as to the outcome of an action or experience (such as singing). (W) Shaw declares that "it is the general experience of teachers of singing that fear, in the mind of the [vocal] student . . . is the greatest and most persistent obstacle to overcome. . . . The first requirement of the teacher is to eliminate this appalling and almost universal sense of fear." [530; Stanley 578] McLean writes: "Fear is a destroyer of balance; and vocal faults, in the beginning, are the outcome of some type of fear.

Fear contracts muscles and constricts throats. . . . Fear causes tension, and mental wheels will not turn when one is tense." [386] De Bruyn speaks of fear as a state of mind that is inimical to correct voice production. "The concept of a beautiful tone and the accompanying fear of a high pitch do not go well together because the latter concept will tend to suppress the former." [132] (See also Chapter VI.) "Naturally," says Orton, "if we assume an attitude [mental] contrary to what we desire, we defeat ourselves." Fear is largely caused by lack of confidence; a mental assumption which divides the mind during the performance of a duty. Hence, in singing, one's attention should be fixed on what is desired rather than on what one wishes to avoid. [439, p. 85; Hemery 238, p. 117] To overcome fear and self-consciousness "unrestrained practice" is essential. [Hill 272, p. 17]

Vocal inhibitions are most often contracted during infancy and adolescence, according to Madden. [366] Such psychological conditions as impatience, fear, anxiety, emotional upsets and self-consciousness provide chronic mental hazards that act as "deterrents to beautiful singing" in later life. [Samuel 486, Lesson 31] Invariably the various muscular interferences in singing stem from the mental attitude of the singer. [Shaw 533] Consequently, in correcting vocal inhibitions, "the first step towards learning is often unlearning." [Orton, op. cit.] Waters believes that the breathing function is directly influenced by mental and emotional upsets like fear, worry, excitement, doubt or confusion. These generate either chronic inertia or abnormal tension in the respiratory muscles with resultant depletion of energy and strain of the vocal mechanism. [647, p. 5] Stanley finds that listening to oneself while singing inhibits the spontaneity of vocal expression. [577, p. 325] (See Chapter VIII.)

Specific preventives and correctives for overcoming inhibitions or fears in singing are seldom given by authors. Clippinger advises the teacher "not to talk about a vocal problem until after it is solved." [104, p. 30] A few minutes of deep breathing is suggested as a good corrective for nervousness and stage fright. [Hill 272, p. 18] Hemery proposes a self-critical attitude of thoughtful reflection and comparison, and improved concentration, as antidotes for fear and stage fright. [238, p. 115 ff.]

In conclusion, Clippinger believes that a considerable part of the voice training program must be devoted to gaining freedom. [109] Sincerity and beauty of expression are derived from freedom. [Henley 264] "Freedom is a rarity in song. Artificiality and rigidity are far more prevalent." [Hill 272, p. 5] But freedom is not the utter abandonment of technical skill or self discipline, according to Mme. Schoen-René. In her opinion freedom is not inimical to self-control. Before you can free your voice you must first learn to control it. [493]

EXPRESSIONAL FACTORS IN SINGING

Singing as self-expression. Self-expression in singing is the process of manifesting one's own thoughts and feelings in and through the medium of song. Expression takes the form of the use of language (words), sounds (voice) or other means of communication, in an endeavor to convey the singer's concepts or feelings with force, vividness, clarity or other desirable qualities. (W) [Dictionary of Education 706] (See also Chapter X.) In the 36 statements gathered in this area the emphasis is laid largely upon the importance of maintaining a flow of meaningful ideas when singing, rather than the mere technical execution of musical or vocal sounds and phrases. "Any separation of technic from expression is a disastrous and distorting abstraction," says Mursell. [410] In other words, vocal training is not primarily a matter of developing specific muscular skills, but rather a training in self-expression, which encompasses such factors as "hearing and imaging sound, certain types of emotional response and control, . . . certain imaginative and intellectual insights." [Ibid. 411]

Aikin insists that it is "the sense of words and not the sound that stimulates the musical sense." [4] "Train those young singers to sing musically [expressively] not muscularly," warns Stock. [589] Allen is of the opinion that the vocal act is a natural endowment rooted in an urge to sing which may not be denied when the vocal instrument is in good form. [7, p. 136] Self-expression through voice is "a basic human instinct." [Clark 102; Clippinger 104, p. 5] Davies explains the process of singing as follows: Vocal tone springs from language and language springs from thought and the desire to express. Hence vocal study begins with the singing of thoughts. [127, p. 128] Other concepts on this subject are summarized in the following typical statements:

1. There is no reason for singing if we do not wish to communicate something to the listener. Therefore, "do not sing words, sing a thought." [Scott 501, p. 129 ff.]

2. "Singing is a colorful and beautiful expression" of intimate feelings and emotions. [Hall 225; McIntyre 384.]

3. In reference to singing, all the components and ingredients of its technique are but vehicles of emotional expression. [Bairstow, Dent and others 32]

4. The singer's task is the "formation and utterance of musical ideas." [Lewis 344, p. iii]

5. Listen to yourself and see if what your voice says is conveying your meaning. When you learn the words to a song, try to express that thought. [Clark 100; Sanders 488]

6. Vocal agility, good diction and other technical details are developed not by routine exercises, but by "the natural desire to express the meaning, and consequently each word of a song." [Bergère 45]

7. "The initiation of the muscular activity in phonation is a conscious desire for oral self expression." [Curry 124]

8. Successful singing must always be motivated by the desire to express something. Always direct your thoughts and your voice toward an imaginary listener when you sing. [De Bruyn 131]

9. Mere technique is devoid of meaning. Therefore voice production must always be related to the expression of ideas until every sound conveys a meaning. [Taylor 602, p. 39]

10. "Technique, if it is to fulfil its purpose, must be framed in expression." [Vale 619, p. 39]

11. The foundation of vocal education is to develop the "ability to express music with the voice . . . to develop a musically intelligent singing voice, rather than a mechanically trained instrument." [Mursell and Glenn 413, p. 280 ff.]

Witherspoon holds that "even the singing of exercises should be done with some definite mood value." [676] Mme. Galli-Curci offers this advice: Do not think of your vocal cords in singing any more than you do in speaking. Instead, think entirely "about what you have to say [sing]." [197] An artist singer "is not merely an emitter of high C's; he is a medium through which musical communication must flow." [Lawrence Tibbett 614] "The significance of the music must come first," says Beniamino Gigli. [203] Kerstin Thorborg adds that the "ultimate goal" is to express "emotional and intellectual conviction" in singing. [612]

Singing as joyous release. Joyous release is a sense of well-being or exhilaration of spirits that is caused by the experience of being free from restraint of any kind. In artistic singing, "there is a thrill and liberation of the spirit which is inimitable." [16] This principle is emphasized in 16 statements which affirm the belief that the experience of joyous release is an inevitable accompaniment of correct singing. "Effective singing must be associated with pleasant emotion," says Mursell. [411, p. 229] Therefore, vocal instruction should aim toward a joyous release of song rather than a meticulous mechanization of the phonatory process. "Our principle is in effect a demand that all singing shall be done for joy. . . . The child must sing because he loves to sing, or not at all; and . . . anything that interferes with the pupil's pleasant feeling tone in the act of song works against voice control. [Mursell and Glenn 413, p. 286 and p. 291 ff.] Scott finds that the best singing comes "from the sheer joy of singing" [501, p. 126]; and Novello-Davies is certain that a voice radiating the beauty of living "and the joy and happiness created within oneself" is far more effective than one that is only mechanically perfect. [430, p. 64] Berto likewise claims that singing should be a joy, rather than a task. When pupils learn this principle, "we shall see fewer distorted faces while singing." [46] A buoyant, joyous mood releases muscles, corrects faulty mechanisms and makes for efficient functioning of the voice. [Wharton 655, p. 50; Wilcox 669, p. 13] As Kirkpatrick puts it, "Beauty of expression is the reflection of a beautiful thought. Depression precludes the possibility of a buoyant voice for the mind sits in regal state and rules with unchanging laws." [317] According to Wilcox, even if you are only vocalizing a few "ahs" and "ohs," first spend a few minutes in imaginative practice until a mood of buoyancy is generated. Then vocalize the sounds in "the spirit of joyous song." [670] In conclusion, Christine Little advises the vocal student to maintain a pleasant, relaxed and mobile facial expression while singing. "Always look as if you were happy," she says. "Singing is an expression of joy." [349] When thought and mood values are right during the performance, the joy of singing will supersede mere exhibitionism. [16]

Singing as compared to speaking. Fifty-three concepts of the relationship existing between singing and speaking pedagogies are summarized in two main groups, consisting of: I) 43 opinions that favor the use of certain speaking analogies for training the singing voice, and II) 10 that are opposed to the use of so-called *sing as you speak* methods, in which speaking analogies are used to explain singing techniques.

Group I: Seashore finds it "very significant that the scientific approach is practically the same for music [song] and speech." "As a rule," he says, "scientific findings in one of these fields transfer in principle to the other." [505] Wilcox claims there is no fundamental difference between the singing and speaking voice. Both function under the same laws and are "subject to development through the same (teaching) processes." [669, p. 58] Other typical comments supporting the same general viewpoint are represented in the following summarizing statements:

1. The only technical difference between song and speech is that the latter is not governed by pitch and time values. [Hathaway, 231, p. 15]

2. The expressional characteristics of the speaking voice—pitch, volume, quality—determine the expressional properties of the singing voice. Vocal education really begins when we first teach children how to use the speaking voice. [Marafioti 368, p. 52 ff.]

3. Singing is speech set in musical phrasing. [Hemery 238, p. xii; Lloyd 351, p. 28]

4. Singing is speech that is "prolonged and intensified." [Taylor 602, p. 35; Proschowski 454; Cimini 99]

5. "If speech were not the natural way to use the voice we would all have ruined our voices long ago." [Patton and Rauch 445, p. 154]

6. Singing is emotional expression in tone and word; a form of intoned speech. [Shakespeare 517, p. 3]

7. Singing is a form of oral expression in which the spoken word is intensified, prolonged and beautified. [Schofield 495; Clark 100; Kirkpatrick 317]

De Bruyn declares that the teaching of singing may be expedited if the speech-song approach is used. In this respect, "the prerequisite to the teaching of singing . . . is beautiful speaking." Many aspects of the singing voice can thus be taught through the speech process. [131] Brown quotes the great Lamperti, with whom he studied, as saying that "the singing tone evolves from the speaking voice." [74] There is a "unity of technique in both speaking and singing" which may not be overlooked by the voice teacher. [Noller 427] Howe claims that it is practically impossible to produce a "natural" vocal tone in singing at any pitch level unless one can first demonstrate the ability to attack it "in the free and flexible manner of good speech." [284, p. 33; also Combs 119, p. 10] As Green explains it, "Singing is almost as easy as speaking and yet, since we speak incorrectly, we sing with the same faults magnified." [210] Therefore, it is a matter of great importance to the singing teacher to observe how the student produces his speaking voice. [Bushell 83; Sanders 488] Singing, from the start, should be as effortless as speaking, "the word being mother to the tone." [Kelly 312]

According to Austin-Ball, the masters of the old Italian school of bel canto insisted that voice production was indentical in speech and song. "Pronunciation was so important they expected to find a little speaking in all singing, and a little singing in all speech." [31, p. 61] Lawrence Tibbett, in an interview, suggests that "it is helpful to think of singing as dramatic speech . . . sustained on definite intervals of pitch." [614; also Efnor 159, Lesson 5] "The great singers are also the great declaimers." [Bairstow, Dent and others 32] "Singing includes the whole art of declamation besides the music of song, and all difficulties in pronunciation are overcome by the study of the acquired faculty of speech." [Ibid. 33; Sheppard 546] Friedich Schorr, leading operatic baritone, warmly endorses the principle promulgated by Richard Wagner; that "there exists no difference [in opera] between so-called 'declaimed' and 'sung' phrases." In all his operas, the composer claims that declamation is equivalent to song and vice versa. Therefore the singer is always required to recite (declaim) his lines before he sings them. [497] Samuels even goes so far as to say that singing may be considered as "beautiful shouting." He claims that this attitude has a marked effect on the singing of nervous vocalists, "for the combative faculty is called upon to assert itself, at once banishing nervousness." [487, p. 52] For best results in vocal training, then, "the approach to a beautiful singing voice should be made through the early cultivation of a beautiful speaking voice." [Seashore 503]

Group II. Opposed to this argument are those opinions that express doubt as to the efficacy of a speech approach in training the singing voice because of the basic differences existing between the singing and speaking functions. According to Webster, *"Speech* and *song* are chiefly distinguished by the wider [and more disjunct] variations of pitch in singing." Aikin infers that "language [speech] is a purely artificial acquisition of mankind," while the singing voice is native to the individual. [4] "We are born with the instinctive ability to use the voice easily and freely and with good expression, without any instruction." [Harvard Dictionary of Music 704] "Sing just as you speak . . . is very misleading advice," says Douty. "It may even prove harmful." [143] In a symposium on singing, conducted by Bairstow, Dent and others, the negative argument is advanced that to sing as you speak is not very useful to the vocalist because speech is usually carried on at a relatively low pitch and "we are apt to forget that speech at a high pitch [as in singing] is a vastly different thing from speech at a low." [32] Henderson maintains that the 'sing as you speak' approach is unscientific because the tones of speaking are entirely different from those used in singing. [243, p. 49] Armstrong derides the attempts to induce the extraordinary vocal controls of singing from the relatively ordinary controls of speaking. "Singing, compared to speaking is a supernormal effort," he says. Therefore, from the very beginning, extraordinary devices are required. [25]

The reports of several experimental observations tend to confirm the viewpoint that speech and singing are not reciprocally transferable skills. Bartholomew reports, in a paper read at a meeting of the Acoustical Society of America, that the singing voice appears to be considerably different from the normal speaking voice. This conclusion is a result of a three year investigation conducted by the author. [36] Ortmann reports, further, that "the muscular coordination involved in singing is not present in the usual throat position or in normal speech. Consequently, inferences from the speaking voice cannot be directly applied to the singing voice." [437] Stanley finds that "the average intensity of the singing voice is far greater than is that of the speaking voice." Also, the pitch norm of the speaking voice "is considerably lower than is that of the singing voice." [578] Finally, Curry speaks of singing as "an artistic form of voice modified by melody and rhythm to produce a pleasing harmony of music and voice. . . . In speech the dominant fundamental pitch of the larynx vibration is present in about 60 per cent of the duration. . . . In singing the larynx vibrates during at least 90 per cent of the duration." [124, p. 1] (For a further comparison of singing and speaking concepts, see also Chapters IX and X.)

TECHNICAL APPROACH

Technical principles and objectives. Techniques are the practical methods used in the execution, performance and mastery of any art. (W) "The ability to produce musical results with a given instrument, as the voice, . . . depends on a variety of skills [or techniques] and their integration in the performance of musical composition." The specific way of presenting instructional materials embodying these skills (techniques) constitutes the *technical approach* in teaching. [Dictionary of Education 706] Dunkley maintains that, since vocal study includes the study of various physical actions and their proper control, technical training becomes an inevitable part of the singer's preparation. [151, p. 11] "We can only improve what we can control," says Henderson. [240, p. 80] Elizabeth Rethberg believes that all singers require a considerable degree of technical training. "I insist," she adds, "that the best 'natural' voice is the result of much experimentation and hard work." [463] Lawrence Tibbett likewise claims that technical training is inevitable. Even after you have cultivated the student's sense of tone and educated his taste "you still will have to teach him to sing." [613] Haywood describes voice culture as a form of physical training. "In this department of our study we must establish a perfect coordination of all the physical parts used in singing." [234] Zerffi goes so far as to call singing "nothing more than musical athletics," requiring an intensive routine of physical drills. [701]

Shaw lists the following as technical objectives in voice training: a) good phonation for all tones sung, whether singly, in scale, or in arpeggio passages; b) elimination of strains and superfluous effort; c) agreeable quality; d) control of dynamics or gradations of power; and e) correct diction. [541] Stanley discusses four interdependent "technical elements of vocal progress." They are: increase of range and volume and improvement in quality (resonance) and vibrato. [573] Edward Johnson, of the Metropolitan Opera Company, would have each singer master three indispensable techniques: breath, vowel and pitch. These he calls "the singer's trinity." When properly developed, they synchronize to make tone. [306] Other statements regarding the technical objectives of a singer's training are summarized as follows:

1. The purposes of technical vocal instruction are breath economy, tonal purity, an even quality throughout the range, clear diction and freedom from strain. [Whittaker 662, p. 72; Howe 284, p. 31]

2. Breath control, free throat, resonance and diction are the four basic technical problems. [Hok 278, p. 7; Waters 645]

3. Learn to manage the breath, free the vocal mechanism, deliver the right sound. [Scott 501, p. 38 ff.]

4. The three R's of singing are Resonance, Relaxation and Respiration. [Jacobus 298]

5. The foundation of vocal training is tone production, pronunciation, breath control and resonance. [Shakespeare 517, p. 93; Douty 142]

6. In summing up the technical requirements of singing one may list the following: "skill in attack," sostenuto, legato, dynamics, flexibility, agility, and a mastery of bravura (virtuosity and daring) and diction. [Haywood 235]

Removing muscular interferences. Muscular interferences in singing are chronic conditions of strain, stiffness or rigidity in the vocal tract that are in opposition or in conflict with normal muscle action; therefore inducing physical resistance and excessive effort during the vocal act. (W) Twenty-three authors consider this subject of paramount importance in planning the technical training of the singing voice. According to Alfred Spouse, "most vocal troubles originate in interference, that is, in tightness or rigidity of the vocal mechanism. In òther words, lack of freedom of tone emission is the underlying evil, although its manifestations may take on different forms in different people." [572] Shaw defines interference as "any muscular contraction which prevents the unhampered vibration of the vocal cords and free motion of the cartilages and muscles of the larynx, or the free use of the resonance space." [528] Wilcox believes that technical voice training is as much a matter of removing interferences as of developing proper coordinations of the vocal musculature. [669, p. 19] De Bruyn lists numerous vocal deficiencies, many of which are caused by types of muscular weakness and interferences in the vocal tract. Among these are: breath insufficiency, breathy or aspirated voice, breaking, forced or tight voice, faulty intonation, nasality, lack of resonance, lack of vibrato (white voice), tremolo, exaggerated jaw movement (mouthing) and exaggerated articulation. Samuels lists tremolo, breathiness, nasal twang, and "metallic," "hard," "gutteral" and "weak voice," as faults of vocal interference. [487, p. 18] Clippinger finds that "the singer's worst enemy is resistance [interference]." [104, p. 8] Stults writes: "All beginning vocal training must be corrective . . . through seeking to restore Nature's original adjustment" of all the vocal organs during phonation [596]; and he is seconded by MacBurney whose opinion is equally emphatic: "When the student can prevent interfering movements without inhibiting reactions he is ready to sing." [361]

Bartholomew observes that the vocal act "involves the inhibition of one of the most powerful, automatic and constantly used reflexes, the swallowing coordination, the muscles of which are in many individuals normally in a state of partial tension. The inhibition of this swallowing coordination is consequently difficult for most persons, and the stiff tongue or jaw remains a major problem." [38] Shaw blames the interference of the speech muscles for most of the "technical inhibitions" in singing. [543] Stanley's explanation of interferences during phonation is also interesting. In the Journal of the Franklin Institute he claims that nearly every vocal fault is associated with some sort of throat constriction. "Unfortunately, the average individual maintains either too high or too low a degree of muscle tone." In either case, the reflex vocal impulse improperly engages extraneous muscles, causing "great inefficiency of action and producing considerable fatigue." In the effort to correct this condition, voluntary controls are resorted to by the singer, with resultant disturbances in the coordination of the vocal mechanism. The remedy lies in the direction of corrective exercises that are designed to strengthen weak muscles and to loosen tight muscles. [578, p. 431 ff.]

In handling the problem of muscular interferences, Witherspoon suggests that technical exercises may be used as correctives if they are planned so that they oppose the activity of the muscles that cause the fault, thus persuading correct action and eliciting a corrected vocal sound that the singer can gradually learn to accept. Correct breathing is an important antidote for chronic muscular interferences in that it induces freedom of the vocal organs. Special types of vocal sounds may also be used as correctives to promote resonance, relieve local tensions and alter the position of offending muscles. [677, p. 81 and p. 94] Other technical correctives suggested are summarized as follows:

1. As a warming up process, spend five or ten minutes in slow deep

breathing. Then hum a few musical tones while loosening the muscles of the neck and shoulders. [Felderman 173, p. 58]

2. "Lowering of the chin and simultaneous elevation of the chest [sternum] help to relax the neck muscles." [Schatz 492]

3. Rotate the head (the "neck roll") freely while the vocal tone is issuing from the lips. This will free the neck and throat from interfering tensions. [Otero 440; Novello-Davies 430, p. 119]

4. The entire under side of the chin must feel soft during phonation. "Any lump or hard spot under the chin [*genio-glossus* muscle] is dangerous to pure tone." [De Bar 128]

5. Capture the sensation of "complete relaxation" that occurs when singing on the lowest tones of the scale and continue to think "low tone relaxation" while raising the pitch. Muscular interferences can thus be prevented. [Dunkley 151, p. 37]

HANDLING BEGINNERS

Those who first enter upon a course of vocal study are called *beginners*. At the outset of instruction, several important problems confront the teacher of singing, such as, the preliminary determination of the nature and scope of the student's basic vocal equipment, its pitch range, characteristic quality of timbre and dynamic scope; and an appraisal of his hearing acuity, experience, educational background and musicianship. [Edgerton 157] Each of these factors aids the teacher in determining the student's potentialities and direction of growth and also indicates the limitations, if any, that he will have to overcome during the course of instruction he is to receive. These problems are more fully discussed under appropriate headings in succeeding chapters; but the preliminary classification of voices and the content of first lessons are given primary consideration here, in the following summation of the 45 statements that were gathered on these two topics.

Classifying voices. Classification is a concept embracing things that are similar or that possess certain characteristics in common. (W) In classifying the singing voice, these characteristics are qualitative variables that need specific measurement and categorical ranking in order that efficient vocal instruction may be given to suit the specific needs of each individual. Since vocal instruction proceeds mainly through the administration of individual practice drills and routine exercises, and the singing of songs, it is considered necessary to determine the type of vocal material that is most suited to each student's voice. To this end, voices are usually tested and classified. Stanley maintains, however, that the natural range, timbre or power of the beginner's voice is not always revealed at first. "In the early stages of training the pupil's natural voice is often so obscured by technical faults that it is impossible to tell what type of voice he actually possesses." [578, p. 438] Then also, there are many borderline or doubtful voices. According to Haywood, such voices seldom reveal their true classification until after their fundamental tones and normal resonance throughout the scale have been established. "A period of three months is not too much to give this all important point. . . . Obviously, no one can honestly declare voice classification at a single hearing." A premature classification and the resultant misapplication of routine practice materials can even warp a student's vocal development to the point of ruination. [236]

Within these general proscriptions, the consensus is that voices are classifiable. There is a diversity of opinion, however, as to the selection of criteria for classifying voices. Curry holds that voices should be classified "according to the anatomical, physiological and psychological characteristics of the individual." These, he explains, deal with the general physique, dimensions and form of the larynx and adjacent resonating structures; the range, quality and intensity of the voice; and, finally, "the temperament and faculty of emotional expression." [124, p. 110] Saenger would measure the compass, the timbre and the tessitura (see Chapter VI) of a voice. These three elements "decide what kind of a voice the student has." [482] *Tessitura* as defined by Drew, is that part of the vocal range "that can be sung with ease for some time." This, he claims, is the part that determines the true classification of each voice; extreme notes of the range being only for occasional, not for daily practice. [147, p. 169; Owsley 441, p. 40] Stanley likewise points out that a well produced voice is categorized by neither quality nor range but "by the area in which [its most powerful and useful] tones lie." [577, p. 323] Evetts and Worthington express the opinion that a singer's vocal classification is determined by the location of his middle range on the musical scale *(tessitura)*, not by his highest pitches; for the compass of voices may vary within the same classification. [167, p. 31]

A preponderance of author opinion (19 statements out of 30) favors the use of quality or vocal "color" (see Chapter V) as the sole criterion for classifying voices. The following are typical summarizing comments in this group:

1. Color and timbre only determine scope of vocal use. [Jarmila Novotna 431]

2. Voice placing (classification) depends upon "the natural color of the voice," never upon the type of music one can sing. [Gertrud Wettergren 654]

3. Natural timbre (quality) takes precedence over range. [Gota Ljungberg 350]

4. "Being a baritone or a tenor . . . depends solely upon the natural color or timbre of the voice." [Friedrich Schorr 497]

5. Voices are classified by fundamental differences in timbre or quality rather than range. [Edward Johnson 306]

6. Quality is the chief factor. Range is secondary. [Grundman and Schumacher 218, p. 12]

7. When in doubt, let quality be the deciding factor. [Wharton 655, p. 15; Marchesi 369, p. 45]

8. Range alone is deceptive. Voices should be classified, rather, by "native quality" and timbre. [Hall and Brown 227, p. 46]

9. Compass (range) is variable whereas color is a "more or less stable" characteristic. [Grace 207, p. 3]

10. Voices, like other musical instruments should be classified according to quality, not range. The quality of any instrument best reveals its individual characteristics. [Barbareux-Parry 34, p. 149; Dossert 140, p. 39]

Finally, Woods suggests that "range plus quality should determine the classification of voices" and the assignment of vocal exercises and songs. [688, p. 11] Stella Roman adds the interesting opinion that the effortless "speaking voice" of each singer because "it does not submit easily to forcing" is a useful guide to vocal clasification. [475]

First lessons. Fifteen authors discuss the nature and specific content of first vocal lessons, although the usual treatment of this subject is rather fragmentary and inconclusive. In order to provide a logical reorientation for the teacher of singing, it may be helpful to prefix a brief general description of the vocal lesson:

Like most forms of specialized technical training, the typical vocal lesson usually consists of a short period (approximately 30 to 45 minutes) of individualized instruction devoted to a specific limited area of the subject. The presentation and treatment of subject matter depends upon the capacity and progress of the individual student but the typical lesson period encompasses materials studied before, during and after each lesson. The teacher lectures, demonstrates, accompanies and corrects the student. The student listens, discusses and performs for the teacher. In general, a miscellaneous type of instruction is given, varying with the individual and deriving its main pedagogical values from precept, experience, observation and deduction. [*Dictionary of Education* 706]

The following typical summarizing statements represent a composite further viewpoint on this topic:

1. "All beginning vocal training must be corrective in nature. Before anything else is attempted, the voice producing apparatus must be restored to that condition or adjustment in evidence at the moment of birth." [Clippinger 116]

2. "There is less work in starting with a beginner than in undoing a faulty method of production." [Novello-Davies 430, p. 43]

3. To avoid confusion, first lessons should be simple, that is, a brief presentation of the rules of tone production together with an explanation of posture, diaphragm, vocal cords, resonance chambers, relaxation and breathing. Patient repetition, illustrative charts and simple analyses will improve comprehension. [Samoiloff 484, p. 15]

4. The beginning pupil should first be allowed to sing so that he may reveal all his strong and weak points "before he is bewildered by counsels and methods." Instruction may then be adapted to his own particular requirements. [Bruna Castagna 94]

5. "Devote the first half (of the lesson period) to the principles of voice production and the last half to the study of songs." [Clippinger 104, p. 2]

6. The first step in voice training should be "the isolation of the two registers." (See Chapter VI.) In the early stages, concentrate upon the weaker register; usually the lower one for women and the higher one (falsetto) for men. [Stanley 578, p. 425]

7. "The initial problems of the instructor in vocal music are much the same, whether he be an independent teacher, an instructor in a four year college, or in junior college [high school]." [Parish 442]

Shaw feels that "it is better to begin with exercises containing wider intervals, rather than with single sustained tones or scales" in order to promote "general elasticity" of the vocal organs and a sense of rhythm. [536] Pitts and Wilcox take an opposing viewpoint. The former insists that the first step in singing is to produce a steady, unwavering tone [448, p. 2]; the latter writes: "the all-important thing is to produce the best possible tone on one pitch and then work from that 'pattern tone' to other vowels and other pitches." [669, p. 59] James emphatically advises "beginning with short intervals, semi-tones, tones and thirds." [300, p. 44] Orton advises beginners to avoid changes in dynamics. "I consider that *crescendi* and *diminuendi* are out of order at the commencement of training," he says. [439, p. 122] Armstrong and Stock both recommend the study and practice of songs, well within the range of the voice, as early as possible

[26; also 587] and Owsley advises the teacher not to be afraid to try songs early in the program since idle vocalizing often destroys interest and quality. [441, p. 91]

The song approach. Grove's *Dictionary of Music* [708] defines *song* as "a short metrical composition [for solo voice] whose meaning is conveyed by the combined force of words and melody." (See also Chapter X.) Songs are the most prevalent vehicles of artistic vocal-musical expression and are in common use wherever singing is practiced. Technical vocal training, therefore, has as its main purpose the preparation of the student for the singing of songs. Song singing is also commonly used as a studio test of proficiency at various stages of vocal progress and the vocal problems arising in the song itself are often used as technical exercises. The *song approach*, then, is a procedure for teaching the techniques of voice production through a study and analysis of the technical problems contained in the rendition of songs.

There is a difference of opinion concerning the efficacy of the song approach as a teaching device. Out of 34 statements on this subject, 24 are in favor of using songs as technical exercises and 10 are opposed to this procedure. The latter group hold that songs should be studied, not as a means to an end, but as the end itself or the ultimate achievement in technical training. The arguments *for* and *against* are presented in the form of summarizing statements:

FOR:

1. Singing should be taught by whole rather than by part methods. This means a minimum of local action techniques and a maximum of singing songs involving whole coordinations of the physical instrument. [Witherspoon 677, p. 14]

2. Interpretation should not lag behind production techniques since both are equally important and need simultaneous development. Songs should provide exercise material for both. [Samoiloff 484, p. 35]

3. "Drill [by rote] has an extremely minor place in voice building. . . . We should develop the voice in and through actual song material. . . . [This] is the best and most central means of voice building." [Mursell and Glenn 413, p. 294]

4. "Avoid the traditional voice-lesson procedure of exercises, vocalises, and then songs. Devote many days entirely to work on songs. . . . When a song presents a difficulty, develop an exercise which will help to overcome the difficulty." [Wilson 674, p. 5]

5. A singer's technique is acquired by practicing suitable materials, not by a study of the technicalities of singing. [Henderson 240, p. 79]

6. "I am convinced that all there is to be learned about the voice can be done on a song." Vocal techniques can best be taught through illustrative song materials rather than through abstract exercises. Each song fragment should concretely illustrate the principle to be learned. "By the time the principle is practiced and understood, a song is learned." [Waters 647, p. 1; 641; 644]

7. In efficient technical study "the teaching material should consist of music—in other words, of 'pieces'—and formal exercises can be almost wholly discarded. . . . A technique can best be built out of the piecemeal study of performance problems when and as they arise." In studying these problems, "clear expressive utterance" is always the goal. [Mursell 410; Stultz 595]

8. "Vocal exercises should be developed out of the actual music you are singing. . . . Your problems exist only in your music." [Norton 428]

9. Vocalises can justify their use only through their specific application in the song itself. [Grove 216]

10. "Make exercises out of pieces." This was David Bispham's motto. [Sheley 545]

11. The teacher should learn to use "fragments of music, such as hymn tunes, anthems and songs as voice production exercises." [Jacques 299, p. 26]

12. "The right kind of music will educate the voice." [Patton and Rauch 445]

13. There are no special practice rules. Use the material at hand. A musical phrase or extract from an aria or lyric will provide excellent practice material for exercising the voice. [Marian Anderson 12; Davies 127, p. 108]

14. A great variety of exercises can be found in wisely selected songs. If exercises can be thought of as phrases of a song they will become vehicles of "expressive meaning" instead of lifeless vocalises. [Luckstone 360; Stock 588]

AGAINST:

1. A premature attempt at interpretation in songs spells the downfall of many vocalists whose technique is still incomplete. [Wood 686, vol. I, p. 17]

2. A complete mastery of technique should always precede the study of songs. [Barbareux-Parry 34, p. 262]

3. "Leave the glamorous arias [and songs] for later days." Scales and

exercises will develop the vocal organ until it is under complete control. [Conrad Thibault 605; Lombardi 357]

4. "Technique is the means, interpretation the end." [Greene 209, p. 8]

5. The interpretation of songs is possible only when correct technique has become habitual, thus relieving the mind from physical distraction during the projection of moods. [Hagara 220; Henschel 265, p. 7]

6. Great vocal harm can be self-inflicted by "attempting to learn and to do at the same time." [Emilio de Gogorza 134]

7. "It is futile to throw yourself into spirited singing until the vocal action has been conditioned to a high state of perfection." [Thomas 609]

8. Songs are used to test, not to develop technique. [Stanley 577, p. 121]

PRINCIPLES AND PROCEDURES USED IN PRACTICING

Practicing is defined as a method of study based on systematic exercise, for the purpose of mastering a specific skill or technique. (W) Inasmuch as the art of singing represents a highly organized, complex performance pattern, involving many skills, it is often considered necessary that the vocal student spend considerable time and effort in the exercise and development of those faculties and techniques that enter into the vocal achievement. Teachers of singing frequently assume that formal exercise of some sort must supplement the vocal instruction given during the studio lesson. By this means, the student can isolate difficulties appearing in the lesson. Then, by applying a repetitive drill routine or *vocalise* to each difficulty, he attempts to overcome it, with the idea that improvement in any one activity will lead to improvement in the total performance. [*Dictionary of Education* 706] A vocal exercise is sometimes called a *vocalise*. This term is derived from the Italian *vocalizzo* whose original meaning was "an extended melody sung on a vowel, i.e., without text . . . implying technical display for its own sake." [Harvard *Dictionary of Music* 704] The 50 statements gathered in this area are subdivided as follows:

a) principles of vocal practice (10 statements)
b) supervision of vocal practice (9 statements)
c) silent practicing as a device (5 statements)
d) the use of piano accompaniments (8 statements)
e) various methods of practicing (18 statements)

Principles of vocal practice. "Fundamental voice training," writes Wilcox, ". . . is not immediately concerned with the art of singing. It is concerned with the preparatory development of a suitable instrument for singing." [668] According to Huey, practicing is an indispensable supplement to vocal instruction. The main purpose of vocal exercise is "to develop to the utmost of beauty and skill of which they are capable," the natural range, power and quality of the singing voice. [287] Clippinger claims that the purpose of practice is "to establish automatic response of the vocal organs to musical ideas." [109] Herbert-Caesari adds that the development of muscular coordinations is the prime purpose. [269, p. 126] Kerstin Thorborg would use preliminary practicing solely "to explore, to settle, and to warm up the tone quality of the voice." [612] No matter what his stage of development, the singer can never afford to neglect his daily practice. This is Wilcox's opinion. A singer is, in a sense, a vocal athlete who must use systematic exercise to keep himself in condition. [665] To avoid meaningless practice, every vocal exercise must have an express purpose. [Haywood 235] "A vocalise should not just be a number of notes, but should be treated as a beautiful phrase in its own right." [Mursell and Glenn 413, p. 294] The use of conventional vocalises as practice materials for all singers has little value, according to Yaroll. "All voices are not equally benefited." Exercises should rather be designed to correct the singer's own peculiar faults. [697] Henderson endorses the use of vocalises. He also gives the term a general meaning; referring to any type of vocal exercise. [243, p. 97]

Supervision of practice. Practice is *supervised* when it is carried on in the presence of, and under the personal direction of, the teacher, for purposes of authoritative guidance. (W) "The beginning student cannot practice alone," says Clippinger, for the reason that his concepts of tone and freedom are as yet indefinite and unformed. "Therefore he will be strengthening his wrong habits." [112; 107] Henley is strongly opposed to unsupervised practice, no matter how intelligent the pupil may be. "No one . . . can possibly . . . judge his own voice without . . . the trained ear of an experienced teacher." [252; also Kwartin 325, Preface] Stanley also maintains that correction is the teacher's prerogative and should never be assumed by the pupil if the lesson is to have any value. Self-direction as in unsupervised practice then becomes a farce. [577, p. 332] Since the vocal student can hardly be trusted to practice alone it is desirable for the teacher to give a short lesson every day, especially during the early period of the pupil's development. [Halbe 221]

Clippinger lists a large number of questions on which the teacher must form a personal judgment during the singing lesson. Among them are the following: Is the student's tone true to pitch or is it flat or sharp? Has it the right intensity or is it too loud or too soft? Is it resonant or breathy?

Is it steady or unsteady? Is it produced with the right mechanism? Has it the necessary breath support? Has it a vibrato? Is the vocal organ free from tension; if not where is the tension located? Is the tone effortless or strained? Is the tone expressive or characterless? etc. Obviously the pupil cannot possibly check himself on all these criteria during an unsupervised practice period. Hence he needs constant supervision. [112] Wilson disagrees with this viewpoint, however. He writes: "The idea that students should not practice by themselves from the beginning is a strange fallacy. It is the duty of the teacher to establish habits immediately" that will enable the student to practice by himself. However, the student should receive constant guidance and should be cautioned that "frequent short periods of practice are better than one long period that may be too tiring." [674, p. 5]

Silent practicing as a device. Silent practice is an act of mental concentration in which a vocal exercise is visualized and mentally performed without any perceptible audible or visible effects. The suggestion is made that it is possible and advantageous to practice in silence, by singing a song mentally, in proper tempo, until it is learned. This obviates vocal fatigue, aids concentration and, in general facilitates the memorization of songs. [Laine 330] "Silent singing . . . stimulates musical thinking." [Brown 68] Silent exercises can be practiced "for the development of muscular strength and flexibility in the larynx" and in other vocal muscles. [Skiles 561] All the vocal muscles may be exercised mentally, without producing any audible sound. [Hagara 220, p. 116] Silent exercise is an invaluable form of exercise. It can be practiced abundantly, even "while travelling in the train or street car." [Novello-Davies 430, p. 50]

The use of piano accompaniment. Accompaniment is defined as "the musical background provided by a less important for a more important part. . . . The term also refers to the support given to a soloist (singer) by a pianist." [Harvard *Dictionary of Music* 704] The main purpose of a piano accompaniment during the vocal lesson or vocal practice period is "to sustain the pitch and give body, variety and completeness to the effect." (W) But the fact that the accompanying instrument tends to guide the voice constantly by keeping it on its true melodic pitch line, creates a type of aural dependency which, in the long run, may be detrimental to the singer, especially while he is practicing. For this reason it is deemed objectionable by some teachers. "All singers should accustom themselves to singing without instrumental aid," is Pierce's advice [447, p. ix] "Use the piano as little as possible in practicing," says Ryan. [480, p. 72] Laine is even more emphatic. "I advise each one (student) to do no vocalizing at the piano at all." [330] "No musician except the singer ever has another instrument as a crutch to lean upon and to determine the pitch of the notes he must produce." [Redfield 462, p. 125] José Mojica claims that "one can hear himself much better without the interference of an accompaniment." [401] Wilson prefers to have the student "practice all exercises [and songs] standing, without attempting to play the piano accompaniment at the same time." [674, p. 5] Father Finn would allow instrumental accompaniments to vocal exercises, providing they are unobtrusive and scarcely audible. [181, p. 248] Hill suggests that a given passage be played "before and after singing it, but not while singing it." [272, p. 17] In an experimental study entitled "The first vocal vibrations in the attack in singing," described in *Psychological Monographs*, Stevens and Miles conclude that "so far as evenness of tone is concerned, the [vocalist's] attack is not made more certain by having just listened to an instrument," such as a tuning fork. The results of this experiment introduces an interesting question as to whether the use of an accompanying instrument during vocal practice actually improves the student's pitch attack or helps him to deliver a steady and unwavering tone. [583]

Various factors in practicing. Various hints and suggestions are offered as to the best general manner of conducting the practice period. These factors are summarized in the following typical statements:

1. Four necessary aids to learning are: repetition, exaggeration, concentration and relaxation. Vocal practice methods should always emphasize these factors. [Novello-Davies 430, p. 34]

2. The intrinsic value of any exercise lies only in the manner of performing it. [Judd 309, p. 10]

3. Vary the mood when singing vocal exercises such as scales, arpeggios, etc. "It is perfectly useless to practice technique in a mechanical fashion without any expression." [Bushell 83; Witherspoon 676]

4. Repetitive practice tends to prevent spontaneity of vocal action. Vocalises and exercises should be sung "with the idea of spontaneous expression" and should therefore never be repeated except after a lapse of time. [Barbareux-Parry 34, p. 272; Shaw 537]

5. Perfection is preferable to speed. Even florid exercises should be practiced slowly with gradual increase of speed as the technique improves. This was Tosi's (ca. 1723) advice. [Klingstedt 320, p. 21]

6. "The coordinations which we use in soft or in low work differ from those used in loud or in rapid work, even if the passage [of music] itself remains the same. Thus the value of all slow practice is psychological and only indirectly physiological." These conclusions are the results of experimental findings. [Ortmann 437]

7. "In learning a song, the problem should be simplified and the learning made more effective and frequently faster, by eliminating one or more of the variables." Experimental research provides evidence to support this conclusion. [Bartholomew 39]

8. Humming a tune every day will keep the vocal instrument "properly exercised" and the musical faculty alive. [Samuels 487]

9. Ideally, vocal practice should not be attempted in confined quarters, but rather out in the open, in the out-door environment of the country. [Bergère 45]

10. When practicing, the use of a mirror, even for the artist, will prevent unnatural grimaces and gestures. [Little 349; Hagara 220]

11. Ten minutes at a time for practicing exercises is the limit for beginners. This period may be repeated two or three times a day. [Drew 147, p. 169]

12. A singing student's voice should never be used much more than an hour at a time. [Elizabeth Schumann 498]

13. In the beginning of the practice period, the work should be "moderate and gradual." [Emma Otero 440]

14. Sing in a standing position, whenever possible. All other positions are "more or less unnatural." [Laine 330]

SUMMARY AND INTERPRETATION

A final consideration of the 690 concepts of vocal pedagogy, subsumed in 29 categories in this chapter, leads to the conclusion that instructional guidance is woefully lacking in this area, in the 702 texts and articles examined. It is also apparent that authors of vocal texts are loathe to reveal their traditional trade secrets. Some authors are more pedagogically minded than others but are ill-equipped to transmit their inept empirical formulations through the impersonal medium of the printed word. Occasional pretentious claims for this or that methodology are weakened for want of factual support, although the laudable reputations and experience of the authors sometimes lend specious credibility to these claims. The brief and fragmentary treatment of many topics confirms the belief that authors are prone to evade the transmission of direct information to the lay reader. In the absence of specific methodological content, a few tenuous generalities often provide the only bases for formulating pedagogical procedures. Altogether, most of these statements cry out for confirmation and proof.

But the material on vocal pedagogy is not without interest and possible value, since the correlation of many diversified instructional viewpoints often brings to light the principles and purposes underlying them, with ultimate gains to the researcher. With this end in view, the following synoptic summaries are presented for interpretation by the vocal teaching profession. *Table One* presents a tabulation of all the concepts reviewed in this chapter.

THEORETICAL CONSIDERATIONS

Terminology. As they are employed in this treatise, *voice placement, voice culture,* and *training the singing voice* are synonymous expressions, all denoting that area of vocal pedagogy that relates to singing. An implicit distinction is made between the *singing voice,* a strictly musical connotation founded on Webster's definition, and the *speaking voice,* a purely non-musical connotation. These distinctions are more fully discussed in Chapters IX (Diction) and X (Interpretation). Therefore, in this and succeeding chapters, the terminology of vocal teaching refers specifically to the training of the singing voice and the term *voice,* appearing alone, in every case relates to the voice of the singer. *Vocal pedagogy,* as used in a general sense, also pertains to the science of teaching singing. Its specific applications include the formulation of principles and procedures (theories and methods) for training the singing voice in its many technical aspects.

Training the singing voice. For research purposes, a multiple approach to the training of the singing voice is used. The components of the act of singing are separately considered under the main headings of *breathing, phonation, resonance, range, dynamics, ear training, diction, interpretation;* and under numerous subheadings within each chapter. These categorical divisions are arbitrarily set up and are not to be construed as recommended separate departments of vocal teaching. In this study, the student's finished singing performance is largely thought of as an integration of development, combining the complex execution of many simple techniques, skillfully coordinated into an essential unity whose total structure is more readily understood because of the differential treatment administered to each of its interrelated parts.

Benefits of vocal study. The benefits of vocal training are classified as:

1. *physical:* singing is health-giving, promotes deep breathing and builds good posture.

2. *psychological:* singing is a mental salubrient; it strengthens memory and power of concentration, requires quick thinking, provides a constructive emotional outlet and means of self expression and removes inhibitions.

3. *character building:* vocal training develops courage, initiative, persistence, endurance.

4. *moral:* singing provides an uplifting, self-satisfying experience, is entertaining and promotes happiness.

5. *aesthetic:* vocal study improves the appreciation of the singing and interpretative arts and promotes an interest in music generally.

6. *personality:* singing creates poise, self-confidence, improved diction and ease of oral expression generally.

7. *vocational:* vocal training leads to a professional singing career for concert, opera, stage and radio.

Vocal prerequisites. Opinion is divided as to whether everyone can learn to sing. Certainly a good vocal organ is an important asset. But the physical organ is practically functionless without proper mental control, an educated and sensitive ear and an interest in, if not a talent for, musical expression. To be effective, therefore, the pedagogy of vocal training obviously requires adequate psychological and aesthetic implementation.

When to begin studying. Singing as a form of self expression should be taught at an early age, but artistic voice culture commences in earnest during the early post-adolescent period (i.e., from age 16 to 19). The younger, formative years of the pupil's life may be used advantageously for general education, physical culture and general musical development as a background for later voice work.

How long to study. Apparently, there is general agreement that singing demands from 3 to 6 years of study, even when the student possesses optimal native vocal endowments. An impatient attitude is inimical to vocal success and the practice of frequently changing teachers in quest of quick results or improved methods often defeats its own purpose. In vocal training, as in all forms of artistic development, humility, patience and slow, gradual growth produce the most lasting results.

The objectives of vocal training. These are considered in two classes:

1. *General objectives:* to develop a flexible voice and an automatic control of the vocal instrument as an expressive medium of interpretation in song; to develop skill in the artistic interpretation of songs; to develop general musicianship in a vocal medium.

2. *Specific objectives:* numerous intermediate processes and techniques of vocal training are mentioned that lead to: ear training; breath control; flexibility and smooth coordination of various muscles contributing to the vocal act; removal of inhibitions; good diction; improved vocal attack, extension of pitch range, relaxation, improved resonance, control of dy-

namics; discovering the natural range and resonance of the voice; building a song repertoire; etc.

Coordination as a factor. Coordination is a primary technical objective of vocal teaching. Since the muscles of the body usually act in pairs or in coordinated groups, it is often difficult to infer the actions of individual muscles that contribute to a complex behavior pattern, except through an analysis of the constituent elements in the group. In effecting such an analysis, part methods of learning are employed which require the specific training of each muscle action in a coordinated pattern. A three-fold procedure is employed:

a) *period of analysis:* the isolation of simple technical problems out of faulty complex behavior patterns.

b) *period of practice:* drilling of each underdeveloped muscle member of a coordinated action pattern until its proficiency level is commensurate with the expected efficiency of its parent group.

c) *period of synthesis:* individual skills are recombined into an integrated activity; i.e., coordinated or combined muscle movements are restored and practiced *in toto.* Balanced coordination is the key note of advanced practice in singing.

Standardization of vocal teaching. The belief that certain basic techniques in a singer's training can be standardized without loss of individuality in the final vocal product is a divided issue. Affirmative opinions find that such factors as pitch, resonance, dynamics, diction and posture can be approached through routine exercises whose purpose is to liberate, strengthen and refine the vocal instrument without impairing its individual characteristics. The danger of overtraining in a given technical routine is admitted.

Those who oppose standardization argue that each voice is a law unto itself; that teaching methods must vary from pupil to pupil; that no two voices are exactly alike; that standardization spells limitation in development. They are willing to accept basic principles and objectives in vocal teaching but insist that the methodology must remain free and variable.

METHODOLOGICAL CONSIDERATIONS

The psychological approach. Inasmuch as the psychologist believes in the sovereignty of the mental processes in controlling and coordinating human behavior, the psychological approach in vocal teaching is predominantly an indirect approach through mental rather than physical training. The student's attention is focussed upon thinking and hearing values in singing, not upon mere physical sensations. Such considerations as musical talent, mental discipline, the value of concentration, ear training, the use of visualization and imagination, aesthetic and interpretative effects are mentioned as important psychological factors in vocal training. Because singing involves these factors, the discipline of the vocal instrument inevitably employs certain psychological teaching methods. In this approach, the voice is trained largely through meaningful situations intended to facilitate learning without exciting the conscious or voluntary control of the functions involved. The singing voice is treated as an instrument of self expression and ear training methods are employed as a means of promoting the automatic response of the vocal instrument to concepts of beautiful tone. (Chapter VIII)

In contradistinction to the psychological approach is the more direct or *technical approach*, emphasizing the conscious manipulation and control of the processes and techniques involved in the vocal act. Teaching procedures employ preparatory technical exercises in which the mechanical repetitive execution of specific skills becomes an essential feature.

Voice training as habit formation. The most deliberate, newly acquired techniques in singing, if repeated often enough, can eventually be made to function as involuntary actions, without the intervention of conscious controls. This is the principle of habit formation employed by voice teachers who seek to develop facility of performance in their pupils through the use of repetitive exercises.

Singing as a natural function. To be natural, the vocal act must be unconscious and involuntary, spontaneous and free. Such a result is not possible by synthetic means and all studio training is fruitless unless the final result is an automatic and unstudied vocal action. Vocal reflexes can be trained through intermediate stages of consciously controlled technical discipline, but the ultimate desire of every singer is to attain such freedom and spontaneity of action that the singing voice will seem to be a natural endowment rather than an acquired skill. To achieve this result, habits must be firmly established and involuntary reflexes must take the place of precise conscious control over each part of the vocal mechanism. The acquisition of spontaneity and naturalness takes precedence over all other vocal accomplishments in training the singing voice.

Freeing the vocal mechanism. An important distinction is made between muscular relaxation *(tonus)* and muscular inertia inasmuch as authors are prone to confuse these two terms. Relaxation is described as a condition of relative ease and spontaneity of muscular action, freedom from abnormal strains and the absence of intrusive conscious controls in an otherwise automatic or involuntary vocal mechanism. The teaching of relaxation and freedom is best approached indirectly, through the elimination of self-consciousness, mental anxieties and fears. Extraneous and unnatural bodily tensions must be obliterated from the behavior pattern of the singer; the mind must be at ease and oblivious of all striving and the attention entirely devoted to the expressive and communicative purposes of the song.

Expressional factors in singing. Besides requiring consummate technical skill and a highly specialized use of the vocal apparatus, singing is also to be considered as a form of self expression, governed by conditions of concentration, spontaneity and joyous release. The voice functions at its best when the singer's mood is buoyant and exhilarated. Carefree attitudes are more conducive to natural, spontaneous vocal release than are meticulous techniques; or the conscious manipulation of breathing and vocal muscles; or the planned "placing" of each tone. Joyous release throws the vocal apparatus into high gear when correct feeling tones are superadded to the mere intellectual communication of ideas. From these observations the teacher may infer that optimal vocal conditions for singing can be induced by first promoting right thinking and feeling reactions in the student. In other words, wholesome satisfactions must always accompany good singing, even during practice periods.

Singing compared to speaking. Singing may be defined as an intensified form of vocal utterance in which only some of the basic factors of speech are operative. Pedagogical comparisons between singing and speaking consist, largely, of the "sing as you speak" approach, which is the use of certain speaking techniques to help explain or demonstrate analogous singing techniques. Majority opinion favors this teaching approach, a main premise being that, since speech habits predominate in daily life, they therefore greatly influence the singer's vocal habits. But this viewpoint is rife with opinionated discussion, without benefit of scientific knowledge or experimental evidence. Negative arguments advance the belief that speaking and singing habits are built on exclusively different forms of training. Each has its own basic physiology and its own psychological concomitants. This argument is supported by the reports of scientific investigators who find that both physiological and psychological conditions are different in singing than in speaking. Moreover, singing is governed by the laws of music, stressing the importance of such factors as pitch, resonance, intensity, rhythm, melodic contour, duration and musical accompaniment. These are factors that have no prominent or fixed value in speech.

The "sing as you speak" approach has some pedagogical merit, however, especially for its possible psychological effect upon the freedom, spontaneity and communicative expressiveness of the singing voice. Any diversion of the singer's attention from direct vocal control would tend to have a salutary effect upon his singing.

Technical principles and objectives. The technical approach to voice teaching is based, largely, upon a specificity of training theory according to which certain exercises and drills are designed to improve the control of breathing, phonation, resonance, range, dynamics, diction, etc., as separate skills. These are later to be integrated into a whole performance pattern through the smooth coordination of its many interrelated parts.

Removing muscular interferences. Vocal faults, caused by chronic extraneous tensions or interferences in the vocal tract, are common among students of singing. Physiological, rather than psychological, correctives are proposed by those who favor mechanistic methods of vocal training. Remedial exercises are used to induce compensatory muscular actions that will offset these extraneous tensions in the vocal tract. Physical relaxation and deep breathing drills are also recommended.

Handling beginners. The inception of the vocal training program is just as important as its outcome since preliminary appraisals of a student's vocal equipment must, to a large extent, determine initial instructional procedures. Authors are not agreed on voice classification factors. Majority opinion favors quality as a criterion. Others propose the use of speaking range, middle range *(tessitura)*, extreme range, intensity, and emotional temperament as criteria. A warning note is sounded against the needless insistence upon the preliminary classification of all voices. As a studio fetish, classification serves no useful purpose. All worthy vocal teaching methods are supposed to subserve aims that are exploratory and diagnostic, constructive, reeducational and habit-building. Such aims allow for procedural revisions in teaching as often as the need arises. The question here is, should the teacher consider it necessary to stretch the pupil's voice to meet the arbitrary dimensions of an imposed classification (e.g., tenor, contralto, soprano, etc.) instead of allowing the voice to develop within its own natural tendency for growth with correct use? Some authors believe that, through a resourceful and efficient utilization of the vocal equipment actually available to the beginner, the singing voice would eventually grow into healthy maturity and acquire normal characteristics of quality, range, etc., without any preliminary classification at all. The reaching out for extraordinary pitch and tonal effects should be deferred until the student has attained considerable mastery over the vocal equipment he already possesses, especially if the student's true vocal stature has not yet emerged. The vocal classification may not reveal itself "until the technique has reached a very high state of perfection. . . . A voice may, indeed, continue to grow for many years." [Stanley 578] Aikin's comment is also relevant at this point. "The amount of strain which has to be borne by the voice, if the work is pitched too high, cannot fail to wear out and distort the instrument prematurely. . . . Every teacher who understands his work ought to know where to stop." [4] To avoid such strains, it is suggested that songs should be transposed to suit the vocal compass, rather than the vocal compass stretched to suit the song.

Opinion also varies as to the treatment of first vocal lessons. Suggestions include the stressing of corrective aspects of early teaching, simplification of instruction, diagnostic and exploratory approaches and the use of such materials and devices as single tones, intervals, the isolation of registers, moderate use of dynamics and the song approach.

The song approach. Whole versus part methods of training are delineated in this controversial topic. Singing a song is a *whole* activity, embodying the complete act of vocal expression. Practicing a vocal exercise is a *part* activity, involving only a small technical subdivision of the singer's art. "Learn to sing by singing" is the motto of the proponents of the whole method, the song approach. "Wait until your technique is ready, then sing!" say its opponents. The issue is clearly defined and there is some merit on either side.

In using the song approach, technical problems are considered only as the need arises, during the actual singing of songs. By a judicious choice of song literature the student's singing repertoire can be planned so as to encompass every needful technical problem of voice production, breathing, resonance, etc. Thus the song performs a dual pedagogical role; the means and the end are combined.

The negative viewpoint is equally clear. Unless the student has at his command a thoroughly trained and habitualized vocal technique, he will find himself beset with technical limitations and cannot devote himself exclusively to the spirit of singing. Furthermore, as Aikin puts it, "the singer must know how to direct his technical ability, and must have some distinct mental intention in singing, or the performance will be nothing more than the mechanical recitation of words and notes." [Op. cit.] The paradox of part method technical training is therefore apparent: before he can enjoy the freedom of singing, the student must first learn to conserve, control and direct his vocal resources. Thus, vocal discipline spells vocal freedom. The issue here rests.

PRINCIPLES AND PROCEDURES USED IN PRACTICING

a) The use and value of systematic practice, as a pedagogical supplement to the vocal lesson, cannot be ignored by the teacher of singing. If used consistently, the benefits of practice should apply with cumulative effect to each succeeding lesson. Formal exercise is the singer's "daily dozen." It helps to warm up the vocal instrument and builds habits of coordination and response.

b) Most pupils, left to themselves, unwittingly practice a fault, rather than its correction, even with the best of intentions. Because bad vocal habits are concealed and elusive, their correction should never be arrogated by the pupil. They require the expert attention of the teacher himself, until they are completely routed. There is a single dissenting opinion, however. Teachers owe it to their pupils to make them self-reliant as soon as possible. To this end, vocal habits must be trained with such certainty that a degree of vocal independence can be established early in the student's training program.

c) An interesting suggestion is offered, that silent or mental practicing is a salutary forerunner of audible vocal exercise. Silent exercises are used for laryngeal muscular gymnastics, for memorizing songs, and to promote visualization and musical thinking. It can be practiced inconspicuously and in any environment. Its benefits accrue to the student in any later performance of the same exercise, since it tends to familiarize him with strange technical combinations and prepares him mentally with an accurate prevision of his finished performance. (See also Chapter VIII.)

d) By a law of exercise, when either a faculty or a function of the body is used often, it will tend to develop strength and stability; conversely, when it is neglected through disuse, it will tend to weaken and waste away. It follows, then, that the student's constant dependency upon ready-made pitch guidance in the use of piano accompaniments while practicing, might conceivably weaken his own pitch sense for attacking tones. This argument, although tenuous, is supported by some experimental data. While he is practicing, the vocal student needs to awaken and stimulate his own powers of aural visualization. Strong tonal preconceptions are valuable in singing. Good hearing acuity guarantees precision and self reliance in the vocal attack. These are virtues and values that need to be protected and nourished by the student during his practice period.

e) Finally, various ways of practicing the singing voice are briefly discussed. Suggestions include: mental aids to learning; the simplification of practice procedures; the importance of expression, mood and a spontaneous manner when practicing exercises; the values of slow tempo, humming, use of a mirror, standing position and outdoor environment; the stultifying effect of rote repetition, need for short practice periods and the use of moderation in all practice work.

Throughout the foregoing discussions of vocal pedagogy, little distinction is made between the trained and the untrained singing voice. Allusions to the effectiveness of vocal training methods, in most instances, disregard the elements of age level, physical health, mental quipment, vocal experience and previous training, emotional stability, hearing acuity or qualities of musicianship in the individual. These are all factors that play a part in the musical education of the average student, whether it be for singing or instrumental performance. In other words, discussions of vocal pedagogy should take into account the adaptability of the individual to the instructional procedures proposed at his own level of experience. Such special considerations as the diagnosis of his faults and the appraisal of his natural endowments for singing might, for instance, precede the application of practice routines, especially if the student is a beginner. In the absence of specific references to aptitude, experience and intelligence factors of learning, it is often necessary to assume that authors are referring to beginners or amateur singers and not to advanced pupils or professionals.

In conclusion, the teacher is reminded that motivation factors are of the utmost importance in training the singing voice. Student interest and the love of self expression are impelling forces in the growth of the singing voice. Singing as an art requires a high degree of cultivation, through correct use, of faculties that are largely native to the individual. Therefore, in applying a varied and selective methodology, the teacher must employ those pedagogical approaches and devices that minimize the deadly monotony of routine drills. "The lazy teacher keeps the pupil vocalizing exercises over and over again with little or no singing," says Stanley. [577, p. 120] Those who appreciate the importance of motivation in the vocal training process will agree with Robison's statement that: "There are many ways to help the pupil arrive at the goal of good singing. Perhaps the best road is simply the one that he best understands. Anything that helps toward free, simple, vital, sincere, natural expression of a clear musical conception . . . is good practice." [Harvard Dictionary of Music 704] To accomplish this end, the teacher will recognize the self-motivating attributes of well chosen songs whose expressional qualities stimulate the creative as well as the technical abilities of the student.

CHAPTER III

CONCEPTS OF BREATHING

Definition. *Breathing* or respiration is the act or process of drawing air into the lungs for oxygenating and purifying the blood, and its subsequent exhalation. (W) A full explanation of the respiratory function may be found in any standard work on physiology. The following résumé, gathered from Starling's *Human Physiology* [713, p. 841 ff.] is given here as a brief reorientation for the teacher of singing:

The constant renewal of air in the lungs is brought about by rhythmical movements of the thorax or chest cavity which cause an alternate increase and diminution in their size. As the lungs swell up with each enlargement of the thorax, air (breath) is sucked in through the trachea or windpipe. This is *inspiration*. As the thorax relaxes it contracts and its capacity is diminished causing an expulsion of air and deflation of the lungs. This is *expiration*. Normally there is a slight pause following each expiration. The frequency of respiratory movement varies with age, muscular effort and emotional excitement, the normal frequency in an average, resting adult being about 17 or 18 per minute. Although breathing is essentially automatic it responds to volitional control. Therefore it can be modified but not entirely repressed by the will. Volitional modifications of the primary act of breathing may take place in singing, often causing greatly altered and accentuated respiratory movements. During inspiration, the thorax is enlarged in all dimensions, from above downwards by the contraction of the diaphragm and in its transverse diameters by the movements of the ribs.

Breathing is important to the singer because normal voice production or phonation depends upon the presence of a steadily expiring stream of breath. Therefore, concepts of breathing relating to the regulation and control of this stream of breath are of primary interest to the teacher of singing.

Of the 428 concepts of breathing gathered from 702 vocal texts, articles and reports of interviews with professional singers, 58 statements discuss

TRAINING THE SINGING VOICE

TABLE TWO

SUMMARY OF CONCEPTS OF BREATHING USED IN TRAINING THE SINGING VOICE

	total number of statements	sub-total	grand total	statements by prof. singers	documented statements	undocumented statements
I. *Theories of breathing*			58			
A. The importance and nature of breathing		33				
1. breathing a primary consideration	20			4	3	17
2. pre-vocal training advised	13			1	2	11
B. Physiological factors		25				
1. action of ribs and diaphragm	17			2	7	10
2. other coordinating factors	8				2	6
II. *Methods of cultivating breath control*			370			
A. Psychological approach		95				
1. natural breathing advised	48			3	1	47
2. singing develops breathing	23					23
3. interpretational controls						
a) by correct phrasing	8			1		8
b) by synchronization with the music	2			1		2
c) expressional intent regulates breathing	9			1		9
d) other devices for improving breathing	5					5
B. Technical approach		275				
1. postural controls						
a) through physical culture	46					46
b) through maintaining a correct chest position	33				1	32
2. voluntary control of breathing						
a) *direct control of breathing organs advised*	24					24
b) *direct control of breathing organs not advised*	11					11

TABLE TWO (continued)

	total number of statements	sub-total	grand total	statements by prof. singers	documented statements	undocumented statements
3. diaphragmatic control						
a) *diaphragmatic control is essential*	27			4	1	26
b) *diaphragmatic control is not essential*	9				1	8
4. orificial controls						
a) breathing through mouth advised	8					8
b) breathing through nose advised	5					5
c) breathing through mouth and nose advised	12			2		12
5. quantitative factors						
a) breath economy	56			9	5	51
b) breath pressure and support	27			2	1	26
c) breath renewal, frequency and speed	17				1	16
TOTALS	428	428	428	30	25	403

the theories of breathing, 95 statements describe psychological methods and 275 statements discuss physiological or technical methods of training the breathing controls of the singer. The main and subordinate groupings under this topic are summarized in *Table Two*. Representative opinions in each group are presented below.

THEORIES OF BREATHING

THE IMPORTANCE AND NATURE OF BREATHING

Breathing is a primary consideration in singing. The vocal act has its inception in the expiratory flow of breath from the lungs of the singer past his vocal cords where phonation takes place. The act of breathing therefore invites attention as a preliminary approach to all problems of training the singer's voice. The first thing the singer has to do is to learn to breathe properly. [Mackenzie 364, p. 95] He must be able to fill his lungs and empty them quickly or slowly, gently or with force, to meet the artistic requirements of his song. So varied and exacting are these requirements that, in a sense, "the singer must be a professional breather." [Clark 102] "Respiration is the power behind the tone." [Jacobus 298] According to Allen, breath is the life giving force of all vocal tone. [7, p. 23] Witherspoon believes that correct breathing is important in that it prepares the way for free vocal action. [677, p. 60] Pressman and Brown both claim that incorrect breathing is one of the chief causes of vocal failure because faults of breathing induce tensions in the throat. [452 and 78, p. 13] Henderson is of the opinion that singing always demands a special type of breathing. "All teachers are agreed that it is absolutely essential for every vocal pupil to acquire a correct method of breathing," he states. "Keep the outgoing column of air under perfect control. That is the foundation of all singing technique." [243, p. 17 and 25]

It is well to remember that singing is but "a constant coming and going of breath." [Marchesi 369, p. 3] The nervous mechanism that controls the breathing muscles works automatically. But these muscular movements are also subject to voluntary control. Therefore breathing "is subject to educational influences." [Owsley 441, p. 24] Witherspoon feels that breathing should never be forced. It will take care of itself if it is free enough. Indeed, there is a definite physiological law, as he puts it, that governs breathing. This law may be stated as follows: In singing, as in any physical exertion, breathing effort is always directly proportionate to the intensity of the action desired. Hence, in singing, breathing effort is proportionate to the pitch and volume of the vocal utterance desired. [675] Shaw empirically observes that the singer artist never takes a breath consciously. He merely extends his body ever so slightly at the beginning of a phrase and there is an immediate proportionate expansion of the torso, unnoticeable but sufficient for the needs of the phrase about to be sung. [529] The nature of this bodily extension is not explained.

Pre-vocal training in breathing advised. In order to sing well, it is first necessary to develop the breathing muscles beyond the normal requirements for living. [Wodell 679] In other words, training in breathing must take precedence over other forms of training for actual tone production. The first step in learning to sing is to acquire a method of managing the breath. [Clark and Leland 101, p. 5] Voice production should not be attempted until the pupil has already acquired good breath control, according to Philip. [446, p. 145] Mme. Shoen-René is also definite in her opinion regarding the separation of breath training from vocal training.

"Practice in correct breathing should always precede all exercises in singing," she warns. [493] Armstrong would have at least six months of practicing breathing exercises before singing lessons are commenced. [23] The
type of pre-vocal training is not always endorsed although there is wide
agreement that the acquisition of superior breathing habits is a primary
consideration in learning to sing. According to Stanley, such work must
not be associated with the act of phonation. [578] "Chest capacity must be
increased as an independent activity." [Jacques 299, p. 12] Thirteen authors emphasize the separation of respiratory and phonatory training
routines, insisting that the foundation of singing is perfect breath control [Byers 89], and that "breathing should be the first function to receive
attention." [Wharton 655, p. 20]

PHYSIOLOGICAL FACTORS

Action of ribs and diaphragm. Howe makes the general statement that
the correct method of breathing requires a combination of rib raising and
diaphragmatic contraction. [284, p. 10] Hemery is more specific. He asserts
that the diaphragm contributes one-third of the expansion of the chest
while the rib movement contributes two-thirds. [238, p. 21] Stanley believes that the rib muscles are always held firm while the diaphragm
varies in tension with the variations in vocal pitch. [577, p. 326] Aikin
supports this view, stating that a well trained singer keeps his ribs expanded while the diaphragm moves in opposition to the abdominal muscles. Thus breathing in singing becomes entirely diaphragmatic and abdominal. [4] Conversely, Evetts and Worthington believe that where the
respiratory movement is intensified for any reason whatsoever, only the
lower rib movements should be increased. [167, p. 90] Wilcke favors the
so-called *combined* type of respiration in which both thorax and diaphragm play an important part. "It should be made clear that pure abdominal or exclusively costal breathing never occurs." [664, p. 16]

The diaphragm should be considered exclusively as an organ of expulsion, according to Armstrong. [22] Apparently it serves only a passive
role in inspiration. Warren speaks of two main points of expansion in
the body during breathing. These are located near the solar plexus in
front and at the base of the shoulder blades in back. The sensation of
breath support comes from an interplay between these two opposite
sides. [640] Witherspoon favors a combination of rib and diaphragmatic
movement known as diaphragmatic-costal breathing. In this coordination, rib movement may be voluntarily controlled. [677, p. 56] This rib
control is especially noticeable during the moment of breath suspension
which this author claims is an important part of the singing act. It

occurs in the momentary cessation of breathing after inhaling, just before attacking a tone. The ribs are extended outward and firmly set at the moment of suspension. The rib muscles then become the central controlling muscles of the breath. [Ibid., p. 57] On the other hand, Josephson argues in favor of diaphragmatic breathing, claiming that it is more economical of effort for a definite volume of air and that it therefore reduces respiratory fatigue. [308] Later on he suggests the employment of different types of respiration for different tonal ranges, for example, chest breathing for higher tones, costo-diaphragmatic breathing for middle register tones and abdominal breathing for the lower tones. [Ibid.]

Other coordinating factors. Coordination and equilibrium between various parts of the breathing mechanism are mentioned as important factors in breathing for singing. Bartholomew describes this coordination as a state of balance between the diaphragm and the abdominal muscles. The diaphragm "holds back" against the inward and upward pressure of the abdominal wall until perfect equilibrium is reached. [39] Apparently the expiration of air under these conditions is subject to a more delicate control than would be possible by diaphragmatic pressure alone. According to Scott, in good singing, breathing must be regarded as a conflict between antagonistic sets of muscles. Hence, equilibrium is an important factor in considering the coordinations which enter into the act of breathing. [501, p. 44] In this state of equilibrium the contracting muscles hold back against the expanding muscles and vice versa. [Robinson 474]

Strangely enough, the lungs and the larynx are not often mentioned in connection with breathing. Hemery claims that there is no coordination between respiratory and laryngeal movements. [238, p. 86] Shaw regards the lungs as passive organs in the breathing mechanism. "As there is no muscular fibre in the lungs themselves," he says, "they cannot perform the act of breathing." Lung expansion in breathing, then is merely a resultant of external expansion of the muscles of the thorax. The expansion of the chest wall produces a decrease of air pressure within the lungs and the response of the elastic lung tissue to this expansion is immediate. The respiratory cycle is completed by contraction of the chest wall with a resultant contraction and deflation of the lungs. [536] "The lungs are always passive in breathing and depend for their performance upon the activity of the chest walls and diaphragm." [Samuels 487, p. 9] One more factor is mentioned by Hagara in connection with the mechanism of breathing. This she offers without further explanation or proof, namely, that during inhalation it is important to straighten the lumbar region of the spinal column. [220, p. 30]

METHODS OF CULTIVATING BREATH CONTROL IN SINGING

PSYCHOLOGICAL APPROACH

The 95 concepts in this group are subdivided as follows: 48 statements advocate *natural* breathing methods for singers; 23 statements endorse the principle that *singing develops breathing;* 24 statements advocate *interpretational* controls of breathing in one form or another.

Natural breathing advised. A *natural* function is one that is not artificial, synthetic or acquired by external means. (W) *Natural breathing,* therefore, is breathing that has not been influenced by direct technical training or localized effort. It is a spontaneous, normal and unconscious activity without any attempt at voluntary control; a reflex action.

The advocates of natural breathing do not allow a pupil to think of his breath while singing. "Forget all about the breath," is their slogan. To them, this is a fundamental law of singing. [Stanley 577, p. 39] In the opinion of Jussi Bjoerling, Metropolitan Opera Company tenor, the minute a singer begins to think about his breath while he is singing, he becomes short-winded. Therefore, breathing should always be a perfectly natural process. [47] In this belief he is upheld by Lauritz Melchior, renowned tenor, who also declares that breathing, upon which all singing rests, must be an entirely natural affair. Any constriction is wrong. "The best teacher for breath control is a young baby," he suggests. The student of singing is also advised to recapture the experience of natural breathing in a recumbent position, preferably while lying "flat on your back on the floor." [388] "Inhale with the complete relaxation of a sleeping child," says Rimmer . . . "or with the ease of a healthy yawn . . . and the secrets of deep breathing have been learned."[465] Frieda Hempel, well-known operatic and concert soprano, insists that a singer should not be troubled with complicated theories of breath support unless a definite need arises. [239]

Evetts and Worthington believe that respiration in singing, as in life, is governed mainly by the body's oxygen requirement. [167, p. 88] It is their contention that excessive breath intake before attack is a common fault among singers which can only be corrected by ignoring the breath altogether and by beginning the song at any point in a normal respiratory cycle. [Ibid., p. 83] Shaw, a prolific writer on the singing voice, declares that breath support in singing is a spontaneous action controlled by natural reflexes. This involuntary process may not be disturbed by conscious breathing techniques without disastrous results. [518, p. 126] Shaw insists that the management of the singer's breath is about as absurd as the management of his heart beat.[536] "Correct breathing for living is correct breathing for singing. There is no other." [519]

There is surprising unanimity of opinion among the advocates of natural breathing. The statements listed here as basic concepts represent their point of view:

1. "When students become over breath-conscious they seldom sing well. It is amazing how very few fine singers know how they breathe." [Wilson 674, p. 29]

2. Much confusion has arisen in the singing profession as a result of teaching methods that attempt to regulate the exhalation of breath. [Kuester 324]

3. Nature's breathing is fool-proof while we sleep. Therefore practice natural breathing in a lying down position. [Lloyd 351, p. 2]

4. Perfect breath control is unobtrusive because it is natural and therefore never apparent to the listener. [New York Singing Teachers Association 421, p. 30]

5. Breathing in singing is an automatic physiological function. [Marafioti 368, p. 88]

6. "In natural breathing, the supply is always equal to the demand." [Hall 222]

7. In the vocal studio, normal bodies have adequate lung capacity for singing. If the body is subnormal, build it up in a gymnasium. [Hall and Brown 227, p. 6]

8. Singers who lock the breath cannot possibly express a natural tone. [Hill 272, p. 20]

9. Great singers of the past always breathed the natural way. [Byers 89]

10. Singers should not take special breaths before singing but should breathe, instead, "in the normal way, as though they were not about to sing." There will always be sufficient quantity of breath if the vocal emission is right. [Brown 65, p. 19]

11. Watch out for Satan's instruction: "Take a good breath and get ready." That is the surest way of defeating your effort to sing. [Stults 597]

12. The object of the singer is to sing, not to breathe. Over-attention to breathing mechanics distracts the singer's attention from the realm of sound production which demands unceasing vigilance of mind and ear. [Drew 147, p. 118]

13. The old Italian method emphasized natural breathing. [Harper 228, p. 79]

14. "Usually when a singer thinks he has a big breath, he merely has tight muscles." [Williamson 672]

15. "Breathe naturally, as if asleep." [Rimmer 464]

16. "Emotion [or intense feeling] is the correct source of the singer's breath and always gives adequate support to the tone." [De Bruyn 131]

Singing develops breathing. This principle is a corollary of natural breathing methods. It follows that, if breathing is to be ignored by the singing student, the breathing organs will develop their own natural action as part of the act of singing. According to Witherspoon, they need never be practiced separately, for exaggerated local effort interferes with the coordinations involved and defeats its own purpose. [677, p. 63] Conklin claims that the mental preparation of any tone includes the automatic preparation of the right amount of breath for that tone. This is a reflex action and should not be obstructed by employing conscious breath controls. [121, p. 32] Obviously then, breathing will improve as voice production improves since the two are reciprocal functions of the same vocal act.

Drew recommends that breath control may be practiced by attempting to sing an absolutely steady note at varying intensities. [147, p. 176] We automatically develop breath control by properly sustaining the tone. [Huey 286] "Do not take a conscious breath," warns Thomas. Singing induces unconscious breath action which gradually becomes "automatic through conditioning and repetition." [609] Direct the attention of the student to the sound of the voice, not to breath control. [Shaw 518, p. 182] Proschowsky maintains that the art of breathing rests fundamentally upon the art of tone production, the latter being governed entirely by the "inner hearing or tone thinking" of the singer. [455] In this, he claims, the perfect tone demands perfect economy of breath usage in phonation. "Breathing must go hand in hand with phonation," says Huey. [285] "The more the vocal cords are trained in the right way, the less air will they require to vibrate," adds Marchesi. [369, p. 8]

Stanley believes that artificial breathing exercises tend to obstruct phonation and that singing demands unique breathing coordinations which cannot be developed by gymnastics but only by the act of singing. [577, p. 314] Christy quotes as follows from an outline of theory issued in 1925 by the American Academy of Teachers of Singing: "The correct practice of singing in itself tends to develop and establish the mastery of breath." He is tempted to add his own comment, however, that "the student will develop more rapidly if taught how to breathe." [97, p. 41]

In conclusion, this group holds the opinion that breathing is not a volitional activity. It is governed solely by the demands of the voice in singing. [Henderson 243, p. 31] Therefore, singing develops breathing but not breathing, singing. [Marafioti 368, p. 86] "Correct breathing for singers is correct breathing for all other people, and vice versa." [Shaw 538] "We breathe to sing, just as we breathe to speak. The only difference is that we prolong the act." [Fleming 183] Finally, breath control does not imply a restraint of the breathing apparatus or an attempt to conserve the breath since breath expenditure is predetermined at the glottis by the intensity, pitch and duration of phonation. Therefore, breathing cannot be controlled locally. [Evetts and Worthington 167, p. 84]

INTERPRETATIONAL CONTROLS

By correct phrasing. The *interpretation* of a song is the artistic representation of it in which the singer presents his own conception of its underlying meaning and mood. (W) (cf. Chapter X) Interpretational values are communicational values in expression. Hence audience comprehension is of paramount importance. Mindful of his audience, the singer objectively transmits his musical ideas and feelings by means of vocal patterns that accentuate and enhance the comprehension of these ideas and feelings in his audience. A *phrase* is a musical thought. (W) Hence, correct phrasing demands the use of vocal patterns and expressional techniques that are appropriate to the musical thought of the song. Phrases are analogous to the sentences of a literary composition. They are usually punctuated by suitable pauses and the intervals between these pauses are uninterrupted musical units. [Grove's Dictionary of Music 708, Vol. IV, p. 146]

In referring to breathing in singing, Williamson claims that breath control is a *result* of good phrasing and not the cause of it. [534] He believes that the maintenance of unbroken phrase units, regardless of their length would tend to develop good breathing. Some of the simpler sacred songs of *Bach* are suggested by Mrs. Henderson as illustrations of excellent breathing exercises for beginners. These songs consist of fairly long phrase units that require sustained breathing for their proper interpretation. She adds, however, that it is advisable to shorten the last note of each phrase so that a breath may be taken when necessary without delaying the attack of the new phrase. [240, p. 60] Brown suggests that, after deciding where to breathe, the student should hum through each complete phrase of a song without a break, studying the effect thereof. This will condition breathing techniques in a practical but indirect manner. [65, p. 19]

It is Coleman's opinion that the taking in of the breath "must be prompted emotionally by the phrase which is to be sung with that breath." The phrase then becomes the unit of breathing and each unit begins, "not with the first note but with the intake of breath before that note." [118, p. 34] When two very fast phrases occur in succession, the breath may not be renewed between them, even when a minute pause is provided. Thus, breath endurance is developed as a concomitant of correct phrasing. [Maurice-Jacquet 376] Jessica Dragonette, in an interview, insists that the quantity of breath taken must always suit the length and intensity of the musical phrase and that the interpretation must therefore govern the breathing behavior. [146] Mursell and Glenn favor working exclusively through interpretation in promoting breathing habits. Their advice is that we should always "work for control of breath by a phrase-wise attack." [413, p. 286]

By synchronization with the music. As the singer progresses, his phrasing, and therefore his breathing, can be improved by *synchronizing* his breathing rhythms with the rhythm of the music he is singing. [Witherspoon 677, p. 66] His pauses will then automatically coincide with rhythmical points in the melody and phrasing will never become disjointed. [Hemery 238, p. 122]

Expressional intent regulates breathing. Expressional intent refers to the thought content of a song, which thought is best expressed by understanding the meaning and mood of the words. Irene Hibbs, in discussing Rameau's viewpoint on singing believes that breathing functions as an expressional reflex, whether for speech or for song. Therefore, if the singer is preoccupied with the thought of his song he will breathe in a manner that is appropriate to its expression. No more breathing effort is needed than when he desires to speak its message. [271] Drew is of the same opinion. He claims that the breathing habits of singing are not unique. We all know that we unconsciously provide sufficient air for each phrase we speak. Then why not sing your phrase as you would speak it and breathing will take care of itself. [147, p. 150] "Breathe to pronounce rightly and you breathe rightly," says Davies. [127, p. 119] Thought and feeling impulses always tend to generate appropriate vocal impulses and proper breathing coordinations are thus automatically brought into play or, as Harper puts it, "the thought takes its own breath." [228, p. 131] "Know what you are going to say and the breath will not fail," says Clark. [102]

Margit Bokor, leading soprano, in an interview advances the interesting theory that emotional fluctuations closely affect the respiratory function. In moments of emotional stress the system burns up more oxygen and therefore demands more breath. That is why breathing is entirely governed by the emotional interpretation or expression of a song. [54] To illustrate this principle, Witherspoon suggests that we practice "exclaiming" with varying degrees of emotional feeling. He even proposes that this method might be used to divert a student's attention from his own breathing actions, thus inducing "correct breathing naturally and quickly." [677, p. 65] Here again, Mursell and Glenn emphasize the importance of using breathing exercises "very sparingly or not at all." If such exercises are used at all they must always be used with a "perceived relationship to musical expressiveness." [413, p. 286]

Other devices for improving breathing. Five other devices are recommended as methods of cultivating breath control for singing, without local effort. They are: laughing, sighing, yawning, panting and being startled.

1. In *laughing* heartily it is possible to develop the abdominal muscles of breathing as they perform in singing. [Wycoff 693]

2. The freedom of deep breathing for singing is best exemplified by a contented *sigh*. [Waters 647, p. 5]

3. "The singer's breath must be as deep as the breath we take in *yawning*." [Marchesi 369, p. 4]

4. *"Panting* is excellent practice to increase the flexibility of breath action." [Wilson 674, p. 29]

5. "Inhale instantly as though *startled*. This will develop quick inhalation for singing." [Snyder 568, p. 6]

TECHNICAL APPROACH

Techniques are the methods or details of practical procedure, or the manner of performance, essential to expert execution in an art or science. (W) The technical approach to breathing would therefore include a consideration of the various practical procedures of instruction and practice advocated by specialists in training the singing voice. To this end, an examination of the 702 texts in the bibliography yielded a total of 275 statements on the various technical aspects of cultivating breathing for singing. These are considered under five separate headings as outlined in *Table Two*. The first of these deals with posture.

POSTURAL CONTROLS

The relative arrangement or disposition of the different structural parts of the body (W) during the act of breathing is a primary consideration in teaching *posture*. Of the 79 fundamental concepts in this category, 46 statements relate to physical culture and 33 statements to the maintenance of correct chest position.

Physical culture as a method. Shaw's opinion represents the prevailing point of view that correct breathing invariably requires an expansion of the torso in the chest and abdominal regions. This expansion is the cause, not the result of breathing. It can be taught as an action separate and apart from breathing because the muscles involved are all subject to voluntary physical control. In other words, as Shaw expresses it, "Torso action should be taught—not breathing." [519] "Expand to breathe—do not breathe to expand." [518, p. 193] To the opera and oratorio singer, physical exercises to enlarge the chest and strengthen the intercostal, diaphragmatic and abdominal muscles are "an absolute necessity." [Douty 144] Singing inevitably requires physical cultivation of the breathing and vocal organs. [Armstrong 23]

Correct posture is of course essential to good tone production. But it must be developed gradually, without strain, "to the point where it becomes a habit." [Austin-Ball 31, p. 2; Waters 646] "Under the conditions of correct posture, deep breathing is facilitated," [Wilcox 666] and the body is kept responsive and free from rigidity. [Wodell 681] Furthermore, correct posture brings coordinated parts into natural alignment and thus assures a perfect functioning of the vocal mechanism. The breathing activity of singing should never disturb the structural alignment of the body which correct posture establishes. [Wilcox 669, pp. 3 and 15] Poor posture cramps the diaphragm. Therefore, as Harper believes, physical culture would seem to be the logical approach to voice culture. [228, p. 11] The singing teacher should apply the physical principles of correct posture to every voice lesson, requiring daily practice of postural controls as a means of enhancing breathing and vocal controls. [Stephens 582]

Wilson holds that posture is "a very important consideration in establishing correct breathing habits." [674, p. 29] Correct breathing is impossible until the entire body (posture) has acquired "poise and flexibility." [Wharton 655, p. 20] The voice always suffers when posture and breathing action are bad. [Wodell 680] Therefore, the consideration of posture comes first among the fundamentals of training the singer's voice. [Fergusson 178]

The kind of posture recommended for good breathing in singing is compositely described in the following thirteen admonitions:

1. The correct tension of muscular attachments between larynx and spine or larynx and sternum (breast bone) must be maintained. [Stephens 582]

2. The vital capacity of the chest is best in standing position. [Passe 443, p. 48]

3. Align the spine so as to avoid neck tension. [Wilcox 666]

4. Use the position of the soldier. [Hagara 220, p. 29]

5. Keep the natural vertical position of the head, the neck free and loose. [Cimini 99]

6. Always stand to sing. [Gould 206, p. 1]

7. Keep the chest medium high. [Christy 97, p. 43]

8. Always drop the shoulders. [Rimmer 464; Finn 181, p. 25]

9. During exhalation the ribs must be kept raised and stationary. [Jacques 299, p. 13]

10. The lower ribs are held outspread, the chest up and forward. [Harper 228, p. 10]

11. The chest remains high, ribs are raised, the shoulders held down. [Henley 246]

12. The chest is held up and supported from below, never from above. [Byers 89]

13. "Stand tall—never slump." [Wycoff 694]

Little need be added in support of postural physical training. The forty-six opinions in this group are all insistent that toneless physical exercises should be practiced to cultivate physique, posture and breath capacity. [E.g., Hemery 238, p. xii and Sheley 545] "The whole body is the vocal instrument," says Hill. "Hence, there is little hope of your becoming an A-1 singer if you are C-3 physically." [272, p. 16] Another point in favor of postural training is that physical exercise will tend to improve breathing without tiring the voice. [Sherwood 548, p. 36] That is why body building exercises should be practiced apart from singing. [New York Singing Teachers Association 421, p. 29]

Maintaining a correct chest position. The *chest* is that part of the body enclosed by the ribs and breastbone. It is also called the *thorax.* (W) Other parts adjacent to the chest and therefore immediately affected by its position and movement are: the collar bone, shoulder blades, spine and diaphragm. The parts indirectly affected are the abdominal wall, neck and larynx. The chest cavity contains the heart and lungs and in normal respiration it expands and contracts rhythmically.

Thirty-three authors mention chest position as a factor in postural control. All but four favor the maintenance of a high and stationary chest position for singing. The advantages named include the following:

1. The lungs are given ample freedom, resonance is increased and personal appearance is improved. [Greene 209, p. 290]

2. High chest position is more than a breathing technique. It is a matter of general physique and good posture. [Henderson 240, p. 82]

3. This high chest posture will help free the throat, jaw and tongue from all stiffness and strain. [Henley 260]

"Raise the chest before breathing," says Clippinger. [104, p. 7] "See that it [chest] does not drop, particularly at the moment of attack." [Jacques 299, p. 34] With a high chest, less breath intake is required, since the expanded thorax "automatically retains" more breath "in continuous reserve." [Henley 252] According to Hagara, the old singing masters taught that a high and stationary chest must be established before the first note is sung. [220, p. 113] That "the heaving of the chest should never be seen except as an emotional expression" is Warren's opinion. [640] "*Clavicular* or collar bone breathing means pulling up the chest by the neck muscles. This tightens the neck and spreads muscular tensions into the larynx, throat and tongue." [Hemery 238, p. 83] "Clavicular breathing has no place in artistic singing." [Henderson 243, p. 28] In respiration the chest should always remain stationary. [New York Singing Teachers Association 421, p. 31]

Four authors hold variant opinions, however. Marafioti quotes Enrico Caruso as saying that, in full breathing, the chest must be raised simultaneously with the drawing in of the abdomen. This evidently occurs with each intake of breath. "The ability to retain the breath until needed makes or mars all singing." [368, p. 158] Orton makes the assertion that raising the chest and pulling in the abdomen while breathing was a method taught by the old Italian masters of singing. It was quite common for their singers to sustain a tone for 30 or 40 seconds with this method of breathing. [439, p. 61] Scott claims that, in singing, rib and chest expansion have little or nothing to do with the intake or output of breath. Therefore, the expansion of these parts should be constant. [501, p. 46] Finally, Evetts and Worthington are opposed to holding the chest high and stationary in singing. They claim that it adds nothing to vocal resonance but increases the possibility of tension in the throat. [167, p. 85]

VOLUNTARY VERSUS INVOLUNTARY BREATHING

Opinions are unevenly divided regarding this controversial topic, there being 24 statements in favor of and 11 against voluntary control of the breathing organs during singing. Some authors, like Shaw, would teach voluntary or conscious control of breathing until habits are established. Thus breathing control would eventually become automatic. [525, p. 8; Barbareux-Parry 34, p. 124 and Jacques 299, p. 11] Breath control is the foundation of interpretative singing, according to Greene. [209, p. 6] It is the motive power and support of voice and must therefore be under direct control at all times. [New York Singing Teachers Association 421, p. 29] It is "indispensable to the good singer." [Rimmer 470] Breath control, open throat and a relaxed tongue mark the master singer. [Shakespeare 517, p. 19] Others who support this opinion are Cimini [98, p. 12], Hinman [273, p. 4], Haywood [237, I: 4], and Weilich [663].

"The breath must be consciously focused," says James, without further comment. How this is brought about is not disclosed.[300, p. 20] Waters describes breath control as "lifting the lower floating ribs and expanding the waist line. . . . Then pull in the waist line and let the breath serve the tone." [646] "Control of breath rather than quantity of breath is of most worth to the singer," according to Clark. [102] Garcia, famous singing master, when over 90 years of age, still held fast to the principle of breath control as a primary requisite of singing. [Wodell 678] The remaining affirmative opinions on this subject are summed up in the words of Storey and Barnard: "Ordinary breathing is an automatic business. But singing requires extra breath and therefore extra breathing control." [590, p. 17; Samoiloff 484, p. 7; Van Orden, Jr. 624; Armstrong 23] Therefore, we must learn deep breathing "in order to sustain tones." [Warren 637] This concept of breath support is common among those who favor voluntary breathing control.

The negative opinions, fewer in number, are firmly opposed to the conscious regulation of the breathing organs during the act of singing. "Never consciously control the breath," says Wharton, "but rather control the tone." [655, p. 21] Correct breathing is invariably a product of correct tone production and should never be dissociated from the coordinated vocal act. [Wilcox 669, p. 6; Shaw 538] De Bruyn likewise believes that "conscious physiological breathing, initiated arbitrarily in the region of the diaphragm, is taking to be a cause what actually is a resultant of forces more remote." [131] Clark favors a psychological approach to the control of breathing. "It is attained through the mentality," not by conscious manipulation of physical parts. [100] "Few people can twitch either diaphragm or vocal cords for they are relatively insensitive and semi-automatic muscles." [Hemery 238, p. 13] And finally, Austin-Ball reports that the old Italian school of singing never employed mechanical breathing as a method. [31, p. 60] These representative opinions cover the case against voluntary breathing.

DIAPHRAGMATIC CONTROL

In specialized training for singing, the rhythmical breathing actions of normal respiration are often disturbed. In their place, strong voluntary abdominal compressions are employed in order better to regulate the flow of the expiring breath stream. This is called *diaphragmatic control.* [Curry 124, p. 13] Of the 36 opinions gathered on this subject, 27 are in favor of conscious diaphragmatic action as a technique in singing and 9 are opposed to it.

Frances Alda, in an interview, expresses the opinion that all vocal muscles must be completely relaxed in singing except those of the abdominal wall where the bellows lie. [6, p. 297] The bellows referred to are the diaphragmatic muscles. "The diaphragm must be kept as tight as a drum," she declares, "to produce, as a drum produces, volume of sound." [Ibid. 5] Margit Bokor, another distinguished artist, advises the student singer to focus attention upon the diaphragm. "The student should perfect the technique of diaphragmatic control before he thinks seriously of singing." [54] Lily Pons and Emílio de Gogorza likewise favor diaphragmatic control, declaring that the chest should be ignored entirely when singing. [451 and 134] Others who advocate this type of breathing control in singing are: Gould [206, p. 15], Armstrong [22] and Martino [375, p. 62]. Jessica Dragonette believes in establishing a combination of rib and diaphragmatic action. [146] According to Greene, who claims to have conferred with many professional singers, control of the diaphragm is a basic technique in singing, endorsed by expert opinion. As the breath is slowly exhaled in phonation, the abdominal wall gradually is drawn inward, providing a trained regulatory device for breathing. [209, p. 292] Whittaker also claims that breathing action is always controlled at the diaphragm. [662, p. 67] Garnetti-Forbes holds the same opinion but adds that the normal breathing movement of the diaphragm is very slight and should remain so. Excessive volume of air in the lungs causes chronic tension in the diaphragmatic muscle and limits its normal downward and upward movements. Therefore, for singing, the intake of air should always be minimized and the outflow of air economically expended. [198, pp. 81 and 86]

William E. Brown's compilation of Lamperti's maxims for singers is a rich source of vocal information. "The diaphragm is never relaxed," says Brown. Vocal attack is a releasing of compressed breath previously prepared by an ever active diaphragm. Volume is determined by the quantity of breath that is thus released. [78, p. 46] William J. Henderson's book *The Art of Singing* presents a historical survey of the methods of vocal instruction employed during the Golden Age of Singing. Hender-

son epitomizes the opinions of singing masters of the past in his statement that "the breath must be retained simply by the action of the diaphragm and rib muscles," not by closing the larynx. He further suggests
that diaphragmatic action may be strengthened by the practice of consciously retaining a full breath for two or three seconds at a time before
each exhalation. [243, p. 23; Butler 87, and Bartholomew 39] All these
authors seem to favor the relaxation of the upper chest in order to prevent throat or laryngeal tightness. But at the same time the effort of
breathing must be concentrated in the abdominal and diaphragmatic regions. [Novello-Davies 430, p. 114; Dodds and Lickley 139, p. 26; Clippinger 104, p. 5]

Diaphragmatic control is sometimes employed as a counter-agent to
divert the student's attention from the throat and laryngeal regions and
thus to prevent laryngeal tension during phonation. It is also widely
believed that, once the chest posture has been established and habitualized in physical culture, the local action of the breathing *bellows* or
diaphragm should be studied and controlled. [Lloyd 351, p. 1; Scott 501,
p. 117]

Opponents of diaphragmatic control declare that the conscious compression and hardening of the abdominal muscles in breathing will
gradually spread tensions into the back muscles and up through the chest
to the neck and throat muscles. [MacBurney 361] Furthermore, it is held
that "the singer is normally not conscious of the position of the diaphragm," [Bartholomew 39] and that the diaphragm and vocal cords are
involuntary muscles and therefore free from sensibility. Hence it is impossible to contract or relax these muscles by thinking about sensations
in them. [Drew 147, p. 174; Shaw 526] The diaphragm's activity "is
resultant" and should never be directly governed in singing. [Shaw 538]
The tensing of the diaphragm is possible only during inhalation, exhalation being accompanied by the relaxing of this muscle. Therefore it is an
error to suppose that compression of the diaphragm must control the
exhalation of the breath stream since this is just opposite to physiological
fact. [Bartholomew op. cit.]

Like any other involuntary muscle, the diaphragm performs best unconsciously and "balks" stubbornly at being conscripted into voluntary
service." [Henley 255] In exhalation the diaphragm is a passive rather
than an active factor since it is in a process of relaxing back to its normal
dome shape. Therefore "it has no driving power. Diaphragmatic breath
control is a pure figment of undisciplined imagination," says Shaw. [522]
The only experimental studies in this area were reported by Dr. John H.
Muyskens at the Music Educators National Conference in 1938. "That

the diaphragm is not the principal organ of breathing has been demonstrated in X-ray studies of individuals during sleep. . . . The diaphragm in contraction contributes not more than twenty-five per cent of the vital capacity." [415]

ORIFICIAL CONTROLS

All normal quiet respiration is through the nose but all normal vocal utterance is through the mouth. Singing teachers are not agreed as to whether it is best to use the nose exclusively when breathing for singing, or to use the mouth exclusively, or both. In the 25 opinions tabulated on this subject, 8 are for mouth breathing, 5 are for nose breathing and 12 approve the use of either. The controversy does not seem of vital importance to the singer except in so far as voluntary controls of any kind might disturb the spontaneous reflexes of the respiratory function. The statements herein given represent points of view on the three sides of this question.

Breathing through mouth advised. Mouth breathing is more conducive to open throat and prevents forced breathing, according to Dossert. [140, p. 39] The tongue will automatically assume a desirable low and inert position if the singer breathes through his mouth while singing. This is Henderson's claim. [240, p. 88] Furthermore, inhaling through the nose is noisier and slower than inhaling through the mouth. [Ibid., p. 58] Others merely express the opinion that the singer must "breathe principally through the mouth, as in speaking." [E.g., Ryan 480, p. 63; Coleman 118, p. 9]

Breathing through nose advised. The only explanation offered in favor of nose breathing is by Kwartin. [325, p. 29] He declares that nose breathing is more hygienic than mouth breathing because it protects the lungs and mucous membranes from chill and micro-organisms. However, he adds, in extremely quick breathing it may be necessary to use the mouth momentarily. In this latter statement he agrees with Henderson above. Martino, although admitting that the mouth may be considered "a passage of necessity" nevertheless believes that it is better to take breath "through the natural passage—the nostrils." [375, p. 60] Novello-Davies specifies that the mouth should be closed while inhaling properly through the nostrils. [430, p. 107; also James 300, p. 15] Philip strongly favors nose breathing in singing, but adds the words "whenever possible." [446, p. 53]

Breathing through mouth and nose advised. "For big, rapid breaths the mouth must be used also," says Nicholson. [425, p. 108] Mme. Olden believes in using both mouth and nose but adds, "nose breathing should play the greater part." [434] To keep the breathing flexible, especially in deep breathing, use either the mouth or nose in inhalation. [Maybee 381, II, 6] "In the use of proper voice, the breath is emitted through both the mouth and the nose." [Waller 631] "Breathing deeply through the nose alone is too slow a process for singing." [Marchesi 369, p. 3] Witherspoon sums up the case for mouth and nose breathing by declaring that it is impossible to breathe noiselessly and rapidly without a simultaneous use of mouth and nose. [677, p. 65; also 675] In this belief he is upheld by Austin-Ball [31, p. 5] and Waters [647, p. 54].

QUANTITATIVE FACTORS OF BREATHING

The amount of breath required in normal breathing varies with the individual. Curry estimates about 500 cc. of *tidal air* or that amount which actually passes in and out of the body with each normal respiratory cycle. About 1500 cc. of *supplemental air* may be added to this amount during maximum inhalation and exhalation. [124, p. 10] But even after the lungs are voluntarily depleted in maximum exhalation there remains about 900 cc. of so-called *residual air* in the breathing organs. All this adds up to the maximum or *vital capacity* of the breathing organs which, in adults measures about 3000 cc. or 3 liters. "The measure of vital capacity is used as a test of physical fitness." [Ibid.]

The 100 opinions expressed on quantitative factors are largely related to economy of breath in singing. *Quantity* implies amount or volume of breath. But the length, duration and brevity of the breathing cycle are directly associated with the quantity of breath taken. Likewise the force or pressure, frequency and speed of breathing have a direct relationship to the expenditure of air in breathing and to the intensity of the vocal sound emitted in singing. The arrangement of quantitative concepts is in three categories as follows:

a) Concepts of breath economy—56 statements.
b) Concepts of breath pressure and support—27 statements
c) Concepts of breath renewal, frequency and speed—17 statements.

a) *Principles of breath economy. Economy of breath* in singing is the utilization of a minimum of breath for each tone produced. Such economy is essential to pure tone production. [Dossert 140, p. 38; Rimmer 470] Voice production is often described as a laryngeal product. But correct voice production, as Herbert-Caesari describes it, is a coordination of correct laryngeal adjustment and minimum exhalation of breath. [269, p. 18] According to Marafioti, the great Caruso always employed "only the exact amount of breath required for producing each tone, and no more." [368, p. 5] Dodds and Lickley maintain that breath economy and breath control are of utmost importance. Purity, ease and endurance of voice production in singing depend on them. [139, p. 34; also Valeri 623]

Advice to beginners in singing should include a word on breath economy. "Among the first and most important things to be learned is the spending of air uniformly—not in spurts—and economically." [Martino 375, p. 60; Wodell 681] In fact, the technique of effortless singing is built upon the habit of quick but unforced inhalation and economical exhalation. [Henderson 240, p. 54] Orton compares voice production with tone production on a large wind instrument like the trombone. A good player on such an instrument produces full and powerful tones "with no more expenditure of breath than would be needed for a soft note on the flute or fife," he says. [439, p. 123]

Breath economy as applied to volume. "In singing, never attempt to fill the lungs to their utmost capacity," says W. J. Henderson. [243, p. 44] It takes very little breath to sustain a long singing tone. [Shaw 538] "When the tone is rightly produced it is all tone and nothing else." Forced inhalation inevitably leads to forced exhalation and forced phonation. [Henley 248] Volume of breath is not required. In fact, "the intake of breath before attacking a note should be moderate." [Jacques 299, p. 34] Also avoid a strong exhalation of breath. Rather, breathe lightly, as if against a window pane. This was the method of the ancients. [Hagara 220, p. 32] Observe what a tiny song bird can do with a tiny cubicle of air. The singer will soon be convinced that it is "not necessary to swell up like a balloon every time he sings a phrase." [Maurice-Jacquet 379] In other words, it is more important to economize the expenditure of a medium intake than to emit forcefully a large quantity of breath in singing. [Jacobus 298; Wharton 655, p. 25]

Curry reports that volume of air does not bear a close relationshsip to vocal intensity and that deep breathing frequently causes faulty phonation. It is true, however, that "singers in general have a larger lung capacity than the average." [124, p. 14] Sir Henry J. Wood conceives of voice production as the playing of a wind instrument. "The besetting sin of the modern singer is over-blowing," he says. [686, p. 12] Nor is the ability to sing long phrases "a matter of lung capacity," says Clippinger. "It is in knowing how to control the breath after it is taken." [104, p. 8; also Christy 97, p. 41] There is fairly close agreement on this point among vocal experts. All seem to agree with Mme. Lehmann, that the smallest quantity of breath must be emitted when singing [Sheley, 545] and that the use of too much breath is a common error of singers. [Wood 685, p.

30] Harper is even more emphatic in declaring that so little breath is required for singing that it seems like "no breath at all." Furthermore under such conditions, the body is absolutely motionless to the observer while breathing for singing. [228, p. 122]

Breath retention. It is Stanley's opinion that correct voice production involves restraints in breathing. Poor singing degenerates into a mere pushing of breath against a throaty constriction. [577, p. 312] Therefore, phonation requires breath retention and breath economy. The combination of gradual and minimal exhalation constitutes *breath control.* [Herbert-Caesari 269, p. 143] "Do not hold your tone," says Brown, "spin it. Hold your breath" instead. [78, p. 29] Holding back or retaining the breath is described by Wodell as the ability to "send out the breath with great slowness, and, at the same time, with sufficient energy [but no more] to produce the pitch and power of tone desired." This is really achieved by means of a balanced interplay between the action of the muscles of inhalation and those of exhalation. [679] Learn to restrain the ribs from pressing inward against the lungs during exhalation. [Warren 640] Learn to economize or hold back the breath, not at the throat, but at the source of the breathing action. [Robinson 474; Grundmann and Schumacher 218, p. 14] To check speedy exhalation, Father Finn suggests as a practice device, the gradual release of breath to a slow count of numbers. [181, p. 25; also Kwartin 325, p. 29]

Breath control is really breath economy. Some authors refuse to be concerned about breath control in singing. "The least said about breath and breath control the better," says George Compton. "It is nothing more than learning to economize the breath." [120] Unless the singing pupil's breathing is decidedly deficient, it should not be molested by breathing exercises. Economy of breath is much more important than volume of breath. [Herbert-Caesari 269, p. 17] Average, undeveloped breath capacity is sufficient to meet every artistic singing requirement providing the technique of production is correct. [Stanley 577, p. 37; Shaw 518, p. 199] Bainbridge Crist expresses the same concept in rhyme. "It requires almost no breath to sing. Don't push your breath, but speak —which is a very different thing." [123] The only historical reference to breath economy is given by William James Henderson in his survey of the teaching methods of the old Italian masters. According to Henderson, deep inhalation followed by a slow, sustained vocal tone is the practice method employed by the old masters for developing breath retention and control. [243, p. 20]

The comments of professional singers on the subject of breath economy are of interest to the teaching profession. These concepts are not always pedagogically sound, but they provide valuable technical insights for the teacher of singing. The following interviews are therefore reported:

1. The manner and distribution of exhalation are more important than inhalation to the singer. Never push on the tone. Large inhalations are not necessary. [Kerstin Thorborg 611 and 612]

2. The chief point is to take enough breath to last the phrase. Trial and error will demonstrate this. [Conrad Thibault 605]

3. Taking too much breath for a short phrase is as incorrect as taking too little for a long one. [Jessica Dragonette 146]

4. "The secret of the singer's breath lies in its conservation." Breathing for singing should be as natural as for ordinary speaking. [Bruna Castagna 94]

5. Breath control means budgeting the breath so that "just the right amount is used for the vocalization of tone." [Margit Bokor 54]

6. Breath emission must be reduced to an absolute minimum. [Lilli Lehmann 337]

7. "I advise you to give supreme attention, not to the drawing in of breath, but to its budgeting." [Ernestine Schumann-Heink 499]

b) *Breath pressure and support.* It is commonly accepted that voice is inseparable from breath. Therefore the consideration of the former must always include the latter and vice versa. This concept of interrelationship no doubt led to the adoption of the *voice on the breath* formula which the old Italian masters taught. [Herbert-Caesari 269, p. 42] But the expression "sing with the voice on the breath" is also misleading in that it invites a correlation between voice pressure and breath pressure which is contrary to common pedagogical belief. White insists that "no pressure of any kind is needed to generate vocal tone, much less a blast of air." [659, p. 39] Stanley concurs in this opinion when he says, "In singing, there is not a stream of fast moving air, i.e., a draught; the breath escapes very slowly when the technic is good." [578] "The common sense point of view," says Bonavia-Hunt, "is that the amount of breath pressure employed to produce a given note should be the minimum required for the purpose." [55]

When the voice is being properly used, the flame of a candle held a few inches away from a singer's mouth, will not flicker while he is emitting a tone, regardless of its loudness or intensity. This is frequently offered as a test of breath economy during voice production. If excessive breath is escaping either at the (vowel) attack or while singing, the candle flame will flicker. [Mackenzie 364, p. 121; Earhart 152, p. 3; Kwartin 325, p. 29] Therefore it is observed that while sustaining a correctly produced tone the air is not moving rapidly out of the singer's mouth even though the sound is traveling forth. [Austin-Ball 31, p. 28]

Singing on the breath is really a restatement of the economy of breath principle. It implies that, regardless of the quantity of breath in the lungs, no more breath will be allowed to escape than can be utilized in phonation. In short, a proper restraint of breath release is a sufficient check upon breath wastage in phonation. "Control of the tone is secured by a continuous breathing into the tone," says Wilson. But this continuous breathing out is governed by correct vocal action and must therefore be performed with maximum breath economy. [674, p. 29]

Stevens and Miles report, in an experimental study, that "singing on a full breath does not interfere with the evenness of the attack but rather seems to improve it." Here again, the full breath refers to the quantity of air retained by the singer not the quantity expelled during phonation. [583] In other words, regardless of the quantity of breath retained in the lungs at the moment of attack "an even pressure of breath will surely obtain an even tone." [Clark 102; Montani 402, II, Preface] All agree that excessive breathing is a symptom of faulty production [Evetts and Worthington 167, p. 74] and that "no breath must be allowed to escape, apart from its function of voice production." [Jacques 299, p. 34]

c) *Breath renewal, frequency and speed. Breath renewal* in singing serves the double purpose of sustaining sound and oxygenating the blood. Therefore, in spite of the economy of breath principle enunciated above, a singer is often called upon to increase his breath intake beyond the requirements of voice production. [Lewis 343, p. 4] The need for oxygen is sometimes accentuated by the fact that the inspiratory act is short and the expiratory act prolonged. Often it is necessary for the singer to renew his breath during expiration by taking "short inspiratory gulps at pauses in the flow of the voice." [Curry 124, p. 13] It is obvious, according to Jacques, that there is "an important difference between breathing when sitting at ease and during singing." The normal respiratory rhythm of 15 or 16 breaths per minute may be considerably reduced when singing, necessitating deeper respiratory movements than for normal breathing. [299, p. 12; also Evetts and Worthington 167, p. 70; Hemery 238, p. 15] "In fact, the less frequently the singer takes a new breath, the better he will sing," says Maurice-Jacquet. [376] Sir George Henschel holds an opposing viewpoint. He believes that it is proper for a singer to breathe as often as interpretation requires, as long as he can breathe quickly and imperceptibly. [265, p. 6; also Whittaker 662, p. 69]

The several technical devices mentioned are those which singers often find it expedient to employ. For instance, the *half breath* is used in passages where there is not time enough for a full breath, to prevent depletion of the lungs. [Henderson 243, p. 30] Brown believes that the singer should be trained to take breath with lightning rapidity. To do this he interpolates an imperceptible pause on the last note of any phrase where it will not disturb the rhythm of the entering phrase. [65, p. 22]

Wood believes that the singer should practice breathing at all speeds and in all combinations, such as quick intake for a slow phrase and slow breath for an allegro phrase. [686, I, 19] "The singer will have to be able to breathe as slowly as four or five times per minute if necessary. Therefore this [breath] control must be developed," says Combs. [119, p. 9] "Quick inhalation has to be acquired" along with slow, sustained breathing as part of the vocal training for singers prescribed by the Department of Education in Ireland. [294, p. 30]

Maurice-Jacquet makes the observation that great artists always take a breath some time in advance of the moment of attack. "The process is breathing, holding and singing." [376] As a limbering up exercise, Hagara suggests taking many slow, sustained, deep singing breaths. [220, p. 113] Finally, Henley refers to the practice of the masters of the Golden Age. Short, quick breathing which was imperceptible, even to a close onlooker, enabled the singer of the Golden Age to breathe as often as desired during the rendition of an aria. It also helped to improve the control of a long breath. [254]

SUMMARY AND INTERPRETATION

THEORETICAL CONSIDERATIONS

A consideration of the foregoing principles and methods of teaching breathing in singing provides challenging evidence of the insufficiency and inconsistency of modern vocal teaching procedures and the need for clarification and research in an as yet uncharted pedagogical field. Numerous problems engage the interest of the investigator but few are adaptable to modern research methods. The human equation is strongly apparent throughout the singing profession. Teaching personalities subsist on the widespread use of pedagogical dogma that has its origins in the mythical reputation and teachings of the masters of the Golden Age. There is often abundant verbal testimony to the validity of this or that technique of breathing but very little historical, physiological or experimental evidence.

An analysis of the concepts of breathing used in training the singer's voice leads us to the conclusion that author opinion on this subject is diversified and fragmentary. No one text attempts an exhaustive treatment of the subject. Therefore, it will be necessary for the teacher of singing to piece together a continuity of ideas in theory and method out of the many incomplete opinions offered. There is surprisingly little experimental data on this subject. Most of the 428 statements on breathing culled out of 702 texts and articles consulted evade the responsibility of proof. Conclusive or authentic evidence on any aspect of breath culture for singing is therefore lacking.

Yet, the subject of breath control cannot be slighted since it is fundamental to the singing act in all its phases. The fact that there is little agreement in this subject need not prevent a reasoned consideration of its major problems even though the great diversity of opinion permits only the most general discussion of some aspects of these problems. The study of concepts presented herein may help to clarify this area of teaching, if only to point the way to a more systematic organization of ideas and a more objective pattern of thinking on the subject.

Breathing is but a small part of the act of singing. But it is an important part, for the breathing habits of a singer are rooted in the vital processes of living. In the consideration of these habits it is necessary to draw a distinction between breathing-for-living and breathing-for-singing. The former, because it is a fundamental process, takes precedence in function over superimposed voluntary breathing controls that the student acquires as part of his training for a singing career. In other words, a singer must learn to coordinate breathing-in-singing habits with breathing-in-living habits if he would achieve the efficiency and endurance that spell artistic success in vocal expression.

METHODOLOGICAL CONSIDERATIONS

It is widely accepted that artistic singing is a voluntary act. Yet, for best results it must simulate the ease, fluency and effortless expression of an involuntary utterance. The elimination of conscious effort and undue tension in any portion of the vocal mechanism is therefore of paramount importance. Authors of singing texts generally concede the automatic nature of the respiratory act in life. But in their zealous application of voice training techniques they frequently demand voluntary breathing controls that disturb the spontaneity of natural respiratory reflexes with serious disadvantages to the vocalist.

There is some confusion at this point as to pedagogical procedure. Are breathing techniques necessary at all in singing? Should they be taught by indirect or direct methods? Before or during the singing lesson? Do they involve local muscular effort or coordinated effort? Opinions on these and other questions are diversified enough to require a grouping of concepts under four theoretical divisions or schools of thought, designated as follows: a) local-effort method; b) pre-vocal training method; c) functional growth method; d) expressional intent method.

a) *Local-effort method.* From the standpoint of the singer, good breathing spells efficiency in converting breath pressure into intensity of vocal utterance. This means that expiration must be controlled. Those who are grouped in the local-effort school believe that breath control is largely a matter of breath retention and gradual release so that vocal tone may be evenly sustained. They also believe in devising techniques for localizing the control of expiratory movements of the ribs, diaphragm or other parts of the breathing mechanism. Thus, by direct control of these parts, the singer may voluntarily vary his mode of breathing to suit his expressional needs. The voluntary action of the diaphragm is especially featured as a method of breathing control. Other devices are rib distension, spinal elongation, abdominal compression, focusing the breath, mouth breathing. These methods are endorsed without explanation or proof and there is no physiological evidence as to their efficacy or acceptability. In all, 275 out of 370 statements on methods of teaching breathing discuss various technical procedures for localizing breath control. Apparently the preponderance of author opinion favors voluntary breathing controls in singing by a ratio of approximately three to one.

b) *Pre-vocal physical training method.* Those who favor pre-vocal training offer good reasons for this preference. Breathing is directly affected by posture. Therefore the benefits of physical culture, which is a form of remedial postural training, must accrue to the breathing organs. Why not develop the student's physique, his poise and posture, before he attempts a singing lesson? This type of training will develop breath capacity, flexibility and endurance up to the standards required for artistic singing. Body building exercises of this kind must precede the program of voice culture.

c) *Functional growth method.* Persons who advocate this method claim that a specialized activity of any function of the body will stimulate the growth and development of those organs and faculties that support it. Thus, by a law of exercise, the activity of singing should stimulate the growth of the breathing organs. Professional singers invariably develop powerful breathing controls for this reason. The student learns to sing immediately, giving little or no attention to breathing, trusting that the organs of breathing will grow through use much as the leg muscles might grow stronger by practicing walking or the arm and shoulder muscles might be developed by pitching hay.

d) *Expressional intent method.* In this group are those who claim that all breathing controls are psychological. The breathing organs respond instanteously to thought and feeling, automatically providing the right degree of chest expansion and air intake for any spontaneous vocal expression. Under this method, the breathing reflexes of living are not disturbed, but merely intensified, as they respond to the intensified thoughts and moods that accompany singing. Breathing in singing, then, is a natural response of the physical organism to expressional impulses that originate in the mind of the singer. This principle may be explained as follows: When witnessing impending danger one might feel impelled to shout suddenly to a passerby, "Look out!" As this impulse to shout is conceived, proper physiological reactions occur which cause a swift preparatory intake of air sufficient to meet the demands of intense vocal utterance at that moment. Similarly, when the thought and mood of an aria or song are properly conceived, the genuine desire to communicate impels a vocal utterance which is exactly proportional to the intensity of thought and mood thus conceived. In training the singer's voice by this method, natural breathing is advised. Functional growth of the breathing organs is provided in abundant practice of the interpretative singing of songs.

In conclusion, there appears to be widespread agreement among singing teachers that the singing voice is the product of a "highly developed wind instrument" and is therefore entirely "dependent upon the breath for the quality and volume of sound produced." [Armstrong 20] This means that every tonal development of the singing voice depends in one way or another upon the acquisition of correct breathing habits. [Margit Bokor 54] Furthermore, to accomplish this purpose, the muscular processes of natural breathing must be developed beyond the requirements for normal living by extension, rather than by distortion. Thus the singer's increased vocal demands are supplied. [Wilcox 669, p. 3] A word of caution is added by Mackenzie when he warns that, although the art of breathing must be thoroughly and properly acquired, habits thus trained ought to be entirely automatic before they can be useful to the singer during his performance. [364, p. 121]

Finally, it is desirable to dispel a misconception that is commonly held by singing teachers who advocate *singing on the breath.* There is a. definite distinction between a sound wave and an air current. Vocal sound waves travel through the air at a speed of about 1100 feet per second. But the air current generated by the outflowing breath stream of a vocalist is dissipated by the surrounding atmosphere within a few inches of its point of issuance. Obviously, if the breath stream flowed with the speed of sound waves a miniature hurricane would be generated. [Shaw 540] It is apparent, therefore, that voice is not breath and breath is never "converted" into voice. The concept of singing on the breath is misleading because voice cannot possibly travel on the breath and "the absurd idea that the voice is vocalized breath is without meaning." [Stanley 576]

CHAPTER IV

CONCEPTS OF PHONATION

Definition: *Phonation* is the act or process of generating vocal sound; it is the inception of vocal tone at its point of production in the larynx. More explicitly, phonation is the vibratory activity of the vocal cords so as to produce pulsations sufficiently rapid to cause the sensation of tone. When these tones are sustained, they form the substance of the singing voice. (W) The *larynx* is the organ which produces vocal sound. It is situated at the top-most ring cartilage of the trachea (wind-pipe) and consists of adjustable cartilages, muscles and membranes which together operate the valve-like mechanism of the vocal cords. [Negus 418]

The *vocal cords* (a misnomer), also more accurately called vocal *bands, folds, lips, cushions, ledges, ligaments, shelves, muscles, processes, edges,* consist of a pair of muscular folds that project into the cavity of the larynx. (The so-called *false cords* are for fixation and distension of the laryngeal ventricles and are not directly affected in phonation. [Hemery 238, p. 55]) The *true* vocal cords can be tensed and drawn together (approximated) along their exposed edges so that the upward flow of breath between them causes them to vibrate, producing voice. "The vocal cords are the only parts of the larynx with any important function in phonation." [Negus op. cit.] The *glottis* is the aperture or chink existing between the vocal lips (cords) when they are drawn apart in normal respiration or when they are forced apart by the expiring breath stream during phonation. "The glottis can be opened, narrowed or closed . . . through the action of muscles controlling the arytenoid or adjusting cartilages." (W) The term *glottis* (glottal) is also sometimes used to refer to the vibrating edges of the vocal lips (cords).

Descriptions of phonation are often complicated by the presence of technical terms used to describe anatomical structures in the vocal tract. In the discussions which follow, this terminology is simplified to afford greater intelligibility of subject matter. Definitions and technical terms

TABLE THREE

TABLE THREE

SUMMARY OF CONCEPTS OF PHONATION USED IN TRAINING THE
SINGING VOICE

	total number of statements	sub-total	grand total	statements by prof. singers	documented statements	undocumented statements
I. *Theories of phonation*			188			
A. General description	53	53			25	28
B. Physiological factors		84				
1. the tonal generator	33				17	16
2. pitch regulators	39				25	14
3. extrinsic mechanisms	12			1	4	8
C. The vocal vibrato	51	51			36	15
II. *Methods of controlling phonation*			275			
A. Psychological approach		85				
1. total coordinations required	23			3	9	14
2. anticipation controls phonation	43			1		43
3. anticipation controls pitch	19			1	3	16
B. Technical approach		190				
1. oral controls						
a) *mouth opening is important*	29					29
b) *mouth opening is not important*	9					9
2. lingual position						
a) *low tongue advised*	31			2		31
b) *free tongue advised*	19			1	1	18
3. palatal controls						
a) *palate should be raised*	2					2
b) *palate should be free*	4				2	2
4. open throat concept						
a) *control of throat advised*	22			1	6	16
b) *control of throat not advised*	17				3	14
c) yawning as a device	20			2		20
5. laryngeal position						
a) *larynx should move*	9			1	2	7
b) *larynx should not move*	9				2	7
6. devices for improving attack	19				2	17
TOTALS	463	463	463	13	137	326

are included only when needed. The 463 concepts of phonation reviewed are categorically summarized in *Table Three*.

THEORIES OF PHONATION

GENERAL DESCRIPTIONS

The following grouping of theoretical statements provides a résumé of 188 concepts in this area. These are correlated with the purpose of synthesizing a more comprehensible and therefore more readable sequence of ideas, without altering their essential character.

1. *The vibrator.* "The vocal instrument consists of a vibrator [larynx] and a number of cavities that act as resonators or reinforcers" of tone. [Clippinger 114] It is maintained in vibration by the pressure of subglottic air. "If a moving column of air be partially or completely interrupted in its exit from an aperture in a rhythmical manner and at a rate within the limits of human audibility, musical [vocal] sounds will be produced." [Negus 418, p. 346] The larynx sound consists of a fundamental and overtone frequencies which are "selectively reinforced by the various cavity resonances," thus producing a resultant vocal tone of great individuality that varies with each vocal utterance. [Curry 124, p. 57; Stanley 578]

2. *Tonal energy.* Experiments prove that the vocal tone that is generated in the larynx produces vibrations throughout a wide area of the chest, throat and head (by means of radiation, sympathetic vibration, resonance and bone conduction). [Lindsley 347] The greatest amount of the vibrational energy of phonation is recorded at the larynx [Ibid.], although subglottic vibrations in the trachea [Redfield 461] and "parasitic vibrations of the structures linked to the larynx" [Curry op. cit.] have also been noted. (See also Chapter V.)

3. *Glottal action.* "Voice is produced by action of the vocal cords, not like the strings of a stringed instrument, but as a pair of membranous lips which, being continually forced apart by the expired breath, and continually brought together again by their own elasticity and muscular tension, break the breath current into a series of puffs, or pulses, sufficiently rapid to cause the sensation of tone." (W) "The tremor of the elastic membranes [cords] rapidly opens and closes the fine slit between their edges [glottis] and releases the air pressure in a quick succession of minute puffs." [Aikin 4] "In order that the vocal cords may be set into vibration, they must be put in a state of tension, and the aperture of the glottis narrowed so as to afford resistance to the current of air." [Starling's *Physiology* 713, p. 350] "The thyro-arytenoid muscle [vocal cord] is always in a

state of tonic contraction, and therefore it possesses elasticity at all times."
[Negus 418, p. 374]

4. *Equilibrium of parts.* Phonation is the product of conflicting or antagonistic forces (i.e., breath pressure versus glottal resistance), functioning in a state of perfect equilibrium. [Brown 78, p. 63] The output of these two interdependent actions, when functioning automatically, is correct vocal tone. [Bergère 45] In other words, the act of phonation mainly involves a fixation or holding of muscular positions, rather than a movement of parts. [Stanley 577, p. 304]

5. *Motive power.* "The voice, like every musical instrument, consists of three distinct actions." These are: motive power, pitch regulating mechanism and resonance mechanism. [New York Singing Teachers Association 421, p. 34; Ruff 477] The lungs and diaphragm supply the motive power, which is breath; this, coming into contact with the vocal cords, causes them to vibrate, creating sound (phonation); the sound is then amplified by the resonating cavities in the nose, mouth, neck and chest; and it is articulated and projected by the mouth, tongue, lips and teeth. [Jacques 299, p. 28; Herbert-Caesari 269, p. 28] "The force which causes the [vocal] folds to separate is pressure of air in the trachea, caused by an effort of expiration. The force which makes them close again is the elasticity possessed by the folds themselves. . . . Increase of loudness is attained by rise of air pressure associated with decrease of elasticity of glottic margins." [Negus 418, pp. 373 and 387] (The loudness of a sound will vary with the area of the vibrating surface, with the substance of which it is composed, with the amplitude of the vibrations and with environment. [Ibid., p. 344] (See also Chapter VII.)

6. *Total coordinations.* Correct vocal technique involves the simultaneous activity of many parts, accurately timed and coordinated. This includes a proper tension of respiratory muscles, intrinsic closure of the glottis, vibrato action, dropped larynx, throat and pharynx open and shaped for resonance. mouth and jaw inert. Incorrect technique practically reverses any or all of these factors. [Dodds and Lickley 139, p. 35] Mursell holds that it is difficult to segregate the vocal mechanism from the rest of the body and describe it as an isolated structure. "Its action is knit into the very texture of the tonal somatic response. . . . The action of the voice influences and shapes the entire pattern of bodily behavior" and, vice versa, "whatever affects the body as a whole must also affect the voice." [411, p. 227] Wharton is of like opinion, claiming that phonation is a process that involves the "cooperation of the many parts of the body" entering into the singing act. [655, p. 69]

7. *Primary functions.* The vocal instrument is unique in that it is com-

posed entirely of parts of the human body. [Drew 147, p. 171] It must also be remembered that "the functions of the larynx are not purely phonatory." [Evetts and Worthington 167, p. 17] The larynx is also involved in several non-vocal functions, such as eating, swallowing and breathing. [Witherspoon 677, p. 14] The method of phonation used by man has the advantage that "sound can be produced during respiration without the interruption of any vital process." [Negus 418, p. 346] "Almost all the peculiarities of structure of the larynx can be accounted for by necessities of functions other than those of phonation." [Ibid., p. 344] Therefore, "to design exercises for these organs, it is necessary to consider their primary functions." [Drew 147, p. 174]

8. *Acoustical analogies.* The phonatory mechanism has been compared with other musical instruments to illustrate its acoustical properties. For example:

   a. Voice is like a wind instrument. [Redfield 462]
   b. It is like a stringed instrument. [Mackenzie 364]
   c. It is a combination of both. [Dodds and Lickley 139]
   d. It vibrates like a reed. [Aikin 4]

On the other hand, Clippinger maintains that voice is voice and is not to be compared to any other instrument because "it is not like any other instrument." [115]

Three other general observations regarding phonation are of interest:

First, Bonavia-Hunt's *vortex theory* of vocal tone production states that the vocal cords themselves do not generate sound. "They produce eddy currents, or 'vortex rings' of air, one eddy at each complete vibration . . . just as the lips of a horn player shoot an eddy into the mouthpiece" of his instrument. The energy, size and velocity of these vortex rings are controlled by the tension, frequency and degree of air blast produced by the vibrating vocal cords (lips), with the result that sound is generated. [55; Herbert-Caesari 269, p. xii] "That the laryngeal sounds are not due to vibrations of the vocal ligaments themselves is common knowledge; the sounds so produced would be feeble. It is cutting of the air current into rhythmical puffs—as in a siren—which is the important factor." [Negus 418, p. 368]

Second, Dodds and Lickley point out that it is erroneous to assume that vocal tone actually consists of "puffs of breath," since these puffs of breath could travel only a very short distance. Vocal sound waves do not require air currents for their projection through space. They travel with an approximate speed of 1100 feet per second, radiating simultaneously in all directions from their source, which is much faster than air (breath) currents could possibly travel. [139, p. 33]

Third, Marafioti, who was Caruso's physician for many years, and who claims to have examined and studied the vocal organs of almost all the greatest singers at the Metropolitan Opera House "of the present day," declares that the vocal cords of most of the greatest modern operatic singers show no marked structural or physiological differences when compared with the vocal cords of ordinary non-singers. It is to be presumed, therefore, that great talent in singing is not exclusively an inherent functional characteristic of the organs of phonation. [368, p. 74] Negus also reports that, "of two human beings one will possess a far better voice than the other, although both are apparently equally well equipped anatomically." [418, p. 437]

These basic concepts of the phonatory process provide a general orientation for the teacher of singing, relevant to the pedagogical discussions that follow. Detailed anatomical descriptions of the vocal organs are available in such favorite texts as Curry [124] and Negus [418], or in any standard physiology book. Excellent non-technical descriptions of the vocal organs also appear in the introductory portion of Webster's *New International Dictionary* (second edition). Further discussions of the larynx and its adjacent structures, pertaining to this study, are also found in Chapters III, V and VI.

PHYSIOLOGICAL FACTORS

The tonal generator. With the exception of White [657; 658; 659], whose trilogy on sinus tone production favors a resonance theory of phonation (see Chapter V), all of the statements gathered on this subject seem to agree with the fundamental premise that the vibratory activity of voice originates in the glottis. Henderson's simple summary of the act of tone production is a typical one: "the cords [vocal lips] rush out of their hiding places and, bringing their edges close together, form a narrow slit through which the air rushes, setting the membranes [cords] into vibration and producing sound . . . and that is the act of phonation." [243, p. 36] A typical more technical description of the same subject is presented for comparison: "During extreme adduction of the vocal folds [cords], as in the emission of a high note, the intermembranous part is reduced to a linear slit by the apposition of the vocal folds . . . which are approximated by medial rotation of the cartilages." [Gray's *Anatomy* 707, p. 1101] The approximation of the vocal cords is accomplished by the action of "antagonistic muscle groups" whose perfect coordination during phonation is one of the first requirements of the singing voice. [McLean 386]

Experimental findings. Ogle describes each vocal cord (lip) as a "delicate prism-shaped muscle," having an over-all length of about 12 millimeters. It is called the *thyro-arytenoid* muscle, named after its two points of attachment (i.e., the *thyroid* cartilage at one end and the *arytenoid* cartilage at the other). [433] Evetts and Worthington find that this muscle averages 15 millimeters in length (about 3/5 of an inch) in male singers, and 11 millimeters (about 2/5 of an inch) in female singers. [167, p. 30] Negus reports the length of the vocal cords to be about 12.5 to 17 millimeters in the adult female, while in the adult male it varies from 17 to 25 millimeters. [418, p. 457] Farnsworth estimates the length of the vocal cords to be "from one half inch to five eighths inch," when vibrating at about 120 cycles. [168] Neblette roughly describes the position of the glottis in singing as "from 60 to 100 millimeters [2.35 to 3.92 inches] down the throat," a rough approximation at best, considering the variability of individual anatomical structures and the mobility of all these parts. [417]

Other experimental findings in this area that are pedagogically significant are summarized as follows:

1. "The vocal cords cannot vibrate themselves." Only released breath can induce the pulsations that cause sound. [Lloyd 351, p. 7]

2. During phonation the vocal cords "move almost entirely in a horizontal plane," and come into direct contact with each other once in each vibratory cycle after a maximum displacement of about 4 millimeters. [Curry 124, p. 45]

3. When the glottal closure is ever so slightly delayed in phonation, an aspirated type of voice results. [Ibid., p. 64]

4. The vibratory action of the vocal cords has the effect of transforming a direct air current into "an alternating air current or sound wave." [Farnsworth 168]

5. The vocal lips vibrate synchronously, not alternately. [Metzger 395]

6. Positive proof is now furnished that "the vocal cords do vibrate in segments." This would seem to indicate that the harmonic overtones released by a segmental vibration contribute basic attributes to the tone quality of the voice. [Seashore 505]

In conclusion, Stanley's opinion, that phonation requires a different technique of breathing than is employed for ordinary respiration, is interesting. In respiration the glottis is normally open while in phonation the glottis must be kept closed. Therefore, he claims, it is not possible to build normal breathing reflexes into tone-supporting techniques of breathing. [577, p. 310]

Pitch regulating factors. The consensus of 39 statements on this subject is that the fundamental pitch of the singing voice depends upon the frequency or rapidity of the opening and closing of the glottal aperture during phonation. [E.g., Negus op. cit., p. 346] It is also commonly held that the frequency (pitch) range of any given voice is influenced by the length, thickness and density of the vocal cords. Mackenzie claims (from laryngoscopic observations of 300 to 400 singers) that only a portion of the glottal edge is in vibration for low tones and that as the vocal pitch ascends to the falsetto quality (see Chapter VI), the vibrating segment travels toward the anterior end of the vocal lips. [364, p. 67] This observation, made with the naked eye, is later confirmed by Farnsworth, who used high speed motion picture photography to study vocal cord action. [168] Negus' explanation of the *falsetto* mechanism is also interesting: In falsetto (head register) the cords remain blown apart and are outwardly bowed by the breath stream. "Only a part of the margins of the glottis are in vibration. . . . The mechanism appears to depend on contraction of the internal fibres only of the thyro-arytenoid muscles, associated with considerable variations of tracheal air pressure." [418, p. 440]

Farnsworth reports that the duration of each glottal contact of the vocal cords during phonation decreases as the pitch rises "until, in the falsetto, complete contact is usually not attained at all." [Op. cit.] According to Curry, the method of pitch adjustment of the larynx changes as the tones ascend the musical scale because one regulatory mechanism is unsuited to make both the coarse and fine adjustments necessary to cover the entire range of the vocal gamut. [124, p. 66] In lower pitches the cords are relatively thick; in higher pitches they are "thinned and stretched." [Bartholomew 39, p. 122; Kwartin 325, p. 32]

There is however no certainty as to the exact physiological method of tuning or stretching the vocal cords during pitch changes in singing. The various actions compositely described below present typical conflicting viewpoints, incompletely picturing the entire process of pitch adjustment:

1. The palate-to-pharynx muscles (rear pillars of the throat) "aid the smaller laryngeal muscles to stretch the cords" for higher pitches. [Bartholomew 39, p. 130]

2. The vocal cords are stretched by the tipping of the cricoid (sic) cartilage. [Jones 307, p. 10]

3. "Rotation outwards of the arytenoid cartilages tenses the edges of the glottal bands [cords] and at the same time prevents closure of the glottis." [Garnetti-Forbes 198, p. 86]

4. The rate of vibration depends upon the tension, length and shape of the cords as well as upon the pressure of the air stream. [Passe 443, p. 56]

5. Two opposing sets of muscles operate to tense the vocal cords. These are the arytenoid and the crico-thyroid muscles. [Stanley 578]

6. Pitch changes are determined "by the degree of [internal] contraction of the thyro-arytenoid muscles" and not by the external stretching of these muscles. [Negus 418, p. 439]

Russell's X-ray studies of the larynx in action submit no evidence that a raising of the pitch is accomplished by the stretching of the vocal cords. Therefore, Russell feels justified in claiming that "our concepts on even this fundamental subject will have to be changed." [479] Redfield's summary of pitch control is purely theoretical but acoustically interesting: "There are three possible means by which the pitch of the human voice could conceivably be controlled either entirely or in part: 1) by varying the tension of the vocal cords, 2) by varying the capacity of the resonating air cavities, or 3) by varying the size of the orifices by which the tone pulsation is permitted to escape from the resonating air cavities to the outer atmosphere." [462, p. 272]

Evetts and Worthington, Stanley, and Clippinger submit the possibility of using breath pressure as a pitch controlling factor. In this connection these authors claim that a fitful increase of breath pressure during phonation is frequently the cause of singing off key. This is explained by the fact that increasing air pressure tends to stretch the vocal membranes (cords) and heighten the pitch of a given fixed tone. As the pressure expends itself, the correct pitch is restored. [Evetts and Worthington 167, p. 81; Stanley 578] Unconsciously applying this principle, singers often try to reach high pitches by sheer force of breath, while holding to a constant adjustment of the vocal cords. When high tones present difficulties, "it is because they are produced with too thick a string, that is, with too much resistance of the vocal cords." [Clippinger 104, p. 32] Evetts and Worthington also point out that the pitch range of the average male voice lies "about an octave lower" than the average female voice because the lengths of the vocal cords of each sex have a ratio of 15 to 11. [167, p. 24] There is no comparable difference in length, however, between the vocal cords of a bass voice and a tenor. [White 658, p. 61] (See also Chapter VI.)

The following interesting summaries of the pitch regulating process are quoted from Negus [418]:

a) "Experiment shows that the pitch of vocal sounds is determined by the larynx (itself) and is not altered by the various pharyngeal, oral, and nasal resonators." [p. 439]

b) "It has been observed that the vocal cord (cadaveric) of an adult man is 23 mm. in length, and that this length can be increased (mechanically) to 27.5," a difference of 4.5 mm. "This is a big range of movement to expect of the arytenoid cartilage, while such a movement —if it occurred—would require the exertion of a force much greater than that possessed by the small postici [crico-arytenoid] muscles. . . . These reasons appear to me to be sufficient evidence on which to state that stretching of vocal cords is an . . . extremely unlikely factor in the normal [pitch-regulating] mechanism of man. . . . Some other factor must be discovered and this, I think, is to be found in the capability of contraction" within the vocal cords [thyro-arytenoid muscles] themselves. [p. 373]

c) Therefore, "changes of pitch are not produced by stretching of the vocal cords. Changes of pitch are determined by the degree of contraction of the thyro-arytenoid muscles, whereby the degree of elasticity of the margins of the glottis can be regulated." [p. 439]

d) "The other muscles of the larynx play a secondary part in holding the arytenoid cartilages in a suitable position." [p. 376]

e) "The conclusion—corroborated on many occasions—is that if the larynx remains in the same condition as regards its vocal cords, increase of air pressure [also] raises the pitch." [p. 384]

f) "Therefore it is obvious that rises of pitch are attained by variations both of air pressure and of elasticity of the glottic margins. . . . In actual phonation the two are associated in such a way that slight increase of air pressure causes considerable rise of pitch. [p. 386 ff.]

Extrinsic mechanisms. The muscles and parts of the larynx that are not entirely contained within it, but extend from it to other parts of the body are referred to as *extrinsic* mechanisms, to distinguish them from *intrinsic* mechanisms that are included wholly within the larynx. In its function as a generator of vocal tone for singing, the larynx is not a fixture. It is freely movable and is suspended in the throat by means of flexible *extrinsic* muscles that connect it with the cranium, tongue, hyoid bone and jaw above, and with the breast bone *(sternum)* and shoulder bones *(omos)* below. [Edwards 158] The accepted latin and greek terms used to name such parts (e.g., *sterno-thyroid* muscle; *omo-hyoid* muscle) are not consistently found in vocal texts; hence, to avoid technical digressions they are employed herein only when necessary.

According to Negus, "there is great confusion with regard to the relation of the vocal cords and [all] their underlying muscles, and to the function of each in phonation." [418, p. 369] Inasmuch as extrinsic muscles are related to the posture of the body in singing, they are occasionally referred to in texts and articles on singing. But little is known about their specific function in the act of phonation and most authors either mention them cursorily or ignore them entirely.

Witherspoon stresses the fact that the larynx is not relaxed during phonation. Rather, it is in a state of tensed equilibrium, a condition which is distributed among its intrinsic and extrinsic muscles proportionate to the intensity of the tone desired. [677, p. 61] Gescheidt claims that certain laryngeal muscles (extrinsic) connect the larynx with the cervical vertebrae of the spine, thus providing the means of "conducting sympathetic vibrations from the larynx to the spinal column" and contributing to the amplification of the initial tone phonated. [200, p. 12] Curry also mentions extrinsic attachments in a brief description of vocal action. These muscles serve to brace the larynx back against the spinal vertebrae for support while the thyroid cartilage "swivels on the cricoid." [124, p. 64; also Negus 418, p. 380] Orton gives a more elaborate description of the extrinsic mechanisms of the voice in which he claims that downward pulling extrinsic muscles (e.g., *sterno-thyroid* and *omo-hyoid*) are counterbalanced by upward pulling muscles that connect the hyoid bone with the tongue muscle *(hyo-glossus)* and cranium so as to stabilize the position of the voice box (larynx) during phonation. The *hyoid bone* is also considered a part of the laryngeal unit in that it lies directly above the thyroid cartilage and is firmly attached to the latter at all times. "The hyoid bone helps to keep the tube open above the larynx." [439, p. 45]

The *epiglottis* is another extrinsic mechanism mentioned by vocal theorists. It is a thin, leaf-like extension of "yellow elastic cartilage that ordinarily projects upward behind the tongue and just in front of the glottis." (W) It is commonly believed to fold back and protect the glottis during the act of swallowing, although this action has not been clearly established. Its possible function in voice production has also been open to scrutiny by vocal theorists. Negus claims that the epiglottis is of slight importance in singing, respiration or deglutition (swallowing). After extensive research in comparative anatomy, embryology and physiology he arrives at the conclusion that "its original function [in animals] is to maintain the integrity of the olfactory sense by shutting off the mouth from the air tract; in man it is large, but degenerate in function." [418, p. 466] Hagara insists that the function of the epiglottis is confined to handling food and that when it is used in singing it blocks the larynx and stifles tone. [220, p. 23] In this opinion she is upheld by Shaw [518, p. 88] and Hemery. [238, p. 33] Evetts and Worthington report that amputation of the epiglottis causes no serious loss to the voice. [167, p. 3] Felderman also states that the epiglottis has no function in phonation. He offers as evidence the fact that "the finest specimens of song birds have no epiglottis." [173, p. 64]

THE VOCAL VIBRATO

The *vocal vibrato* is defined as a periodic oscillation of vocal tone above and below its normal pitch level, occurring at the rate of about 6.5 variations per second, and always *within* a semitone interval. It is not to be confused with a *tremolo* effect which usually varies more than a semitone [Tolmie 617] or with the vocal *trill* which is the rapid alternation of two distinct pitches in the interval of a semitone, whole tone or third. [Waters 647, p. 76; Henley 251] The vocal *tremolo* is defined as an irregular unsteadiness or faulty trembling of the pitch caused by interfering tensions, muscular weakness and the inability to maintain a stable adjustment of the laryngeal mechanism during phonation. [Wilcox 669, p. 39] In the *trill* a conscious regular musical interval is always maintained between two rapidly alternating tones. In the *vibrato* the concept of interval is entirely absent. [Seashore 511, p. 154]

The vibrato appears to be one factor in voice production that has undergone considerable experimental treatment. Of the 51 statements gathered on this subject, 16 are reports of experimental findings. An exhaustive summary of early research in this field is published in Volume III (1936) of the *University of Iowa Studies in the Psychology of Music*, edited by Carl E. Seashore. [511] Although the entire subject of vocal vibrato is still in its experimental stages, the reports of some of the investigators are informative and interesting to the teaching profession. Along with the physiological and acoustical data uncovered, there are also some speculations as to the causes and pedagogical treatment of the vibrato.

Westerman explains the vocal vibrato as a neuro-muscular phenomenon caused by the rate of discharge of action currents (nervous impulses) in the human body. By a physiological law, these impulses normally travel along the nervous system (e.g., from brain to muscle) with a frequency of from five to eight times per second. The vocal muscles, when normally activated during phonation, also receive their nervous energy with this frequency, which results in a quivering vocal effect that is called *vocal vibrato*. [652] The vibrato is as essential to the singing voice as it is to the violin tone. [Evetts and Worthington 167, p. 80] Its chief characteristics are experimentally observed to be as follows:

1. It averages 6 to 7 cycles per second in the voice of the artist singer. [Metfessel 394]

2. A slowed down or irregular rate of vibrato creates an unpleasant effect to the listener. [Stanley 577, p. 367]

3. The regularity of the vibrato is fairly constant in any single tone. [Metfessel op. cit.]

4. The average width or extent of a vibrato cycle in artistic singing is a musical semitone. [Seashore 506, p. 33]

5. There is no apparent sex difference in regard to vibrato width. [Ibid.]

6. An intensity vibrato varying from 2 to 3 decibels [Tolmie 617] is also present during 50% to 75% of the phonated time of concert singing. [Seashore 506, p. 97]

7. A vocal vibrato is present during 100% of the phonated time in gliding intonations of artistic singing. (68 gliding intonations were studied) [Miller 400]

8. During slurs and accents in the song the vibrato remains constant. [Stanley 578]

9. The ideal vibrato in artistic singing is smooth and free from chronic irregularities. [Seashore 512, p. 154]

10. Both artist singers and advanced vocal students all show a predominance of the vibrato in tone production. [Tiffin 615]

Seashore believes that the vocal vibrato is a desirable and inevitable attribute of good vocal tone, analogous to timbre. It automatically accompanies phonation in all well trained amateur and professional singers. [512, p. 120; 513, p. 12]It is a characteristic of all intensified and emotional utterance in song [Scott 501, Foreword]; the outcome of passionate utterance. [Samuels 487, p. 39] It is present whenever feeling is expressed and absent in cold, expressionless voice. To cultivate vibrato, cultivate the power to feel genuinely, not to simulate emotion. This is Seashore's advice. [511, p. 112]

Should the vibrato be cultivated when training the singing voice? "Yes, by all means!" says Muhlmann. "All good singers have one." [407] In a doctoral dissertation, based on an experimental study in the control of the vocal vibrato, Wagner draws the conclusion that "both children and adults can be taught to sing with vibrato." This, he explains, can be accomplished through the influence of rhythmic metronome beats and through paying special attention to the action of the mechanism that controls expiration during phonation. [626]

In this connection, Wilcox issues the warning to teachers of singing that the uneven wobbling tremolo defect (which Philip calls "an unpardonable vocal fault" [446, p. 147]) should not be confused with the natural, evenly spaced vibrato that is a characteristic of all correctly produced tones. [669, p. 39] Scott likewise urges that a distinction always be made in vocal teaching between "involuntary tremolo and voluntary vibrato." The former is definitely bad, but the latter is "indispensable to expressive performance." [501, p. 72] Westerman would discard the term "tremolo" entirely from the voice teacher's vocabulary because it is misleading. [652] Stanley claims that training of the vocal vibrato "is a most important phase of the [singing] teacher's art." He believes that ultimately definite criteria will be established whereby a singing pupil's voice can be evaluated almost entirely in terms of its vibrato effect. [578]

In conclusion, it should be noted that Metfessel and Seashore both remind the aspirant singer that the case for vibrato singing has been definitely established both acoustically and aesthetically. It has now been proven conclusively that "anyone who would succeed in concert or opera must have a vibrato on practically every note that is sung." [505; 392]

METHODS OF CONTROLLING PHONATION

PSYCHOLOGICAL APPROACH

Total coordinations required. Coordination is the process of integrating different, but related, activities of the body into a functional unity. (W) Because certain coordinations in singing may be either developed or disturbed by conscious training and practice, they are subject to educational influences. Voice is not produced by the throat alone, but by "cooperation of all parts of the body." [Wharton 655, p. 69] The 23 authors expressing this point of view offer various reasons for their belief. Davies declares that singing involves "physical, mental and spiritual" elements and therefore involves the whole personality. [127, p. 138] According to Mursell and Glenn, "every part of the vocal mechanism acts and reacts most intimately upon every other part," and coordination is at the very essence of the act of singing. [413, p. 284]

Nerve impulses that control the act of phonation can now be traced along their entire course to their very origin in the brain. [Seashore 505] It has been found that the control of phonation involves nerve centers in the cerebral cortex, "the highest and most general coordinating agency in the body." [Mursell and Glenn, op. cit.] "There are also direct sub-cortical [neural] interconnections between the larynx and the diaphragm, the larynx and the ear and the larynx and the facial muscles," indicating, according to Mursell, that "the entire organism comes to a focus in the act of song." [411, p. 225 ff; also Curry 124, p. 7]

Orton reports that vocal tone is controlled from both hemispheres of the brain, indicating a somatic connection with bodily behavior. [439, p. 139] According to Negus, "movements of the vocal cords [phonation] are bilaterally represented [in the brain], but speech in man is controlled by a centre in the left hemisphere only" (Broca's area). [418, p. 468] It is also known that the vagus nerve serves both respiratory and phonatory functions. [White 658, p. 103] Hence, it is obvious from neurological evidence alone that the entire vocal musculature functions as one united system, governed only by psycho-neurological controls; and that the training of the voice involves deep-seated coordinations that can only be affected by a psychological teaching approach. [Garnetti-Forbes 198, p. 79] Henderson declares that the action of the vocal cords is entirely automatic and is governed entirely by the will to make a sound. [243, p. 35] Voluntary physical controls will obstruct the spontaneous mental processes which always govern tone production, according to Stanley. [577] "Nothing but naturally free [vocal] movements can suffice," says Hill. [272, p. 11]

Witherspoon believes that faults of phonation are usually not of local origin. They arise from faulty coordinations. Local effort of any kind is anathema to the vocal student. [677, p. 5] Therefore, the first law of voice teaching is "that no direction may be given the pupil which pertains to the direct control of any narrow group of muscles taking part in the act of phonation." [Stanley 578] In other words, the total coordination of all the vocal organs is far more important than the trained activity of any single part. [Everett 165]

Anticipation of tone controls phonation. This is a widely held concept among singing teachers; 43 authors endorse it. *Anticipation,* in this sense, may be defined as a form of mental prevision or visualization of a sound in expectation of its actual production in the larynx. (W) It differs from self-listening (see Chapter VII). When tonal anticipation is strong enough the tone may be "heard" mentally and a preparatory reaction of the vocal organs may take place before the tone is actually produced. The popular concept of anticipation as a psychological teaching device is summed up in the following representative comments:

1. "It is useless to expect the student to produce a good singing tone unless it first exists in his mind." [Clippinger 114]

2. "If his conception of the tone is perfect, its production will be perfect." [Maurice-Jacquet 380; also Cimini 98, p. 11]

3. "In the perfect attack, the artist is really singing in the consciousness [mind] before the voice starts . . . hence the need of steady concentration." [Wharton 655, p. 61]

4. "The [tonal] idea is always antecedent to the [vocal] movement and absolutely essential." [La Forest 326, p. 173]

5. A "mental picture" should be formed before any physical [vocal] action is attempted. [Brouillet 64, p. 65]

6. "Good vocal tone depends upon a conception of beautiful sound." [Quoted from American Academy of Teachers of Singing—Outline of Theory. Christy 97, p. 45]

7. Phonation has three stages: 1) thinking, 2) attacking, 3) sustaining; all are governed by "mental purpose." [Owsley 441, p. 66]

8. The spontaneity of any tone is governed only by its anticipation. [Brown 78, p. 78]

9. From the first, the pupil must learn to think tone before it is produced. [Mowe 405, p. 2; Althouse 9]

10. "Listen to what you are going to do; not only to what you have done." [Howe 284, p. 63]

11. The singer's vocal tone is always an imitation of a mental model previously conceived. [Kling 319, p. 3; also Smallman and Wilcox 566, p. 8]

12. The ability to idealize tone is a prerequisite to beautiful singing. [Kirkpatrick 317]

13. Train the singer to think his tone before he produces it. [Staton 581, p. 3]

Anticipation controls pitch. Nineteen statements express the opinion that "the mere thought of any pitch," with no conscious direction of the will, automatically produces in the vocal cords the exact necessary tension to make them vibrate at that frequency. [E.g., Clippinger 112] This concept is related to concepts of ear training by the use of tonal imagery. (See Chapter VII.) Stanley explains this teaching method as follows: "Before commencing to sing, the pupil must be directed . . . to hold clearly in his mind an absolutely clean-cut mental concept of the pitch . . . he is about to sing." [578; also Wood 686, p. 21] Luckstone thinks of vocal pitch adjustment as a reflex action to a mental concept. [358] The muscles of phonation respond automatically to a mental concept of pitch. [Judd 309, p. 13; Strauss 591, p. 2] In other words, pitch control is not a separate technique in controlling phonation. It is imbedded in the tonal concept and must be taught as part of the phonatory process. "We control pitch by thinking," says Mowe. "This is the only control that should be attempted." [405, p. 5]

Stevens and Miles, who made an experimental study of the relation of vocal attack to pitch accuracy in singing report that correct intonation (of pitch) cannot be obtained "by any effort of the will," except by means of the "untaught instinctive sense of mental perception." [583] Edward Johnson, famous tenor, likewise believes that "the creation of tension on the vocal cords [for pitch control] is a completely subconscious process." Pitch changes in phonation are therefore automatic and unconscious and are controlled by thought alone. [306]

Finally, Dunkley claims that most singing faults are caused by incorrect habits of pitch control. [151, p. 1] "Singing off pitch is more often a mental than a physical disorder," says Eley. [160] Shakespeare likewise taught that correction of this fault could be achieved only by losing all consciousness of tongue or throat action and by practicing with the mental visualization of correct tones before singing them. [517, p. 24]

TECHNICAL APPROACH

Oral controls. The *mouth* or *oral cavity* is part of the tone channel through which voice is conveyed from the larynx to the outer atmosphere. The oral cavity is separated from the nasal cavity that lies above it by a horizontal bony and muscular partition called the *palate*. The mouth (oral) cavity also includes the tongue, teeth, cheeks, lips, chin and jaw and it is often loosely referred to in terms of one or more of these parts. Mouth position may therefore include chin position, jaw position, lip position, etc.

Thirty-eight statements mention the control of mouth position as a technical factor in training the singing voice, the main purpose being to relax the jaw so as to help prevent muscular constrictions in the throat. But the efficacy of voluntary oral control is in doubt and 9 authors are definitely opposed to it. Both sides of the issue are represented as follows:

For voluntary oral control:

1. The musculature that controls the shape of the oral cavity is closely related to and coordinated with the muscular action of the larynx. Mouth position is therefore important. [Crist 123]

2. The old masters taught that the mouth should be opened enough to admit one or two fingers. [Henderson 243, p. 62; Blatherwick 53]

3. "Failure to open the mouth will result in rigidity." [Wilson 674, I, p. 7]

4. "The ancient teachers placed great stress upon the importance of the mouth position of the singer.". The upper teeth should be kept visible by curling the upper lip in a natural, unforced smile. [Hagara 220, p. 44]

5. The oral cavity is an adjustable resonator. Hence, the larger the mouth, "the more ample the sound will be." [Scott 502, p. 26]

6. To free the tone, you first have to free the jaw. [Hall and Brown 227, p. 14]

7. "A loose [relaxed] jaw is indispensable to beautiful singing." [Cimini 99]

8. Relaxing the lower jaw helps relax the tongue. [Clippinger 110]

9. To establish easy jaw movement, imagine that the upper jaw is the one that moves. [Orton 439, p. 94]

10. Do not tilt the head back when dropping the jaw. [Hill 272, p. 11; Wilson, op. cit.]

11. Drop your jaw so that your lips form the shape of an egg standing on end. [Ryan 480, p. 77]

12. The higher the tone, the lower the jaw must drop. [Marchesi 369, p. 34]

13. For loud singing a wide jaw opening is indispensable. [Jeffries 301]

14. There is an ideal size of lip opening which produces the purest sound. [Passe 443, p. 69]

Against voluntary oral control:

1. Consciously opening the jaw cramps the tongue and laryngeal muscles. [Harper 228, p. 21]

2. Labial mobility is important for good diction, but the jaw should remain passive, requiring no special attention. [Greene 209, p. 311]

3. "He who moves the mouth will never become a singer." [Quoted from Lamperti by Owsley 441, p. 65]

4. "Exaggerated mouth and lip action is totally unnecessary . . . and spoils many a good singer." [Lloyd 351, p. 9]

5. Opening the mouth too wide is the most common error. [Haywood 237, II, p. 14]

6. The high notes require only a small mouth opening. [White 659, p. 41]

Lingual controls. The *tongue* is a freely movable and protrusive muscle in the mouth. Its base is attached to the hyoid bone and therefore, indirectly, to the larynx. Through other extrinsic connections it is also joined to parts of the jaw and cranium. (W)

Front, low tongue position is favored by 31 authors, the prevalent opinion being that the tongue must be held low and forward in the mouth so as to prevent the lingual muscle from sliding back into the throat and larynx. These opinions are summarized in the following:

1. The tongue is indirectly attached to the larynx. Its slightest backward movement will muffle the voice. Therefore, train it to lie quietly in the mouth during phonation. [Samuels 487, p. 21]

2. Forward tongue position keeps the throat open. [Faulds 172]

3. Raising the back tongue pulls up the larynx and obstructs its normal adjustment. [Conklin 121, p. 27]

4. The tongue muscle that lies under the chin must always feel soft and relaxed to the touch. [Clippinger 104, p. 10]

5. Widen and relax the tongue "so that the cheeks will not be drawn in against the teeth." [Harper 228, p. 137]

6. Keep the tongue low and the soft palate raised to provide a "maximum outlet for sound." [Bonavia-Hunt 55]

7. When singing, the tongue should be in complete relaxation on the floor of the mouth. [Marafioti 368, p. 113; Nicholson 425, p. 106]

8. The tongue tip rests on or behind the lower front teeth. The back of the tongue is elevated. [Lilli Lehmann 337, p. 54]

9. "The base of the tongue must lie low." [Jessica Dragonette 146]

10. Placing the tongue limply against the lower lip helps free the jaw. [Hall and Brown 227, p. 14; Wycoff 692]

Complete freedom of tongue is preferred by 19 authors on grounds that conscious tongue control makes for local effort and muscular strain. E.g.:

1. "Kill the tongue! It has nothing to do with tone except to spoil it." [Lloyd 351, p. 16]

2. Freedom of tongue is synonymous with open throat since throat tension inevitably stiffens the tongue. [Shakespeare 517, p. 19; Waters 647, p. 13]

3. The tongue and jaw must be independent of each other in good singing. [Howe 284, p. 63]

4. The tongue has little, if any, effect on the quality of the singing voice. [Dacy 126]

5. Do not try to flatten the tongue locally. [Witherspoon 677, p. 15]

6. Tongue control is effected through the mind, "not through voluntary effort or physical force." [Skiles 559]

7. Mere mention of the tongue to a vocal student induces unconscious muscular tension in it. [Samoiloff 484, p. 121; Henderson 243, p. 46]

8. "There are no tongue exercises of value to the singer." [Ryan 480, p. 95]

9. Great flexibility, freedom and facility of action are called for in the lingual organ. [Wilcox 666]

Palatal controls. The *soft palate* or *velum* is a membranous and muscular extension of the hard palate, forming a continuous surface with the latter in the roof of the mouth and serving as a partition which separates the mouth cavity from the nasal cavity. The posterior border of the velum ends in a centrally located pendant fleshy lobe which is called the *uvula.* (W)

The role of the soft palate in voice production is not clearly established. According to Russell, it was commonly believed that, to prevent nasality during phonation, the soft palate had to be raised in a valve-like action, closing off the posterior entrance into the nasal cavity. But X-ray studies show that the velar opening into the nose is not closed by the raising of the soft palate but by a "sphincter-like action from front to back." Russell reports that the velar passage always remained closed during phonation, in all the X-ray photographs taken. [479] Evetts and Worthington also used radiograms to demonstrate the fact that the soft palate "remains in exactly the same position" (i.e., passive) during normal phonation as during quiet respiration. This position is not altered by vocalization at any pitch. [167, p. 44] Conklin maintains that the soft palate rises "naturally" with ascending pitch and therefore does not require any conscious regulation. [121, p. 20] Savage also favors non-interference in palatal action and claims that these movements must be controlled "mentally," i.e., not consciously. [490, p. 92]

The typical opinions favoring conscious palatal control in voice training are those of Lissfelt, who believes that the palate must be raised consciously to prevent a faulty attack in phonation [348, p. 19]; and Mackenzie, who advises that "the uvula must be carefully trained" to remain at a high level for good voice production. [364, p. 117]

OPEN THROAT CONCEPT

The *throat* is described as the main passageway that connects the mouth cavity with the stomach and lungs. It contains the pharynx (upper throat), upper part of the esophagus, larynx and trachea, as well as the intricate musculatures that control swallowing, coughing and phonation. (W) Its many interrelated parts are subtly connected with the delicate laryngeal organ so that the slightest mismanagement of the act of phonation can impair the coordination of throat muscles and vice versa.

The most notorious vocal fault is constriction in the throat muscles. The expression *open throat* (a misnomer) is used to describe the sensation of freedom or passivity in the throat region that is said to accompany good singing. In discussing the role of imagery in voice teaching, Bartholomew has this to say: "If the various tricks of the trade that voice teachers use to improve quality are analyzed, most or all of them will be found to be devices for directly or indirectly enlarging the throat." [38] Fifty-nine statements were gathered in which the open throat concept is discussed. Twenty-two favor direct control of this factor, 17 are opposed to direct control, and 20 suggest *yawning* as an indirect teaching device for inducing open throat during phonation.

Direct approach favored. "The art of singing," says Shakespeare, "lies in the avoidance of rigidity and the adoption of the open throat." [516] Howe would have all children taught to sing with a "free, open throat, flexible tongue, and loose jaw" as a method of preventing bad singing later on. [284, Introduction] Austin-Ball believes that "the more open the throat is, the more full-throated, vibrant and generally desirable the tone is likely to be." This, he claims was taught by the old Italian masters and has never been disproven by any modern scientific theory. [31, p. 14] Caruso and Chaliapin also endorsed open throat singing techniques. [Marafioti 368; and 5]

Ortmann reports, from experimental observations, that enlarging the throat involves a conscious inhibition of some of the natural reflexes, "such as the swallowing reflex," a condition which is nevertheless essential to good tone production. [437] According to Bartholomew, research in this field has definitely proven that the accoustical attributes of good vocal quality, such as prominent "low formant," all tend to appear when the throat is consciously enlarged. Therefore teaching the open throat concept is good pedagogy. It is certainly more important than teaching "head resonance," since repeated experiments show that "the actual resonating of sound in the head cavities is of very little importance, if any, in the physical production of good quality." [39] (See also Chapter V.) Waters suggests deep breathing as a device for relaxing the throat and preventing rigidity [647, p. 7] and Shakespeare advises that the utterance of "whispered vowels," will be as an antidote for throat constrictions. [516]

Indirect approach favored. Arguments against direct control are summed up in Clippinger's statement: "It is physically impossible to hold the throat open consciously without a considerable degree of tension." Furthermore, the throat must be kept in a "plastic" condition to allow the various adjustments for vowels and tone qualities to be made. [104, p. 8] Stanley agrees with this viewpoint. He is opposed to localized control because, as he puts it, opening the throat and relaxing the throat are a "direct contradiction in terms." [578]

Aikin claims that the throat is naturally always open and free; that is, if you leave it alone. [4] "The throat is always open," says Savage, "else we would choke to death." [490, p. 113] Samoiloff and Zerffi are equally emphatic in declaring that any conscious effort to relieve the throat while singing will surely impose a strain on it and physical stiffness will result. [485; 700] It defeats its own purpose. [Shaw, 518, p. 194] Don't consciously sing with your throat; merely use it as a passageway. [Macklin 365; Ryan 480, p. 56] "Let the throat alone." [Skiles 564] It functions automatically. [Huey 285]

Yawning as a device. *Yawning* is defined as an involuntary act, usually excited by drowsiness, consisting of a deep and long inspiration following several successive attempts at inspiration in which the mouth, palate and throat passageway are forced wide open. (W) The main idea in using this device is to capture the preparatory sensation of yawning without actually performing the deep inspiratory reflex that usually accompanies it. Thus the throat is indirectly held open for singing.

Queena Mario, soprano at the Metropolitan Opera House, calls "that open feeling of a suppressed yawn" the best test of correct tone production. [370] "Opening the voice [throat] is more like yawning than anything else to which it can be compared," says Fory. [191] Lilli Lehmann always teaches her beginners the yawning position. "It helps the tongue to lie in the right place." [337, p. 186] "We learn valuable lessons in tone production from the yawn," says McAll. [383, p. 25] Every condition that is essential to the correct singing position is thereby established. [Spohr 571, p. 110] It also improves vowel attack. [Dodds and Lickley 139, p. 42] Gregory suggests pronouncing the word "hung" with the jaw dropped as a preparation for yawning. [211] Finally, Shakespeare's summary of phonation in motto form is instructive:

> *By silent breathing free the throat,*
> *Start exactly on the note,*
> *Sound the* ah *as if in yawning,*
> *Breathe as in the act of warming.* [517, p. 15]

LARYNGEAL POSITION

Should the larynx move during phonation? The opinions of 18 authors are evenly divided on this question, the arguments pro and con being based largely on empirical observations and personal teaching experience. Affirmative opinions are represented by the following concepts:

1. The larynx revolves on its own axis. Therefore it descends according to pitch. [Witherspoon 677, p. 26]

2. It moves up and down to a slight extent. [Passe 443, p. 54; Marchesi 369, p. 15]

3. The larynx rises as the pitch ascends the scale. [Allen 7, p. 49]

4. There is no fixed position. In trained singers the larynx may actually descend as the pitch rises. [Pressman 452]

Contrary opinions are summed up in the following:

1. The larynx is rather low during phonation and is kept in that position by correct breathing. [Scott 502, p. 20]

2. Natural singers show no laryngeal movement during voice production. [Evetts and Worthington 167, p. 10]

3. Retain the Adam's Apple, or larynx, in one position for singing. [La Forest 326, p. 151]

4. "The larynx should remain quiescent throughout a song." This is a sign of correct action. [Brown 78, p. 12]

5. It must not go up or down "no matter how high or low you sing." If anything, it remains firmly fixed against the spine. [Feuchtinger 179]

6. To obtain the best results in singing, "the larynx should not be elevated by contraction of its extrinsic muscles. . . . Thereby the capacity of the resonating chamber above the larynx is diminished." [Negus 418, p. 441 and p. 383]

7. Leave it (larynx) alone where it belongs! [Hemery 238, p. 82]

Devices for improving vocal attack. The *attack* is the method of beginning a vocal sound. (W) It is the means by which sound waves are initiated in the glottis by setting in motion the edges of the vocal cords. [Skiles 558; Curry 124, p. 5] Nineteen statements were gathered on this subject.

"What is a perfect attack?" asks Lawrence. Providing her own answer, she explains that it is the sounding of the tone "with nothing happening before the tone starts." [335, p. 14] Henderson's statement is more explicit: Phonation and breath control are simultaneous activities in correct voice production. The glottal attack should occur neither before nor after the breath is ready for it. [243, p. 37] In other words, the correct attack means a precise synchronization of the approximation of the vocal cords, and the onset of breath. [Howe 284, p. 36] "The basic preparation is very simple," says Jeffries. "First there should be an upright position; second, an easy, relaxed intake of sufficient breath; and third, a normal opening of the mouth, with a feeling of opening the whole channel down into the chest." [302] A poor attack causes unwarranted variations in pitch and intensity. The good singer attacks a tone right in the center of the pitch and holds a constant intensity throughout the duration of the tone. [Stanley 578] "Sliding up to the tone shows that you are not certain of its location." [Clippinger 104, p. 37]

Deviations in attack are said to occur, even in artistic performances. Scientific instruments can now measure irregularities of performance that escape the naked ear. (See Chapter X.) Seashore's experimental analyses of the vocal performances of a group of great singers reveals the fact that about 25 per cent of the tonal attacks were not direct hits but were accomplished by gliding (imperceptibly) into the tone desired. Furthermore about 40 per cent of the transitions from tone to tone were accomplished by inaudible portamentos or gliding intonations that connected the tones. Only about 35 per cent of the notes sung were level attacks (with a slight pause between tones). This information is interesting to the teacher in that it illustrates the irregularities of phonation even in good singing and the fallibility of common hearing as a guide to pitch accuracy. [511]

The glottal stroke. According to Aikin, Manuel Garcia and his followers have always insisted that a tone should be preceded by what he described as "a very slight cough," in order to secure a distinct attack upon it. [4] This type of attack is called the stroke of the glottis or *coup de glotte*. [Henderson 243, p. 37] The *coup de glotte* is little understood by authors. Hence meagre mention is made of it, often in confusing and contradictory terms. Clippinger calls it a "disagreeable shock of the glottis" [104, p. 6], while Skiles refers to it as a method of clarifying vocal attack, giving "the best raw material from which to build tone." [564] Here the issue rests for want of confirmatory evidence.

Five more interesting suggestions are made relevant to the subject of vocal attack:

1. When deep inhalation precedes the singing of any tone (in practicing) it is best "to allow a small quantity of breath to escape before attacking" the tone. [Allen 7, p. 28]

2. Stevens and Miles made an experimental study of the first vocal vibrations in the attack of a singing tone. They report that "the best

guarantee of success in attack, as to pitch and evenness of result, is to have had immediately preceding vocal experience at about the same level in pitch range. This is realized in the singing of different vowels consecutively on the same note." [583]

3. Dunkley suggests that before singing a succession of different pitches in a song, it is desirable "to gauge the feeling of the highest note in the group" before beginning the group. This can be accomplished by thinking the high tone well in advance of its attack. [151, p. 37]

4. Make your mind (thought) direct the accurate placing of wide interval attacks. This mental preparation will overcome any physical inertia in the throat. [Wood 686, Introduction to Volume III]

5. Kortkamp also favors the mental approach for improving vocal attack. "Imagine you can hear your voice singing that first note for about three seconds *before* actually singing it." [321]

SUMMARY AND INTERPRETATION

The analysis of 463 concepts of phonation offers convincing testimony that there is hardly a subdivision of vocal theory or practice in which authorities do not disagree. Negus, whose 493 page experimental study of the mechanism of the larynx is considered the most comprehensive and authoritative work in this field, after reviewing all the known explanations of phonation comes to the conclusion that "the whole subject is so vague and confused, and shows such a complete absence of unanimity of opinion, that it will be necessary to start from the beginning without regard to any previous explanation of the mechanism of phonation." [418, p. 369] Even the fact that voice originates in the larynx is in dispute. [E.g., White 657] But disagreements among authorities are inevitable within the tangled areas of vocal research and rational comparisons of conflicting viewpoints often help to clarify and reconcile them.

The discussions of vocal theory reviewed herein tend to confirm Negus' opinion. Many of the fragmentary and incomplete descriptions of vocal action are derived from superficial laryngoscopic views, supplemented by some X-ray studies of the vocal tract. Some of these descriptions are succinct statements of physiological fact. Others are dilated empirical observations tinged with philosophical comment. Some authors dwell on relatively insignificant data, to the exclusion of more fundamental factors. Others indulge in generalities while ignoring underlying details. A composite abridgement and simplification of these incomplete fragments would be helpful to the teaching profession, especially with reference to the intricate process of vocal tone production.

Discussions of phonation are further complicated by the numerous ramifications existing in related areas. The study of the physical structures of the larynx and their functions belong in *physiology*. Tonal analysis is an *acoustical* subject. Singing as a form of self-expression demands *psychological* treatment. Breathing, facial expression, posture, tongue, lip and jaw movements, and the functions of the ear are all related activities. Conceivably, even the sense of vision enters into the estimating of distance for vocal projection. Obviously, then, phonation integrates with many other bodily functions and such interrelationships as these, existing between various departments of vocal theory, seem to preclude the setting up of independent hierarchies of teaching procedure for each of the several components of singing. Indeed, in its pedagogical implications, no part of this study may be considered entirely independently of all its other parts.

In order to strengthen this concept of *wholeness* of the vocal processes, and to provide a simplified, not-too-technical reorientation for the teacher of singing, the following résumé of the phonatory function is presented. This represents an interpretative digest of foregoing theoretical and methodological materials pertaining to this subject. Except when otherwise indicated, page numbers refer to Negus' book which is listed as item No. 418 in the Bibliography.

THEORETICAL CONSIDERATIONS

Mechanical aspects of phonation. In its simplest mechanical aspects, the larynx is a transformer of energy. Its valve-like action at the glottis converts thoracic breath pressure into acoustical energy, which is then propagated into the surrounding atmosphere as *voice*. Phonation employs at least five mechanical factors: 1) a reservoir of breath energy (lungs); 2) a directional valve that releases the expiring breath stream upwards (breathing muscles and trachea); 3) another valve that partially resists the air pressure and thus focuses its potential energy at a given point (the vocal cords or glottis); 4) a channel for the conduction, projection and propagation of newly converted acoustical energy or vocal tone into the outer atmosphere (the resonators); 5) a means of renewing and leading off depleted and unused portions of the energizing agent (breathing passages in the throat, nose and mouth). Negus reminds us that breath is not vocal substance. It is merely the mechanical force used to activate the vocal vibrator and it apparently ceases to play an

important part as an acoustical agent when once it passes the point where
the glottal vibrations have been induced. He writes: "For efficient phonation it is necessary that the lungs should hold a considerable volume of
air and that this air should be expelled through the trachea at an
accurately controlled rate and pressure." [p. 439] Such breathing "is best
carried out by a combined lower thoracic and diaphragmatic mechanism.
. . . Pure clavicular breathing is acknowledged to be wrong." [p. 390]
(See also Chapter III.)

   Structural aspects. For simplification, the larynx or voice box is reduced to five basic structural elements. These are described as: 1) a
ring-shaped *(cricoid)* cartilage; 2) a pair of small ladle-shaped *(arytenoid)*
cartilages; 3) a shield-shaped *(thyroid)* cartilage; 4) a pair of vocal cords
(thyro-arytenoid muscles or folds); and 5) a U-shaped *(hyoid)* bone.
These five structural units are so situated and interjoined with connecting tissues that together they provide rigidity and mobility to the valving
parts of the larynx, and patency and direction to the breathing channel
for purposes of respiration and phonation.

   1) The *cricoid* cartilage provides an anchorage for the entire laryngeal
mechanism, being a relatively stationary base for the more mobile thyroid
and arytenoid cartilages that rest upon it. It is firmly attached to the
windpipe (trachea), forming, in fact, its uppermost ring. "It is of great
importance in maintaining patency of the air tract at the larynx." [p.
466]

   2) The *arytenoid* cartilages provide posterior points of attachment for
the vocal cords (thyro-arytenoid muscles). The arytenoids rest upon individual convex facets of the cricoid cartilage and are capable of a rotary and sliding motion "so that each arytenoid can be shifted towards
or away from its fellow, and can also rotate about a vertical axis." [p.
450] Thus the arytenoids serve as tiny regulators of the length and tension of the vocal cords and they can also regulate the opening and closing
of the glottis during phonation, respiration and deglutition. During phonation, fixation of the arytenoids is maintained as part of the cord-tensing
action, by means of tiny groups of laryngeal muscles.

   3) The *thyroid* cartilage also rests on the cricoid cartilage and is
articulated with the latter by means of a pivot joint, making possible a
slight arc-like rocking movement. The anterior ends of the vocal cords
converge to a common point of attachment in the thyroid cartilage, just
behind the prominent bulge that is commonly known as the *Adam's
Apple.*

   4) The *vocal cords* (a pair) form the outer vibrating edges of the *thyro-
arytenoid* muscles or folds. They overhang the entrance of the trachea

and, being elastic, they may be set into vibratory activity by the pressure of the expiring breath stream. The internal contraction of these thyro-arytenoid muscles tenses and stiffens them for phonation and the degree of this tension also influences the pitch of the phonated tone. Coincidently with this tensing action, the vocal edges (cords) of the glottis are brought together by the approximation of the two arytenoid cartilages to which they are posteriorly attached. This increases the resistance of the vocal edges to the expiring breath stream and forces them into vibration, much as the lips of a bugler vibrate when he blows into his instrument. "If the air pressure remains constant . . . the vibratory action will recur at rhythmical intervals and an audible tone will be produced." [p. 459]

5) The *hyoid* bone lies horizontally above the entire phonating mechanism and completes the laryngeal framework. Its chief function is to hold the superior entrance into the larynx open where it joins the lower throat cavity (pharynx), just as the cricoid cartilage holds the inferior entrance to the larynx open where it joins the trachea tube. The hyoid bone also serves as an anchorage for the tongue and other muscles. Because it is always firmly attached to the thyroid cartilage (by means of thyro-hyoid muscles and ligaments), the hyoid bone usually moves as a unit with the latter, imparting its own movements to the thyroid cartilage and vice versa. [p. 16]

Extrinsic mechanisms. Also attached to each of the rigid structural parts of the larynx described above are numerous extrinsic muscles and ligaments that activate the phonating mechanism or else hold the larynx in a steadying position in the throat that is favorable to phonation. These extrinsic attachments also increase the vibratory area of phonation and thus augment the initial vibrations generated by the tiny vocal cords themselves. (The vocal cords of an adult measure from about 12.5 to 17 mm. in the female larynx and from 17 to 25 mm. in the male larynx, or from about one-half inch to less than one inch in length.) [p. 457] The process of phonation thus encompasses a much wider musculature than is represented by the laryngeal mechanism itself.

The vibratory area of phonation. The tones of phonation really consist of two types of vibratory energy: a) originating vibrations and b) supplementary or enforced vibrations. Curry estimates that only twenty per cent of the energy applied to the vocal cords in the form of breath pressure is utilized at the glottis. [124, p. 49] The remaining eighty per cent is either dissipated in unused breath or it may be absorbed into contiguous areas in the form of sympathetic (enforced) vibrations of connecting muscles and surfaces. Such supplementary vibrations considerably augment the volume and also influence the quality of the phonated tone.

"The loudness of the sound will vary with the area of the vibrating surface." [Negus, p. 344]

Through their inherent power of contraction *(tonus)* all these connecting extrinsic muscles are capable of vibrating in sympathy with the vocal vibrations originating in the larynx. Furthermore, they tend to transmit vibratory energy into outlying structures of the body, to which they are also attached. The following examples illustrate this principle:

1. The *stylo-hyoid* muscles connect the larynx with the styloid processes of the cranium, thus transmitting laryngeal vibrations into the temporal bones of the skull.

2. The *palato-pharyngeus* muscles connect the larynx (thyroid cartilage) with the soft palate, thus transmitting laryngeal vibrations into the roof of the mouth.

3. The *sterno-thyroid* muscles connect the larynx with the breast bone (sternum), thus transmitting laryngeal vibrations into the chest wall and ribs.

4. The *hyo-glossus* and other muscles connecting the larynx with the tongue tend to generate sympathetic vibrations in the latter.

5. The spinal vertebrae and shoulder blades likewise receive sympathetic vibrations through direct muscular connections with the larynx. (E.g., the *crico-pharyngeal* and *omo-hyoid* muscles. "The cricoid cartilage is held back with great force against the front of the vertebral column by contraction of the *crico-pharyngeus* muscle." [Negus, p. 380])

Numerous other extrinsic laryngeal muscular connections may be traced, pertaining to many different skeletal parts of the body that are similarly affected by direct conduction and radiation of vibratory energy from the larynx, thus indicating that a considerable portion of the human body functions as a complex vibrator of sound during the act of phonation. (See also Chapters V and VII.) [Negus, p. 382 ff.]

Other discussions of vocal theory appearing in this chapter include the nature and importance of the vocal vibrato in singing. The summarizing analyses of these discussions are self explanatory and need not be repeated here.

METHODOLOGICAL CONSIDERATIONS

The importance of posture. Problems of posture predominate in the 275 methodological statements reviewed. Special emphasis is laid on the positions and control of the mouth, tongue, palate, throat and larynx. Here again, it is desirable to relate the various parts of the vocal mechanism to the whole posture of the body for singing. The larynx is attached to the upper end of the trachea much as a nozzle is attached to the end of a garden hose. During the application of breath pressure against the occluded vocal lips (cords), the larynx is prevented from wobbling by an arrangement of extrinsic supporting muscles. These muscles, like supporting guy wires, radiate from the larynx upward to points in the head, backward to points in the spine, and downward to points in the chest and shoulders. Obviously, the slightest postural abnormality during phonation will tend to pull these extrinsic muscles out of alignment and also tend to pull the entire larynx away from its basic support against the spine, thus disturbing the phonating mechanism. "Elevation of the larynx during singing is a faulty mechanism." [Negus, p. 383]

Because many common faults of phonation are attributed to faulty posture, authors of singing texts continually stress the importance of head position, chest position, tongue position, etc., as technical elements in maintaining a correct over-all posture of the body for artistic singing. Freedom and flexibility of the neck, shoulders, spine, ribs and chest are therefore contributing factors in phonation. Artist singers caution beginners against assuming backward tilting head positions, flat chest or drooping shoulders. Such postural deformities impose abnormal strains upon the neck muscles which, in turn, might set up chronic laryngeal tensions and result in injuries to the vocal apparatus under the exertion of sustained singing. [Ibid. p. 390]

Psychological controls. The foregoing considerations present forceful evidence of the complexity of the phonatory apparatus and indicate the extreme difficulty and hazard involved in imposing part-methods of technical training upon the muscular network that actuates the singing voice. It is argued, in 85 statements, that local effort of any kind in singing tends to disturb coordinations of the many interrelated parts of the vocal instrument. Psychological or indirect training procedures are therefore recommended, embodying three main objectives:

1. *Mental ease.* Mental ease or poise is cultivated in the student by removing all fear and caution regarding the vocal act. Formal discipline and criticism are reduced to a minimum. Feelings of frustration and failure are dissipated by preventing self-analysis, conscious effort and striving beyond the capabilities of the vocal instrument. Singing is taught as a soul-satisfying experience, rather than a laborious and self-conscious performance of vocal gymnastics.

2. *Tonal imagery.* The inculcation of strong tonal concepts requires previous experience in recognizing good vocal models. The ear is trained

through listening and imitation. (Chapter VIII) The student also practices anticipating (imaging) each tone that is to be phonated. Thus, vocal reflexes are cultivated indirectly through the building of mental concepts of pitch, volume and quality.

3. *Motivation*. Finally, motivation controls phonation because it stimulates the proper desire to express, accompanied by an incentive or fruitful purpose. (Chapters II and X) Those who favor indirect teaching methods believe that strong purpose, aesthetic feeling, interest and joyous enthusiasm spell freedom of vocal action in singing.

In conclusion, the teacher of singing is reminded that voice is a living phenomenon and not the mechanical product of inert laryngeal structures. Cadaveric dissections are largely unrevealing to the vocalist, and experimental procedures for observing and measuring the exact characteristics of glottal vibration in a living voice present many practical difficulties that have not been overcome as yet. In training the singing voice, old habits must often be broken down before new ones can be acquired. Remedial techniques therefore play an important role in voice-building. But, in the process of applying remedial procedures through actual singing, the songs that are studied should always be regarded as vehicles of self-expression at whatever level of proficiency the student has attained, rather than as analytical technical studies in the overcoming of basic vocal difficulties. Attention-arresting admonitions such as "stand up straight," "pull your chin in," "breathe deeply" or "keep the tongue low" inevitably disturb spontaneous vocal coordinations and result in stilted, self-conscious performance.

CHAPTER V

CONCEPTS OF RESONANCE

Definition. According to Webster, *resonance* is the intensification and enrichment of a musical tone by means of supplementary vibration. It is also the result of synchronous vibrations that blend with the initial pulsations issuing from a generator of sound. The action of the resonator, which is distinguished from that of the generator, is usually to amplify certain frequencies produced by the generator while damping out or absorbing other frequencies. Therefore the effect of resonance is to increase the initial tone or to change its quality or both. [Curry 124, p. 42]

THEORIES OF RESONANCE

GENERAL DESCRIPTIONS

The human vocal organ is a wind instrument analogous to the open tube type of wind instrument in the orchestra. This analogy now seems widely accepted. Such an instrument consists of a mouthpiece where the sound is generated and a cylindrical pipe or cavity where the sound is resonated. The quality of tone produced by such an instrument is always dependent upon two main factors: the manner in which the generator vibrates and the shape of the air cavity which constitutes the resonator. [Redfield 462, p. 267] The resonance properties of cylindrical tubes and similar cavities can be accurately determined experimentally. But the vocal cavities are so irregular in shape, varying as they do from individual to individual that the only way of arriving at any estimate of their resonance properties is by comparing them with analogous shapes and tubes of fixed pattern and design. Therefore, the most common vocal descriptions are borrowed, by analogy, from musical instruments. The human vocal instrument is described as consisting of a set of vocal cords or *mouthpiece* and an outlying structure of bony and muscular cavities which constitute a *resonator*. In the vocal mechanism the resonators are the mouth, throat, nose and sinus

TABLE FOUR

SUMMARY OF CONCEPTS OF RESONANCE USED IN TRAINING THE
SINGING VOICE

	total number of statements	sub-total	grand total	statements by prof. singers	documented statements	undocumented statements
I. *Theories of resonance*			137			
A. General descriptions	19	19		2	6	13
B. Acoustical factors	44	44			30	14
C. Physiological factors		74				
1. head resonance						
a) *head cavities are important*	7			2		7
b) *head cavities are not important*	3				2	1
2. function of sinuses						
a) *sinuses are used*	9				2	7
b) *sinuses are not used*	4				3	1
3. nasal resonance						
a) *nasal cavities are consciously employed*	14			2	4	10
b) *nasal cavities are not consciously employed*	3					3
4. importance of mouth and throat cavities	11				6	5
5. importance of chest cavity	7				2	5
6. the entire body as a resonator	16			1	1	15
II. *Methods of controlling vocal resonance*			125			
A. Psychological approach		19				
1. expressional intent controls resonance	6				1	5
2. is direct control possible						
a) *resonance is directly controllable*	5			1		5
b) *resonance is not directly controllable*	8					8

TABLE FOUR (continued)

	total number of statements	sub-total	grand total	statements by prof. singers	documented statements	undocumented statements
B. Technical approach		106				
1. quality as a guide	16			2	1	15
2. acquiring a vocal focus						
a) *the voice should be consciously focused*	41			4	2	39
b) *the voice should not be consciously focused*	19			2	2	17
3. the value of humming						
a) *humming is a useful device*	25			1		25
b) *humming is not a useful device*	5				1	4
TOTALS	262	262	262	17	63	199

cavities, the chest cavity also being considered a resonator of importance. [Dodds and Lickley 139, p. 33]

It is hardly necessary to enter into a detailed discussion of the acoustical properties of resonators since such information is readily available in any good encyclopedia. It is more important here that the teacher of singing receive a few basic acoustical facts that will guide his choice and use of vocal training methods. The following brief acoustical résumé is therefore given, based upon the experimental findings of recent investigators in this field.

ACOUSTICAL FACTORS

Tone travels, but the vibrating or pulsating particles of air which transmit the sound waves do not travel. [Brown 68] The wave of sound is not a draught or current of air to be directed at will. It is more like the wave that passes over a field of wheat when wind is blowing. Each stalk sways a bit but returns. Similarly, each particle of air swings to and fro on a fixed axis. As it is set in motion by vibrations it imparts its energy to adjacent particles which in turn continue to transmit the vibratory energy in all directions simultaneously in the form of expanding concentric spheres emanating from the vibratory source. [Hemery 238, p. 40] As Redfield describes it, sound is a kind of shivering or trembling of the atmosphere that is propagated in all directions at once. [462, p. 266] The action of a resonator, although it does not produce the vibratory energy itself, is to reduce the resistance of the medium in which the vibration is propagated. [Curry 124, p. 53] Clippinger adds that the office of the resonator is "to reinforce the tone and give it quality."[112]

All sounds whether vocal or not possess four main characteristics: pitch, loudness, time and quality, representing the frequency, amplitude, period and form of the sound wave. [Seashore 505]

Vocal quality or timbre is determined by the form of the sound wave issuing from the singer's lips and the relative frequencies and intensities of its harmonic constituents or overtones. [Evetts and Worthington 167, p. 39] *Quality*, according to Stanley, is a generic term that really includes two independent factors: a) the tonal or vowel spectrum which is determined by the distribution pattern of fundamental and overtones in a given note and b) the aesthetic effect or beauty of a tone. Apparently, the tonal spectrum does not influence the beauty of a tone. [577, p. 299] The distribution of tonal frequencies in a vowel spectrum is called its *formant*. Borchers describes the timbre of a vocal tone at a given moment as a combination of three factors, absolute pitch, absolute intensity and vowel characteristics (tonal spectrum or formant). [58] According to Seashore, tone quality depends entirely upon "the prevailing tone spectrum." [507] Curry describes tone quality as the subjective impression of the nature of the sound wave, this impression depending upon the number and relative frequencies, intensities and duration of its components. The *fundamental* of a sound wave is that component which has the lowest frequency and which usually determines the absolute pitch of the sound we hear. [124, p. 41] It should be noted that the complex frequency and intensity composition of voice varies continuously during oral expression and it is not easy therefore, to take objective measurements of vocal quality. [Farnsworth 169] Lewis reports that the vocal tract in singing or speaking is constantly changing. "The evidence as a whole indicates . . . that there are no fixed vocal resonators of any appreciable importance." [340]

Good vocal quality in singing is usually accompanied by minute imperceptible fluctuations of pitch and intensity (about six per second) around the central pitch of the note as a norm. This fluctuation of a vocal tone is called its *vibrato*. (Chapter IV) When the pitch center shifts unduly the effect is unpleasant to the ear of a listener. [Stanley 577, p. 301] The vibrato seems to add life or warmth to a tone. Intensity lends volume or dynamic properties, a low formant or distribution of frequencies lends depth or resonance and a high formant provides brilliance. [Ortmann 437, p. 99] All these properties compositely form the *quality* of a vocal tone.

Peabody Conservatory experiments over a period of nearly five years have analyzed the recordings of more than a thousand vocal tones taken from forty male and female singers' voices with the following results: Good singers' voices possess four unmistakable attributes: an even vibrato, a minimum intensity of tone, prominent low overtones or formant at about 500 cycles and prominent high overtones at about 2900 cycles. [Bartholomew 40] Stanley claims that the maximum energy in a good tone is concentrated in only two or three frequency bands while in a faulty tone the energy distribution is more extensive. [578] The voice is said to be properly *placed* when the above mentioned objective characteristics have been arrived at through systematic training. [Bartholomew 37]

Four more acoustical facts are to be noted: Lindsley reports experimental evidence that voice quality can be changed by increasing the amount of vibration in one or more of the vocal resonators. [347] He does not state whether this is an automatic result of training the singer's voice or whether a skilled vocalist should be able to focus his voice consciously in any particular region of the vocal resonators at will. Lewis and Lichte report an experiment in which various overtones or partials in the voice of a trained vocalist were successively brought out by means of changes in the size and shape of the vocal cavities and mouth orifice. [341] Curry holds that it is wrong to believe that a sound wave can be reflected by the epiglottis, tongue or other surfaces to various other parts of the vocal tract since the wave length of any sound within the average range of a voice is much too long to be affected by these relatively small surfaces within the vocal tract. [124, p. 49] Another interesting observation that Curry makes is that the vocal sound phonated by a singer constitutes only about 20 per cent of the total energy applied to the vocal cords during phonation. Apparently the remaining energy is dissipated in "parasitic vibrations" which emanate from the initial tone and are absorbed throughout the vocal tract. [Ibid., p. 50] Thus it would appear that the vocal resonators as a whole absorb nearly four-fifths of the energy of phonation.

Pedagogical aspects. The action of the resonance factor in voice production has caused considerable controversy among teachers of singing. [Drew 147, p. 125] The term *resonance* is often loosely used to describe the unknown properties which a singing tone acquires after it has been properly cultivated by means of a regular system of instruction. In this sense it is synonymous with *voice placing,* a term which vaguely describes the product of good vocal teaching.

In the foreword to *The Science and Sensations of Vocal Tone* by Herbert-Caesari, Bonavia-Hunt makes a statement that is typical of many texts on singing: as vocal sound travels outward from the larynx it acquires volume and other characteristics in the throat and mouth until it is released into the surrounding atmosphere. [269] Most texts agree that resonance is due to the synchronous vibration of the air in the resonance cavities. The New York Singing Teachers Association accepts this view. [421, p. 35] Some explanations also mention that the sympathetic vibration of the bony or cartilaginous framework of the human body is part of the resonance system. [Herbert-Caesari 269, p. xiii] Curry speaks of the parasitic vibrations of the structures linked to the larynx [124, p. 49] and Negus includes the subglottic volume of the trachea and the bronchi as part of the system of vocal resonators. [418, p. 440] Stanley lists as vocal resonators the trachea and bronchi, the laryngeal pharynx, the oral pharynx, the nasal pharynx, the nasal cavity, the sinuses and the mouth. [578]

Regarding the relative influence of phonation and resonance upon the final singing tone emitted, opinions are widely varied. On one extreme, Bergère claims that resonance is a negative factor and depends entirely upon the type of vibration that is produced in the larynx. If the phonated vibration is correct, the final tone will be correct. [45] At the other extreme, Graveure and Madden hold that everyone's singing voice is pretty much the same as far as phonation is concerned. What we call vocal differences are those characteristics that are superadded to the bit of pitch that comes off the vocal cords. These differences originate not in the larynx but in the resonating organs, where the singing voice "attains its character and individuality." [208; also 367]

It is generally agreed that concepts of vocal quality are linked up with resonance factors inasmuch as differences of quality are caused by differences in the shape of the resonators or those parts which vibrate in sympathy with the vocal tone that is phonated. [Henderson 243, p. 57] In other words, differences of vocal quality depend on individual anatomical pecularities. [Negus 418, p. 289] Illustrating this point, Wheeler's report on X-ray experiments indicates that so-called naturally beautiful voices seem to have symmetrical palatal and pharyngeal arches, those having flat arches having less beauty in their voices than the well arched cases. [656, p. 630]

Concerning the commonly used terms *chest voice* and *head voice,* Drew maintains that they are misleading to the singer because voice does not actually come from the chest or head. Furthermore, the sinuses in the head are not acoustically equipped to amplify vocal sounds and the chest resonator is equivalent to a box filled with a wet sponge. We can hardly expect much resonance from such unfavorable conditions. [147, p. 126] When he made this statement, Mr. Drew apparently was unaware of an earlier experiment reported in the Psychological Bulletin in which various parts of the body were tested for vibratory activity during the vocal act. The most active resonators were listed according to the amount of vibration produced in the walls thereof, in the following order: the pharynx, the lower jaw, the chest, the top of the head, the nasal framework, the left and right sinuses, and the frontal sinuses. [Lindsley 347]

PHYSIOLOGICAL FACTORS

Head resonance. Opinion is divided on the importance of head cavities, sinuses and nasal cavities in singing. Mme. Dossert along with six others is certain that in the head and chest cavities there are definite places for the reinforcement of each singing vocal tone. [140, p. 36] This is apparently a matter of opinion, based upon extensive teaching experience. Typical opinions are also offered by Wettergren [654] and de Gogorza [134], two prominent professional singers who in interviews state that all tone must be resonated in the *mask,* or hollow bone cavities that lie directly under the eyes and back of the nose.

On the other hand, Austin-Ball at the Eastman School of Music emphatically claims that the influence of the head cavities on the quality of tone is negligible. [31, p. 39] This latter view is supported by Bartholomew who admits that the attempt of the singer to feel head resonance frequently improves his tone but that it is a psychological rather than a physiological control. In other words, the actual resonating of sound in the head cavities is of very little importance, if any, in the physical production of good vocal quality. [38] Stanley is opposed to singers trying to feel any tones in the head at all. This conscious effort merely constricts the throat and ultimately eliminates some of the upper tones of the vocal range. [578] Wilcox points out, in an apparent contradiction, that the head cavities are important as regulators of quality but that they do not contribute to the volume of tone and hence they may not be regarded as resonators. [669, p. 7]

Function of sinuses. The *sinuses,* six in number, are relatively small bony cavities in the skull which communicate with the nostrils and contain air. Their function as resonators has always been a subject of controversy among vocal teachers. Even the reports of experimenters are conflicting. Wheeler believes, from experimental studies, that the range of the voice is governed by the length of the space in the frontal sinuses. [656] Bartholomew claims that the resonance value of the sinuses is practically nil. Because they are partially filled with semi-liquid they would be more likely to dampen and absorb than to amplify sounds. [39] White builds the amazing thesis, in a scholarly three volume treatment, that vocal tone is generated in the sinuses rather than, as is commonly believed, in the larynx. [657, 658, 659] It is a lengthy rationalization, strongly opinionated and convincingly presented, but it cries out for experimental evidence to support its radical assertions. In a nontechnical discussion, Hill rather vaguely refers to the sinuses as tone building chambers. [272, p. 27] Schatz, a voice physician, claims that the sinuses are no longer regarded as resonators. [492] Passe, who writes extensively on vocal physiology, quotes the authority of Negus and Schaeffer on the same opinion. [443, p. 62; also Negus 418, p. 440]

Nasal resonance. The nasal cavity is more or less fixed in its size, shape and total volume. During voice production in singing, strong vibratory sensations can be felt in the walls of the nasal cavity. This fact has led many singing teachers to the belief that the nose is "the sounding board of the voice." [Scott 502, p. 32] But there is a difference between singing a tone through the nose and feeling it vibrate in the nasal cavity. The former condition is extremely objectionable to singers. It is called *nasality.* The latter condition is highly desirable. It is called *nasal resonance.* The distinction here is physiological, not acoustical. Singing *through* the nose comes from relaxing the velum or soft palate and thus opening the passage between the back of the oral cavity and the nasal cavity. Nasal resonance, on the other hand, is merely the effect of sound conduction into the walls of the nasal cavity and the bones of the skull and may take place even when the velum is closed. [Orton 439, p. 98; Fory 194]

Kerstin Thorborg, noted prima donna, in an interview recommends a nose pinching test while singing a sustained tone, to guard against objectionable nasality. If the nostrils can be pinched and released intermittently without altering the quality of the tone the voice is being correctly resonated. [611] The use of a rubber tube from nostril to ear will likewise indicate to the singer just when the velum relaxes, causing objectionable nasality to occur. [Bartholomew 39] The use of syllables like *ning* when substituted for the words of a song will help to establish the sensation of nasal resonance. [Novello-Davies 430, p. 189] Dan Beddoe recommends the use of the sound of *hung* for inducing nasal resonance. [42] Wodell suggests the use of *m, n,* and *ng* sounds. [680]

Edgerton believes that "part of every tone must be sung through the nose." [156] Warren favors the conscious use of nasal resonance because "it performs the service of amalgamating" the various vocal resonances "into a composite, artistic tone." [632]

Henderson definitely is against consciously controlling nasal resonance and advises that the best way to utilize the nasal cavities is to "let them entirely alone." [243, p. 60] Bartholomew vaguely asserts that objectionable nasality is not caused by a relaxed velum but by having strong nose resonance while the throat resonance remains weak. [39] This statement needs clarification by the author. He further states that the velar passage to the nose should be kept open when singing all vowel sounds, for this spells the beginning of vocal quality. [Ibid. 37] Shaw likewise claims that we lose about half the carrying power of the voice when the soft palate is unduly raised. [534, p. 156] To Sbriglia, famous Italian singing master, the nasal tone was anathema. He therefore settled the matter by always advocating keeping the voice in the chest. [Huey 290, p. 610]

Mouth and throat cavities. In defining the functions of the various vocal resonators, the mouth or oral cavity is distinguished from the nasal cavity and the pharyngeal or throat cavity is distinguished from the laryngeal and chest cavities. The boundary lines of these various cavities are not finely laid except possibly for the vocal cords which form an accurate line of division between the chest and laryngeal cavities. The simplest physiological concept regarding these cavities is that they form a more or less continuous passageway interrupted only by the various curves and contours shaped by muscular and cartilaginous protuberances. Instances of these valve-like protuberances are the tongue in the oral cavity, the uvula and velum in the nasal cavity, the epiglottis in the pharynx or throat cavity and the vocal cords in the laryngeal cavity. The contours of the vocal resonator are analogous to the walls of a horn loud speaker, the larynx being the sound generating unit. The passage through which the voice passes from larynx to lips is the resonance cavity, formed in large part by the shape of the throat and mouth. [Evetts and Worthington 167, p. 35] But here the analogy ends. One theory, not widely held, is that the pharynx, nose and mouth are the only resonance cavities; that the head and body bones cannot resonate because they are damped by overlying tissues. [Ibid., p. 37]

Even physiological and acoustical experts find it difficult to decide the respective resonating functions of the oral and pharyngeal cavities during singing. [Curry 124, p. 56] Stanley insists that the mouth is unimportant and that one of the chief aims of the vocal teacher must be to throw the mouth out of action, thus rendering it passive to vocal tone. According to experiments conducted by Stanley, the movements of the jaw, lips and cheeks in singing do not appreciably affect the quality of vocal tone or vowel purity. Therefore mouth resonance has little effect on properly produced voice. [578] Wilcox, Bartholomew, and Negus have combed the field of scientific vocal research and report that the throat, generally speaking, is the main place of resonance of vocal tone. [669, p. 7; 39; 418, p. 440]

Chest cavity. Regarding the function of the chest as a resonator, the observations of authors are related to two main points of view, namely, whether the air space alone in the chest constitutes a resonator or whether the bony and muscular walls of the chest contribute to vocal resonance. Evetts and Worthington hold that the chest cannot act as a resonator at all because the chest cavity is closed during phonation by the glottis. [167, p. 36] But Redfield finds experimentally that every frequency imposed upon the atmosphere surrounding a musical wind instrument is likewise imposed upon the air confined within the mouth, throat, laryngeal and chest cavities of the player. [461] If this be true of musical instruments it must also be true of voice since the column of air supporting the lips of the player of an instrument is analogous to the column of air supporting the vocal cords during phonation. Therefore, acoustically speaking, the chest cavity is not closed to vibration by the vocal glottis during phonation. This may be simply tested with a stethoscope held on the chest wall. With the exception of the flute, every musical wind instrumnt (including the vocal tract) is a doubly open tube in the sense that an antinode exists at the mouthpiece end (vocal cords) with approximate constancy of air pressure there and with the consequent establishment of pulses of identical frequency both inside the instrument (above the vocal cords) and inside the player's lips (below the vocal cords). [Ibid.] In other words, sound may travel either with the stream of breath that generates it or against the stream of breath that generates it. In the latter case the sounds of phonation generated at the glottis would travel downwards into the subglottic area of the chest. The subglottic air therefore constitutes a resonator which because of its total volume reinforces the fundamental and lower partials or overtones of the voice. [Curry 124, p. 49] This effect is usually described as *chest resonance.*

The only modern references to the other point of view regarding chest resonance, namely, that laryngeal vibrations are conducted into the chest by means of the bony and muscular structures which compose its walls, are given by Scott [501, p. 47], Hemery [238, p. 61] and Austin-Ball [31, p. 38]. All three agree that vibrations may be definitely felt in the chest walls during phonation, especially in the lower range of the voice, and that during phonation the firmness of the bony structures of the chest may produce synchronous vibrations that contribute to vocal resonance.

Entire body as resonator. Broadly speaking, the whole body is the sounding board of the voice. [Barbareux-Parry 34, p. 197] While it is true that vibrations are initiated in the vocal cords, the fact that these vibrations are extended throughout the bony structure of the body can be readily detected in any of its parts. [Harper 228, p. 41] In good singing, the entire body is coordinated and acts as a sounding board for the vocal tone. [Gould 206, p. 37] As Brown expresses it, "the texture of the singer's tone and the substance of his body . . . are an invisible whole, continuously, coherently cooperating and functioning." [70] Dr. Marafioti in his unusual book entitled *Caruso's Method of Voice Production* sums up the case for vocal resonance by saying that the entire body is one complex vocal resonator, receiving and augmenting the vibrations that emanate in all directions from their origin in the vocal cords. Throaty constrictions, when present, prevent the vocal vibrations from radiating to all parts of the body resonator. [368, p. 102] Individual differences in vocal resonance between singers depend upon the structural differences in the human body with its contributing bones, cavities and tissues. [Ibid., p. 107]

Of course, if this be true, the tone quality and resonance of the vocal instrument depend upon the muscle tone of the entire body. Therefore the entire body must be trained to serve as a vocal instrument. [Garnetti-Forbes 198, p. 81] Muscle tone or tension throughout the body affects vocal resonance in that limp and inert muscles do not vibrate to sound waves as readily as muscles that are in the state of partial tension *(tonus)* or equilibrium that is characteristic of a healthy body. [Ibid., p. 64] Jessica Dragonette, concert and operatic singer, summarizes her opinion regarding resonance as follows: "I like to think of the singing body as a single large larynx. The throat gives out the sound, but the entire body sings!" [146]

METHODS OF CONTROLLING VOCAL RESONANCE

PSYCHOLOGICAL APPROACH

Expressional intent controls resonance. The correct *function* of any organ in the body is its natural, proper or characteristic action or use in life. (W) If, as Mackenzie claims, the function of the vocal organs is to express the thoughts and emotions of life, obviously the right expressional use of the voice would be the greatest factor in determining and maintaining its quality or resonance. [364, p. 23] Efficient tone production, then, demands emotional value as well as carrying power. In fact, tonal

beauty, carrying power and emotional properties are all concomitants of
one vocal impulse or expressional urge. [Haywood 233] The governor of
tone quality is the mind and imagination of the singer. [Lewis 343, p. 3]
Or, as Brown puts it, emotion controls vocal quality. [78, p. 98] Owsley
and Felderman likewise believe that quality depends upon the state of
mind as well as on a relaxed body. Variations of vocal color are "in direct
ratio to the emotional complex of the singer." [441, p. 62; 175]

Is direct control of resonance possible? Of the 13 opinions expressed on
this topic, 8 are for placing strong emphasis on the importance of an indirect or psychological control of the voice through expressional intent.
The other 5 favor direct control of resonance factors. Frank Philip states
that the direction of the breath stream and the utilization of the resonance chambers of the voice certainly do come within the actual control
of the will of the singer. [446, p. 27] Therefore it is part of the singing
teacher's work to instruct the pupil in the best methods of controlling the
positions of the throat, tongue, cheeks and lips that will produce optimum resonance conditions during phonation. [Passe 443, p. 63] Shaw believes that favorable vocal resonance results from correct voluntary adjustments of the vocal orifice, the mouth and lips. [518, p. 184] Voice
placement, in other words, is largely a matter of training the student
singer so that he can voluntarily shape his upper air passages to produce
the best possible resonance conditions for each note within his vocal
range. [Redfield 462, p. 268] Greta Stueckgold, artist singer, believes that
a type of resonance control can be achieved by consciously willing the
tone into the head. [594]

Those who are opposed to direct control of vocal resonance believe that
when voice production is free enough the tone will automatically find all
the resonance cavities that are available for its proper reinforcement,
whether in the chest or head. [Faulds 141] "Quality exists first as an idea,
a mental picture," says Clippinger. [112] A type of reflex action occurs in
a normal vocal organ which unconsciously induces the proper vocal resonance. [Conklin 121, p. 20] Of course resonance is always an important
factor in voice production but the singer will remember that, however
important it may be, it is always a product of involuntary muscle adjustments [Wilcox 669, p. 6] and that therefore resonance cannot be improved by direct muscular controls. Radiograms taken of the singing
voice in action have demonstrated this fact, according to Evetts and Worthington. [167, p. 45] Resonances will always occur naturally, when muscular interferences are removed. [Douty 144] Judd believes that good resonance is a product of correct vocal attack and good diction. Hence it must

be taught indirectly through these two channels of training. [309, p. 11]
"The great singer colors his voice psychologically, and not by conscious
control." [Stanley and Maxfield 580, p. 125]

TECHNICAL APPROACH

Quality as a guide. Quality is that property of a tone which may distinguish it from another tone having the same pitch, loudness and duration. It is the identifying character of a sound determined chiefly by the
resonance of the vocal chambers in uttering it. (W)

Sixteen opinions agree on the importance of cultivating in the singer a
"subjective hearing recognition of good quality or beauty of tone."
[Wharton 655, p. 75] Quality is more important than pitch in evaluating
a voice. [Samoiloff 484, p. 5] It is more important than intensity or volume [De Bruyn 132] and you may even have to sacrifice correct diction if
by doing so you can best preserve the beauty of tone in singing. [Kort-
kamp 322] An old Italian maxim runs: *cerca la qualita, la quantita verra*
(Seek quality, quantity will come). [Orton 439, p. 120] In other words, a
loud voice is not necessarily a good voice, [Austin 28] and a soft, clear
pure quality is the foundation for dynamics, flexibility and good diction.
[Glenn 204] Fory agrees with W. J. Henderson's opinion that "if singers
would devote all their attention to securing a round, mellow, beautiful
tone," they would have no further difficulties in voice production. [189]

The first thing the singer should do in warming up for practice is to
make certain of the quality of his instrument. [Kerstin Thorborg 612] Indeed, the proper "placing" of the voice consists mainly in acquiring those
techniques for adjusting the vocal resonators whereby the best quality of
tone is secured. [Bartholomew 36] To determine the characteristic quality
of any voice one should first determine what the natural or spontaneous
and undisciplined vocal utterance is like. This will bring forth the true
quality or timbre whereby vocal classifications or evaluations may be
made. [Witherspoon 675]

Acquiring a vocal focus. To *focus* the voice is to direct the attention exclusively toward a limited or localized area of the body where much vibrational or resonance activity is centered during the emission of vocal
sound. (W) The main factor in tone production is in controlling the sensation of forward focus, according to Kwartin. [325, p. 41] It is indispensable as a means of removing interference in the larynx and pharynx.
[Savage 490, p. 90] Dodds and Lickley claim that the bel canto term, *singing on the breath*, is a teaching device for focusing the tone forward in

the direction of the outflowing breath, so that the throat and laryngeal regions may be entirely freed from conscious muscular effort and resultant constrictions. [139, p. 53]

The technical application of the *upward* and *forward* focusing idea varies from teacher to teacher. But all are not agreed as to the interpretation of this principle. [Bartholomew 39] The following typical pedagogical concepts present the case for those who favor the voluntary control of vocal focus in singing.

1. Alternate open and closed mouth production will help keep the voice focused at the highest point in the head. [James 300, p. 39]

2. The tone should be directed into the cavities bounded by the cheek bones and allowed to vibrate freely there. [Mme. Schoen-René 493]

3. Vocal tone seems to start in the place where the *ng* in *sing* is located. [Brown 78, p. 56]

4. Never sing backward or downward since voice production comes from the front part of the mask. [Altglass and Kempf 8]

5. The tone is always focused at the place where forehead and nose meet. This vibratory sensation and that of head resonance are indispensable in any manner of singing. [Samoiloff 484, p. 27]

6. All right tone, whether in word, song or shout, is formed behind the nose bridge. [Lloyd 351, p. 14]

7. *Forward* tone is one of the principal aims of the vocalist. Simply direct the tone energetically to the front of the mouth behind the front teeth. [Scott 501, p. 65]

8. When you think your tone forward to the front of the hard palate, you automatically put your mouth in the correct position for good resonance. [Henderson, W. J. 243, p. 61]

9. As the pitch rises the focus of the voice gradually moves farther back along the hard palate. [Kwartin 325, p. 43]

10. The intimacy between vocal sounds and their verbal vehicles establishes a close relationship between the larynx and the mouth and gives rise to the dictum that voice must be placed in the mouth. [Marafioti 368, p. 72]

11. The sound should be aimed at the front of the mouth. [Jacques 299, p. 36]

12. Devote the first part of each practice period to concentrated work on replacing tone in the mask. [Vivian della Chiesa 135]

13. Strong vibration is felt back of the nose and under the eyes. This forward ring gives solidity and character to the vocal tones. [Jessica Dragonette 146]

Opposed to this group are those who believe that the attempt to direct voice into any one place limits its flexibility and color. Vocal color varies with mood and in proper expression the voice must be free to go anywhere at any time. [Witherspoon 677, p. 24; also Douty 144] Irvine holds that conscious direction of the tone is an interference. There is a certain strain involved in maintaining a definite vocal focus. False tensions are thus generated which reveal themselves in a certain artificiality of sound. [295] Scholes believes that it is impossible to direct the stream of sound towards any one part of the anatomy. [496] Vocal sound originates in the larynx. But its course is centrifugal, notwithstanding that the singer may think he can direct it. [Samuels 487, p. 15] That is to say, sound waves simultaneously travel in every direction from a given source. The attempt to *focus* tones by mental or physical effort is therefore unnatural and futile. [Ten Haff 603] Tone is not a material substance and cannot be put or placed. It will automatically flow into all open spaces if there is no interference. [Booker 56] "As voice teachers we should know enough of the elements of acoustics to realize that no soundboard action of the hard palate or teeth can possibly take place and that sound itself cannot be directed, projected, focussed or pointed anywhere in the mouth or head." [Bartholomew 39] Therefore, do not deliberately try to place the voice anywhere. Rigidity of the throat will be an almost invariable result. [Gregory 211] These opinions sum up the case against consciously maintaining a vocal focus during singing.

The value of humming. Humming may be defined as a form of singing with closed lips and without articulating or, in other words, uttering a sound like or suggestive of the letter *m* prolonged, without opening the mouth. (W) Many teachers utilize the humming sound of the voice as a guide to voice placement and the development of vocal resonance, although here again, opinion is divided. Lamperti's favorite maxim is found echoed in many modern vocal texts: "You cannot sing with your mouth open if you cannot first sing with it shut." [MacBurney 361] This slogan is countermanded by one which is reputed to come from the same source: "You cannot hum right until you can sing right." [Brown, W. E. 78, p. 104] According to Cain, humming has no qualities that will improve vocal tone quality and should be avoided as a vocal exercise. [90, p. 88] Conklin thinks humming has little value in voice training except as a focussing device for establishing tonal direction. [121, p. 70]

Acton claims for humming that it is one of the finest of early exercises [3] while Brown bluntly exclaims "Don't hum! You can't hum until you have learned to sing." [78, p. 104] Stevens and Miles, in an experimental study on the relation of vocal attack to pitch accuracy in singing, report that humming in itself is less certain as a mode of vocal attack than is open singing. [583] James is of the opinion that no consonant that closes the lips should be used for controlling vocal tone or breath, since this produces a strain in the neck which results in contraction. [300, p. 39] *M* will always produce the richest vocal resonance. It is the basis of all vocal tone and all our vowels are merely modifications of this consonant. [Scott 501, p. 21 and p. 8] Some singing teachers prefer the sound of *n* as a humming device since it drives the tone where it always should be. [Lloyd 351, p. 3] Others recommend *l, m* and *n* because they are so near to the natural resonance quality of the singing voice. [Skiles 564]

Shaw and Efnor agree that humming promotes the fundamental vocal tone. [518, p. 184 and 159, lesson 4] It is assumed that by fundamental vocal tone a fundamental resonance is meant although this point is not made clear by the texts mentioned. Other texts hold that humming practice is helpful in developing the so-called forward placing of the voice [Stock 589], and that humming gives the best sensation for placement. [Hok 278, p. 29] Humming is beneficial because it induces freedom and relaxation and prevents throatiness. One cannot hum well without being thoroughly relaxed throughout the vocal tract. [Grace 207, p. 9] If one is completely relaxed while humming a continuous tone it should be possible to drop the jaw slowly until the mouth is wide open without in any way disturbing the quality of resonance that occurred during the hum. This is offered as a test of correct humming and correct resonance. [Hill 272, p. 27] Hence the singing student is advised to practice humming as frequently as possible. [Philip 446, p. 38] Mowe maintains that the correct hum is one of the most valuable of exercises and guides to correct tone. [405, p. 12] Fory finds it "an invaluable teaching device." [188] Lily Pons, famous soprano, states that she sings many scales and vocalises with closed lips or humming. "This exercise is very helpful to me." [450]

SUMMARY AND INTERPRETATION

THEORETICAL CONSIDERATIONS

In the various descriptions of resonance given it is apparent that the processes of phonation and resonation are related to each other as cause and effect. The line of demarcation between the two is not clearly made. Hence it is difficult to determine which teaching techniques are purely phonatory and which pertain to resonance alone. No one has as yet succeeded in completely damping out the resonance factor during voice production. Therefore, the relative importance of phonation and resonation in the act of singing cannot be determined. In all, 262 concepts of resonance were studied. These are classified in *Table Four*. Seventy-four authors refer to physiological factors. The parts of the body mentioned are the head cavities, sinuses, nasal cavities, mouth and throat cavities and the chest cavity. Sixteen refer to the entire body as a single complex resonator. The larynx is not included in this list of resonators, indicating that it is to be considered exclusively as an organ of phonation. This view is still widely held by the singing profession.

In the late nineteenth century, John Howard, a prominent vocal teacher who was also a practicing physician and voice specialist, advanced the theory that the larynx is itself a complex resonator or *consonator,* as he calls it. Its function is not only to generate tone (phonation) but to distribute vocal vibrations to all the outlying muscles and cartilages that are directly attached to it. The vibratory area of phonation is thus increased by synchronous vibration of all adjacent parts and the phonated vocal tone thereby augmented and resonated. Howard's books are now out of print and little known to the vocal profession, but his theories invite further investigation.

It is questionable whether anything is gained for either singing teacher or student by dividing the vocal tract into separate functional units. Physicians may have a special interest in these anatomical structures for purposes of local medication, but, to the singing teacher, the vocal act involves simultaneous coordinations of breathing organs, postural organs and vocal organs. It would be difficult to localize, either through sound or sensation, the functional control of any single part of this complex musculature. We come to the conclusion therefore, that in life it is impossible to dissociate phonation from resonation; that phonation and resonation are reciprocal concomitants of a single function called the vocal act, since neither can function as such without the other.

METHODOLOGICAL CONSIDERATIONS

All techniques for cultivating resonance seem to subserve the purpose of establishing standards of quality in voice production. If there were more accurate descriptions of quality, its acoustical properties, its aesthetic effects, its technical disciplines, adequate teaching procedures could be devised which would have standard values for the singing student.

It must be remembered that any given vocal tone really consists of a combination of overtones or partials. The relative pitch and intensity components of such partials contribute to the total subjective impressions of quality which the ear receives. Hence, in teaching singing, the ear must first be trained to recognize resonance values or qualities of vocal tone, independently of pitch or loudness. Of course, such impressions of quality will have to remain purely subjective or aesthetic until accurate measurements and terminologies are developed whereby they may be objectified and standardized for research.

Empirical theory predominates in the vocal texts examined, yielding methodologies that are obscured by opinion and controversy. Many of the basic concepts gathered have the support of successful singing artists. But they need clarification through experimental investigation. The function of the sinuses, the importance of nasal resonance, the open throat theory, the entire body functioning as a resonator, the use and value of a vocal focus, humming as a teaching device and the voluntary control of all vocal training factors are controversial subjects that are open to further investigation.

In conclusion, the emphasis which is laid on resonance as an important factor in voice production leads one to inquire why there is not more objective data on hand regarding this phenomenon. The term *resonance* itself is under suspicion since it often is used to cover up any deficiencies in scientific accuracy when describing the operation of the vocal organs. [Drew 147, p. 125] From foregoing discussions we may conclude that some fragmentary information is available concerning the theory of vocal resonance. But there are few conclusive experiments in this area and most of the pedagogical information is based on empirical observations or pure conjecture. It is as yet impossible to fill in the gaps in this subject but a further objective analysis of the methods used by voice teachers for improving and cultivating the singer's resonance might confirm or refute some of the contentions of the vocal theorists. Bartholomew, who by means of sound recordings, has made a thorough study of the determinants of quality in the singer's voice, is more or less optimistic about the possibility of working backward from the carefully produced sound wave records of good voices and bad voices to the differences in the physiological structures that produced the various qualities. "Fortunately," he says, "there is enough agreement among musicians as to what constitutes *good vocal quality* to enable us to speak of a typical good quality." [38] If such deductions can be made by experimental means there should be hope of clarifying and standardizing this area of vocal teaching.

CHAPTER VI

CONCEPTS OF RANGE

Definition: *Vocal range* in singing is defined as the number of frequency changes possible between the lowest and the highest pitches of the voice. Synonyms such as *compass, gamut, reach,* or *scope* are sometimes used to define the limits of vibratory activity of the vocal cords as measured in definite pitch intervals on a musical scale. (W) The *pitch* or frequency of any vocal sound is determined by the number of double vibrations (dv.) per second of the vocal cords or generator that produces the sound. [Grove's Dictionary 708 vol. IV, p. 189] *Frequency* is used to designate the number of sound waves per second as measured objectively, while pitch usually refers to the sound experienced or heard. [Wagner 626] A term that is often confused with range in describing and classifying voices is the Italian word *tessitura* (texture). *Tessitura* is defined as that part of the compass of a melody or voice part of a musical composition in which most of its tones lie. (W) This term does not denote the range of a voice but, rather, the adaptability of a given voice to a given piece of music. By extension, *tessitura* has also come to mean: the purest, most facile and singable portion of the vocal range.

THEORIES OF VOCAL RANGE

AVERAGE COMPASS OF VOICES

Philip measures the total combined range of the human voice as "extending over some five octaves," from about A, to a''' or from 55 to 1760 dv. per second; a compass that is "considerably within the limits of the aural perception of musical tone." [446, p. 21] This overall range of the singing voice has two overlapping main divisions: a sector that encompasses the combined reaches of the male voice, amounting to about 3½ octaves or, roughly, from A, to f''; and a combined female compass of about 3½ octaves, from d to a'''. Male voices are subdivided into three distinctive classes called *tenor, baritone* and *bass;* female voices into

TABLE FIVE

SUMMARY OF CONCEPTS OF RANGE USED IN TRAINING THE SINGING VOICE

	total number of statements	sub-total	grand total	statements by prof. singers	documented statements	undocumented statements
I. *Theories of vocal range*			99			
A. Average compass of voices	29	29		1	7	22
B. Theory of registers			70			
1. general descriptions	32				7	25
2. number of registers in voice						
a) *voice has one*	11			3		11
b) *voice has two*	16				6	10
c) *voice has three*	7				1	6
3. value of falsetto tones						
a) *they are legitimate tones*	2				2	
b) *they are not legitimate tones*	2				1	1
II. *Methods of cultivating range*			129			
A. Psychological approach		33				
1. mental causes affect registers	6					6
2. using the track of the speaking voice	8				1	7
3. the "high" and "low" fallacy	19				1	18
B. Technical approach		96				
1. sectional treatment						
a) *practice with entire range*	2					2
b) *practice with middle range*	30			6	1	29
2. directional treatment						
a) downward practice advised	13				1	12
b) approaching high tones	16			4	1	15
3. various technical devices						
a) importance of scale work	17			8		17
b) blending the registers	18			1	4	14
TOTALS	228	228	228	23	33	195

soprano, mezzo-soprano and *contralto.* [Stanley 577, p. 128] Within these common classifications further subdivisions and extensions may occur bearing such special designations as *basso-profundo, coloratura soprano, male alto, dramatic tenor,* etc., to describe extraordinary characteristics of quality and range possessed by unusual voices. Male and female voices differ chiefly in pitch and quality, the lowest female tone usually being an octave or more lower than the highest male tone and each male classification having its counterpart in a parallel female classification lying approximately an octave above it. [Passe 443, p. 57]

Authors' opinions vary somewhat regarding the average range of well developed voices. The following concepts represent 29 statements gathered on this subject.

1. An individual voice rarely has a compass, for singing of more than two octaves. (W)

2. The range of average voices is about an octave and a half; from e' to g'' for soprano; g to c'' for alto; c to g' for tenor; G to c' for bass. [Woods 689]

3. "Every vocal reed may be expected to have a compass of two octaves." [Aikin 4; also Hoffrek 277]

4. "The average compass of the singing voice is from 2 to 2½ octaves"; 3 octaves is exceptional and 4 is phenomenal. [Mackenzie 364, p. 50]

5. "The ordinary adult human voice has a range of 2½ octaves, seldom extending over 3 octaves." [Pressman 452]

6. Potentially most voices have a compass of at least 3 octaves. [Orton 439, p. 110]

7. Even in its early development, every normal singing voice should be able to span 3 octaves without straining. [Wilcox 669, p. 10; Stanley 579; Nichols 424]

8. Every finished voice has a range of about 3 octaves. [Sigrid Onegin 435; Shaw 523]

Nearly 80% of the energy expended in singing is in the lower frequency band of the male voice, from 250 to 1000 dv., according to Farnsworth's recent experiments. [169] The applications to vocal pedagogy of these and other reliable but inconclusive observations are not yet clearly established. For instance, Pressman notes the interesting fact that a newborn infant cries on a pitch level "approximating 435 cycles per second, the vocal range extending to 6½ tones and reaching an octave at the end of four years." Just before puberty this compass expands to an octave and a half. [452] White holds the opinion that the length of the vocal cords does not determine the average range of the singing voice because, as he explains it, "there are very few children indeed who could sing as high as an ordinary soprano." [657, p. 32] On the other hand, Jersild and Bienstock find, experimentally, that individual children, as early as the age of four years, may be able to produce as many tones as the average adult, although with less flexibility or musical skill. [303]

THEORY OF VOCAL REGISTERS

Of the 70 statements on the theory of registers found in articles and texts on singing, 32 are general descriptions, 34 discuss the number of registers in the singing voice and 4 present the pros and cons of falsetto tone production. Author opinion is divided on these topics; some concepts are general, others are more explicit as to details of registration and pitch control.

General descriptions. Grove's Dictionary defines the term *registers* as: "the classification of parts of the vocal range according to method of production, as 'head register,' 'chest register.'" [708, vol. IV, p. 350] This concept is clarified somewhat in Webster's more detailed description as follows: A register is the "series of tones of like quality within the compass of a voice which are produced by a particular adjustment of the vocal cords. In singing up the scale the register changes at the point where the singer readjusts the vocal cords to reach the higher notes. All below this point is in the *chest* or *thick register*, all above it in the *head* or *thin register*. The two registers generally overlap, some notes about the middle of the vocal range being producible in either." Webster also refers to quality as a criterion for determining the registers and states the objection that divisions of register based on pitch determinations alone are unsatisfactory since the same notes often can be sung equally well in either of two adjacent registers. According to Curry, the term *register* "is used loosely in singing to describe firstly, certain ranges of sung tones, or secondly, different audible qualities of a singer's voice." [124, p. 5]

Are registers natural? De Bruyn quotes Lilli Lehmann's authority for the following statement: "Do registers exist by nature? No. It may be said that they are created throughout long years of speaking in the vocal range that is easiest to the person, . . . which means that the notes below and above the habitual speaking voice zone comprise two other registers." [129] In this opinion he is upheld by Armstrong. [24] Aikin is also convinced that "the so-called *registers* cannot be accepted as natural." "That they are often acquired is beyond doubt," he says, "but it is astonishing how they disappear when singers are relieved of the necessity of thinking about them." Certain descriptions of the vocal membranes are frequently given to explain the changes in methods of vocal production during changes in registration, but according to present knowledge, "the membranes behave in the same way throughout the entire compass" of the voice. [4]

Waters claims that so-called *chest* and *head* voice registers are produced by the same pair of vocal muscles in "thick edge" and "thin edge" adjustments, respectively. [642] On the other hand, Wilcox declares that two different sets of muscles function in stretching the vocal cords. The first, or crico-thyroid group is predominantly for adjusting lower register pitches and loud intensities; the second, or arytenoid muscle group is for higher or *falsetto* register pitches and soft intensities. [669, p. 8] Stanley, who writes about mechanistic voice building, concurs in this explanation of registers and adds that the *break* between falsetto and lower registers is caused by a weakness of the arytenoid muscles which causes them to yield to the downward pull of the powerful lower register muscles under the tension of high tones. Therefore, he claims that the development and coordination of the registers demands special training which no singer can avoid. [577, p. 307 ff.]

Head, chest and falsetto registers. There is an apparent confusion of terminology in this area that gives rise to conflicting opinions among authors. Clippinger, for instance, defines *head voice* as "that part of the compass lying above the speaking range." [106] Hipsher describes head register as the "upper division of the voice in which the tones receive the larger part of their reinforcement from the resonance cavities in the frontal part of the head." [274] Lindsley finds experimentally that "the concept of *head tones* is not clearly justified according to the amount of vibration produced in the walls of the sinuses." [347] Gescheidt declares that the term *chest tone* is a misnomer since the chest is incapable of producing tones. [200, p. 24] According to Hagara, the transition from chest register to head register encompasses two or three tones where the registers appear to overlap. "The ancients called these transitional notes *the falsetto*." [220, p. 54] Stanley claims that the male voice goes into falsetto range on the same note as the female voice, "at about E flat on the top space" of the staff. [577, p. 323] Wharton claims that the registers of "men's voices run parallel to those of women at an interval of an octave below." [655, p. 48] Statements such as these are open to misinterpretation due to the absence of a standard terminology.

According to Webster, *falsetto* is "that voice of a man which lies above his natural voice." Also, it is "the human voice of the upper, or head register, whether male or female." Negus, a recognized authority on vocal physiology, explains falsetto as a particular form of sound production at the larynx which employs a different mechanism for notes above the ordinary range of the individual (male) voice. [418, p. 419 ff.] In falsetto voice, "the vocal cords, when viewed through a stroboscope, are seen to be blown apart, whereby a permanent oval orifice is left between the edges. . . . The size of the aperture varies, and is found to increase as the pressure of air expelled from the lungs is raised. In ordinary phonation, the vocal cords vibrate as a whole. . . . In falsetto, the extreme membranous edges of the vocal cords appear to be the only parts in vibration." [Grove's *Dictionary of Music* 708, vol. II, p. 193] MacKenzie, whose book on the hygiene of the vocal organs is in its ninth edition, also states that, in the falsetto, the vocal cords are comparatively (not entirely) relaxed since "only their margins vibrate." [364, p. 59] Hall empirically defines falsetto as "tone without speech reinforcement, tone without low resonance or speaking voice color." [224]

The action of registration. Stanley claims that "registration action is a means whereby to control the intensity (of the voice), and has nothing to do with pitch range." He further declares that women with improperly trained voices use only the falsetto register adjustment over nearly the entire range. Men, on the other hand, usually employ lower register adjustments exclusively, ignoring the falsetto. [574] Sometimes, when the muscles of one register are weaker than surrounding muscles, a condition of "mixed registration" is produced. An overlapping of the registers then results and the stronger low register muscles of the male voice tend to dominate weaker falsetto-producing muscles. In the female voice this condition is reversed and the falsetto action then predominates throughout the lower range. [Stanley 577, p. 308]

The exact causes of registration in the singing voice remain undecided. Bartholomew finds experimentally that the chest register tones are acoustically more complex than those of the head register. The former contain "more and stronger overtones," while the latter, contrary to common belief, "have very few or even no overtones." Obviously, then, the head register does not provide overtones for the voice. [39] Concepts of registration are closely interwoven with those of resonance, according to Henderson, and sensations accompanying the various registers are largely related to sympathetic vibrations of the chest and head cavities during certain ranges of the singing voice. [243, p. 71] (See also Chapter V.) Finally, Dr. Schatz, a physician and voice specialist, advances the interesting theory that, in the lower register of the voice, vibrations are transmitted downward into the chest through direct contact between the cricoid cartilage of the larynx and the cervical vertebrae of the spine. Thus it is the bones of the chest that vibrate, rather than the air column contained within the chest cavity. The same principle may be said to apply to the vibration of head tones by upward bone conduction through the spinal vertebrae during the production of high register tones. [492]

Number of registers in the singing voice. There are 34 authors' opinions on this subject, divided among: 11 who believe that the singing voice has but one register throughout its entire range, 16 who hold that there are two vocal registers and 7 who believe that three registers exist.

The prevailing opinions of the "one register" group are represented by the statements of three professional singers, Lilli Lehmann, Herbert Witherspoon and Marion Anderson. Vocal registers are unnatural, according to Mme. Lehmann. They are caused by the predominant speaking activity of the vocal organs when they habitually operate within a limited range. [337] Witherspoon holds the opinion that there is only one vocal register, involving three qualities or places of resonance: the head, mouth, and chest. [677, p. 22] Anderson's point of view is that "there is no such thing as a boundary of range. [i.e., registers] within the complete tonal compass." "Try to get rid of the habit of charting your voice into separate little islands of range," is her advice. "Actually they do not exist. Try to approach your work with the idea of a single tonal line." [12] Wharton holds that "training based upon the theory of registers is an artificial and unnatural" procedure since divisions of range "do not by nature exist." [655, p. 48] In other words, there are no register breaks in the voice and it is possible for a singer to carry the same quality of voice from one end of his range to the other. All register terminologies such as *chest tones* and *head tones* are misleading. [Dossert 140, p. 35; Evetts and Worthington 167, p. 42] Qualities and registers are two different things, not to be confused. "Nowadays nearly every teacher teaches the theory of one register," says Butler, with the result that a more even scale is developed with "a smaller number of breaks in both voices and singers." [87; also Samuel 486, Lesson VI]

In the second group, Wagner asserts that there are two vocal registers, if by register we mean "a series of consecutive homogeneous tones produced by one mechanism." The head or falsetto and the chest tones "are produced by two mutually exclusive mechanisms." [629] Weer likewise claims that there are two registers and that "they cannot be blended." Rather, "they must be made to cooperate" because two different organic mechanisms are involved. [650, p. 62; also Stanley 577, p. 309] Hemery names these two registers as follows: a) The normal range carried as high as possible without force or strain; b) The falsetto range. [238, p. 51] The old masters taught the use of two registers, one for chest voice and one for head voice. This fact was first noted by Mancini in the 18th century. [Hopkins 283, p. 76; also Hagara 220, p. 36] Others in this group concur in the opinion that two registers exist in the singing voice.

Manuel Garcia, world famous singing teacher of the 19th century and inventor of the laryngoscope, is the strongest proponent of the three register concept. Garcia recognizes three mechanical variations in voice production which he calls *registers*. In the first, "the glottis is progressively narrowed to the point at which the vocal processes [cords] completely touch each other." In the second, this movement "less energetically done, produces the falsetto," and the head notes of the third register "are produced by the vibration of the ligamentous parts of the glottis." [Mackenzie 364, p. 87] Samuels offers a somewhat simpler explanation: "In the *chest register* the vocal cords vibrate in their full length and breadth; in the *medium* [register] only the inner edges vibrate; in the *head register* only a portion of the inner edges vibrate." [487, p. 26] The others who name three registers (head, middle, and chest) are Henley [254], Miller [398, p. 108], Blatherwick [52], and Valeri [622].

Falsetto tones. Opinion is brief, but evenly divided on the legitimacy of falsetto tones for singing. Wagner and Stanley both hold that the artificial or effeminate quality of falsetto tones disappears with training and that when the so-called *falsettos* have been sufficiently developed their "quality becomes indistinguishable from that of the lower register." [629; also 578] On the other hand, Curry and Gescheidt consider the falsetto an "abnormal" and "unnatural" voice. The former claims that "it is produced above the normal vocal compass and requires an altered mode of larynx vibration" [124, p. 5]; the latter states that it is useless. "It should never be used at any age." [200, p. 20]

METHODS OF CULTIVATING RANGE

PSYCHOLOGICAL APPROACH

Registration is influenced by mental causes. This is the opinion of 6 authors. Aikin is convinced that the only reason the registers appear in a singer's voice is because the teacher continually calls his attention to them. [4] Wodell adds that it is "positively harmful to speak to students about registers or breaks" in the singing range. [679] Breaks in the voice inevitably occur when a singer becomes self-conscious about registers. If a slight break should be present, it will tend to become obtrusive when attention is called to it. [Jacques 299, p. 29] "The register fallacy is a mental ailment, not a physical or tonal imperfection," according to Savage. "Any form of [conscious] interference in spontaneous expression" manifests itself in "spasmodic physical action." The register is the result of such interferences and "by thinking tone placement which is impossible . . . we inhibit the action of the vocal cords at certain pitches." [490] Wilcox is also certain that the muscular mechanisms of registration are by no means subject to conscious control in singing [669, p. 9], and Marafioti sums up Caruso's point of view as follows: By leaving the intonations of the voice under psycholgical control we can attain any altitude within the vocal range without experiencing register breaks. [368, p. 153]

Using the track of the speaking voice. Eight authors point out a relationship between the speaking and the singing voice which is represented in the following four concepts:

1. The speaking range of the voice is already fairly well developed through constant use. It is necessary for the singer to extend this range above and below its every-day limits. [Warren 635; also Stanley 578]

2. Beginners should first learn to talk on any pitch so that the singing tones may be moulded around the speaking pitches. When this is practiced, the highest pitches of the singing voice can present no problem. [Marafioti 368, pp. 134 and 270]

3. Sliding inflections within a prescribed pitch interval of the singing voice may be practiced as effortlessly as upward and downward inflections are used in the speaking voice. With this comparison in mind, the student soon learns to govern his singing vocal movements by following the equivalent inflectional pattern of his speaking voice. A psychological tie is thus built between the two. [Evetts and Worthington 167, p. 106 ff.]

4. Instead of using acrobatic stretching feats, simply speak the tones at the desired pitch, as in conversing. Such treatment of any phrase in a song will show up the natural range of the singer. [Whitfield 660]

Dispelling the "high" and "low" fallacy. The illusory *height* and *depth* of the voice which the singing student feels when ranging along his entire vocal compass, comes from an erroneous association of "upness" with a direction that is contrary to the pull of gravity. Pitch elevation or height is a misnomer since sound can have neither height nor depth. [Herbert-Caesari 269, p. xvii] In other words, "a high tone is produced exactly in the same *place* as a low tone," [Divver 138, p. 36] and, therefore, the word *height* in its ordinary sense is not applicable to voices. [White 658, p. 46]

These opinions represent the general point of view of 19 authors, who find that calling the voice *high* and *low* at various pitch levels introduces an erroneous idea in the student's mind which is ultimately detrimental to his voice. "Students must lose their feeling of singing high and low and must learn to think of it [pitch] in terms of more or less energy." [Wilson 674, p. 7] To realize that the singing tone is "always produced on the same general level" prevents the singer from trying "to *reach* for tones of a high pitch frequency" and from "pressing down for tones of a low pitch frequency." [Austin-Ball 31, p. 25] In other words, there should be no special preparation for high tones in singing, within the natural range of the individual voice. [Wharton 655, p. 61; also James 300, p. 42]

Bartholomew points out that the so-called *head tone* "is largely psychological rather than physiological." [38] Waters suggests the following simple but interesting remedy to offset the false concept which causes strained reaching for high or low notes: "Think ascent while singing down the scale and vice versa." [647, p. 26] Eight authors suggest the same psychological corrective, a device that is also quoted from Lamperti's teachings as follows: "When rising to a note think of the movement as being downwards and vice versa." [Shakespeare 517, p. 31; Brown 78, p. 102; Christy 97, p. 42] Anxiety induces tension; hence high tones should not be prematurely anticipated as they are approached. Conklin's advice is pertinent: Don't think high when singing octaves but direct the tone mentally on a level that is "straight ahead and on the same level with the mouth." [121, p. 103]

TECHNICAL APPROACH

There are 96 concepts dealing with techniques of direct instruction and practice in cultivating the range of the singing voice. These have been divided into three main categories: a) 32 statements that discuss the most favorable practice areas or sections of the vocal gamut, a sectional treatment of range; b) 29 statements that present directional methods of approach, i.e., upward and downward types of practice; c) 35 statements that discuss scale work and register blending.

Sectional treatment. Of the 32 concepts found in this area, all but 2 advocate use of a moderate portion of the vocal range when training the singing voice. Wilson and Samoiloff, the two exceptions, both favor the use of the entire vocal range. "Sing to the high and low extremes of all voices," is Wilson's advice [674, p. 7], while Samoiloff declares that it is best to work on the entire voice always, neglecting no part of the range in favor of another. [484, p. 34]

Six professional singers are among the 30 advocates of middle range practice. These are: Vivian della Chiesa [135], Zinka Milanov [397], Kerstin Thorborg [611], Stella Roman [475], Marian Anderson [12], and Elizabeth Schumann [498]. Their composite viewpoint is expressed as follows: It is a mistake to try to develop the (full) range before the middle voice is under control; scale building begins with the notes that lie smoothly in the voice; extensions of the middle range are added note by note, only after the middle register is secure. Other opinions in this group are represented by the following typical concepts:

1. The first exercises should establish the lower register tones. Subsequently the voice may be extended downward by comfortable degrees, then upwards gradually until the falsetto and highest limits of the vocal range are encompassed. [Wilcox 669, p. 25]

2. According to Tosi (1742), after the middle octave was firmly established, the next step was to extend the range in both directions. [Klingstedt 320, p. 21]

3. "Begin practice in the range that comes easiest to your voice. . . . Avoid high notes." [Stock 584; also Freemantel 196]

4. "Stay with the medium part of the voice until a clear concept of good, easy tone has been gained." [Combs 119, p. 10; also Shakespeare 517, p. 79]

5. Avoid exercises in extreme upper or lower parts of the vocal range where they produce strains during attack or phonation. [Henderson 243, p. 52]

6. For best results, work very gradually from oft-repeated model tones to less accessible and more difficult ones. [Drew 147, p. 165]

7. The so-called "talking song" which encompasses the middle or conversational voice is best study material for beginners, since fewer problems are encountered therein. [Barbareux-Parry 34, p. 262]

Directional treatment. Vocal practice implies vocal movement and movement requires direction. Hence, as the voice changes in pitch from one note to the next it must either move up the range or downward; from lower to higher pitches or vice versa. Apparently, this question is fairly important to singing teachers since 29 opinions were gathered on the subject. Of these, 13 agree that downward practice is preferable to upward practice in training the singer's range; and 16 advise special techniques for approaching high tones.

Downward practice is advised. Hill wants downward scale practice to be "a constant study of the beginner." [272, p. 46] Philip believes that downward practice is the most certain method of "merging one register into another," an indispensable feature of all voice training. [446, p. 82] "If there is a break," says Ryan, "it should be mended by first beginning on the tones above the break and working down." [480, p. 89] "Open the voice downward," is Fory's advice, "work as low as the voice will go without forcing or squeezing." [186] The remaining opinions in this group are summed up in the following concepts:

1. "Never force the voice up. . . . Working downwards . . . is the great principle of tonal unity." [Scott 501, p. 55]

2. Loud practice up the scale tends to constrict the upper register while downward vocalization in soft tones endows the lower registers with elasticity and lightness. [Finn 181, p. 22; also Evetts and Worthington 167, p. 102]

3. The first step in vocal training, for children or adults, "should be from a given easy pitch downward to the end of the present effective compass." [Wodell 679; Mme. Margarete Olden 434]

4. "Descending scales are the finest possible exercises . . . throughout the vocal compass." [Jacques 299, p. 37]

5. Downward scale practice is similar to floating downstream with the current instead of paddling upstream against it. [Armstrong 23]

Approaching high tones. Sixteen authors and professional singers express the belief that the upper reaches of the singing voice are more difficult to develop than the middle range and that higher tones require special treatment. Lily Pons, in an interview states, "I centered all my attention on developing the upper range . . . and found that the middle voice developed along with it." [450] Frances Alda reports that her teacher, the great Marchesi, laid great emphasis on the use of the head voice and insisted that every note above *F* must be sung in head voice. [6, p. 298] Clippinger finds that the correct training of the upper range endows the upper male voice with unusual brilliance and resonance so that it more easily matches the middle voice. [104, p. 35] Conversely, high tones can be seriously impaired if the middle register is forced. This is especially true of tenors and sopranos, according to Jones. [307, p. 6]

The question of intensity or breath pressure as related to pitch level in singing is also discussed, although opinions are divided on the subject. Mme. Galli-Curci insists that "the higher the tone, the less breath pressure is required. . . . Many singers ruin their voices by adding extra effort on the upper tones. . . . They should take a lesson from the violinist who knows that the pressure of the bow for the upper notes must be less." [197] In this she is upheld by Wilson who also writes that male voices especially should learn to sing softly on the high notes. [674, p. 6] This point of view is contradicted by Seashore [506, p. 89], Stanley [577, p. 358] and Huey [291], who believe that "higher-pitched tones are usually sung with greater intensity," and that "breath pressure should be increased as the tone ascends." Stanley adds that higher pitches require more exertion than lower ones. Conversely loud volume tends to raise vocal pitch. Whitfield takes a middle course. He would not force the voice up or down, but would allow only "the least breath and tension to each tone" so that complete relaxation could be maintained to let the voice function properly at all times. [660] The controversy rests at this point.

The notes immediately preceding the highest ones sung are also important and require special treatment, according to Stella Roman, noted Rumanian soprano. This prima donna believes that "the note before the high one is actually of greater importance because it serves as a tonal base. . . . A high tone should never be attacked without vocal preparation from a note of lower range." [475] According to Ryan, it is the lower tone following the highest one that holds up the higher tone. Caruso once said, "I always carry my high tone over to the next note below, in the same volume, unless otherwise marked." [480, p. 81] Marafioti, who is reputed to be an authority on Caruso's technique of singing, quotes the great tenor as saying: "In the matter of taking high notes one should remember that their purity and ease of production depend very much on the way the preceding notes leading up to them are sung." [368, p. 158] It is Maurice-Jacquet's belief that a lower note sung directly following a high one, "if not reduced in volume, will crash from the sheer force of the higher vibrations." [377] One more opinion is quoted concerning the special treatment of high notes. It is a physiological observation made by Haywood, that "each time the voice rises to the top tone, there is a slight elevation of the base of the tongue." [237, vol. III, p. 14]

VARIOUS TECHNICAL DEVICES

Importance of scale work. A *scale* is a ladder, a series of steps, a means of ascending. In music, it is "a graduated series of tones, ascending or descending in order of pitch according to a specified scheme of their intervals." (W) Redfield's definition is also useful: "A scale is a division of the octave into intervals suitable for musical purposes." [462, p. 68] As on any musical instrument, the entire range of the singing voice is divided into conventional step intervals or scale tones for purposes of musical orientation and study. The singer thus has a means of identifying various tones and intervals in his own voice by relating them to the corresponding standardized musical scale which he has previously learned to recognize. The singing of scales as a means of vocal exercise serves the purpose of familiarizing the student with the range and tonal composition of his own voice, and it is therefore an indispensable part of vocal training, according to the opinions of 17 authors and professional singers.

Many singing teachers begin with the practice of scales, although, according to one author, this is not always a wise procedure. James admits the importance of scale work for accomplished artists but would not give scale work to the beginner. [300, p. 11] Sigrid Onegin believes that "the greatest, most bneficial of all vocal exercises is the slow scale." [436] The simplest kind of exercises, consisting of slow scales, sustained and single tones, arpeggios and other simple devices were the basis of Marchesi's teaching, according to Mme. Frances Alda. [6, p. 299] Elizabeth Rethberg likewise claims that "the perfect scale is more important than a hundred operatic roles. . . . Let the roles wait until you have learned to sing!" [463]

The vocal benefits attributed to scale work are summed up in the following representative claims:

1. *Developing flexibility.* [Queena Mario 370; Clippinger 105, p. 87]

2. *Promoting exact intonation and building coordinations of mind, muscle and ear.* [Waters 647, p. 27]

3. *Extending the range of the voice note by note and firming the upper tones.* [Klingstedt 320, p. 21]

4. *Developing tone and building a groundwork for all technique.* [Gota Ljungberg 350]

5. *Probing the full possibilities of the voice.* [Friederich Schorr 497]

Five different methods of scale practice are suggested, as follows:

1. "Work on the syllable oo." [Margit Bokor 54]

2. "Begin with slow scales not too loud and not in either extreme of range." [Emilio de Gogorza 134]

3. "Soft humming of rapid scale passages . . . develops freedom and flexibility." [Wilson 674, p. 6]

4. "Accent the first note of any group and sing the intervening notes, between accents, lightly." [Henley 264]

5. Precede each note with the sound of h. "Instead of singing *ah* on the notes, sing *hah.*" [Henley 251]

Sir Henry J. Wood adds a hint on the practicing of *arpeggios* or harp-like broken chords: "Mentally visualize the curve and shape of an arpeggio" as you practice it. Arpeggios provide excellent exercises for increasing range in both directions without effort or strain. His opinion on scale study is summed up as follows: The epitome of vocal technique, acquired only after long, careful study, is to produce a pearly, even scale. [686, vol. II, Introduction]

Blending the registers. Blending registers is the process of fusing or merging two overlapping but dissimilar sections of the vocal range into a continuous whole, so that these two sections shade insensibly into each other with no perceptible line of demarcation between them. (W) Of the 18 opinions gathered on this subject, only one declares that "the blending of registers so as to conceal the change in timbre is physically impossible." [Evetts and Worthington 167, p. 27] The others consider blending not only feasible but highly desirable. "The single [blended] register in a singer's voice is considered the hallmark of efficiency. Where there appears to be more than one, the voice is classed as poor and untrained." [Samuels 487, p. 22] The professional singer must possess a vocal range of two to three octaves, every tone from lowest to highest matching perfectly in color, quality, smoothness and texture, like a perfect string of pearls. [Samoiloff 484, p. 13; Wharton 655, p. 50] There are registers in every musical instrument, but they must not show. Nor must they ever be apparent in singing. [Wood 686, vol. I, p. 12] Therefore, the "marriage of the registers" is an all important work in training the singer's voice. [Curtis 125; Kerstin Thorborg 611]

The method of register blending is not exhaustively treated in any text. Stanley attempts a lengthy explanation, the essence of which is that each register must be trained separately "until the full development [of each] has been attained. . . . The lower register, even of a man, can never be pure until the falsetto, or upper register, has been isolated and developed." Blending will automatically follow if each register has been separately "purified," since blending becomes a "natural physiological action" in the voice only when it (voice) has been trained equally throughout its entire range. [578] Henderson writes that the blending of the registers must be effected without any feeling of constriction in the throat. Only practice and keen listening can bring this about. [243, p. 72] Waters suggests that falsetto and chest registers may be bridged by humming through the two at first until this can be done smoothly. If breaks occur, let the voice "flop" where it will until sufficient muscular strength has been built into "the entire vocal instrument" to prevent such sudden changes. [642] Philip's suggestion concludes this discussion: "The only safe method of blending the head voice with the [other] registers is to utilize soft singing and not to increase it in strength·or volume" until the transition and the entire head range "can be produced with ease and freedom." [446, p. 89]

SUMMARY AND INTERPRETATION

THEORETICAL CONSIDERATIONS

The 228 concepts of vocal range used in training the singing voice fall into two main categories: The first of these, containing 99 statements, deals with such theoretical concepts as definitions of range, the average compass of voices, the value of falsetto tones, and the theory of registers. The second, containing 129 statements, deals with psychological and technical methods of cultivating range, such as sectional and directional scale work and the blending of registers. Further subdivisions of these topics are classified in *Table Five*.

Theoretical discussions of range are often opinionated and controversial issues predominate. Experimental data are at a premium and many questions are left unanswered. The following conclusions indicate a definite need for further investigation in this area:

1. Opinions vary (from 1½ to 4 octaves) as to the average range of untrained and trained singers' voices.

2. Opinion is divided on fundamentals of the theory of registration.

3. Definitions are vague and contradictory.

4. Authors disagree as to the cause, nature and even the existence of registers.

5. Conflicting opinions are open to misinterpretation due to the absence of a standard terminology.

6. The action of registration is not clearly explained and the exact causes of registration remain undecided.

7. Opinion is evenly divided on the legitimacy of falsetto tones for singing and on the relation of pitch level to vocal intensity.

8. The method of register blending remains a trade secret.

Theories of average vocal compass. This subject could be clarified if a distinction were made between *vocable compass* and *singable compass*. The former is the extreme range of the individual's voice, consisting of non-utilitarian, utterable but nondescript vocal sounds, measured from the lowest grunt to the highest obtainable vocal squeak, a range that covers three or more octaves in the average voice. The latter includes only those vocal tones that can be rendered with some degree of musical, if not artistic, expressiveness. Under these standards, the average untrained *singable* compass might be two octaves or less, a compass that can easily be cultivated to meet the requirements of average song literature. [Woods 689]

Theories of registers. The question of vocal registration is one of the most insistent controversial topics in the discussion of vocal range. It promises no immediate solution, although interesting possibilities for further research are revealed. Because the term *register* has not been clearly defined, there is little certainty as to just what is intended when this term is alluded to as a point in vocal theory or technique. That a so-called register *break* usually occurs in the average untrained singing voice is commonly conceded. But out of this empirical observation, diversified and sometimes far-fetched conclusions are drawn that need further verification. Three schools of thought are represented by these conclusions, upholding respectively, the following three theories:

1. *Natural action theory.* There are no registers. The term is a misnomer. Breaks are caused by psychological fears of high tones and chronic tensions induced by habitual straining during ascent of vocal pitch, incorrect methods of phonation, faulty breathing, self-consciousness about registers, and attempts at local laryngeal effort which disturb normal spontaneous laryngeal coordinations. Muscular mechanisms of phonation are not readily subject to conscious control in singing. Therefore, conscious interference in spontaneous laryngeal action causes spasmodic phonation and resultant "register" breaks. When a voice is free from the above disturbances, breaks cannot occur; hence registers cannot exist. Witness the so-called *natural* voice that has escaped the damaging influence of incorrect teaching methods and therefore shows no register breaks.

2. *Speech action theory.* The singing range is influenced by the speaking range to the extent that the habitual daily activity of the speaking voice creates predominant vocal tensions that affect the singing range. That segment of the vocal gamut that is continually exercised in speaking acquires strength and firmness beyond the development of relatively unused portions of the singing range in the upper and lower extremes of the voice. Transitional breaks or wobbly tones occur whenever the singing voice passes from a stronger to a weaker segment of the range. These transitional breaks define the so-called registers.

3. *Mechanistic action theory.* Pitch elevation in the singing voice is controlled by the antagonistic action of thyro-arytenoid or cord stretching muscles (vocal cords) and other extrinsic muscles such as downward pulling crico-thyroid, sterno-thyroid and lateral crico-arytenoid muscles. When one group of muscles is weaker than its antagonistic opposites the

former collapse under the stretching tensions of the latter, thus causing wobbly points in the vocal range, pitch fluttering or breaks. To offset such breaks it is necessary to equalize the strength and tension of the weaker muscles so that a condition of perfect equilibrium or balanced tension may be reached between antagonistic muscular actions. The function of each set of phonatory muscles is amenable to training and must be clearly defined so that one function never encroaches upon the regulatory action of neighboring muscles, causing the condition called *mixed registration*. [Stanley 578]

METHODOLOGICAL CONSIDERATIONS

The suggested use of psychological or indirect methods of cultivating vocal range introduces interesting possibilities of overcoming the mental hazards and tensions that usually accompany the treatment of registers and the singing of high pitches. An attempt is made to correlate the pitch range of the singing voice with the inflectional track of the speaking voice. In this respect, it is claimed that the activating principle of the singing voice is closely related to the self-expressional impulses of the individual. Thus, the impulse to express always awakens automatic vocal coordinations that provide appropriate pitch movements or inflections suited to the meaning or interpretation of the idea expressed, whether in singing or speaking. These complex, spontaneous coordinations of vocal utterance should not be disturbed by the isolation of pitch factors in training the singer's voice, since pitch control is imbedded in the interpretational pattern of the song. High tones would then be regarded merely as higher reaches of the speaking voice and practiced as glissando inflections of the latter. The teaching techniques that deal with the sectional and directional treatment of range, scale work and register blending are self-explanatory and require no further comment.

In conclusion, the voice teacher is reminded that the attainment of unusually high pitches and the abnormal stretching of the student's vocal compass can become a studio fetish rather than a constructive principle of voice building. The student's singing range should be utilized at the outset within his own easy capabilities for wholesome and comfortable musical performance. It is claimed by some authors that the over-zealous striving to stretch every vocal range to arbitrary limits can lead to chronic vocal fatigue and defeat the entire voice training program. In other words, there is little virtue in the fanatical pursuit of operatic gymnastics that seek to exploit the unusual rather than the musically beautiful ranges of the singing voice. Such music should be avoided, especially by beginners. The student's satisfaction in performance is an important incentive to learning and a factor in freeing the mind from anxieties that induce chronic muscular tensions in the vocal tract. Therefore, the conservative song repertoire of the salon type might prove far more beneficial and conducive to growth, in the long run, than grand opera acrobatics that strain and stretch the vocal range at every studio lesson.

CHAPTER VII

CONCEPTS OF DYNAMICS

Definition: In the physical sciences, *dynamics* refers to physical force, power or energy. In acoustics it refers to the relative intensity or force producing a sound. In musical science it relates to the variation of volume, quantity or power of musical sounds. (W) From this last definition its application to voice is derived, namely, dynamics refers to variations in the volume or carrying power of the singing voice.

Like most vocal and acoustical terms, dynamics has both subjective and objective connotations. Hence it is broken down into *loudness* and *intensity*. According to recent recommendations of the Acoustical Society of America, the term *loudness* should be used to designate the strength of the tone as *heard,* the mental or subjective impression, while *intensity* denotes the physical strength of the tone as measured objectively. These distinctions are logical and are coming into current use in scientific work. [Seashore 512] Since both subjective and objective meanings of these terms are employed in training the singing voice, *dynamics* is also used to denote that department of vocal science that relates to the variation and control of either loudness or intensity factors in voice production. Webster's succinct explanation is also helpful: "The power of a vocal tone depends on the force of the separate pulses of the vocal cords while they are vibrating, and this is determined by the pressure of the expired air stream, together with the resistance on the part of the vocal cords."

THEORIES OF VOCAL DYNAMICS

ACOUSTICAL FACTORS

Curry defines *intensity* as "the rate of supply of vibrational energy per square centimetre of wave front." [124, p. 40] This energy is proportional to the product of the amplitude squared and the frequency squared. i.e., $I = a^2f^2$. It is apparent from this formula that the intensity

TABLE SIX

SUMMARY OF CONCEPTS OF DYNAMICS USED IN TRAINING THE
SINGING VOICE

	total number of statements	sub-total	grand total	statements by prof. singers	documented statements	undocumented statements
I. *Theories of vocal dynamics*			9			
A. Acoustical factors	9	9			8	1
II. *Methods of controlling vocal dynamics*			101			
A. Psychological approach		6				
1. projection factors	6				1	5
B. Technical approach		95				
1. controlling factors						
a) resonance as a factor	9			4	1	8
b) breath pressure as a factor	18			1	2	16
c) resonance and breath pressure combined as factors	2					2
2. loud versus soft practice						
a) *loud tones should be used in practicing*	18				4	14
b) *loud tones should not be used in practicing*	38			12	1	37
3. swelling and diminishing as a device	10			1		10
TOTALS	110	110	110	18	17	93

of an evenly produced voice rises as the pitch (frequency) rises. According to Stanley, this rate of intensity increase is about fifteen decibels per octave as the voice ascends in the musical scale, or about fifty decibels over a range of three octaves. (The *decibel* is the unit of measurement employed for testing vocal intensity.) [577, p. 295]

From experimental tests and observations Stanley finds that the ability to sing loudly is not a product of vocal training since untrained voices show as wide a dynamic range as trained ones. However, the better trained voices show high intensity readings over a wider pitch range. [Ibid.] Seashore reports that the range of tonal power found in average concert songs is no greater than the power range of the average untrained speaking voice, i.e., about twenty decibels. [506, p. 88] In this he is supported by Curry, who also finds that the average singer produces an intensity range of twenty decibels in ordinary singing but that this range is greatly extended in dramatic concert style of singing. It must be borne in mind, however, that most vocal music covers less than two-thirds of the full range of the singing voice. The actual intensity range of such music is only from twenty to thirty decibels, while the total intensity range of a good singing voice is about fifty decibels. [124, p. 109] Wolf, Stanley and Sette report an experiment in which intensity ratings were made of various singers' voices. They conclude that the ability to attack and sustain the intensity of a given tone is a characteristic of good singing and that the lack of this ability "suggests a singer of inferior artistic rating and also gives the impression of a weak voice." [683] These general considerations provide a background for the discussions which follow. The concepts in this chapter are summarized in *Table Six*.

METHODS OF CONTROLLING VOCAL DYNAMICS

PSYCHOLOGICAL APPROACH

Projection factors. Vocal projection is directly related to dynamics. The former is measured in terms of distance traversed between singer and listener. The latter is the measure of force or power with which the voice is released and radiated into space. In teaching singing, it is not easy to dissociate the act of phonation from the act of vocal projection. Samuels believes that vocal projection is an automatic process governed by mental controls and requiring no special attention on the part of the singer. Almost as soon as the singer opens his mouth and utters a sound "he can be heard a hundred yards away, before there is time to think of directing the voice, even were that possible." [487, p. 16] "With regard to power," says Stanley, "any properly produced voice can fill the largest hall or opera house." Furthermore, voice projection, being a reflex action, should be effortless in singing. It is an acoustical phenomenon depending upon the intensity of sound vibrations and not upon conscious muscular effort. [578]

William E. Brown, an exponent of Lamperti's methods of teaching, would have us ignore projection factors entirely in teaching singing. He claims that the larynx merely generates invisible vibratory energy which instantly expands and radiates in all directions. Except for causing the initial intensity and regularity of the generating sound vibrations, the larynx and throat muscles have nothing to do with the carrying power or propulsion of voice. "When you realize that nothing leaves the throat, you will stop pushing and pulling to make your voice carry." [78, p. 87] In other words, as Waters puts it, it only defeats your purpose "to push your voice . . . or try to project it to the back rows." It is her contention that such efforts interfere with the working of the laws of sound "that will carry your voice for you." [645]

Thinking a tone louder or softer is all that is necessary to make it so, according to Shaw. That is to say, physiologic action governing voice projection is purely an involuntary response to tonal concepts of the singer. [521] Jeffries also supports this viewpoint and adds, "producing (vocal) volume requires only the will to hear a louder tone, and with this a conscious loosening and opening of the throat." [301]

TECHNICAL APPROACH

Controlling vocal dynamics. From previous definitions in Chapter V (q.v.) we learn that vocal resonance is "the *intensification* and enrichment of tone"; that the action of the vocal resonator is *"to amplify* certain frequencies"; that the effect of vocal resonance is *"to increase* the initial tone or to change its quality or both." An apparent relationship exists between resonance and dynamics that may not be overlooked in training the singing voice. The question arises as to whether resonance is an active agency for augmenting laryngeal tone, either wholly, partially, or not at all. Twenty-nine opinions were gathered on this subject. Nine of them express the belief that resonance is the main controlling factor in amplifying vocal sound, 18 believe that breath pressure is the main controlling factor and 2 suggest that resonance and breath pressure combined control vocal dynamics.

Resonance as a controlling factor. Resonance controls vocal dynamics. It endows the voice with effortless volume as well as quality. Resonance does not depend on force. [Marafioti 368, p. 100] As Curry explains it, maximum intensity of vocal sound is really produced at the larynx. The resonance cavities serve "to increase the flow of energy from the source, thereby increasing the loudness of the sound." [124, p. 32] Hemery also believes that volume of voice means "increased resonance of a wider area than the larynx." [238, p. 123] Shaw states that resonance and sympathetic vibration are the two methods of amplifying vocal sound. [518, p. 68] Rimmer also holds that "power or largeness of tone, depends upon the proper use of the resonance chambers." [466] The opinions of four professional singers are also relevant:

1. "A person of small stature, who resonates tone correctly, can be

heard farther than one of larger frame who shouts on forced breath." [Jessica Dragonette 146]

2. What we call a small voice is simply tone produced by means of undeveloped resonance. [Louis Graveure 208]

3. Using diaphragmatic breath pressure is a grave error. Instead of augmenting the tone, "such forcing robs it of both color and volume." [Lily Pons 450]

4. Forcing the voice for either volume or range by means of breath pressure or in any other way "is the surest way to ruin it." [Ernestine Schumann-Heink 499]

Breath pressure as a controlling factor. Intensity of tone in any wind instrument always depends upon the pressure of wind applied to the generator of the sound, whether it be the reed of a clarinet, the lips of the trombone player or the vocal cords in the human voice. The amplitude of the vibratory swing of the vocal cords, and therefore the intensity of vocal sound, is thus affected. [Redfield 462, p. 267; Curry 124, p. 47; Hemery 238, p. 54] This acoustical principle gives rise to a theory of breath support advocated by 18 authors. As Wilcox explains it, loudness or softness of tone depends upon the rate at which the diaphragm sends the breath against the vocal cords. That is to say, "breath energy must always be commensurate with the intensity of the tone." [Wilcox 667; also Stanley 578] Clark maintains that "getting the force of singing exclusively determined" by the force of breathing is a certain way of remedying "many physical faults of singing." [102]

Great singers accomplish an intensified vocal utterance by means of intensified breath pressure, according to Henley. "The 'diaphragmatic push' must be held continuously," he says. [251] Sir Henry Coward refers to "high pressure breathing" as a means of "pushing the voice forward with tremendous volume for loud passages." [122, p. 17] Scott warns that "the larynx must not give way before the breath pressure." It (larynx) must be firmly held or the voice will crack. [502, p. 20]

Breath pressure is equally important for loud or soft singing, according to Hok. "The soft tone is produced exactly like the big one, only there is less of it." [278, p. 26] In this opinion he is supported by five others. Stanley adds that soft singing requires even more breath pressure than loud singing since the glottis is slightly separated in soft tones. Hence, more work is done for soft singing. [577, p. 313; Samuels 487, p. 33] "A real pianissimo can be produced only by strong breathing muscles," says Metzger [396], and he is seconded by Philip, who adds, "the singer should never deprive the vocal tone, however soft it may be, of adequate breath support." [446, p. 89] Finally, a method of practicing in an audible whisper is suggested by Kellogg, who claims that "it takes as much breath support . . . as to sing at full voice." [311]

Resonance and breath pressure combined. Both are factors in controlling vocal volume, according to Evetts and Worthington [167, p. 77] and Wodell [679]. The latter adds that "power of voice is secured as much, or more, through the use of resonance resources as through the increase of breath pressure."

LOUD VERSUS SOFT PRACTICE

The question of vocal dynamics used in practicing is fairly important. Fifty-six authors mention it. Singing *practice,* especially for beginners, is a voice training routine that involves repetitive exercises and other disciplinary procedures, usually continued over long periods of time. (W) Habits are formed during these training periods and there is danger of inflicting damage to the vocal instrument should the wrong methods of practicing be employed. But the opinions of authors are divided on this subject. Eighteen are advocates of loud singing practice and 38 (including 12 professional singers) favor soft singing practice.

Loud singing practice is favored. Lombardi advises the new pupil "to sing with a full voice, but never to the point of straining it." [353] Hopkins, an advocate of self-training, would build the voice by singing "very loudly" until the registers are developed. [283, p. 87] "All tone should be hearty and vital during early training," says Wharton. Soft tones are among the most difficult of vocal feats and should be left to the artist singer. [655, p. 17] The following typical opinions also represent this point of view:

1. "A firm, strong character of tone must be employed in the early stages of training." [Shaw 543]

2. "Best results are brought about by singing full voice, not softly." [Dossert 140, p. 44]

3. "The secret of a beautiful . . . pianissimo is a round and ringing forte." [Orton 439, p. 123; also Mowe 405, p. 7]

4. Soft tones are more difficult and require more actual work than loud tones. That is why "the beginner must not be allowed to practice soft singing." [Stanley 578]

5. Avoid the singing of soft tones until the student has learned to produce and hear his voice at average loudness throughout his pitch range. [Conklin 121, p. 105]

6. Breath restraint as in soft singing requires more muscular effort than breath release as in loud singing. That is why soft singing should be studied last. [Brown 78]

7. "We believe that the practice of inducing young people to sing in a way commonly and inaccurately described as *soft* which should be termed *devitalized* will result in the presence rather than in the absence of strain." [American Academy of Teachers of Singing 10]

8. An overdose of soft singing tires and deteriorates the voice. [Hagara 220, p. 114]

9. "Soft singing itself leads to the most vicious errors in vocal action." [Mursell and Glenn 413, p. 285]

Soft singing practice is favored by authors and professional singers in a ratio of more than 2 to 1. Greta Stueckgold, artist soprano, for instance, takes an emphatic stand that is directly opposed to some of the opinions expressed above. She declares that nobody who is still building his voice should sing forte. "A voice that sings forte entirely will soon wear itself out through lack of proper control." [593] Lawrence Tibbett is equally emphatic in affirming that "most beginners are slaves of the big tone habit." It is better to test your voice with the lightest pianissimo when practicing. This is an infallible guide to correct tone production. Teachers should never allow a pupil to sing in full voice until he has first acquired a good pianissimo. [613] "I sing all my exercises *mezza voce*," says Lily Pons. "Never do I practice in full voice." [450] That "loud singing ruins the voice" is also the conviction of Zinka Milanov, noted soprano. "Everyone can produce loud tones without practice." But the art of singing lies in developing the finer and subtler dynamic shadings. [397] Jarmila Novotna also holds this opinion [431] Jose Mojica adds that "most practicing should be done in half-voice," and forte passages should never be included in the day's perliminary practicing. [401; also Emilio de Gogorza 134]

Other typical concepts on this subject support the view that the singer learns to measure his own vocal strength by practicing at first in soft voice, then, in gradual intermediate steps, progressing toward his full voice. According to Shakespeare, this idea is over a hundred years old. It can be found in Manstein's, *History of Song*, published in 1845. [517, p. 86] Klingstedt quotes the authority of Tosi (1730 A.D.) in stating that it is best always to practice slowly with a light vocal quality. [320, p. 21] According to Marafioti, the minutest feeble sound which the vocal cords can produce is the embryo from which all vocal growth evolves. [368, p. 76] Strauss holds that it is better not to strive for excessively loud tones, but to keep the voice at a natural level instead. [591, p. 2; also Henley 262] If pleasant soft tones are cultivated, power will follow when it is needed, says Howe. [284, Introduction] Quality strengthens the voice more than volume. [Skiles 561] Father Finn's suggestion is also typical: Always establish a good pianissimo as a working basis when eliminating habits of faulty production. [181, p. 18; also Marchesi 369, p. 7; Hall and Brown 227, p. 21; and Divver 138, p. 40] Shakespeare sums up the case for soft practicing in a maxim that he quotes from an old publication by Hiller, written in 1774. "Never force the voice so as to excite astonishment; never louder than lovely." [517, p. 81] Borchers reports the only experiment in this area of vocal dynamics. In his summary he says that there is "without exception" a greater percentage of energy in the fundamental of tones sung with less intensity than in those sung at greater intensity levels. [57]

Swelling and diminishing. A favorite vocal training device employed by the Italian singing masters of the Golden Age was called *messa di voce*. It consisted of the gradual swelling of a tone from pianissimo to its maximum power, and then slowly diminishing it again to its starting point. [Grove's Dictionary of Music 708, vol. III, p. 443] According to Orton, the old Italian masters were not all agreed on the importance of swelling and diminishing techniques as a part of basic voice culture. [439, p. 120] Henderson reports that *messa di voce* was practiced by singers as far back as the year 1638. [243, p. 81] This principle is explained by Crescentini (ca. 1797) as follows: The singer cannot attain mastery of his breath until he can control it steadily through a thousand degrees of gradually swelling and diminishing tone from softest piano to loudest forte and back again without the slightest variations of pitch, quality or technique. [Henley 264] Henderson suggests that the trumpet call in the opening notes of Wagner's *Rienzi Overture* is a good model to follow for the *messa di voce*. The pupil should study this effect. [243, p. 85] Dodds and Lickley declare that *messa di voce* is the best general vocal exercise. It should be practiced on a single note at a time, in the middle register of the voice and throughout a comfortable dynamic range. The duration of this exercise should be increased gradually. [139, p. 48] Lloyd holds the belief that "you do not own any note in your voice" until this exercise has been mastered [351, p. 28], while Lawrence Tibbett calls it an "acid test for the voice. . . . A singer who cannot do this cannot be said to have control of his voice." [613] White warns against tension during the practice of techniques involving dynamic changes of the voice. "The correct sensation for a crescendo is a feeling of expansion, but never a feeling of pressure," he says. [659, p. 56]

SUMMARY AND INTERPRETATION

THEORETICAL CONSIDERATIONS

Discussions of vocal dynamics are less extensive than those of other components of singing, such as breathing, phonation or resonance. One hundred and ten statements were gathered on this subject. Only six of these refer to objective studies and two give authentic historical references. Eighteen statements by professional singers are included.

There is little information regarding the physiological controls of dynamics in singing. These controls involve the gradation of tonal volume. The popular theory is that the degree of loudness of a vocal tone is related to the amount of energy applied to its point of emission at the glottis, the energizing agent of glottal vibration being the expiring breath stream. When the breath stream is applied to the occluded vocal lips (cords) it forces them to pulsate intermittently, much as the lips of a bugler might vibrate when he compresses them and blows against the mouthpiece of his instrument. In either case, the force of the energizing agent (breath pressure) will determine the amplitude of the glottal pulsations and the consequent amplitude of the issuing sound wave, which we interpret as intensity or loudness.

METHODOLOGICAL CONSIDERATIONS

The discussions of technique center around two important controversial questions: a) Is vocal volume controlled by means of breath pressure, resonance factors or both? and b) Should loud or soft singing be used when practicing? There is also a discussion of the swelling and diminishing device which the Italian masters called *messa di voce,* and an experimental report indicating that the ability to sing loudly is not a product of vocal training but an inherent characteristic of the normal vocal equipment of every individual, whether singer or non-singer. One author offers the interesting opinion that vocal dynamics are governed by hearing concepts rather than volitional controls of the vocal or breathing apparatus.

The argument favoring soft singing practice is reinforced somewhat by Borcher's findings in an experimental analysis of the acoustic spectra of three tones of the same pitch and vowel as sung by artist subjects at three different intensity levels: *pp, mf, ff.* Results of this study indicate that, in soft singing, the natural fundamental frequency in a vocal tone is relatively stronger than in loud singing of the same tone. Although these findings are inconclusive, they tend to support the idea that soft singing, or at least moderate loudness, helps to build a strong fundamental quality into the voice. [57]

Unanimity of opinion is lacking on any of these aspects of vocal training. It would appear from these discussions that the control of loudness is an inherent rather than an acquired characteristic of all vocal utterance. If this belief could be substantiated by conclusive objective evidence, the training of this faculty would be superfluous and the responsibility of the singing teacher would resolve itself into a refinement of technical abilities that the singer already possesses, rather than the cultivation of new skills where none existed. This theory of inherent dynamic vocal control holds important pedagogical implications, namely:

1. That proficiency in controlling the dynamic range of the singing voice is not a product of vocal training.

2. That the average person possesses the ability to sing with sufficient intensity to meet the average requirements of song literature.

3. That the control of vocal dynamics in singing cannot be dissociated from the control of phonation since the former is an attribute of the latter.

4. That the intensity component of the singing voice is an automatic resultant of the initial energy of phonation and the pitch level or vibratory frequency of the vocal cords and is beyond the voluntary control of the singer.

In conclusion, a word of warning is given regarding the abuse of vocal power in untrained voices. Those who attempt to actuate the laryngeal mechanism voluntarily by means of breath pressure and local muscular effort run the risk of straining some of the delicate intrinsic muscular fibres in the glottis with resultant vocal disturbances such as impaired phonation, chronic inflammation (hoarseness), and singer's nodes. Many singing students show one or more symptoms of vocal abuse caused by earlier straining of the vocal cords. It is presumed, therefore, that reeducative and remedial techniques of vocal study are needed along with other teaching procedures.

CHAPTER VIII

CONCEPTS OF EAR TRAINING

D*efinition:* The *ear* is the organ of hearing. To have an ear for music is to have a refined or acute sense of hearing and to possess the ability to catch, retain or reproduce music by having heard it. Since singing is a form of musical expression, this definition has vocal applications as well. *Ear training* in singing may be defined as the process of becoming proficient and skillful in recognizing, retaining or reproducing vocal tones by means of practice in experiencing their auditory sensations. In other words, it is the means of receiving and retaining mental impressions of vocal tones and tonal relations through the medium of the sense of hearing. (W)

The following definitions are also useful. *Sound* is the interpretation, by the brain, of a succession of atmospheric pulsations capable of producing the sensation of hearing. [Passe 443, p. 1] "To be musical, the pulsations must be periodic." [Redfield 462, p. 30] *Tone* is musical sound as opposed to noise, having such regularity of vibration as to possess recognizable and individual characteristics of pitch, loudness, duration and quality. Sensations of tone may therefore vary in these four characteristics. *Hearing* is the capacity for perceiving auditory sensations of sound. The extreme range of human hearing includes roughly about 11,000 pitch tones, varying from 16 to nearly 50,000 dv., and about 600 degrees of loudness or intensity. Music commonly employs less than 100 conventional pitch tones (i.e., between 40 and 4800 dv. or about 7 octaves), gaining variety by the fusion of these. (W)

The terminology of ear training is varied but basic to all departments of vocal study. Such terms as *sound, tone, hearing, listening, tonal imagery* and *visualization* are fundamental concepts in the discussions which follow. Therefore, simple definitions of these and other pertinent terms are provided, when needed, for purposes of orientation. Detailed technical descriptions of the hearing organs and their functions are beyond the

TABLE SEVEN

SUMMARY OF CONCEPTS OF EAR TRAINING USED IN TRAINING THE SINGING VOICE

	total number of statements	sub-total	grand total	statements by prof. singers	documented statements	undocumented statements
I. *Theories of ear training*			39			
A. General considerations	16	16			8	8
B. Fundamental importance of ear training	23	23		1	5	18
II. *Methods of ear training*			118			
A. Psychological approach		78				
1. tonal imagery a prime factor in ear training	16				1	15
2. self-listening as a vocal aid						
a) *self-listening is recommended*	17			2		17
b) *self-listening is not recommended*	4				1	3
3. sensation and sound as guides to vocal action						
a) *sensation is a reliable guide*	15			2		15
b) *sensation is not a reliable guide*	20			2	1	19
c) *sound and sensation combined are reliable guides*	6			1		6
B. Technical approach		40				
1. critical listening to vocal models	20				1	19
2. imitation as a factor						
a) *imitation is recommended*	12			3		12
b) *imitation is not recommended*	8			1		8
TOTALS	157	157	157	12	17	140

scope of this study but are available, for reference, in any standard encyclopedia or physiology text.

THEORIES OF EAR TRAINING

GENERAL CONSIDERATIONS

Ear training has as its primary purpose the building up of the power to feel, think and express in tone. Its method is to give students "opportunities to think music before they sing or play it." [Mursell and Glenn 413, p. 169] In this educative process the ear is the receptor, or transformer of energy, which definitely contributes to the performance. [Owsley 441, p. 1] Proschowski points out that, through the sense of hearing, the ear controls the mechanism of voice, whether in singing or speaking. [455] All other trained muscular mechanisms achieve their coordination by the senses of touch or seeing, but the voice is unique in that it responds almost exclusively to the auditory sense in its method of control. [Drew 148] Mursell likewise states that "aural perceptions seem considerably more important for vocal control than any kinaesthetic elements." In other words, becoming "ear-minded" is an essential factor in musical training. [411, p. 227]

After making an exhaustive study of comparative anatomy, Negus comes to the conclusion that "perception of vibrations [hearing] was acquired before the power of purposive production of sound." He also finds that "discrimination of differences of pitch by the organ of hearing is very much more sensitive than differences of shade in sight or of odours in olfaction. . . . Man makes greater use of differences of pitch than do any animals." [418, p. 288] Philip compares the organ of hearing to "an intricate piano having about 16,000 strings," each of which can be made to vibrate alone or in combination with others. [446, p. 17] The average ear can detect pitch differences as small as 1/17 of a tone and the trained ear acquires a sensitivity that may respond to 1/100 of a tone or less. It is this sensitivity to minute pitch differences that contributes to the ear's perception of overtones and vocal quality. On the other hand, a poor ear can be insensitive to pitch differences as large as a semitone. [Seashore 505] According to Negus, the faculty of pitch discrimination is most acute for tones "whose vibration rates are between 128 dv. and 256 dv., pitches which roughly comprise the range of the conversational voice." [Op. cit., p. 482] Lewis and Lichte find experimentally that "a trained listener might perceive two complex tones as being different in timbre and yet be unable to designate the exact nature of the difference in terms of (say) saliency of specific partials." [341]

Stevens and Miles observe that "there are hardly any sensory nerve endings in the vocal cords and muscles of the larynx." It is their belief that this largely accounts for the absence of voluntary phonatory controls in singing and also for the complete dependency of vocal pitch and dynamic modulations upon the sense of hearing. [583] One more physiological fact is worth noting. Ortmann reports that there is "a predominance of energy" in the tonal spectrum of a well trained singing voice, at a point which he describes as "2900 frequency." That this frequency band is always prominent, "regardless of the pitch of the fundamental is significant because this frequency corresponds to the natural resonance period" of the human ear canal. [437]

There is never any doubt among vocal musicians that the normal ear of the average singer is readily amenable to training. As Glenn Haydon explains it, the physiological limits of pitch discrimination may not change during a lifetime, but cognition always improves with training and experience. Hence, the cognitive limits of hearing can be changed by training. [710, p. 71] Mursell and Glenn hold that the ability to hear music (voice), like the ability to hear language, can be developed by ear training [Op. cit., p. 142], and Novello-Davies declares that in forty years experience "I have yet to find anyone whose sense of pitch cannot be cultivated." [430, p. 25]

FUNDAMENTAL IMPORTANCE OF EAR TRAINING

Twenty-three authors support the belief that training the singing voice is largely a process of cultivating hearing acuity. That "voice training is largely aesthetic ear training," is a typical viewpoint. It is also a matter of improving musical taste. [Clippinger 104, p. 3; 108] Curry claims that auditory perceptions formed by the ear are a "major control" on the singer's voice quality [124, p. 115] and Gescheidt holds that ear training is a necessary concomitant of all vocal training procedures. [200, p. 27] Drew argues that some form of ear training should always precede vocal exercises. This latter opinion is based upon the assumption that perfect phonation is an instinctive action, inhering in each individual at birth and therefore not subject to voluntary control or direct training. Therefore, voice training is fundamentally ear training. [147; 148, p. 157] Other concepts in this category are summed up in the following representative opinions:

1. The important thing in voice training is how the tone sounds. [Skiles 551]

2. The ear governs phonation and resonance. Therefore voice training is accomplished largely by means of ear training. [Evetts 166]

3. Everybody cannot sing well. But the fault lies more often "in defective musical perception" than in the condition of the vocal organs. [Aikin 4; also Mackenzie 364, p. 50]

4. Intensity of breath and tone are not increased by muscular pressure. They are "automatically controlled through the sense of hearing." [Proschowsky 458]

5. "The ear, then, is the chief guide for singing just as the eye is for painting." [Witherspoon 677, p. 27]

Two historical references are also included. According to Stock, Garcia's way of training the voice was through the ear, so as to keep the mind entirely off the muscles. [586] Klingstedt's more recent historical study of bel canto methods reports that the old Italian masters worked largely through the ear to establish the four main techniques of open throat, forward tone, vocal support and singing on the breath. Ear training was always the first step in training the singing voice and vocal responses were always correctly governed by correct hearing concepts, "as in violin playing." [320, p. 17 and p. 45]

METHODS OF EAR TRAINING

PSYCHOLOGICAL APPROACH

Tonal imagery a prime factor. Tonal imagery, also called *auditory visualization,* may be defined as the reproduction in memory or imagination of the likeness of an actual auditory sensory experience, together with accompanying feelings. It is the preconception or mental expectation of sounds not actually present to the outer sense of hearing. (W) A typical point of view is expressed by Fergusson, namely, that "a vocal tone is the physical reaction to a mental concept." Therefore, the more nearly a singer can conceive a perfect tone, the more closely will he approach the perfect muscular coordinations which produce it. [178] Although they vary in form, the 78 statements in this category all support the basic idea that "vocal tone has its beginning in thought." [Austin-Ball 31, p. 15] For instance, Mursell and Glenn believe that, in order to be considered adequate, a system of ear training must make "constant provision for developing musical imagery." Seashore stresses the importance of "musical imagining" as an attribute of the musical mind, and declares that the performer (vocalist) must have in his mind a clear-cut image of tone quality before he produces a sound. [510, p. 161] Waters holds that the voice cannot be used effectively until the "inner hearing" is first developed. [647, p. 105] Glenn Woods refers to this inner hearing as the awakening of "tonal consciousness." [687] Hathaway calls it "voice consciousness." [231, p. 13] Stanley refers to mental concepts as "memory pictures" of sound. [577, p. 324] Lewis declares that vocal tone is not merely sound or pitch; "it is an idea." [344, p. iii] Clippinger believes that training the singing voice is a matter of developing "concepts," not muscles. When correct tone concepts have been formed, the vocal training program is immeasurably expedited. [108] "Tonal imagery is very important in guiding song," according to Mursell and Glenn. [Op. cit.] Ideal vocal tones "are reproduced by reflex action, only after they have been mentally imaged." [Brouillet 64, p. 43] Drew describes the act of phonation as an involuntary auditory reflex governed entirely by "thinking of a sound" rather than by thinking of an action. [147, p. 158] According to De Bruyn, a true "bel cantist" always patterns the quality of his voice after his own concept of tonal beauty, rather than by means of conscious muscular adjustments. [132] (See also Chapter IV)

Self-listening as a vocal aid. Listening is defined as the act of giving close or undivided attention with the purpose of hearing. (W) *Self-listening*, therefore, requires "concentration on what you are doing"; on how you sound, while singing. [Whitfield 661] In all, 21 opinions on this subject were gathered; 17 of them endorse self-listening as a teaching method and 4 are opposed to it. Those who are opposed to this device claim that no singer can hear his own voice accurately until he has been trained to do so. Hence he must rely entirely upon his teacher's judgment and hearing while he is studying singing. [Taylor 602, p. 31] Henley claims that the singer cannot accurately check on his own vocal reflexes by listening to himself, since he is likely to obtain a distorted picture of his own voice. [246] "Don't talk of ear tests," says Benedict. "What is one man's meat is often another's poison." If self-listening were resorted to, there would be as many standards of vocal excellence as there are people. [44] Stanley is also emphatic in his disapproval of self-listening because, as he claims, the student cannot listen impartially to his own voice during the act of singing. It is inevitable that he will either feel conceited or discontented, depending upon whether he approves or disapproves of his tone. Therefore it is far better that the singer should never listen to his own voice. [578]

The arguments in favor of self-listening as a teaching device are summed up in the following representative opinions:

1. Learn to hear yourself. Perfect tone involves a complex coordination which can only be controlled by the ear. [Lilli Lehmann 337, p. 91]

2. Instead of thinking about the throat, think of the effect produced. [Samuels 487, p. 37]

3. Good vocal tone rests on an ideal aesthetic conception. "Learn to hear and value your own tone." [Altglass and Kempf 8]

4. Close your eyes and concentrate on the pitch of the tones you are singing, especially in difficult passages. [Bas 41]

5. First of all, you must learn to hear yourself as others hear you. [Kirkpatrick 317]

6. "It is only by alertness in listening to the tone that the right mechanism can be attained." [Shakespeare 516]

7. "The ear is the arbiter . . . of the tone." Vocal results are guided by careful listening. [La Forest 326, p. 156; also Hemery 238, p. 13]

8. "Think, sing, listen"—is always a good motto for the vocal student. [Austin-Ball 31, p. 35]

9. The vocal student must be taught "to be his own critic and advisor, so that he can hear himself when 'lesson time' is over." [Friedrich Schorr 497]

SENSATION AND SOUND AS GUIDES TO VOCAL ACTION

Sensation is defined as the mental awareness of some immediate physical stimulation of the bodily organism. (W) Fifteen authors express the belief that the tactile and kinesthetic sense impressions caused by changes in the internal state of the body during singing are the singer's only reliable guides to vocal action. Opposed to this group are the 20 opinions that emphasize the primacy of auditory impressions as guiding evidence of vocal action to the singer. A third group of 6 assume that both sensation and sound are interdependent criteria of vocal action. In all, 41 opinions are expressed, embracing the following three aspects of this controversial subject:

a) *Sensation is a reliable guide.* Graveure's opinion is typical: The proper way to learn to sing is "by the muscular feel of the thing." The voice should be trained "entirely through the channel of muscular sensation, and not by the ear." [208] Vivian della Chiesa explains that the singer should always make a concentrated effort to capture the sensation of good tone so that he can summon up these sensations at will, "until they become second nature." [135] Nicholson believes that the student of singing should first "find out what it *feels* like to produce the sounds." His teacher is the only one who can judge whether they are pleasant tones or not. [425, p. 91] Wodell defines "placing the tone" as locating the sensation of tonal vibration. The memory of these sensations constitutes your "method" of singing. [682; Jones 307, p. 10] "Focussing the voice" is directed by sensation only, according to Philip. [446, p. 119] "Never depend on the deceiving evidence of the outer ear," warns Jetson-Ryder. [304] Herbert-Caesari claims that the old masters worked entirely from "the sensation of cause and effect." [269, p. 5] Finally, Jessica Dragonette recommends that the student learn to master the invisible mechanics of singing entirely "in terms of his sensations." [146] These are typical concepts that present the case for *sensation*. The argument is explicitly summed up in Brown's maxim: "Do not listen to yourself sing! *Feel* yourself sing!" [78, p. 16; and 73]

b) *Sensation is not a reliable guide.* This group believes that sensations are unreliable and illusory symptoms of physical technique that tend to distract the attention of the singer from the tones he is singing. The following arguments bespeak the viewpoint of the entire group.

1. Trying to explain the mechanism of singing by working backwards from sensations leads to empirical acoustical fallacies such as "singing in the mask," "supporting the voice on the diaphragm"; "focusing tone with the uvula"; and "holding the tone on the teeth." [Drew 147, p. 130]

2. The true expression of beauty comes only "to those who are able to erase from the consciousness every physical sensation." [Savage 490, p. 113]

3. Singing-by-sensation is placing the cart before the horse, the effect before the cause. [Austin-Ball 31, p. 17; Witherspoon 677, p. 32]

4. Because body structures vary with the individual, the sensations accompanying voice will vary. Therefore physical sensation is an unreliable teaching tool. [Conklin 121, p. 10]

5. Correct singing is an unconscious act. Only faults and tensions impart sensations. When the performance is perfect, the singer does not know how he did it. [Lloyd 351, p. 12]

6. "Kinaesthetic sensations . . . are rarely brought into . . . conscious attention." It has been found that even under complete local anaesthesia of the throat the singer's performance did not noticeably deteriorate. [Mursell 411, p. 227]

7. Singing is devoid of physical sensation and can only be controlled indirectly by listening. [Lilli Lehmann 337, pp. 34 and 90]

8. The singer's main concern is how his voice sounds, not how it is

produced. At his best, he should be unconscious of his vocal organs. [Greene 209, p. 7]

9. The laryngeal muscles "can only be contracted by thinking of a sound," not by thinking of muscular movements or sensations. [Drew 148; Merritt 389]

10. Mechanical guidance cannot help vocal action since it obstructs the natural spontaneous auditory responses which normally occur in the vocal organs when they are guided by a keen musical ear. [Klingstedt 320, p. 44]

c) *Sensation and sound combined are reliable guides to vocal action.* These authors take the attitude that "sensation and hearing always go hand in hand with mental conception in producing a singing tone." [Key 315, p. 65] Greta Stueckgold, in an interview, claims that the only guide to the singer is "the way tones sound and feel." Therefore, the formative study years should be devoted to constant "listening for tones and feeling their sensations" within the vocal organs. [594; also Wilson 674, I, p. 20] The ancients were always successfully guided by feeling and hearing, according to Shaw, in the days when scientific information concerning vocal action was still unknown. [528] Clippinger maintains that, although the "final court of appeal" in judging tone is the ear, nevertheless the ear must often "be supplemented by the sensations" accompanying voice production. [116] Finally, Hall and Brown declare that the student must learn to judge the quality of his own voice through both auditory and tactile sensations. [227, p. 18]

TECHNICAL APPROACH

Critical listening to vocal models is a technique of ear training recommended by 20 authors. The term *critical listening* is often used in discussions of the singing voice. In a pedagogical sense it may be defined as the process of exercising careful or analytical judgment as to the merits, beauty or techniques revealed by a specific performance. The *vocal models* used for critical listening should be archetypes of singing artistry which present ideal patterns of performance to the listening ear, and which are worthy of imitation or emulation.

According to Mursell and Glenn, ear training should be carried on through at least three kinds of musical projects: listening, singing songs and improvising. [413, p. 143] The first of these, listening, requires the presence of artist performers either in person or through phonographic recordings. Drew insists that a good demonstration by one who can produce a full, free tone is a great help to one who cannot, in that it provides a listening model worthy of emulation. Good vocal models are the best teachers. [147, p. 162] When they are lacking in fine vocal equipment themselves, teachers should at least insist that their pupils often hear fine singers. [Ibid., p. 113] The remaining opinions on this subject are represented in the following statements:

1. Recorded renditions of selections by recognized artists are useful as "objective criteria" by which the student may judge his own vocal development. [Buswell 85; Glenn 205]

2. "To supplement your regular work on tone production . . . listen critically to first-class phonograph or radio music." Then try to sing the same songs that you listen to. [Karapetoff 310; Wilson 674, I, p. 5]

3. Records of lyric singing are to be preferred as models of well-produced voices. [Butler 88]

4. "We build up our concepts of vocal tone, good or bad, in part by listening to models." [De Bruyn 130]

5. "The ear must be trained to recognize the beauty that is heard in the tone of the artist singer." [Thomas 608; Earhart 153, p. 15]

6. The phonograph may be used "to set up a model tone . . . in objectifying stages of vocal progress." [Seashore 509, p. 92]

7. The pupil should also be taught to listen discriminatingly to the piece of music he is learning to execute, either vocally or instrumentally. [Mursell 412]

8. The singer can learn much by listening to the violin. [Braine 61]

IMITATION AS A FACTOR

Imitation is defined as an "assumption of the form of something regarded as a pattern or model." (W) It is also "the conscious or unconscious patterning of . . . acts, feelings, attitudes, achievements . . . after some model." [Dictionary of Education 706] In vocal training, the teacher often serves as an exemplar of vocal technique, illustrating with his own performance the archetypes of singing artistry that he wishes the student to follow or imitate. This represents an early stage of vocal instruction in which the student, by listening, strives to pattern his own expression after the performances of some worthy model. Out of 20 statements gathered on this subject, 12 endorse imitation as a teaching device; 8 condemn it.

The affirmative opinions are epitomized in the following summarizing statements:

1. "Imitation is an important factor in teaching singing." [Glenn 205]

2. "Imitation is the life of the singing voice." [Waters 646; Kelly 312]

3. The student should learn to imitate the buoyancy, freedom and tonal beauty of the teacher's voice, rather than the exact tone quality. [Votaw 625]

4. "Try to reproduce in your own voice the good qualities" of every good voice you hear. "The imitative faculty will prove a first aid." [Stock 587]

5. In the beginning, the singer needs a model "just as much as the painter or sculptor." Everything is imitation until the individuality begins to assert itself. [Ryan 480]

6. There is no harm in imitating worthy models, providing it is not "mechanical or slavish" imitation. [Frieda Hempel 239]

7. The teacher must be able to illustrate what he wants the pupil to do. Illustration and imitation are the bases of all vocal teaching methods. [Frances Aldà 6, p. 295; Feodor Chaliapin 95]

Those opposed to imitation are represented in the following:

1. Individuality, the basis of artistic interpretation is inhibited by imitative teaching. The great artist must learn always to express individual thought in tone. [Barbareux-Parry 34, p. 301]

2. The teacher must do "more than set up a model" to be copied by imitation. He must set up "an inspiring ideal." [Mursell and Glenn 413, p. 292]

3. "Do not imitate someone else's voice. . . . Find out how your own voice should sound." [New York Singing Teachers Association 420; Key 314, p. 31]

4. Because two voices are never alike, imitation is ruinous to the singer. He may copy technique or occasional interpretative effects but his vocal quality must always remain individual and distinctive. [Witherspoon 677, p. 36]

5. We work against nature when we try to imitate, since no two voices are ever exactly alike. [Wodell 680; Brouillet 64, p. 44]

6. Imitation develops "parrot-like" performance which is inimical to artistic expression. [Owsley 441, p. iv]

SUMMARY AND INTERPRETATION

THEORETICAL CONSIDERATIONS

"Hearing," says Redfield, "is the ultimate goal toward which all musical activities tend." [462, p. 123] The subject of ear training is common ground to most vocal authorities and generalities abound, in the vocal texts examined, concerning the importance of a good ear as a singing requisite. One hundred and fifty-seven statements of specific pedagogical import were gathered, indicating a fairly wide-spread interest in this subject. These statements are summarized in *Table Seven*.

Singing, like any other acoustical phenomenon, depends upon three physical factors: a) a generator of sound, b) a medium of transmission, and c) a receptor or device for receiving (hearing) sounds and interpreting them. None of these three factors can function as such without the other two. It is apparent, therefore, that the act of hearing is inseparably associated with all other functional aspects of voice production and projection.

The terms *ear* and *hearing* are often used synonymously. Authors generally agree that the ear (hearing) is the organ by which initial perceptions of acoustical phenomena are recognized, correlated and controlled for purposes of vocal expression. In other words the ear (hearing) is the monitor that governs both the input and output of sensory impressions of the singing voice. Hence, the importance of ear training to the singer is obvious. Pedagogical discussions of ear training are complicated by the fact that the ear may function in this dual capacity, as both receptor and transmitter of acoustical energy. As a subjective experience, hearing takes place without any conscious effort on the part of the listener. In this process a phenomenon of "central or mental integration" is said to occur whereby external auditory stimuli are fused into intelligible vocal concepts and expressional impulses in the mind of the listener. [Mursell 411, p. 71] On the other hand, hearing may be consciously or objectively directed toward certain tonal experiences.

There is very little objective evidence concerning the relation of the hearing function to the vocal act and most author opinions grow out of empirical observations or guesswork. The theoretical discussions are largely based on the premise that the ear (hearing) intimately governs such vocal actions as phonation, pitch attack, vocal range, resonation and the determination of vocal quality, tonal dynamics and projection factors of voice production. With incredible versatility and selectivity, hearing apparently plays an important role in the vocal act, and it is doubtful whether any performance of the singing voice can be entirely independent of the hearing function. This subject is open to further research. Seashore's findings on the artistic deviations in singers' performances (see Chapter X) are significant. [506]

METHODOLOGICAL CONSIDERATIONS

The psychological approach is preeminent in the pedagogy of ear training. Teaching procedures may be grouped in two main categories which are called *tonal input methods* and *tonal output methods*, depending upon whether they are used primarily to enhance the listening experience exclusively, or to control vocal tone production in singing.

a) *Methods governing tonal input.* For purposes of ear training, the listening experience is completely dissociated from the act of voice production. A rational procedure consisting of the critical analysis of vocal models is advocated, utilizing the performances of artist singers, either on the concert stage or through the media of phonographic recordings and the radio. Profitable listening experiences may also be provided for in the vocal demonstrations of the student's teacher and in listening to the "singing" tones of an instrumental (e.g., violin) performance. Methods of analysis are not given by those who discuss these procedures. It is to be presumed, therefore, that in the absence of objective criteria for evaluating each performance heard, the student will, through exposure, absorb the tonal experience in its entirety, thus improving his tonal consciousness.

b) *Methods governing tonal output.* Pedagogical procedures include the use of tonal imagery, self-listening, vocal models, imitation, and a consideration of the values of sound and sensation as guides to vocal action. These methods frequently overlap and conflict with one another, but each, in its own area of application, is interesting and valuable to the teacher of singing. Self-listening is described as a quasi-objective auditory experience in which the individual attempts to dissociate his preconceptions (imagery) of vocal tone from his objective awareness of what he is actually singing. It is doubtful whether satisfactory coordinations of the vocal organs are possible under such conditions of divided attention and self-analysis. The view that both sound and sensation are effective guides to vocal action would seem to be a tenable compromise in the absence of objective evaluations of either factor. Until convincing experimental data can be obtained as to the efficacy of any of these teaching procedures, one observation appears to be as good as another.

In conclusion, the teacher of singing is reminded that vivid vocal imagery induces adequate vocal response. The listening experience is just as important as the singing experience for it stimulates the forming of ideal concepts of vocal expression. But listening should be free from compulsions and should be carried on as a cultural pursuit, voluntarily indulged in with eager interest and wholesome enjoyment. In this connection, emulation should not be confused with imitation. *Emulation*, according to Webster, is "to strive to equal or excel." *Imitation* is "to follow as a pattern, to copy." The student's exposure to his spoken language over a great many years illustrates a type of unconscious ear training that has influenced his oral expression of speech sounds. Analogously, if he gives the same degree of intelligent attention to listening to good singing his hearing awareness of good singing tones should be considerably enhanced.

CHAPTER IX

CONCEPTS OF DICTION

efinition. In defining diction, it must be borne in mind that language is a synthesis of differentiated vocal and non-vocal sound patterns into larger syllabic and verbal groupings that can be standardized as to meaning. Thus language becomes a means of symbolization and communication of ideas and *diction* is the process of manufacturing these symbols out of vocal raw materials. (W) The *diction* of singing, therefore, may be defined as the clear and accurate formation, production and projection of the elementary sounds of language, and the combining of these sounds into fluent sequential patterns that are suited to the tonal expression of the words and music of a song. [Haywood 237, II, p. 31; Hok 278, p. 31]

Diction comprises three fundamental processes that are significant to the teacher of singing. These are called *articulation, enunciation* and *pronunciation;* terms that are often loosely interchanged in common usage. In a more exact differentiation of terminology the following distinctions might be made, based on dictionary definitions and on the *Outline of Theory* issued by the American Academy of Teachers of Singing. [10]

1. *Articulation* is a *formative* or moulding process, involving organic mechanisms of the vocal tract that incipiently shape the phonetic patterns of the language. This is accomplished by varying the positions, conformations and movements of the vocal organs so as to provide favorable channels of communication for fluent oral utterance. Thus, basic breath and vocal substance are differentiated into intelligible vowel and consonant symbols. [Drew 148; Scott 501, p. 99]

2. *Enunciation* is a *projective,* dynamic or energizing process whereby vocal sonancy or audibility is applied to the vowels and consonants articulated, for purposes of communication to a listener.

3. *Pronunciation* is an *integrative* or combining process whereby vowel and consonant sounds are united into larger rhythmic groupings called syllables, words and phrases. Thus are the elementary sounds of the language finally shaped into the words of song.

TABLE EIGHT

SUMMARY OF CONCEPTS OF DICTION USED IN TRAINING THE
SINGING VOICE

	total number of statements	sub-total	grand total	statements by prof. singers	documented statements	undocumented statements
I. *Theories of diction*			77			
A. General considerations	23	23		1		23
B. Vocal factors in the singer's diction		54				
1. vowel as a vocal vehicle	25			2		25
2. vowel characteristics	16				8	8
3. importance of consonants	13				1	12
II. *Methods of cultivating diction*			177			
A. Psychological approach		41				
1. importance of mental imagery	7					7
2. speaking as a device	28			1	2	26
3. whispering as a device	2					2
4. chanting as a device	4					4
B. Technical approach		136				
1. value of sol-fa training	9					9
2. vowel techniques						
a) importance of *ah* vowel	26			1	3	23
b) lingual controls	17			2	1	16
c) other physical controls	7				3	4
d) various hints	13			1		13
3. vowel alteration						
a) *high pitch vowels are altered*	15			2		15
b) *high pitch vowels are not altered*	7					7
4. consonant techniques						
a) physical controls	9				1	8
b) consonants as tone-interrupters	23			1	2	21
c) interrupters of rhythm: the "time spot"	5					5
d) exaggeration as a device	5					5
TOTALS	254	254	254	11	21	233

The singer's diction is an important factor in the vocal training program. It embodies a technique of tone production in verbal patterns which is prerequisite to the actual singing of songs in any language. [Nicholson 425, p. 95] As early as 1723 Tosi, the noted bel cantist, wrote: "Singers should not ignore the fact that it is the words which elevate them above the instrumentalists." [Henderson 243, p. 104] Tosi permitted the vocal student to use words only after all vowels had been perfected. The study of repertory then began. [Klingstedt 320, p. 21] Pacchiarotti (ca. 1796), who also taught that diction and voice production were interrelated, wrote: "He who knows . . . how to pronounce, knows well how to sing." [Henley 264] According to Proschowski, verbal expression is a product of human intelligence and an indispensable factor in singing technique. The very fact that the human vocal organs can shape the various vowel forms into intelligible patterns distinguishes the singing voice from some mechanical sound product. [453]

It is Howe's opinion that good singing is the natural corollary of good diction. [284, p. 16; also Wharton 655, p. 32] Jones adds that abstract tone production is practically impossible since every vocal tone automatically pronounces something through its acquired vowel resonance. [307, p. 12] Henschel believes that the singer's diction is even more important than his vocalization when considered from the standpoint of interpretation and listener comprehension. [266] Proper diction is the very basis for correct voice production in singing. [Marafioti 368, p. 164] Abbott also suggests that diction and tone production are closely related factors in training the singing voice. "From the very first lessons," he says, "I never separate tone and diction." Furthermore, the pupil must understand that distinct enunciation is a help, not a hindrance, to beautiful tone. [1] Barbareux-Parry and Brown also hold to this view. [34, p. 226; 78, p. 58] According to Austin, "no voice is really a good musical instrument until it has attained some skill in diction." [28] "Perfect diction means perfect singing; one is but a complement to the other," says Obolensky. [432] Henderson suggests that good diction is an exercise in itself for training the singing voice. [240, p. 3] It is also an invaluable medium for helping tonal resonance. [Wettergren 654]

Vowel is the vehicle of voice. Aikin divides the sounds of the language into two groups: a) *"vowels,* due to open and expanded positions of the resonator, suitable for continuous sounds of best possible quality"; and

b) *"consonants,* due to more or less closed positions and movements of the resonator which give certain characteristics to the approach to and departure from the vowel positions." [4] Webster similarly defines *vowels* as "the open, sonorous sounds of a language." Their distinguishing characteristics are determined by the configurations of the vocal passage that accompany phonation. That is, for each distinct vowel sound, there is a definite change in the shape of the pharyngeal and oral cavities, each change being accentuated by characteristic positions of the lips, tongue and palate. Twenty-five authors stress the importance of the vowel as a basic tonal vehicle in singing. Their opinions are summarized in the following statements:

1. "Tone cannot sound forth until it is fixed within the limits of some vowel." [Mme. Schoen-René 493]

2. Singing is an art of words and therefore an art of vowels. [Edward Johnson 306]

3. We do our singing almost entirely upon vowels. [Wodell 681]

4. The vowel is "the melodic part of each syllable." [Howe 284, p. 35]

5. You purify the tone by purifying the vowels. [Waters 641]

6. If the vowel is poor, vocal tone will be adversely affected. [Austin-Ball 31, p. 13]

7. The singing voice "must be fed with vowels and not with mere tone." [Herbert-Caesari 267]

8. "The vowel makes the tone." [Warren 633]

9. "Voice is always vowels." [Hemery 238, p. xii]

10. Correct vowel production is an inevitable concomitant of the correctly produced singing voice, for the perfect voice automatically provides its own perfect vehicles of utterance. [Gescheidt 200, p. 16]

Vowel characteristics. The analysis of vowel resonance has engaged the interest of vocal scientists for some time. Russell's dissertation, *The Vowel* presents an exhaustive study of the physiological causes of vowel quality differences. It is basically a speech, rather than a singing approach, arriving at the conclusion that there is no standard or fixed position of tongue, mouth or other surfaces for any particular vowel sound. There is proof of "radical difference of movement . . . not only from vowel to vowel, but from subject to subject. It is therefore not justifiable to postulate a constant position" for the velum, tongue or mouth. [712, p. 69] Russell goes on to say that a change in one part of the vocal tract "may be compensated for by another" in some other moveable part and that current physiological descriptions regarding vowel positions (e.g., *open, closed, narrow, wide, high, low,* etc.) are "generally fantastic and practically without basis in fact." [Ibid., p. 351]

The exact physiology of vowel production in singing is not yet clearly understood. Harris and Harper still believe that "vowels are formed entirely by the shape of the oral [mouth] cavities." [229, 228, p. 26] But majority opinion holds, with Russell, that the entire vocal passage, including the pharyngeal and throat cavities contribute to the shaping of the vowel resonator. [479] Therefore, it is "the position of the [entire] resonator in forming the vowel sounds that is most important in the art of singing." [Aikin 4]

More recent acoustical research has contributed some interesting information on the subject of vowel analysis. Along with factors of physical shape, position and duration, the acoustical composition of the vowel is also important. That is, a vowel sound is composed of a fundamental pitch frequency (produced at the glottis) and a series of overtones (produced in the resonators). [Stanley 578] This peculiar composition of fundamental and overtones produces, for each standard vowel sound, a characteristic tonal spectrum or formant. (See Chapter V) Negus' description is also typical: Vowels are "a mixture of fundamental and overtones produced at the glottis and modified as to quality by the resonators." [418, p. 440; also Herbert-Caesari 269, p. xiii; Jones 307, p. 5] Stanley also finds that it is the vowel sound that determines the timbre (quality) of the voice at any moment during the singing of a song. Vowel sounds are always determined by the preponderance of "two or three bands of frequencies" in the tonal spectrum (formant). The slightest modification in the position of these frequency bands alters the vowel. Therefore, a wide range of vowel changes is possible in normal voice production. "These bands do not depend upon the fundamental" (pitch) but rather upon the selectivity of the vocal resonators. [Op. cit.]

The vowel formant is apparently determined independently of the pitch of the vocal tone; that is, different vowels may be sounded on the same pitch and the same vowel may be produced on different pitches. Jacobsen describes the vowel formant as a "frequency region where each individual vowel will have an unusual amount of energy, regardless of the pitch [fundamental] at which the vowel is sung." [297] Metfessel reports that the elimination of several overtones in the formant of the vowel *ah* does not change the pitch of the note that is sung. [390] Don Lewis' extensive researches on vocal and vowel resonance are reported in the *Journal of the Acoustical Society of America.* In his findings he pre-sents a typical vowel theory that is summarized as follows:

The vocal cords, during phonation, set up in the air immediately adjacent to them a complex motion which consists of a fundamental component and a large number of its overtones. This complex motion constitutes the so-called cord tone. . . . The vocal cavities, on which the cord tone acts as a force, have the properties of simple resonators and thus serve to modify the spectrum of the energy flowing from the cords. In terms of this theory, a vowel sound, as emitted from the mouth, is due to both selective generation and selective transmission . . . and it is composed *mainly* of a harmonic series of simple motions, each of which has a determinable magnitude. [340]

Thus it is that each vowel is endowed with its own peculiar frequencies and distinguishing characteristics by the cavity in which it is resonated, rather than by the vocal cords alone.

The importance of consonants. According to Webster, *consonants* are the "less sonorous" or less sonant sounds of the language. They are "never sounded alone" but always in combination with a sonant or vocal (vowel) sound. Hence the name *con-sonant*, which literally means "produced with a sonant." The essential feature in the production of consonant sounds is partial or complete obstruction in the voice channel, with or without accompanying breath friction caused by these obstructions (e.g., *s, f, t*). Consonants also vary in intensity, duration and sonancy. Certain consonants, because of their greater sonancy, are called *semi-vowels*. Like the vowels they may be musically intoned and indefinitely prolonged (e.g., *l, m, n*).

The fact that song is a dichotomy of "two equally collaborative elements," the tone and the word, introduces certain complications into the training of the singing voice. Both tonal excellence and verbal significance are essential to the singer. [Grove 216] But, as Graveure sees it, these two indispensable elements are diametrically opposed to each other. On the one hand, to produce voice it is necessary to free all the tone chambers from obstructions; on the other, in order to form the consonants, certain mouth closures are constantly called for. [208] "All pronunciation involves a blocking or shaping of the vocal resonators." [Westerman 651] But because the singer is trying to do these two different things simultaneously he frequently is caught in a condition of "partial inco-ordination which favors neither tone quality nor enunciation." [Bartholomew 39] This conflict between voice production and the enunciation of the consonant sounds calls for consummate skill and refinement in the vocal act which, according to one anonymous writer, explains the scarcity of good singers in the world today. [15]

Brown claims that word, tone and breath are an inseparable trinity in the singer's art. [78, p. 100] Articulation provides form to the word. [Henderson 243, p. 105] "The vowels make the tone, the consonants make the sense," says Nicholson. [425, p. 95; also Clippinger 104, p. 6] "With the use of consonants, vowels become words." [Hemery 238, p. 74] Therefore, the study of the consonants is quite as important as the study of the vowels. [Henley 259; 252] On the other hand, Wilson claims that "the job is not to sing through the consonants, but to get the consonants out of the way so that the vowel will have a chance to sing." [674, p. 38] Grove also believes that "the efficacy of an acquired technique in consonants" will determine the accuracy of vowel enunciation in words. [214] That is to say, "the function of the consonant is to interrupt the vowel without doing violence to the tone." [American Academy of Teachers of Singing 10; 11]

Methods of Cultivating Diction for Singing

PSYCHOLOGICAL APPROACH

Mental imagery as a device. "Think the sound before you sing it" is a common admonition in vocal teaching. Davies believes that by a mental process of aural visualization the inner ear always unconsciously anticipates the vocal utterance of a word. [127, p. 124] "Simply think of the vowel sound to be made," says Combs. [119, p. 12] Other opinions express variations of the same concept. E.g.:

1. *Stanley:* To attack a tone, the singer must first obtain a perfectly clear mental image of the vowel sound. [576, p. 156]

2. *Conklin:* To conceive a vowel mentally is all that is necessary to provide automatic adjustments of all the organs of articulation that enter into the formation of that vowel, including lips and tongue. [121, p. 72]

3. *Wharton:* The first step in perfect diction is "being able to hear and determine quickly what the sustained sound in each word is before it is sung." [655, p. 33]

4. *Benedict:* Mouth shaping plans must be made before the vowel is uttered. Therefore, you must think of the vowel *before* you sing it, but not while you are singing it. [44]

4. *Warren:* "You cannot be casual with pronunciation when singing." Exact mental preparations must be made which will establish both "quality and quantity of the vowel and the consonant" before they are produced. [637]

Speaking as a device. Webster defines *speech* as the faculty of expressing thoughts by means of words or articulated sounds. Speech and song are distinguishable chiefly by their respective acoustical and aesthetic effects rather than by differences in intellectual or thought content. That is to say, "*song* is a type of oral utterance with musical modulations of the voice" representing a stylized melodic version of oral speech communication. In song there is usually strict adherence to a rhythmic musical pattern, with prescribed values of pitch, dynamics and duration for each syllable or word expressed. Also, singing employs wider variations in pitch (range), intensity and duration and is usually more dramatic, poetical and affective in character than speech (W). It is the music that makes singing different than speech. [Lawrence 335, p. 3] Singing requires "definite, separated steps of pitch, while [speech] involves a continuity of pitch." [Mursell and Glenn 413, p. 279] Singing requires at least fifty per cent more vocal energy than normal speech. [Taylor 602, p. 9] Every syllable in the song must be given a definite time value. Slurs and omissions are permitted only in speech, not in singing. [Judd 309, p. 17] Singing, because of its sustained character, requires more breath than speaking. [Conklin 121, p. 30] "In song, pitches are more constant, vowels have more value than consonants, sostenuto is more frequent, agility is easier [e.g., trills], and the intervals are definite." [De Bruyn 131] In singing, vowels are more sustained, there is more vocal vibrato, intensity is greater, range is wider and articulation is more distinct, than in speech. [Stanley 578, p. 441]

In the opinion of 28 authors, there are certain marked differences between singing and speaking; but there are also certain similarities between these two forms of oral expression that can be pedagogically helpful to the singing teacher. For instance, the basic vowel and consonant values of singing find their counterparts in the speech patterns of everyday discourse. Furthermore singing and speaking are both forms of communication that express ideas or thoughts by means of verbal utterance. The singer's diction may, to a certain extent, be influenced and even conditioned by his daily speaking habits. Therefore it is considered necessary to caution the singing student against bad speaking practices which might affect his singing voice. The student must also be taught how to extract the communicative or expressional values of a song by first speaking the text and giving full attention to the meaning of the words.

The New York Singing Teachers Association has promulgated the principle that good diction for singing can be attained "through such automatic use of the speech mechanism as shall eliminate vocal interferences." The speaking habits of the singing student should be supervised to the extent that "the greatest relaxation and freedom" of the vocal organs shall be developed. [421, p. 39] Brainerd advises singers to "speak in low, free tones, [thus] saving the speaking voice as well as the singing voice." [62] "Well spoken is half sung," says Shakespeare. This should be the motto of every singing school. [517, p. 80]

Spier suggests that the exact formation of each consonant should first be practiced silently and in speech before attempting singing. [570, Foreword] Other suggestions and comments relating to the influence of speech on song are summarized in the following statements:

1. "The singer's work will be easier if, as a child, she is never allowed to form slovenly and unbeautiful habits of speech." [Frances Alda 5]

2. "The very first object of the one ambitious to sing well . . . should be to learn to speak well." [Everett 164]

3. Good diction means the acquisition of "perfect speech in singing." [Haywood 234]

4. A correct verbal impulse always impels a correct vocal impulse. Let the word lead the voice in singing. [Gescheidt 200, p. 40; Samuels 487, p. 35]

5. Isolated abstract vowel production makes for difficult and hazardous vocal practice. All vowels should be taught as a part of appropriate words having specific meanings. Thus defined, vowel practice promotes voice production. "Feel that you are talking on the vowel." [Shakespeare 517, p. 28; Henderson 240, p. 37]

6. "We sing the vowels and speak the consonants." [Ryan 480, p. 75]

7. "Every sound, be it vowel or . . . consonant, should be heard like perfect talking as far as the voice can carry." [Shakespeare op. cit., p. 51]

Grove suggests that the presence of an interested listener during the period of practice will help the singer to infuse real meaning into the words of his song. By this means, verbal vowel sounds will acquire "the uncompromising verity of intelligible speech." [216] In a sense, all singing may be influenced by speech. If the vowel in the spoken word were prolonged "as it is in legato singing, there would be less difficulty in training . . . voices. [Chesnutt 96] "Sung vowels are the counterparts of spoken vowels, provided that the speech is correct." [Proschowski 458] On the other hand, Aikin is convinced that diction for singing is entirely unlike spoken diction. "So much latitude is permitted" in ordinary conversational speaking that the singer's diction has acquired a style of its own and is now "looked upon as something quite different from it." [4]

Whispering as a device. Whispering is a type of non-vocal speech that employs only breath sound without tone. (W) Because it does not possess the carrying power of vocal utterance, whispering requires an especially distinct type of enunciation in order to be understood. In a loud whisper the organs of articulation move with exaggerated precision which results in a clear cut delineation of all essential vowel and consonant sounds. Audibility of whispering is accomplished by the background sound of rushing breath as it is forced past partial obstructions in the glottis, throat and mouth. Since the vocal cords do not vibrate, whispering is considered restful to the voice and conducive to relaxation and freedom of the vocal organs. Howe recommends whispering as a technique for testing and practicing vowels. He calls it "an infallible guide to the correct shaping of all vowel sounds." [284, Introduction] Vale considers whispering a cure for indistinct diction. Loud whispering should be audible eight or ten feet away from the singer for best results. [619, p. 34]

Chanting as a device. Chanting is the recitation of the words of a song in a musical monotone. (W) The chanter undergoes all the correct actions necessary for singing except that he does not have to concern himself with variations in pitch, intensity and interpretation. Thus relieved of the control of several variables in singing he can give more attention to problems of intonation and diction. According to De Bruyn, chanting is one of the oldest of vocal methods. It combines "speaking and singing into one unified . . . phonation process." [131]

Mowe recommends chanting as "a good introduction to the use of words" in singing. [405, p. 14] Grove prescribes a monotone (chanting) treatment for all vowel sounds. By separating the vowels from the words of a song it is possible for the singer to scrutinize them individually, thus developing "a keen sense of exact vowel form." [216] Finally, Greene suggests that diction difficulties in a song may be overcome by practicing the intoning (chanting) of an entire phrase on that note which is easy and pleasant to produce, thus diverting attention from the music to the diction and the meaning. [209, p. 142]

TECHNICAL APPROACH

Value of sol-fa training. According to Webster, the term *sol-fa* (also called *solfeggio, solfege* and *solmization*) denotes an exercise based upon the singing of the tones in the scale by the syllable names *do, re, mi,* etc.

As Grove's Dictionary explains it, "to *sol-fa* is to sing a passage or a piece of vocal music, giving to the notes (of the scale), not words, but the syllables Do, Re, Mi, Fa, Sol, La, Si, Do." [708] The use of a set of syllables to denote the tones of a musical scale is considered by some teachers a convenient method of naming and identifying the various pitches in the vocal gamut without the use of printed notation. It is used to help vocal students form aural concepts of pitch-tone relationships and intervals, just as the printed staff and notation are used to form audio-visual concepts of tonal and intervalic relationships. By common usage, the printed note has become an almost universal means of conveying auditory impressions to instrumentalist and vocalist alike. But in certain methods of vocal training, the use of spoken or sung syllable names has partially supplemented the use of printed notation as a studio exercise. Thus vocal exercises *(vocalises)* are frequently printed and sung with sol-fa syllables and any sequential combination of melodic tones may then be described by means of syllable names.

Sol-fa training is more widely endorsed in England than in this country. Many writers of singing texts ignore it entirely as a teaching tool; some consider it obsolete and unnecessary. Those who endorse it are not always explicit as to whether it is used as a vocalise, ear training drill, diction exercise, or method of learning to sing at sight. [Sands 489] According to Mursell and Glenn, "the value of the sol-fa system lies in its power of defining and bringing before the learner the tonality element in vocal music." [413, p. 165] Holl finds the use of solfege stimulating to the ear as well as to the eye. The pupil should always learn by the process of seeing the note; then hearing the note (mentally); then producing the note (physically). Thus the ear would be constantly anticipating and checking the singer's performance instead of merely listening to his performance. [279] (See also Chapter VIII) Scott declares that sol-fa "should be studied by every singer as a primary and fundamental thing." [502, p. 165] The ear of the sol-fa-ist is usually far keener. This is Hill's claim. Besides, the best sight readers are acquainted with sol-fa. [272, p. 42] Lee also believes that sight-singing (sol-fa) study should go side by side with other forms of aural training for singers. [336, p. 43]

Hagara, a vocal historian who writes about bel canto methods, finds solfeggio an important practice medium for perfecting the syllabic diction of consonants and their accompanying vowels. [220, p. 116] Shaw would have all vocal students thoroughly grounded in solfeggio training "before words are used." This would counteract the tendency that consonants have of "interference with the tone producing mechanism." [543]

Wilcox endorses the use of vocalises embodying "all phonetic vowel primes," a type of sol-fa drill. "It is logical to utilize these primes (vowels) in vocal exercises . . . as a foundation for good diction," he says. [666]

VOWEL TECHNIQUES

Importance of the ah vowel. According to Webster, in the formation of a vowel chamber in the vocal tract, there is always a "place of constriction made by a more or less close approximation of some part of the tongue [front or back] to the hard or soft palate." Webster also distinguishes between *front vowels* and *back vowels,* claiming that in the formation of back vowels, the root of the tongue is elevated or bunched up by partial retraction of the entire tongue, while in front vowels the front of the tongue is elevated. This distinction between *front* and *back* vowels is not commonly accepted by vocalists but there is wide agreement that the varying conformations of the vowel tract do strongly influence the vowel sound. Thus the vowel passageway in the vocal tract may vary from the extremely open and free condition for the vowel *ah* to the relatively constricted condition for the vowel *ee.* [Aikin 4]

The *ah* vowel is often called the "open-throat" vowel. (W) Aikin describes the position for the *ah* vowel as that which is most favorable to voice production. "The whole passage is open and expanded to the fullest extent convenient . . . and from it others [vowels] are differentiated." [Op. cit.] Russell takes exception to this viewpoint in his report and analysis of innumerable "x-ray photographs of the tongue and vocal organ positions" of Madame Bori and many other outstanding opera and concert stars. His claim is that experimental investigations clearly indicate that whenever "even the best of the singers [pronounces] a clear and unmistakable" *ah* vowel, the back of the tongue always swells out into the back of the throat near the epiglottis, producing a very small opening or passageway in this part of the throat. [479]

In all, 26 opinions were gathered on this subject, most of them agreeing with Aikin's viewpoint that the practice of *ah* vowels is a basic technique favorable to the cultivation of the singing voice. The *ah* vowel has an additional advantage in that it is also a characteristic sound in Spanish, German, Italian and other European languages. "It is with some slight variations the usual sound of the letter *a* in most other languages." (W) Acoustical analysis of the *ah* vowel reveals that its essential quality is to intensify the phonated larynx sound, "without exerting any considerable modification of its harmonic composition." [Curry 124, p. 58]

The *ah* (sometimes called the *Italian a*) is the closest approximation to the matrix vowel of the singing voice and is therefore a favorite vehicle for practicing various vocalises and diction exercises. As Wodell expresses it, "the *ah* sensation throughout the throat is the model sensation for all the vowels." Thus, a correctly produced *ah* shows forth the possibilities of producing all other vowels. [680] Shakespeare finds that the consonant *l* before *ah* as in *lah* helps to free the tongue and throat. [517, p. 30] Henley also claims that the reiterated *lah* is "the absolute standard for establishing the freedom of the throat" and for tuning the voice to exact pitch. [249] Grete Stueckgold, well known soprano of the Metropolitan Opera Company recommends the *ah* vowel as a basic vocalise for improving diction. "Do not sing exercises on *ah*," she declares. "Place a consonant before it. Sing *ma* or *ba* or *la!*" [594] Fory would alternate the use of *ah* and *oo*. "*Oo* is one of the singer's very best friends," in any type of voice. [188] Hall also recommends that in beginning the study of a song the entire melody should be vocalized on an *oo* sound. [224] Remaining opinions on the importance of the *ah* vowel in training the singer's diction are represented by the following statements:

1. "It is the ideal vowel sound . . . for pure tone production." [Chesnutt 96; Holland 280]

2. Start all vocalizing exercises on the vowel *ah*, "which best lends itself to the free opening" of the throat and mouth cavities. [Lombardi 353; Wodell 679]

3. The *ah* is the best open vowel sound for practice. It should be uttered freely and without restraint. [Henderson 243, p. 45; Hemery 238, p. 74; Lewis 343, p. 2]

4. In attacking chest tones, think *ah* as if it were said at the base of the larynx. Sustain this *ah* mentally for the duration of the tone. [Hagara 220, p. 37]

Sands reports that modern vocal methods have not varied greatly from those used in the days of Porpora (ca. 1750). Legato, *messa di voce* (Chapter VII) and the open *ah* techniques were in vogue then as now. [489; also Orton 439, p. 81] In a dissenting opinion, Philip claims that *ah* is the most difficult vowel sound to place because it is the most open sound. Therefore "it is inadvisable to commence . . . with the *ah*." [446, p. 101] Finally, Wilson cautions the singing student against the careless substitution of *uh* for *ah*. This is "one of the most harmful of practices. . . . It thickens and deadens the voice." [674, II, p. 20]

Lingual controls. The tongue is the principal organ of diction "employed in changing the various configurations of the mouth" so as to produce the different sounds of the language. (W) In vowel production the front of the tongue is considered less active than in consonant production. [Robinson 473; Austin-Ball 31, p. 50] Hence, in order to prevent obstructions in the oral orifice and to keep the rather bulky lingual muscle from slipping back into the throat during singing, vocal students are often advised to keep the front of the tongue low in the mouth, while lightly touching the lower front teeth. This position provides a useful orientation point for the limited range of lingual movement that is characteristic of consonantal diction in song. [Allen 7, p. 75] (See also Chapter IV) The 17 opinions gathered on this subject are summarized in the following:

1. The old masters taught that the tongue must be *allowed* to lie flat at the bottom of the mouth during the *ah* vowel. It must not be forced there. [Henderson 243, p. 46]

2. For the series of vowels from *ah* to *oo,* "the tongue should lie flat, or even a little concave, in the pit of the mouth." [Scott 500, p. 40; 502, p. 24]

3. The tongue tip should touch "the roots of the lower front teeth as in a half yawn" on all vowels. Complete relaxation of the tongue is also prescribed. [Samuel 486, Lesson 6]

4. Learn to sing or speak all the vowels with a flat, wide tongue position that is forward and low in the mouth. [Wycoff 696; Olden 434]

5. "Unless it is needed for the formation of certain consonants like l, n, r," keep the tongue as flat and as relaxed as possible in the mouth. "It should not be pushed back, raised up, or allowed to move" for vowel sounds. [Kerstin Thorborg 611; Jacques 299, p. 17]

6. For the forming of every vowel the tongue lies relaxed on the front teeth. [Waters 646; 645]

In a dissenting opinion, Russell insists (as a result of his X-ray observations of singers) that the position of the tongue in singing is largely "dependent upon the consonants that precede and follow the vowel." The tip of the tongue does not always rest against the lower teeth as is commonly advised. Nor does it appear that changes in tongue position in any way change the quality of the singing voice. [479]

Other physical controls. Stanley advises all singers to practice pharyngeal vowel production since this will obviate the necessity of moving the mouth, lips and front tongue for the pronunciation of vowel sounds. Any singer can, with a little practice, learn to "hold his mouth and lips in constant position and produce practically all the vowel sounds." Conversely, "a singer who uses his voice correctly . . . can retain a constant vowel" sound while widely varying the position of his lips and jaw. [578] Wilcox and Lloyd likewise favor the use of the pharynx and throat rather than the mouth for vowel formation. Since all vowels are properly shaped in the back of the mouth and throat, the lips should never actively participate in forming vowels. [669, p. 28; 351, p. 8] Coleman suggests that the mouth should be shaped before, not during, the attack of a singing vowel [118, p. 36], while Henley believes that "certain positions of the mouth, tongue, jaws and lips" can be used to accentuate the vowel sound and to induce "greater freedom" of vowel emission. [264] According to Russell, there is proof that the movement of the velum (palate) and other such surfaces differs radically "not only from vowel to vowel, but from subject to subject. . . . It is therefore not justifiable to postulate a constant position" for the velum, tongue or mouth. [479; also 712, p. 69]

Various hints for improving vowel attack. In correct attack, the vowel is formed simultaneously with the release of the tone. The singer is cautioned to prepare his vowel sound in advance of the attack so that nondescript vocal murmurs that glide into the correct vowel may be obviated. [Conklin 121, p. 33] For clean-cut diction in singing, words and music must be made to coincide. Furthermore, diction in singing is usually much slower and more sustained than in speech. This is especially true of vowel sounds whose duration must strictly conform to the time values of the notes that are sung. [Lawrence 335, p. 10] "Always start the tone with the diction," warns King. Instead of listening for tone, try listening for vowel. [316] In the effort to make a big tone, students often neglect their vowels with resultant impaired intelligibility of the words of a song. Giving full attention to vowel attack will correct this tendency. [Skiles 561]

A comment on diphthong vowels is added at this point. "A *diphthong* is a compound, but continuous, vowel sound" consisting of two blended vowels that are pronounced in one syllable. (W) Skiles claims that it is futile to attempt to master diphthong vowels before mastering the individual production and blending of its constituent elements. [554] Henschel offers a useful hint for improving diction and vowel attack. It is to practice the rendition of an entire song on nothing but vowels. [265, p. 8] Wilson would have the student practice various songs "by singing them on a (single) sustained vowel; especially *ah, oh* and *ooh*." [674, II, p. 20]

Continuity of vocal sound is considered an important factor in the singer's diction. The fact that the vowel is the vehicle of voice reminds the singer of the importance of maintaining fluent connections between the vowels of a song. Edward Johnson, manager of the Metropolitan Opera Company, advises singers to carry the voice from vowel to vowel "like a string of pearls," without interrupting the flow of sound. Consonants should be quick, firm and distinct but not distracting. [306] "The job is not to sing through the consonants, but to get the consonants out of the way so that the vowel will have a chance to sing." [Wilson op. cit., p. 38] According to Grove, "tonal expediency cannot justify vowel substitution and its inevitable verbal chaos." [213] Jacobsen advances the interesting theory that each vowel is easiest to sing when it is produced on a pitch level that most closely approximates its characteristic dominant frequency band or formant. Much off-pitch singing could thus be overcome. The correct pitch for each vowel could be arrived at by experimentation (presumably trial-and-error singing) until the singer discovered for himself which vowels were easiest to sing on each pitch of his vocal range. Some songs would have to be reworded so as to bring the various vowels into more favorable pitch positions for ease in singing. These positions would be different in male and female voices. [297]

Vowel alteration on high pitches. The practice of vowel alteration (also called *covering* in male and female voices) is believed to be an outgrowth of the occurrence of register breaks in the singing voice. As the beginning vocalist sings up the scale he transcends the regular compass of his speaking voice and enters a relatively unused and therefore undeveloped portion of his vocal range. Here the tone quality weakens appreciably, especially in the male voice, and there is considerable instability of pitch and volume at one or more points, often accompanied by "fluttering" or "breaks." (See Chapter V) To overcome the suddenness of the transition from well developed to undeveloped portions of the vocal gamut, a firming action of the vocal organs is introduced just before the break or point of greatest weakness is reached. This firming or strengthening action serves to splice the break in the voice. It involves the action of external laryngeal muscles that assist the vocal cords in maintaining maximum tension for high pitched tones. [Curry 124, p. 72] (See also Chapter III)

This physiological action is not yet clearly understood by singing teachers and is therefore approached indirectly by means of an empirical teaching device called "covering." This is taught largely by trial and error methods, often with accompanying distortion or alteration of vowel sounds above a certain point in the range, depending upon the type of voice that is being trained. Sound and sensation are the main criteria for identifying and evaluating "covered" tones. Henley claims in his article on "training the male voice" that we have inherited our use of covered tones from the masters of bel canto in the early eighteenth century. Pupils were then taught that "pronunciation of words, on high notes especially, must be modified for the sake of beauty." [258] Various reasons have been advanced for the use of covered tones in singing. Of the 22 statements gathered on this subject 15 are in favor of using this device to facilitate the singing of high pitches while 7 protest against its use. There is no conclusive argument on either side of the controversy and the opinions summarized below merely serve to present the case for those who are interested in pursuing it further.

VOWELS SHOULD BE ALTERED

1. Pure vowels are easiest to produce only within the speaking range, which is usually only an octave or less. Therefore, "some degree of vowel modification always takes place in the more extreme pitches of the register." [Austin-Ball 31, p. 52; Judd 309, p. 29]

2. Modifying (covering) the vowels in the upper registers helps "to reduce the physical strain of their production to a minimum." [Philip 446, p. 130]

3. It is best to alter the vowel "at the point where discomfort sets in," to avoid the quality of a scream or shout in the tone. When covering, focus the tone well forward. [Armstrong 24]

4. "The covered tone, although it lessens the amount of tone, adds richness, and thus maintains a legato." [Gould 206, p. 45]

5. "A covered tone is not a smothered tone. . . . It is simply an emphasis of post-nasal resonance." The use of *ing* or *ung* are the best methods for developing the covering action. [Wilson 674, II, p. 8]

6. Women singers will find relief in the head voice when adding a slight *a* (as in *hat*) to any vowel. [Henley 253]

7. "Always think *oo* into the upper tones, whatever the vowel." [Bushell 82; Hall 224]

8. The vowel *oo* is always blended with the ascending tone when it is being covered. [Lilli Lehmann 337, p. 81]

9. To experience the sensation of covering high tones, expand the back of your mouth as if about to bite into a large, round apple while singing these tones. [Margit Bokor 54]

VOWELS SHOULD NOT BE ALTERED

1. Pure vowels can be sung throughout the vocal range without modification. [Henderson 243, p. 110; Thomas 607]

2. Within the entire range of the voice, it should be possible to sing any vowel, and therefore any word, with equal facility. [Evetts and Worthington 167, p. 42]

3. "There is no physical reason for any change of pronunciation owing to pitch." [Scott 501, p. 52; 500, p. 41]

4. It is important to be able to attack any pitch in your range in medium voice and on any vowel. [Waters 647, p. 48]

CONSONANT TECHNIQUES

Physical controls. It will be recalled that consonants are the less sonorous sounds of the language; that, unlike the vowels, they are produced by "audible friction, squeezing or stopping of the breath in some part of the mouth or throat." (W) Since the valve-like narrowing or stopping of the oral passage is fundamental to the production of most consonant sounds, some form of muscular action is necessary. Thus, various parts of the oral cavity are brought into play to produce the consonants. (E.g., tongue, lips, palate.)

To the singer, the consonant positions are, as a rule, easier to recognize than the vowel positions since the former are usually plainly visible to the eye. Furthermore, for obvious vocal reasons, the singer's consonants must be made clearly and distinctly "without doing violence to the tone." That is, the movements of the tongue and other parts must be subordinated to the free release of the vowel sound. The chief function of the tongue (consonants), says Lloyd, "is to separate the syllables [vowels] into different lengths, and to do nothing else!" [351, p. 16] In singing, the differentiation of the consonant sounds of the language is accomplished almost entirely by the various tongue and lip positions, while the vowel sound acts as "a sort of carrier" of vocal tone. However, consonant and vowel positions do influence each other and must therefore be coordinated to provide optimum conditions of vocal release. [Harper 228, p. 64 ff.]

Pronunciation of consonants should engage only the front half of the mouth, "leaving the throat unconscious," according to Jones. [307, p. 12] Owsley would have pronunciation function automatically, except that the singer must always "be conscious of the soft palate and roof of the mouth." [441, p. 97] Three other physical controls are suggested. Wharton finds that "an inward smile, not a grin," arches the palate and promotes freedom of tongue action in enunciation. [655, p. 95] Lloyd recommends trilling the *r* as "a fine practice for relaxation of the tongue." [351, · p. 18]; and Novello-Davies advises the student to practice the lip and tongue movements of word formations both silently and aloud as an exercise for improving diction. [430, p. 129]

Consonants as interrupters of tone. Consonants are regarded by 23 authors as antivocal elements; that is, as interrupters of tone. Mme. Galli-Curci, noted diva, reminds the student he must always sing on the vowels since the consonants "are merely the divisions between the vowels." "Consonants have no carrying power. . . . If you hang onto the consonants, you kill the legato," [197] Benedict advises the use of consonants that have pitch for beginning practice. Such consonants as *l, m, n, r, v, z,* and *ng* "can be sung on every pitch of the vocal range." [44; also Clippinger 104, p. 26] The sounds of l, m, n, are really hybrids (semi-vowels), according to Henderson and Palmer. They have time values and combine consonant treatment with the duration values of vowels. Therefore they are less antagonistic to the voice in singing. [242, p. 356]

Never practice isolated consonants, is Hagara's advice. In perfect diction, the consonant must always accompany the vowel that follows it. [220, p. 64] Other opinions in this category are represented in the following summarizing statements:

1. Vowels are vocal sustainers. Consonants are vocal interrupters. [Taylor 602, p. 13; Hjortsvang 276, p. 119]

2. The singer's slogan should be "vowels long, consonants short." [Shaw 537]

3. The consonants should be quickly articulated "so that the 'ribbon' of sound is almost unbroken." [Young 698]

4. Singing requires the ability to use consonantal diction without allowing the throat and vocal passage to be come constricted in any way. [Bartholomew 40]

5. Consonants, unlike vowels, are sounds that may not be sustained. Therefore, their production should be quick and clearly defined. [Maybee 381, p. 8; Fory 187]

6. Throughout the entire compass of the voice, the singer must be able to enunciate all the consonants distinctly and delicately, without sacrificing any of the quality of the vocal tone. [Patterson 440; Wharton 655, p. 34]

7. The singer should never forget these two fundamental facts: a)

only a vowel can sustain a full vocal tone; b) a consonant is "an interruption of the sustained tone." [Douty 142]

Consonants as interrupters of rhythm: the "time spot." Rhythm is the accentual structure of music, based on the succession of beats or time units. (W) In singing, the time value of the rhythm is usually distributed among the syllabic vowel sounds contained in the words of a song. Thus, each vowel, because it is both vocal and prolongable, becomes a variable component of the rhythmical structure of the song. From the singer's standpoint, consonants, being interrupters of vocal tone, are also interrupters of rhythm. To overcome this rhythmical antagonism of the consonants, singers are warned to sound each vowel, regardless of its consonantal attachments, exactly on the time-spot; the *time-spot* being the exact moment that the musical note begins. Thus, the rhythm of the melodic line is always maintained. [Howe 284, p. 35] "The rule is very simple," says Scott. "Consonants should be sounded before the beat; vowels on the beat." [501, p. 106] Young believes that, at the beginning of a word that starts with sounds like *br, cl, th, s, f,* consonants "should actually precede the musical accent" so that the time-spot may be accurately struck by the vowel. [698] Benedict advises the singer to break the phrase unit with the consonant sound, rather than on the vowel so that the imperceptible phrasing pauses may not detract from the time values of vowel sounds which begin or end the phrase. In other words, "commence exactly on the time of the note instead of slightly before," for words beginning with consonants. [44] Henschel also insists that consonants must be sung on the note of the syllable to which the consonant belongs. [266]

Exaggeration as a device. Exaggeration is defined as a process of extravagant delineation of action. (W) In diction, exaggeration is a means of overstressing or accentuating the value of a sound by making it abnormally prominent in the word in which it appears. Exaggeration is suggested as a device for improving diction in singing. Jeffries claims that the best method of improving diction for song is "to read aloud, exaggerating all consonants, till distinctness becomes habitual." [301] Stanley advises that "all consonants should be articulated with great vigor and extreme rapidity" as an exercise for singers. [578] Finally, Novello-Davies offers this suggestion: In training the singing voice, "vowels should be quickly threaded, not jerked, on to exaggerated consonants. Correct placement will inevitably result." She adds that the exaggeration of consonants in word practice "gives strength, grace and facility in singing," and that the greatest Italian artists, including Caruso, always stressed the consonants.

Those who claim that the Italians considered vowels more important than consonants in singing are mistaken. [430, pp. 35, 127, 131]

SUMMARY AND INTERPRETATION

THEORETICAL CONSIDERATIONS

There is considerable agreement among vocal authorities on most of the 19 topics treated in this chapter. By simplification and correlation, 254 statements on singer's diction have been summarized and classified. These classifications appear in condensed form in *Table Eight*. Theoretical and methodological groupings comprise separate treatments of vowel and consonant factors in singing and a comparison of the characteristics of singing and speaking diction.

The cultivation of the singer's diction gains preeminence in the vocal training program because of its fundamental importance in the production of vocal tone and because diction is the basic medium of textual interpretation. Song-speech values also have a special pedagogical interest. In song, the vocal factor is always uppermost whereas in speech, the voice may become a subordinate factor. Webster defines *singing* as a type of oral (vocal) expression uttered "with musical inflections or modulations of voice"; and *speaking* as the utterance of words or articulate sounds "with ordinary modulations of the voice, as opposed to singing." Obviously, the distinction is mainly a musical one, although, in the application of vocal teaching procedures, the singing voice receives specialized preparatory training that distinguishes it from the speaking voice. From the standpoint of communicability, the same law of expression undoubtedly applies to both the singing and the speaking voice. Nevertheless there are significant technical differences between the two; differences that are illustrated in the vocalist's modification of his daily speaking habits to suit the requirements of singing. Such differences are further accentuated by the intensification and predominance of vowel, vocal and musical factors in the language of song and the acceptabliity of certain aesthetic, poetic and dramatic effects in singing that would be considered artificial and ludicrous mannerisms in the language of speech.

The rhythmic regularity of singing and the stricter requirements of uninterrupted phrasing, the wider scope and greater variability of range, dynamics and tempo, all call for physical development and coordinations of the breathing and vocal organs that are beyond the requirements of normal conversational discourse. Otto Ortmann, in his *Notes on Recent Music Research* [437], reports that "the muscular coordination involved in singing is not present in the usual throat position . . . [of] normal speech. Consequently, inferences from the speaking voice cannot be directly applied to the singing voice." The following résumé provides a further reminder that song and speech values are not readily interchangeable. (See also Chapter II)

Characteristics that distinguish the diction of singing

1. The vocal pitch range of the singing voice exceeds the average pitch range of the speaking voice by from one to two octaves. (Chapter VI)

2. Resonance and projection factors are far more important and more conspicuous than in the speaking voice.

3. Musical and aesthetic requirements of singing are much more exacting than in speaking, sometimes requiring a subordination of intelligibility to tone production.

4. Singing employs more stylized, sustained, dramatic, declamatory and intensified forms of expression than speech, with greater emphasis laid upon emotional and aesthetic factors than upon the intellectual content of the words.

5. Individual vocal (vowel) tones are sustained on definite pitches.

6. Pitch intervals between various vocal tones are easily discernible.

7. Individual vocal (vowel) tones have a prescribed duration or time value.

8. Musical factors such as staccato, legato, attack, rests and phrasing are featured elements in the expression of song.

9. Dynamic or intensity values of all vocal tones and combinations of tones are prescribed by the musical pattern.

10. Measured swelling and diminishing effects are often used.

11. The duration of vocal tones conforms to a definite rhythmic pattern.

12. Vocal tones move deliberately through pitch intervals that conform to a prescribed melodic pattern.

13. Pauses have definite rhythmic values, even at cadences and endings.

Further generalizations that are derived from the foregoing theoretical discussions are as follows:

1. Diction (in singing) is the adaptation of the art of verbal communication to the language of song.

2. The physical basis of the diction of the singing voice is the breath.

3. In order to produce articulate phonetic symbols of the language, the expiring current of breath must be modified in the vocal tract, first through a process of phonation, then through a definite configuration of the vocal tract (vowel formation) and finally through the adjustment (valving) of the tongue and other parts of the oral cavity at the place where the phonetic symbols are intelligibly produced.

4. Vowels and consonants are elementary forms of voice that provide basic vehicles of intelligible oral utterance for the singing voice.

5. Vowels and consonants are classified with reference to their physiological or organic formations and also according to their acoustical effects.

6. The basis of vocal training for singing is the vowel, which is also the basic audibility factor in the singing voice.

7. In singing, vowels generally have more vocal value than consonants.

METHODOLOGICAL CONSIDERATIONS

Various techniques of vocal instruction are presented in the 177 methodological statements that have been gathered in this area. Most of them are opinionated assertions, based on haphazard teaching procedures and empirical observations that claim superiority for one particular method of teaching diction while ignoring the others. Undocumented and untested studio procedures such as these do not always provide the best teaching materials. The inexperienced teacher is often compelled to select for himself, out of this accumulation of ideas, those methods that show promise of meeting his individual requirements, without the possibility of first testing or evaluating them by scientific means. Until all these teaching methods are reported "out of committee" by trained investigators, their true value as haphazard contributions to that large body of information that now constitutes the basic pedagogy of singing is still in question.

Techniques of diction are held to be closely associated with techniques of vocal tone production. To the singer, the vowels are important tonal and rhythmic factors and consonants are anti-vocal elements and interrupters of tone and rhythm. Intelligibility is a prime requisite in singing, but the singer's diction never sacrifices vocal purity for clear enunciation. It is also believed that, although singing and speaking are independent arts, requiring different techniques of instruction, nevertheless, the benefits of training the singing voice accrue to the speaking voice and the benefits of clear spoken diction are also transferable to singing. Hence certain speaking techniques are recommended as having possible values for cultivating diction in singing. Other techniques discussed include the use of mental imagery or the proper conception of vowel sounds as a basic approach to the intonation of integrated verbal patterns; sol-fa training; certain lingual controls; vowel alteration; and various consonant techniques which already have been adequately described.

In general, techniques for cultivating a singer's diction represent two different schools of thought which may be described as follows:

a) *Tone is subordinated to text.* Sing-as-you-speak methods are favored by this group. At first, vocal and musical values of the song are entirely ignored, while the meaning of the text is studied. The words of the song are then "tried out" by utilizing them in appropriate speaking situations in which their communication values are made obvious to the singer. As a final step, the musical vocal pattern is grafted onto the spoken message, only after the student has captured its essential meaning. Thus, before he attempts to execute the vocal requirements of his song, the student will have learned to emphasize the interpretation of the text. (See Chapter II) This indirect approach employs whole methods of instruction. Verbal expression in singing is improved, not by practicing the vowel and consonant sounds separately, but by a phrase-wise approach in which whole ideas and their accompanying moods are expressed at once. Vocal exercises may be practiced separately, to improve abstract tone production, but not so as to disturb the integrity of verbal expression.

b) *Text is subordinated to tone.* In this procedure, the song is first stripped of its verbal context and then treated as a series of vocal exercises. The emphasis is now laid upon the various vowel forms, individual consonants and syllabic combinations of these, that will provide vehicles of vocal tone in the rendition of the song. Part methods of instruction are employed, in a teaching procedure that first analyzes the text of a song into parts or units of technique embodying various technical problems such as vowel resonance, covering, tongue position, etc. The individual parts are then practiced separately until reasonable skill has been attained and these separate skills are finally synthesized into the continuous pattern that represents the finished song.

In conclusion, it might be advisable to caution the singer against the common tendency to acquire an artificial style of diction for singing. One of the most common failings of singers is their inability to impart the meaning of the text effectively to their listeners. In most such instances, this failure is not caused by lack of comprehension but rather by inattention to factors of communication in song. Words are studied with mechanical precision but without thoroughly understanding their underlying meaning and mood. Even after many repetitions of a song, a singer will often find it difficult to paraphrase a would-be expressive passage so as to communicate its essential thought content.

The student should also be reminded that quiet expressiveness in singing can be just as conducive to good diction as bombastic or exaggerated utterance. The much derided crooning style of singing has as its main virtue that it combines maximum ease of tone production with maximum verbal intelligibility, a style that approximates the effortless expressiveness of casual conversation. Although this type of "conversational singing" has been widely condemned by teachers of "operatic singing" because it is said to devitalize the voice, nevertheless the vocal student might benefit from a comparison of his own diction while he quietly sings a song in a conversational style, with his rendition of the same text when it is sung with full volume and declamatory vocal effects. Teaching methods that foster the cultivation of tonal ease combined with maximum intelligibility of diction from the very inception of vocal study can do much to enhance the artistic stature of the student singer.

CHAPTER X

CONCEPTS OF INTERPRETATION

Definition. Interpretation is generally defined as: "an artist's way of expressing . . . his conception of the subject of his art." (W) In singing, interpretation is the final rendering of a piece of vocal music so that its fullest meaning is intelligible to a listener. [Henschel 265, p. 3] The process of vocal interpretation involves a) apprehension, or the faculty by which musical ideas are conceived and understood; and b) representation, or the act of portraying and imparting these ideas to an audience by means of appropriate audible and visible symbols. Thus, interpretation in singing has its inception in the proper analysis and absorption of the meaning, intent and mood of a song by the singer himself, a subjective process; and it reaches fulfillment in the out-picturing or vivid indication of these elements in communicable patterns of expression. [Owsley 441, p. 62]

The terminology of interpretation is fairly extensive, reaching into many adjacent but non-vocal areas and also into advanced operatic and concert fields that lie beyond the scope of this study. Such general technical terms as grace-notes, syncopation, phrasing, crescendo, tempo-rubato, for example, have general musical connotations that are not peculiar to vocal science and therefore, not within the scope of a vocal terminology. In all, 354 statements are classified as concepts of interpretation that pertain to the basic training of the singing voice. These are categorically summarized in Table Nine.

THEORIES OF INTERPRETATION

GENERAL CONSIDERATIONS

The nature and importance of interpretation. "If I were asked to define the singer's art," says Frieda Hempel, "I should not explain it in terms of vocal technic. I should say that it lies in the ability to move an audience." The singer who only performs notes is merely a technician. [239] The art

TABLE NINE

SUMMARY OF CONCEPTS OF INTERPRETATION USED IN TRAINING THE
SINGING VOICE

	total number of statements	sub-total	grand total	statements by prof. singers	documented statements	undocumented statements
I. *Theories of interpretation*			37			
A. General considerations	20	20		1	2	18
B. Artistic deviations in performance	17	17				17
II. *Methods of cultivating interpretational skill*			317			
A. Psychological approach		174				
1. visualization as a factor	10			1	2	8
2. motivation as a factor						
a) emotional emphasis	25			5	1	24
b) personality emphasis	14			1	4	10
c) interpretational emphasis	22			6		22
3. mastery of the text						
a) text comes before tone	18					18
b) "speaking the song"	74			7		74
c) recitative as a factor	11					11
B. Technical approach		143				
1. criteria of song selection	20			1	1	19
2. foreign language study						
a) *foreign language study is essential*	21			4		21
b) *foreign language study is not essential*	7					7
3. techniques used in interpretation						
a) memorization as a factor	5					5
b) note connection: legato and staccato	29			2	2	27
c) variety and tone color	12			1		12
d) various factors in song analysis	7					7
4. performance aspects						
a) visible factors of performance	8					8
b) criteria of artistic performance	34			5		34
TOTALS	354	354	354	34	29	325

of interpretation, therefore, really belongs to the final or culminating stage in the training of the singing voice, encompassing all basic elements of vocal technique and also the attainment of virtuosity in expressing the language of song. "It is the highest branch of the singer's art." [Greene 209, p. 1]

The art of interpretation includes many variables of vocal expression, such as pitch, intensity and duration of tone, and their composite effect upon the quality of the singing voice. Negus claims that mammals and birds have evolved the highest forms of intercommunication because of the greatest variations of pitch and loudness attained by these species. [418, p. 344] Vocal nuance reaches its greatest flexibility in man, according to Brown, because of the prevalence of ideational and emotional factors in his thinking processes. Subtlety of thought demands subtlety of expression. Therefore, the singing of a song is something more than the mere combination of breathing, phonation and pronunciation. That which is added is the interpretative factor, an illusory coordinating intelligence that synchronizes "the subtle powers of mind and body . . . to a common end." [75] Through the inherent flexibility of man's thought, then, great flexibility of expression is developed since the idea always begets its own medium of utterance. If the interpretation is poor, either the concept is at fault or the conditions of the instrument are not right, or both. "Have something to say, and know how to say it." [Clippinger 112; 104, p. 48]

"Intelligent interpretation . . . is the end and aim of singing," says Brines. Without it, the song degenerates into the merest choice of words for the expression of ideas and is completely devoid of interest and aesthetic appeal. [63] According to Greene, the interpretation of a song includes more than lyric quality and clear diction. It also requires an intensified, personal expression of the meaning. [Op. cit., p. 145; also Henderson 240, p. 67] "The psychological relations between the performer and listener must be worked out." [Seashore 506, p. 118] Mood and meaning are concomitant factors of interpretation; one "expresses in music the emotions of the soul, while the other expresses in words the poetic thoughts of the mind." This duality of thought and emotion is conveyed in the phraseology, style, musical expressiveness and vocabulary of the song. [Aikin 4] According to Kwartin, the primary elements of interpretation are musical, vocal and verbal. All three combine to present a dramatic "tone portrayal" of the song. [325, p. 96] " 'In the beginning was the word' seems to be an accurate description of the genesis of song," says Douty. The word inspires the melody and "the emotion engendered by it brings the song to birth." [143] Thus, a multiple function devolves upon the verbal context of the song. [Lawrence 335, p. 15]

Another frequently mentioned element in interpretation is *style,* a term that Webster defines as "a distinctive or characteristic mode of presentation, construction or execution in any art." In singing, *style* is the distinctive or characteristic manner or method of performing a song that exhibits "the spirit and faculty" of the artist. (W) Greene stresses the importance of individuality in style. "Individuality," he says, "is the antithesis of self-consciousness and conventionality." [209, p. 36] Haywood uses *style* to denote general or group characteristics of singers, while *interpretation* is used to describe individual characteristics and differences. [233] In a later discussion of interpretation, he lists such factors as rhythm, tempi, phrasing, melody, nuance, diction, and the use of accent, climax and contrasts in word and phrase. All these song factors are subject to personal differences of interpretation. [234; also Herbert-Caesari 269, p. 6] According to Henderson, style is distinguished from interpretation in that the former is general and denotes the character of a period, school or master, while the latter is particular in that it discloses the individuality of the singer. It is apparent, therefore, that individual differences in singing are more obvious in the interpretative than in any other aspects of vocal expression. [243, p. 149]

Artistic deviations in performance. One of the most striking discoveries in the field of interpretation is the prevalent tendency of leading vocal artists to make minute individual deviations from the notated values in a musical score, during their singing performances. Scientific measurements taken by Seashore, Metfessel, Stevens and Miles, and others, clearly indicate that absolute standards of performance among artist singers are practically non-existent. Metfessel sums up his findings as follows in the *Bulletin of the American Musicological Society:* "No two musical performances, or for that matter, no two behaviors of any kind, are exactly alike. The notated pitch and rhythm of a musical selection are never rendered precisely. From measurements of sound waves from the violin and the voice, it is possible to find out just how much deviation there is in artistic performances." [391]

Seashore and Tiffin believe that these minute individual differences in performance, in their totality, serve to distinguish one artist's interpretation from another and contribute to the aesthetic effect. "One is struck with the great liberty that the artist takes with the conventional musical notes. Presumably the beauty in the rendition lies in the artistic deviation from the conventional notes, both as to pitch and time." [508] As a result of his later extensive researches in the same field, Seashore writes, more emphatically, that "no singer . . . sings in true pitch, even dynamics, metronomic time or uniform tone quality. If he did, he could not possibly be regarded as a good singer. [505] Among Seashore's more significant findings are the following:

a) In about 25% of the tones sung, the artist never even touches the correct mean-pitch level. In about 75% of the tones, the correct pitch level is only momentarily attained within the duration value of the note. [506, p. 56]

b) Approximately 40% of the tone to tone pitch connections are accompanied by imperceptible portamento (gliding) transitions; about 35% are level pitch attacks, following a minute pause; and about 25% are gliding attacks following a minute pause. [Ibid., p. 73]

c) About 55% of the tones sung are ended with a level release and 45% have a gliding release, usually falling. [Ibid.]

d) Artistic singing lies not in strict conformance to fixed values of pitch, intensity, time and quality, but rather in deviation from these. [511, p. 21]

e) Singers perform by habit, not by exact technical control of the voice; i.e., vocal effects are learned empirically by constant repetition. [506, p. 74]

f) Singers agree on what is good, but they disagree on what they are doing. [Ibid.]

g) The gliding attack or release is not to be condemned since it is "an important medium for softening the contour of the tone." [509, p. 271]

h) In expressing specific emotions in song, the artist singer "takes great freedom with the score, usually supplementing the song with dramatic accessories," essential to his interpretation. [504]

Metfessel also finds that emotional expression, even in artistic singing, adversely affects the pitch accuracy of the voice, causing minute and subtle deviations from true pitch that play an essential part in creating the emotional effect intended. He cautions the singer, however, that "no implication is intended that performers should strive to deviate from pitch." [391] All these reports of scientific studies clearly indicate that the errors found in pitch attack among singers "are not due to motor skill deficiency or to auditory misjudgements, but are deviations necessary for the legato flow of the song." [19]

PSYCHOLOGICAL APPROACH

Visualization as a factor. As previously defined (Chapter VIII), *visualization* is the faculty of forming mental images of conditions or things not actually present to the senses. In the cultivation of interpretational skill in singing, an essential factor is the formation of clean-cut mental concepts of vocal tones and tonal combinations in their proper musical and textual settings. The opinion held by 10 authors is summed up in Stanley's words: "The ability to conceive groups of tones is a vital part of the innate talent for singing. . . . If it is lacking, the pupil . . . can never become an artist." [578]

A certain freedom and continuity of expression is acquired by those singers whose interpretations follow a preconceived mental pattern. "You must be singing before you begin!" was maestro Lamperti's motto, according to Brown. Continuity is achieved by entertaining the concept that the music of the song is but the "division of one tone." This concept must be held before the phrase is started and during its complete utterance. In other words, the mind is never silent during the performance of a song. It is always either singing or preparing, so that the mental effect is that of a continuously spinning tone. Thus, the momentum of singing is never arrested, since each succeeding phrase is mentally being prepared while the singer is still on the preceding one. Diction and interpretation should never interrupt the flow of tone. [78, pp. 47 and 67] Skiles declares that "the real artist first sings his songs mentally." [557, p. 14] Jessica Dragonette is of the same opinion. [146] A singer "worthy of the name" will always "know beforehand [mentally] what a passage will sound like." [Hill 272, p. 49] Deliberate and detailed mental planning are always necessary in preparing a song. The success of your interpretation depends upon it. [Jones 307, p. 11; Williamson 672]

MOTIVATION AS A FACTOR

Motivation is defined as the mental and emotional excitement aroused in a singer by the recognition of those ideas and values in a song that appeal to his native interest and understanding, and that stimulate him to spontaneous and enthusiastic self-expression. This definition, derived from Webster and the *Dictionary of Education* [706] clarifies the pedagogical intent of 61 statements that were gathered on the subject of motivation in singing. These statements are grouped in three categories: a) those that emphasize the emotional content of the song; b) those that emphasize the personality of the singer; and c) those that emphasize general interpretational factors.

Emotional emphasis. In a broad sense, an *emotion* is a state of mind characterized by feelings of pleasantness or unpleasantness, in varying degrees and combinations, accompanying mental or physical experiences. (W) To emphasize the emotional content of a song is to give force, prominence or vividness of expression to the more or less variable complex of feelings that accompanies its interpretation. Sherman reports (in the *Journal of Experimental Psychology*) that emotional characteristics of the singing voice can often be apprehended from qualitative vocal attributes, without the aid of outside clues. [547] However, two schools of thought are represented in the 25 opinions gathered on this subject. In the first group are those who believe that the emotional interpretation of a song should always be simulated; that genuine emotional feeling would be dangerous if not destructive to the singer's voice. "The effect of every moment of every scene must be prepared, calculated, studied and rehearsed in advance many times." Furthermore, the experienced artist knows exactly what tones, looks and gestures he must employ to secure these effects. This is the opinion of Bidu Sayao, well known Brazilian soprano of the Metropolitan Opera Company. [491] Her opinion is seconded by A. M. Henderson who emphatically adds that it is not the singer's business to feel emotions but to make the audience feel them. Therefore, a singer's interpretation must always be convincing, though simulated. [240, p. 73] "We must distinguish between the having of an emotion and the expression of it," says Seashore. [505] Do not sing your personal feelings, no matter how real they are. Get entirely away from yourself when you sing the song. [Roland Hayes 232; Dunkin 150]

In the second group are those who believe that a singer must genuinely feel the emotions of his song and must impart his actual feelings to his listeners while singing. The following representative concepts summarize this viewpoint:

1. Always "give back" the mood of the music you sing with sincere feeling. [Geraldine Farrar 171]

2. "The trick is . . . to live one's song." [Emma Otero 440]

3. "The emotional significance of the song" must be thoroughly absorbed before the singer can communicate it through his voice. [Lawrence Tibbett 614]

4. Singing is something you feel, rather than something you do. [Kirkpatrick 317; Brainard 60]

5. In order to supply deficiencies in the color of the voice, the teacher will find it profitable to arouse genuine feelings in the singer's voice. [Samuels 487, p. 38]

6. "The mood of the song is the mood of the singer." [Wharton 655, p. 55; also Austin 30]

7. "Only what comes from the heart will go to the heart." [Samoiloff 485]

8. True feeling puts both warmth and color into voice. [Holscher 281; Abney 2]

Personality emphasis. Personality (from *persona:* a mask) is the outward manifestation of individuality, or the sum total of characteristic traits and patterns of behavior that outwardly distinguish one person from another. (W) The concept of personality emphasis in training the singing voice is variously explained by 14 authors. Mursell believes that, because the singing voice really outpictures the singer's personality, the vocal teacher's task is to develop singing personalities, rather than to cultivate routine mechanical skills that are completely dissociated from personality. [411, p. 224 ff.] "The same song can be sung with very different conceptions" by different artists, says Lotte Lehmann. "There is no right or wrong way." For, just as personalities (individualities) differ, so will the interpretations of a song differ. [338] "When we listen to . . . good singing, we are not enjoying a mechanically perfect device, but the creative utterance of a musical personality. . . . It is not the child's voice that sings; it is the child who sings." [Mursell and Glenn 413, pp. 285 and 293]

"Voice should [always] be the spontaneous expression of [the singer's] personality," says Jessica Dragonette, in an interview. [146] "Put your whole personality into the song" is Christine Little's advice. [349] Giddings holds that individual singing develops the personality of the singer, a worth-while accomplishment. [201] These three authors maintain that the singer has a message that can only be expressed by his personality. Therefore, personality emphasis in singing is paramount. According to Seashore, individual differences in interpretation are inevitable. "After all," he says, "a musical score is a very crude way for a composer to convey all the ideas he wishes to convey. The singer must, of necessity, regard the score as the barest reference pattern." [515] The singer's mental processes contribute as much to the performance as the score markings; and interpretation is therefore always essentially individual. [Herbert-Caesari 269, p. xiv; Greene 209, p. 3]

Interpretational emphasis in singing requires the proper subordination of the technical factors of voice production. Twenty-two statements support this opinion. Davies believes that the singer should aim to sing a word rather than to make a tone. The word, which is thought made audible, is always the vehicle of tone, and voice production should be regarded as a mental rather than a physical experience. [127, p. 124] The accomplished artist always sings thoughts, rather than mere tones, "Voice must grow out of language." [Edward Johnson 306] Lawrence Tibbett believes that vocal and interpretative techniques should be learned simultaneously. "It is inconceivable," he says, "that one could first learn to sing the notes of a song and then graft a layer of 'interpretation' over them. . . . [Therefore] I am inclined to approach the entire question of study from the interpretative rather than the purely vocal standpoint." [614] Witherspoon holds that "technique and expression are inseparable." [677, p. 7] Lotte Lehmann is of the same opinion. "The ideal way would be to teach singing and stagecraft [interpretation] together from the very start." [339] According to Margit Bokor, a master of technique always gives the impression that he is without technique; in short, the art is to conceal the art. [54; Judd 309, p. 32]

Other opinions in this group are summed up in the following representative statements:

1. Interpretation is a form of "story telling." Therefore, the singer must forget himself (technique) in the expression of the song. [Brines 63]

2. Interpretation demands freedom from technical cares so that thought may be directed exclusively to the mental rather than the physical factors of expression. [Conklin 121, p. 48; Parrish 442]

3. No technical accomplishment is worthy of a singer unless it seems effortless and unobtrusive to the listener. [Henschel 265, p. 7; Henderson and Palmer 242, p. 11]

4. "Sing a word rather than . . . a tone." [Divver 138, p. 42]

5. Mechanized vocal training tends to stifle originality since it divides the attention between production and interpretation. [Barbareux-Parry 34, p. 111]

6. In Caruso's singing, thought and feeling were always uppermost. He refused to make "the words slaves to the tones." [Marafioti 368, p. 8]

7. The singing voice is a reflex action. When the tone is sufficiently motivated, the entire vocal instrument automatically "springs to life, independent of thought and muscle, yet served by both." [Brown 72; Tillery 616]

MASTERY OF THE TEXT

The original words of a song constitute its *text*. Interpreting the *text* of a song is the vocal expression of its words, poem, subject matter, thought content, message and meaning, with all their implications of emotional and intellectual interpretation, as distinguished from the mere rendition of the musical score or musical and instrumental accompaniment. (W) Songs without words are instrumental compositions. Vocal songs always use a text. [Henderson 243, p. 103]

Text comes before tone in vocal study. Eighteen authors believe, with La Forge, that "the poem is the point of departure" in studying singing. [327] "The first requisite of the vocalist is to be understood," says Philip. [446, p. 99] Technical ability is directionless unless the singer has "some distinct mental intention in singing." [Aikin 4] Greene voices a dissenting opinion, however. He insists that although intelligibility of meaning is important in interpreting a song, "the music must always come first" and may not be subordinated. [209, p. 121] Other affirmative opinions are summarized in the following statements:

1. "The word phrase [always] governs the musical phrase. . . . The major moods of the poem are invariably associated with the harmonic structure and melodic action" of the song. [Haywood 234; also Vale 619, p. 44]

2. Interpretation will be enhanced if the meaning of the words is first understood. [Wilson 673, p. 97]

3. Never begin with the music; first consider the text. [Eustis 163]

4. Singing is "the vitalization of text by musical tone . . . the creation of the [vocal] tone must be for that purpose and that alone." [Henderson 243, p. 7]

5. "Learn the text first so that you will know what you are singing about." [Ryan 480, p. 76]

"Speaking the song." Speech and song are distinguishable largely by the formalities and style of vocal utterance related to each. (Chapter IX) When stripped of its musical score, the text of a song can be rendered in spoken style as a means of capturing and accentuating its essential thought content. [Conklin 121, p. 47] When so performed, the words of a song can be made to resemble intensified or declamatory spoken utterances, thereby eliminating many complexities of oral and musical expression and facilitating the comprehension of the text. Seventy-four authors recommend this type of speaking approach to the study of interpretation in singing.

"Singing should be as easy and as natural as talking. And it is," says Conrad Thibault. [605] Frieda Hempel recommends that the study of a song should begin "away from the music, working entirely from the text. . . . Recite it, as a poem." [239] Emilio de Gogorza reminds teachers that singers should be taught to declaim "before they are allowed to sing." [134] "Learn the story of a song. Singing a song is telling a story in music." [Jeanette MacDonald 363] "Leave the business of singing alone until you have thoroughly mastered the [spoken] text," is Lotte Lehmann's advice. Song is "a wonderful interweaving of word and tone. The text must be sung, therefore, as though it were created to be recited." [338; 339] "Speak every word you sing." [Divver 138, p. 37; Cristy 97, p. 42] "Song is easiest when it most resembles speech." [Bairstow, Dent and others 32; Sands 489] Vocal modulations and pitch changes are as free in singing as in speaking. The psychological motivation is the same in both. [Evetts and Worthington 167, p. 131; Marafioti 368, p. 151]

Owsley describes song as the "union of sustained vocal tone and words. . . . The problems of the singer, then, is to coordinate the results between the organs of phonation and those of speech." [441, p. 80] Remaining opinions of the speech-song exponents are epitomized in the following typical concepts:

1. "The desire to say something" influences the production of all vocal tones in singing. [Williamson 672]

2. "We must sing as we speak." [Proschowski 453]

3. Vocal modulations for speaking are acquired without difficulty at an early age. "The same should be true of singing." [Medonis 587, p. 1]

4. A good interpreter in song is also a good reciter. [Henschel 265]

5. "The [spoken] word is the primary essential of good singing." [Skiles 562]

6. The amateur singer should learn to read aloud. [Hill 272, p. 49]

7. "Good singing is good speech sustained." [Wood 685, p. 14; also Tapper 601]

8. "We should sing with the same abandon that we use in speech." [Smallman and Wilcox 566, p. 8]

9. Singers should practice reading poetry aloud for verbal expression only. [Drew 148]

10. In studying vocalises, think of speaking rather than singing the syllables, since speech promotes spontaneous vocal action. [Barbareux-Parry 34]

11. "Practice pitching or tuning" the words in a song by using the "free and natural inflections" of speech. [Howe 284, p. 63]

12. "When people begin to study singing they are astonished to find that they have never learned to speak." [Passe 443, p. 64]

13. The simplicity and ease of enunciation in speaking should be captured and carried into singing. Tongue, larynx and mouth will then remain at ease. [Henderson 243, p. 119; Wycoff 695; Maybee 382, p. 6]

14. Vocal and dramatic technique should be studied simutaneously. "Ability to read the text of a song intelligently, dramatically, and to carry over such a reading into the singing is essential to good song interpretation." [Wagner 627; Lawrence Tibbett 614]

15. Effective singing elicits the same expressional activity that is present in dramatic speaking. The breath is vitalized and colored with the intensity of impassioned utterance. Effective interpretation demands speech in song. A singer must talk sense in his songs. Intelligibility of meaning is derived from the same values that obtain in intelligible speaking. [Greene 209, p. 27]

16. "There is no singing without saying; that which is sung must also be said." Richard Wagner's idea of vocal training was to make the vocalist "really and distinctly speak in singing." Beginners might remain seated while practicing their vocal exercises, as if they were merely talking to the teacher. [Owsley 441, p. 91; Marafioti 368, pp. 72, 182 and 271]

17. "If the student does not sing the vowel [word] correctly, ask him to speak it." [Clippinger 104, p. 13]

18. "Song is intoned recitation." [Jetson-Ryder 304]

19. "Select a phrase and have the pupil begin to speak it, gradually, more and more sliding into a sustained pitch, and ending in singing." Employ this technique with an entire song. Caruso always sang as he spoke. [De Bruyn 131]

20. After memorizing the text of a song, recite it aloud in order to experience the projection of its spoken message. [Conklin op. cit.]

Recitative as a factor. The art of *recitative* is defined as "a species of musical recitation in which the words are delivered in a manner resembling declamation. . . . Recitative is thus characterized by freedom from strict form," being oratorical rather than melodic in its phrasing. (W) In this respect, it is closely related to speaking. Certain explanations appearing in Grove's *Musical Dictionary* are also useful to the teacher of singing. Recitative is described as "language in song," or the declamatory

portion of a vocal composition (usually an opera or an oratorio) as opposed to the lyrical portion. Recitative may appear either accompanied
(stromentato) or unaccompanied *(secco)*. In either case, the syllabic values
of the language are expressed "in a quasi-mensural plain-song," often producing melodic contours that are as free as those of speech. Some recitatives have a melodic form which makes them musical works of the first
order. Some seek expressiveness "through a strained use of vocal orna-
ment." But the characteristic of good recitative, even when it is sung in
strict time, is that it "gives with extraordinary fidelity the accentual value
to the words which belongs to good speaking and emphasizes the broad
sense of the text." [708, vol. IV, pp. 294 and 337]

Eleven authors claim that it is this close relationship to speech that
makes recitative a useful medium for studying interpretational and diction factors in singing. W. J. Henderson writes that in the delivery of unaccompanied *(secco)* recitative it is especially important that "the first
thought . . . be given to the text. . . . The music is altogether a secondary consideration." [243, p. 136] A. M. Henderson recommends the use of
"recitatives from the classic masters" as an excellent form of practice in
verbal (textual) emphasis. [240, p. 72] In recitative, "the phrases have
more of the nature of impassioned speech," emphasizing the "intelligent
and interested expression of the text." [Shaw 521]

According to Barbareux-Parry, a masterful rendition of recitative is always the sign of a vocal artist. It involves singing with the ease of speech
throughout the entire compass, a condition possible only with perfectly
balanced tone production. [34, p. 263] In recitative, the singer's interpretation is the focus of attention; the accompaniment recedes into the background. [209, p. 157] Its success depends upon "the proper capturing of
mood." [Samuels 487, p. 40] Finally, W. J. Henderson warns the student
vocalist that recitative is still song. It is not to be shouted, cackled or
barked but rendered musically, with musical accent and emphasis kept
intact. However, in delivering recitative, the important point is "what is
said in singing, and not what is sung in the saying." In other words, meaning and mood are to be considered more important here than melody.
[243, pp. 141 and 145]

TECHNICAL APPROACH

Criteria of song selection. Grove's Dictionary defines *song* as: "a short
metrical composition whose meaning is conveyed by the combined force
of words and melody." [708] According to Webster, *song* is "a melody
or musical setting for a lyric poem or ballad; . . . a lyrical poem adapted
to vocal music." La Forge describes song as "a [musical] composition

which explains, beautifies, illustrates or clarifies a poem. If it does none of these, it is not worthy to be called a song." [327] Apparently the singer must make the important distinction that song is not merely instrumental music. "It is poetry allied to music; it tells a story." [Bairstow, Dent, et al. 32]

Many classifications of song are mentioned by authors, including the following: oratorio, opera and recitative; concert song, ballad and aria; folk and art song, classical and modern; liturgical mass, hymn and cantata; lieder; operetta; atmospheric, dramatic, romantic and lyric songs; narrative, florid, character and humorous songs; etc. [E.g., Greene 209, p. 201; Stanley 577, p. 215; Kwartin 325, p. 105] A comprehensive analysis and comparison of these song forms is beyond the scope of this study. But the methods of song selection used by teachers in the training of the singing voice have a pedagogical interest since the singing of songs is a widely accepted medium of vocal study. Suggestions embodied in the 20 statements gathered on this subject are represented in the following concepts:

1. The very first requisite for selecting a new song for study is that "it shall so lie within the singer's vocal compass that he or she can sing its every tone without the least effort or constriction." [Bellporte 43; Elverson 161] (See also discussion of *tessitura* in Chapter VI)

2. The tessitura of the student's voice should also match the predominant range (tessitura) of the music sung. [Evetts and Worthington 167, p. 33]

3. The mental focus in singing must be equivalent to the vocal tessitura in that the point of major interest (climax) in a song is directly related to the range of vocal movement. [Greene 209, p. 102]

4. "My own preference is to open a program with a slow, sustained aria or song" requiring full voice. This helps to warm up the voice and also to overcome nervousness. [Nino Martini 374]

5. Simple songs are an important part of the student's early training. [Allen 7, p. 80]

6. The singer must consider the element of audience appeal in choosing his songs. "Artistry is not voice alone, it is also communication." [Armstrong 21]

7. Never sing a song in public that sounds as if it were too difficult for the singer. [Brines 63]

8. Never allow songs to become stale; avoid boredom caused by lack of variety either in choice of song or in style of rendition. [Jacques 299, p. 67]

9. "Talking" songs which tell a simple melodic story are the best singing materials to use for the first year's study. [Barbareux-Parry 34, p. 279]

10. The pieces you love are the best music to choose for your singing repertoire. [Wood 686, p. 18]

Three general comments are added to guide teachers in selecting song materials for their vocal students. Jacobsen advises against the use of texts that have been translated from another language. They are more difficult to handle in early studies and they often "seem to lose a good deal through translation" and the changing of the vowel sounds. [297] La Forest takes exception to the exclusive use of easy and simple songs for early repertoire. Simple songs are often too exacting and are therefore really difficult to the student. In simple songs, "the bare tone has to stand forth sustained, unaided and with perfect evenness." [326, p. 143] Finally, Easley points out two common differences between opera and concert songs; differences that are likely to influence the choice of early study materials. The opera aria is usually much more difficult than the concert song because a) it contains more "vocal gymnastics" and b) it usually expresses "more than one mood or emotional tone." [154]

FOREIGN LANGUAGE STUDY AS A FACTOR

The literature of song is varied and extensive, encompassing many nationalities and many languages. Grove's Dictionary lists seventeen separate categories of national song literature in Europe alone. "The song of each nation has qualities and idioms of its own as distinct and definite as those of its language." [708, vol. V, p. 1] Although many translations of favorite foreign song texts are available to English speaking vocal students, nevertheless, a vast foreign song literature is still inaccessible to beginning singers who are unfamiliar with foreign languages. The question of studying foreign languages as an essential factor in the early training of the singing voice is therefore of pedagogical interest. Of the 28 authors who discuss this subject, 21 endorse foreign language study, with emphasis upon Italian, and 7 are opposed to the foreign language requirement. The following arguments, pro and con, are interesting, though inconclusive:

Frances Alda would have the singer who is preparing for opera study four basic languages: Italian, French, German and English. [5] Blatherwick adds Spanish to the four mentioned, claiming that "versatility is acquired through studying the songs of many languages." [52] Wharton's unusual argument is that singing a song in a foreign language allows the beginning student to hide imperfections more easily before an audience, thus escaping embarrassing public criticisms. [655, p. 34]

There is also some comment as to the danger of allowing the faults of daily speaking to creep into the singing voice. Drew claims that beginners would do well to practice with meaningless vowels and with the songs of an unfamiliar foreign language, to prevent colorless conversational traits from influencing the singing voice. [147, p. 162] Edward Johnson advises against singing "one's own language" because bad speaking habits invariably carry over into singing when the singer's own language is employed. [306] According to La Forest, "the higher ratio of consonants to vowels in the English language makes it a more difficult medium of song than either Italian or French." [326, p. 143] Wolfe writes that "the singer must learn the foreign language to interpret a foreign song properly. . . . Good literal translations are rare and practically impossible. . . . Much of the intrinsic beauty is sacrificed in translations." [684] Wilcox deplores the lack of good English texts for foreign songs. He believes that when the public begins to demand good English translations, writers and publishers will supply them. But American teachers and singers must first stop the "silly custom of singing foreign languages to audiences who cannot understand them." [669, p. 40 and p. 45]

Arguments in favor of having singers study Italian as a first language are summarized as follows:

1. Vowel purity predominates in the Italian language. [E.g., Wilcox op. cit., p. 46; Cimini 99]

2. Study Italian "because of its superior euphony." [Owsley 441, p. 75]

3. The classic Italian arias are basic to all vocal training methods. [Gruen 217]

4. Italian "brings out the voice and vowel to fullest advantage." [Kempf 313; Valeri 620]

5. Italian is free from aspirate sounds. [Brown 78, p. 7]

6. It is best for pure tone production. [Witherspoon 677, p. 18]

7. Italian "abounds in open syllables" and is therefore conducive to legato singing. [Curry 124, p. 106]

8. The Italian arias "are easier for the voice and lay the foundation for greater finesse." [Frieda Hempel 239; Hagara 220, p. 15]

A negative viewpoint toward foreign language study for beginners is led by Norton who claims that "a song has little value in any language if the audience does not get the text. . . . Good tone quality is possible in English." [429] It is wrong to assume that English is not as good for singing as some other languages. "The trouble lies with the singer, not the language." [Skiles 562; also Parrish 442] "English can be as beautiful as any language if you dwell on the vowels," is Byers opinion. [89, p. 338] Greene claims that English has acquired a poor reputation only because translations are poor. Literal translations from foreign languages make for cramped and clumsy interpretations. He further advises that, in translating songs into English, it is necessary to give the poetic equivalent rather than the exact meaning of the text. In this way idiomatic usage is maintained and English singing is thereby enhanced. [209, p. 139]

TECHNIQUES USED IN INTERPRETATION

Memorization as a factor. Memorization is a mental process involving the ability to retain and reproduce, in full detail, a piece of music previously learned. (W) To the vocalist, this process of committing a song to memory is the basis of building a musical repertoire. A good interpreter always memorizes his songs in every detail. [Greene op. cit., p. 12; Waters 647, p. 104] Author opinion generally supports this belief. Pierce holds that the singer should memorize exercises as well as songs. [447, p. ix] Memorization also develops accuracy and self-assurance in singing. "You must be able to sing a phrase twice before you try to sing it once," says Brown. [78, p. 116; also La Forest 326, p. 144]

Note connection: legato and staccato. Note connection is the conjunction or continuity of consecutive tones or pitches in a melody. (W) "*Melody* is a flowing of tone on a succession of varying pitches, punctuated by phrasing and propelled by rhythm." [Haywood 233] Melody is pitch in motion. [Ortmann 438, p. 7] In the last analysis, melody is really "heightened [vocal] inflection." [La Forest 326, p. 144] In its melodic aspects, the art of singing rests upon the ability to produce a succession of single vocal tones, either conjunctly or disjunctly, in an arrangement that conforms to a given musical pattern. [Harris and Evanson 230, p. xiii] The melodious inflection of the singing voice as it moves from tone to tone (each tone having a definite pitch, duration and volume) therefore involves a technique of note connection that is related to the process of interpretation. Two fundamental types of note connection are emphasized in the 29 statements gathered on this subject. They are: a) the *legato* of smoothly connected type, in which a tenuous but imperceptible gliding intonation is maintained, without breaks, between successive tones.

(When the gliding connection between two tones is perceptible to the ear it is called a *portamento connection*. [Henderson 243, p. 86]); b) the *staccato* or disconnected type, in which notes are cut short or apart by minute gaps of silence. [Kwartin 325, p. 93] Other types of note connection (such as martellato, appogiatura, filar-di-voce, etc.) are employed in singing and instrumental performance, involving variations and gradations of these two fundamental forms in various rhythms and intensities.

According to Grove's Dictionary, a legato style of singing is always presumed in the notation of music unless indications to the contrary are given. "The ability to take breath with as little interruption of tone as possible is a first essential of (legato) technique." [708, vol. III] Various comments and hints on the two basic techniques of note (tone) connection are summarized in the following representative statements:

LEGATO:

1. Vocal continuity (legato) is the singer's greatest asset. The "principle of joining" was one of the precepts of the old masters. Johannes Hiller, founder of the *German Singspiel* (1764) is quoted as saying, "He who knows not how to join, knows not how to sing." [Henley 250; 264]

2. The Italian bel cantists emphasized pure legato singing "from first to last," thus assuring a steady flow of tone. [Klingstedt 320, p. 22; Hok 278, p. 22]

3. "A straight tone line" between two consonants assures the best possible vocal output. [Benedict 44]

4. Singing songs on vowels only will produce a perfect legato. Consonants can be "slipped in their proper places" without losing the tone line. [Byers 89]

5. Strict legato singing excludes all jarring, all sudden outbursts; it is a flowing river of sound in which "no sense of jerkiness is apparent to either singer or listener." [Wharton 655, p. 60]

6. Dissolve one vowel into another. [Brown 78, p. 23]

7. In pure legato singing, the successive tones are clearly separated . . . but closely joined to each other." [Margit Bokor 54]

8. For "straight line" phrasing, your vowel tone must never stop. [Greene 209, p. 316; Waters 647, p. 35]

9. Transitions from tone to tone are made "on a single vibrato." [Stanley 578]

10. True legato is "the instantaneous substitution of one tone for another," without a break. [La Forest 326, p. 180]

11. "Think and sing in terms of groups of notes" and short phrases, rather than in individual notes and syllables. [Karapetoff 310]

STACCATO:

1. The correct staccato is controlled by an automatic breath reflex similar to "a hearty belly laugh." Like the laugh, it must sound spontaneous. [Stults 597]

2. There is a "short stroke of the diaphragm" on each staccato tone [Owsley 441, p. 95]

3. "Staccato is entirely a glottic action, a rapid starting and stopping of the vocal cords." [Clippinger 104, p. 38]

4. The vocal cords leap together and fly apart again on every staccato note. Therefore, to strengthen the vocal cords, practice the staccato action countless times. [Henley 247]

5. Staccato practice builds "vocal surety . . . and develops flexibility in the arching of the soft palate." [Elizabeth Schumann 498]

Importance of variety and tone color. Variety is the diversification of interpretative effects in the rendition of a song, brought about by the intermixture or succession of different qualities or characteristics of vocal expression. It is opposed to *monotony* which is a mechanical and stereotyped sameness throughout the performance. (W) *Color*, in a literal sense, denotes the quality or timbre of the voice; that is, the various shades of vowel quality. [Clippinger 104, p. 12] In a more general sense, however, color refers to those characteristics of the singer's voice that give "life, vivacity, reality or imaginative intensity" to his expression; a composite of subtle gradations in tonal quality and dynamics that vividly portrays the imagery and mood suggested by the text of the song. (W) "Tone color is that modulation in the voice that is expressive of the singer's emotions." [Samuels 487, p. 38; Lewis 343, p. 57] The comments of 12 authors are summarized here.

"I do not always sing a song the same way," says Lotte Lehmann. "The singer who in himself is not capable of changing conceptions would certainly be no creative artist." [338] Originality in interpretation is important. The tone quality must be varied at will "to suit the character of the song." [Karapetoff 310] Originality (variety), always the mark of the genius, may be defined as "a personal rearrangement of experience or ideas." [Hemery 238, p. 108] Mursell and Glenn admonish the vocal student against what is called "straight line singing." Interpretations must be made to vary with the meaning of the text. Important words require special attention. "To sing all words with equal stress . . . is bad singing." [413, p. 289] Variety of tone color is synonymous with warmth of expression, according to Luckstone. [360] Judd likewise insists that "understanding and sympathetic feeling" are necessary for the command of vocal color. [309] Austin-Ball holds that, however beautiful the voice, it will become monotonous "if there is no variety of color in one's singing." [31, p. 40] Stanley adds that each phrase should be given its own peculiar color, according to the meaning expressed, thus "modifying each and every vowel sound in the phrase." [578]

Various factors in song analysis. Henderson and Palmer list the following twelve stages of study in the preparatory analysis of a song:

1) read the lyric (text) silently while listening to the melody;

2) commit the melody to memory, without the words;

3) determine the musical key and all its changes;

4) recite the words aloud, with meaning, until they are thoroughly learned and understood;

5) divide the song into phrase and breathing units;

6) settle all doubtful points of diction;

7) determine the tempo and pace;

8) learn the dynamics;

9) work out melodic climaxes and special rhythmic problems;

10) lay out a plan of interpretation and learn it;

11) decide the predominant mood and all its various changes and gradations;

12) learn to express the song with your own personality and style. [242, p. 150]

Marsh gives only three steps for studying the interpretation of a song:

1. "Know the meaning of the story," with its verbal context.

2. "Know the rhythm and mood that the composer has chosen to express in the story."

3. "Know the melody perfectly, note by note." [372]

"Introduce a song as a whole," says Wilson, "including words, music and interpretation. Then the song may be analyzed and each element studied separately." [674, p. 5] Lawrence and Samuels both suggest that the best way to practice interpretation is to learn the meaning of the words separately from the tune. Then, while singing or humming the tune without the words, try to express the "spirit of the song" which the words are intended to convey. Ultimately you may add the words to the tune. [335, p. 16; 487, p. 47] Henderson warns the singer not to ignore accented and emphasized words and syllables. "Every word has an accented syllable and every sentence [phrase] an emphasized word." [240, p. 68] Finally, Lardizabal lists six obstacles to the easy learning of a song. They are: unattractive material; over-repetition; unhappy or distressed mental set; too much direction and instruction regarding the song; over-emphasis of theory (too much analysis); and too many preparatory exercises and vocalises. [334]

PERFORMANCE ASPECTS

Visible factors of performance. The singer's *performance* is the outward fulfillment of the act of vocal expression, representing a detailed elaboration of musical and interpretative elements as they are conveyed to a listener. (W) In other words, performance is the final achievement of visible and audible communication in singing. In it, the expressive motions of the face and body (gestures) also serve to accentuate the expression of ideas and feelings and as such they provide visible indices of concomitant mental and emotional states occurring during the interpretation of a song. Hence they are significant factors in the training of the singing voice and should be watched. "The personal appearance of the singer is of the greatest importance," says Bushell, in an essay on poise in singing. "Therefore, an easy, graceful, buoyant position is an essential and should be cultivated in front of a mirror from the very first lesson." [84] Scott's advice is to "let every movement connected with singing be quick and energetic . . . always under control." [501, p. 50] Wagner finds that changes in facial expression affect the changes in tone quality. "Hence," he says, "facial expression should not be neglected by the student or teacher of interpretation." [627] Conversely, correct vocal emission is free from accompanying tensions in the mouth, face or eyes. [Shakespeare 517] Mursell and Glenn also emphasize the freedom of the facial muscles (e.g., cheeks, tongue and jaw). They suggest that facial relaxation may be induced "by setting up a pleasurable and interesting situation, to which it is a natural response." [413, p. 287] Finally, Clippinger advises the student singer to "look the song" he is singing. "His face is a mirror in which the listener may see the song as definitely as he hears it." [104, p. 5]

Criteria of artistic performance. According to Webster, the *artist* is one in whom "imagination and aesthetic taste preside over the execution" of a skillful technique. Therefore, an artist singer would be one who applies consummate skill, imagination and taste in the expression of a song. Various minimum requirements for artistic performance are set forth in the 34 statements gathered on this subject. They are summarized as follows:

1. The artist always exceeds the minimum technical requirements of his performance while the student seldom reaches beyond them. [Stanley 577, p. 295]

2. An amateur is often unaware of the effect created; the artist "is deliberately attempting to secure a desired stylistic effect." [Wharton 655, p. 70]

3. Agility and the ability "to play with your voice" at will is the mark of an artist. A flexible voice imparts "ease, grace and fluency of delivery." [Maurice-Jacquet 380; Henderson 243, p. 102; Wilson 674, II, p. 46]

4. The artist interpreter sustains the attention and interest of his listeners throughout his song, without allowing even a momentary lapse of interest from start to finish. [Wagner 627; Woodside 690, p. 15]

5. Avoid analysis during performance. "See, hear and feel the entire work as a whole." [Brown 68]

6. "The song, the singer and the accompaniment must be one"; in perfect harmony and understanding. [Galli-Curci 197]

7. "Think of beauty and you will forget yourself." [Louise Homer 282]

8. The work of the artist must always be distinctive and outstanding, never ordinary. [Galli-Curci op. cit.]

9. Artistic performance, especially in opera, requires superior breath control, "to encompass long phrases" with ease. [Zinka Milanov 397]

10. The mark of an artist is the singing of a good adagio. [Scott 501, p. 88]

11. An artist must have a superb legato in uniform quality over more than two octaves of range. [Waters 642; Giddings 202]

12. Sing to yourself, not to your audience. "If you thrill yourself, you will thrill your audience." [Clark and Leland 101, p. 14]

13. "Perfect intonation, absolute steadiness of sound and beauty of timbre . . . are the tripod of [artistic] voice production." [Blatherwick 51; also Wodell 681]

14. Effortless production, agility and a full, flexible range of perfectly matched tones denote the "ideal" voice. [Samoiloff 484, p. 7] To the foregoing, add good diction. [Judd 309, Introduction]

15. The artistic voice is free from constriction and strain, even on high notes, and never distorts vowels. "If the listener is not charmed and engrossed, the singer is wrong." [Capell 92]

16. Six criteria for artistic performance are: naturalness, clear diction, sustaining one mood throughout, a convincing personality, sincerity and showmanship (stage presence). [Henderson and Palmer 242, p. 30]

17. Musicianship, imagination and good, flexible tonal quality combine to produce an artistic interpretation. [McIntyre 385]

18. The artist sings *with* effect, not *for* effect! [Henderson 240, p. 63]

19. Above all, create the illusion of the "first time"! That is, sing "as if yours was the very first performance anywhere and you the very first privileged interpreter!" [Henschel 266]

20. Flexibility, an essential in artistic performance, is the ability to sing rapid passages easily and accurately. [Bowlly 59, p. 93]

21. The artist always uses bel canto, or purity of tone production, blending each successive tone into an unbroken, flowing line. [Jarmila Novotna 431]

22. Dexterity, expert phrasing, legato, tonal beauty and purity of diction are all essential attributes of bel canto singing, a style that enters into the artistic interpretation of most songs. [Woodside 690, p. 18]

23. To become an artist singer, it is not enough to be a proficient vocalist. You must also be a good enough musician to utilize your vocal abilities in musical expression. [Wilcox 669, p. 49]

24. Personal magnetism is an individual gift indispensable to the interpreter along with an acquired technique, a sense of atmosphere and a command of tone color. [Greene 209, p. 4]

25. Virtuosity in interpretation demands a mastery of breath control, resonant vocal production, pure and easy diction, fluency, speed and smooth phrasing. [Greene 209, p. 7]

Finally, De Bruyn lists 20 criteria that mark the artist singer. These are: agility and facility of technique in low or high registers; good attack on all tones; no breaks in register or quality throughout the vocal range; adequate breath in all situations; superb quality of tone throughout;

complete control of the voice; love of singing; absence of fatigue; excellent diction; ease in ascending or descending scale; articulation does not interrupt the flow of tone; absence of forcing or strain; perfect intonation (pitch); smoothness of legato; facile staccato; perfect *messa di voce* (Chapter VII); good range; sostenuto; ease of singing resembles ease of speaking; feeling of support. When the pupil can measure up to these standards of technique he is on the road to becoming an artist. [130, p. 2] Sir Henry J. Wood adds to the above criteria the factors of ear training, gift for languages, general physique and pleasing personality [686, p. 11]; while Clippinger adds stage-presence and the mastery of interpretative factors such as mood, phrasing, contrast, balance and unity of effect. [104, p. 3]

SUMMARY AND INTERPRETATION

THEORETICAL CONSIDERATIONS

The 354 statements gathered in this area develop the general principle that the singer's responsibilities extend beyond the technical mastery of his vocal instrument, into the realm of artistic self-expression. In his role as an artist, the singer is primarily concerned with human values in expression; with the communication of musical ideas through the language of song. The art of singing now acquires attributes that are both technical and psychological: technical, in that certain skills are cultivated through the use of drills and exercises that develop the vocal instrument as a flexible medium of tone production; psychological, in that the singer's portrayal of aesthetic values in expression through the use of tone and text is emphasized.

Also of prime importance in the interpretational phase of vocal training is the emergence of the individuality of the singer, in which he demonstrates his capacity for original and creative expression. The general concept here developed is that interpretation is in itself a never-ending maturation process, requiring years of trial and error learning and abundant listening experience. In this process, the student gradually frees himself from inhibitions and restraints caused by inexperience. Self-consciousness and fear are also banished with the overcoming of technical limitations. "Experience is the soil out of which interpretation grows and young people [singers] are deficient in that." [Glenn and Spouse 705]

The widely held assumption, that interpretations in singing vary with the individual, is supported by the recent investigations of vocal scientists. "No two behaviors of any kind are exactly alike," says Metfessel.

[op. cit.] The very fact that the voice is human endows it with certain individual characteristics that distinguish it from a mechanical sound product. Minute individual deviations in performance exist, even among artist singers. The experiments of Seashore and others tend to confirm the belief that the entire process of voice production is motivated by the singer's expressional impulses or, in other words, by his desire to communicate to a listener the intimate, individual thoughts and feelings that are engendered by his understanding of the song. These, in brief, are the general theoretical concepts underlying the pedagogy of interpretation in singing.

METHODOLOGICAL CONSIDERATIONS

Techniques of interpretation in singing are many and varied, but only those are considered that pertain to the basic training of the vocal artist. The 317 methodological statements gathered in this area include concepts of visualization, motivation, the importance of text, song selection, foreign language study, memorization, note connection, variety and tone color, techniques of song analysis and certain aspects of artistic performance. These concepts are briefly summarized as follows:

Visualization. Interpretation follows a preconceived mental pattern. It is not a haphazard or impromptu vocal utterance of the thoughts contained within the text of a song. In this respect, singing differs from speaking. The former is a prepared expression, preceded by a reflective process that requires the mental anticipation (visualization) of each phrase before it is sounded; the latter is largely improvised utterance. The singer really sings in his mind, the body merely serving as a passive instrument or channel of expression.

Motivation. In a certain sense, the voice is an emotional barometer because the slightest variation of feeling is instantly registered in the quality of the vocal sound emitted by the singer. Hence, the vocal interpretation of a song is motivated by the desire to express emotional as well as intellectual and musical effects. The singer must project his own personality by accentuating individual feelings, real or apparent, as part of his poetic portrayal of the varying moods in the song. In other words, to be artistically successful, interpretation must express personality attributes along with other musical values, and the techniques of tone production are thereby completely subordinated to interpretative factors during the performance of a song.

Mastery of the text. The text epitomizes the intentions of the composer. It imparts, through its verbal context, the story or conversational theme of the song and thus appeals to the aesthetic and intellectual comprehension of the audience. The whole purpose of singing is to vitalize the text, in that singing is a means of emotional intensification in vocal tone that expresses thought and feeling values in poetic forms. Therefore, a primary stage in interpreting the text is to comprehend its spoken message, a step that the singer can facilitate by speaking its context aloud, so as to capture its essential meaning in the plain tones of everyday conversation. Following this, a secondary stage of declamatory or intensified utterance is recommended, utilizing the quasi-musical recitative style of singing. As a final stage, the rendition of the text in its full musical form may be attempted. Thus, the mastery of the text proceeds through three easy stages, conversational, recitative and musical, toward the artistic rendition of the complete song.

Song selection. The preparation of a singing repertoire marks the culmination of technical study in vocal training. Here, the teacher's primary concern is that musical compositions of suitable texture and scope be chosen to match the student's technical development. Such factors as compass and tessitura, simplicity of style and communicability of text are suggested criteria for selecting songs.

Foreign language study. The preponderance of teacher and artist opinion favors foreign language study, notably Italian, as part of the regular vocal training program of the singer. The advocates of Italian claim for it certain vocal advantages, such as vowel purity, superior euphony, ease of legato singing and the availability of an extensive song literature in this language. The opinions against foreign language study are epitomized in David Bispham's statement, quoted from a leaflet issued by the American Academy of Teachers of Singing in 1932. "English is just as easy to sing as any other language if we but . . . know how to pronounce it. The only thing bad about English as a song medium is bad English. . . . Get away from this foreign language fad and you will find yourself nearer the heart of your [English-speaking] public." [703]

Memorization. The memorization of songs is the generally accepted method of building a student's repertoire, a procedure that is said to develop accuracy and self assurance in singing.

Note connection. The type of note connection used by the singer (i.e., legato or staccato) determines the melodic continuity or flow of vocal tone in the song. Legato is described as a process of vowel connection or vowel blending, the transitions from vowel to vowel being effected with minimum intrusions of consonant breaks or pauses into the tonal line. Always sing notes in groups or phrases, rather than as individual tones. (See also Chapter IX) In staccato singing, vowels are perceptibly disconnected. The attack and release of each staccato tone may be regulated either by diaphragmatic action, as in laughing, or by glottal action, as in coughing. The repeated glottal attack is recommended as an exercise for strengthening the vocal cords.

Variety and tone color. In order to create an illusion of spontaneous and unstudied expression in the interpretation of a song, the singer must capture the whimsicality of thought, the freedom and variability of feeling, the purposiveness and expressional intent of the text. This is accomplished with sufficient flexibility of technique to allow for a varied and colorful interpretation that is both interesting and convincing to his audience. In other words, the singer must play upon those variables of vocal expression that lie within the compass of his voice; through his use of variety and tone color he projects the final characterization of his song.

Song analysis. The interpretation of a song is an involved process, requiring a preliminary structural analysis and a part-by-part study of all its constituent elements. Ultimately, the singer must learn to fuse all musical and textual elements into a fluent continuity of expression in which techniques of tone production obediently subserve the desired artistic interpretation.

Performance aspects. In the final analysis, judgments of a singing performance are largely based on the subjective aesthetic reactions of a listener. [Seashore 506, p. 7] Such intangible factors as originality, sustained effect, self-control, personality (visible and audible) and musicianship, combined with the physiological impressions of the tones heard, help form the final complex impression of the singer's artistic development which is conveyed to an audience during a performance.

THE IMPORTANCE OF FLEXIBILITY AND FREEDOM

In conclusion, the voice training program is composed of various components of singing which are separately featured as technical objectives. Such factors as breath-control, phonation, resonance, range, dynamics and diction form the constituent elements of the vocal act. Hence each provides its own problems of technical development and, where the student of singing reveals limitations such as poor posture, pitch strain, breathiness, lingual ineptitude, etc., it is often felt that each problem requires isolated treatment during the singing lesson. But the art of interpretation represents an integration of all these technical factors in a tonal unity that compositely functions to provide suitable vehicles for vocal expression. The keystone of such technical training is coordination and its mainstays are flexibility and freedom.

According to Webster, "that is *flexible* which adapts itself readily to change," while *freedom* represents "ease and facility of execution." The singing teacher would do well to weigh the importance of these two attributes of the student's performance. Flexibility and freedom are the technical lubricants that promote instantaneous vocal coordinations resembling the smooth and effortless, unstudied responsiveness of reflex actions. Such ease of performance develops full-functioning artistic stature in the vocal instrument and spells freedom of expression for the singer. It is "the art that conceals the art," creating an illusion of impromptu utterance that is characteristic of all vocal virtuosity. For these reasons, the use of vocalises, trills and scale passages are often advocated as tests of flexibility and freedom in vocal practice, and such exercises are commonly regarded as prerequisites to the study of interpretation.

Finally, the teacher of singing is reminded that the specific application of the foregoing principles and techniques of interpretational study may raise additional teaching problems that would require further investigation. Ultimately, methods of experimental research and scientific testing can lead to the standardization of most pedagogical procedures for training the singing voice. But the adoption of tested or standardized methods of teaching interpretation should not be construed as an attempt to standardize the actual interpretations of songs. Individual differences in performance always are to be encouraged as evidence of creative ability and artistic initiative in the student. Although the acquisition of certain vocal techniques may be reduced to routine procedure, the standardization of performance would be less desirable in the interpretation of a song than in any other aspects of vocal training. [Henderson op. cit.]

CHAPTER XI

OUTCOMES OF THIS STUDY

Certain immediate results of this study have been reported seriately in the tables and concluding discussions of Chapters II through X, representing each of nine main areas of investigation. A conspectus of all the pedagogical viewpoints expressed by authors of texts and articles on the training of the singing voice suggests a predominance of three main schools of thought:

1. First there are the *empiricists*, who derive their teaching methods largely from trial and error observations. Their techniques are based on symptomatic judgments of the student's performance during the vocal lesson period. Underlying causes are guessed at or else ignored, the main objectives being the attainment of desirable results, by whatever means. Local effort and voluntary controls of the vocal apparatus are common instructional procedures and the chief criterion for evaluating any vocal technique is that the voice must sound better for having used that technique.

2. The second, or *scientific* group is composed of those who delve into the causes underlying acoustical and physiological vocal phenomena and voice teaching procedures are sought that agree with scientific or experimental findings. This group believes that the teaching of singing can ultimately be reduced to various testing and measuring procedures; that vocal tone can be analyzed objectively and definite standards of vocal production established for all singers.

3. The third or *natural method* group takes a middle path, disclaiming any detailed knowledge of vocal physiology, but seeking to eliminate local effort so that natural vocal reflexes take their course. "Train the mind, train the ear, but let the vocal organs alone" is the slogan of this last group. Herbert Witherspoon sums it up by saying, "the most difficult thing to do is to leave the voice alone. Voices cannot be pulled, placed or squirted. They perform most effectively when free from conscious effort, mental or physical." [677, p. 15] A basic limitation common to all three

groups is the freedom with which authors make assumptions (often implicitly) that are never justified.

In the absence of a core of established scientific data on the training of the singing voice, it was necessary to plan the procedures of this investigation so as to provide basic orientations in this field for future investigators, as well as to provide a segment of organized information for the teaching profession. To achieve these ends, the plan and purposes of this study were carried out in three main operational stages, as follows:

1. *Gathering sources of information.* A working bibliography of 702 items was compiled by systematically searching through the following sources of bibliographical information: a) The Library of Congress in Washington, D. C.; b) The New York Public Library, Central Branch; c) The New York Public Library, 58th Street Music Branch; d) Teachers College Library; e) Columbia University Music Library; f) Juilliard School of Music Library; g) Readers' Guide to Periodical Literature; h) Education Index; i) Ohio State University Card Index to Periodical Literature; j) Psychological Abstracts.

2. *Collecting and arranging the data.* In all, 2,946 concepts used in training the singing voice were gathered by reading the 702 bibliographical items. These were arranged: a) by comparison and grouping, into 9 main areas and b) by their relevancy to certain categories of information, into 162 subordinate areas. These categorical classifications were distributed as follows:

Main Area	Number of Categories
Vocal pedagogy	29
Breathing	22
Phonation	20
Resonance	19
Range	16
Dynamics	8
Ear training	11
Diction	19
Interpretation	18
TOTAL	162

The concepts were also arranged in theoretical and methodological groupings in each main area, and were further subdivided into psychological and technical teaching approaches and according to documentation. Statements made by professional singers were also indicated.

3. *Analyzing the data.* By classifying, correlating and tabulating the concepts within broad and narrow content groupings, it was possible to arrive at a numerical summation and critical analysis of each category. These data were arranged, tabulated and discussed in nine separate chapters, one for each main area. A summarizing table of concepts which served as a chapter plan was placed at the beginning of each of these chapters (II-X) and a *summary and interpretation* section at the end of each chapter included a discussion of the prevailing theoretical and methodological schools of thought represented therein. Table Ten contains a final summation of all the concepts tabulated in the nine preceding tables given in Chapters II through X.

Other principal outcomes of this study are:

I. A list of 23 controversial questions.

II. A list of 177 vocal and nonvocal terms that were defined for use in this study.

III. A list of 97 problems and problem areas for future research in this and related fields.

IV. An annotated bibliography of 702 items.

I. *Controversial questions.* The analysis of concepts contained in Chapters II through X reveals considerable diversity of author opinion on many questions of vocal theory and technique. Unanimity of opinion rarely prevails among teachers of singing, regarding any of the pedagogical questions raised. Nevertheless, there is often sufficient agreement among authors on a given issue to indicate the basic argument underlying their contentions. In at least 23 areas of vocal teaching, representing approximately 22.5 per cent of the total number of concepts gathered, the issues are clearly enough defined to be stated as debatable questions. The scarcity of documentary and experimental evidence indicates a definite need for further research in these areas. These 23 controversial questions are listed in Table Eleven.

II. *Terminology defined.* In the absence of a standard terminology in vocal pedagogy, it was found necessary to provide operational definitions of each of the following 177 vocal and nonvocal terms. This terminology was consistently used throughout this study as a means of enhancing the specificity of meaning in the discussions of each category of concepts. Definitions, whether derived from contextual or other sources, were in each case verified in a standard dictionary or standard reference

TABLE TEN

A TABULATED FINAL SUMMARY OF CONCEPTS USED IN TRAINING THE SINGING VOICE

	total number of statements	theories	METHODS					
			methods total	psychological approach	technical approach	statements by prof. singers	documented statements	undocumented statements
TABLE ONE: Concepts of vocal pedagogy	690	145	545	374	171	73	48	642
TABLE TWO: Concepts of breathing	428	58	370	95	275	30	25	403
TABLE THREE: Concepts of phonation	463	188	275	85	190	13	137	326
TABLE FOUR: Concepts of resonance	262	137	125	19	106	17	63	199
TABLE FIVE: Concepts of vocal range	228	99	129	33	96	23	36	192
TABLE SIX: Concepts of vocal dynamics	110	9	101	6	95	18	17	93
TABLE SEVEN: Concepts of ear training	157	39	118	78	40	12	17	140
TABLE EIGHT: Concepts of diction	254	77	177	41	136	11	21	233
TABLE NINE: Concepts of interpretation	354	37	317	174	143	34	29	325
TOTALS	2946	789	2157	905	1252	231	393	2553

TABLE ELEVEN

SUMMARY OF CONTROVERSIAL QUESTIONS RAISED

	total number of statements	statements by prof. singers	documented statements	undocumented statements
TABLE ONE				
1. Vocal teaching can be standardized	13	1	1	12
Vocal teaching cannot be standardized	18	8		18
2. Technique should be acquired through songs	24	2		24
Technique should not be acquired through songs	10	2		10
TABLE TWO				
3. Direct control of breathing organs advised	24			24
Direct control of breathing organs is not advised	11	4		11
4. Diaphragmatic control of breathing is essential	27		1	26
Diaphragmatic control of breathing is not essential	9		1	8
TABLE THREE				
5. Mouth opening is important in phonation	29			29
Mouth opening is not important in phonation	9			9
6. Low tongue is desirable	31	2		31
Free tongue is desirable	19	1	1	18
7. Palate should be raised	2			2
Palate should be free	4		2	2
8. Conscious control of throat is desirable	21		6	15
Conscious control of throat is not desirable	16		2	14
9. Larynx should move during phonation	7		2	5
Larynx should not move during phonation	7			7

TABLE ELEVEN (continued)

	total number of statements	statements by prof. singers	documented statements	undocumented statements
TABLE FOUR				
10. Head cavities are important as resonators	7	2		7
Head cavities are not important as resonators	3		2	1
11. Sinuses are used as resonators	9		2	7
Sinuses are not used as resonators	4		3	1
12. Nasal cavities are consciously employed	14	2	4	10
Nasal cavities are not consciously employed	3			3
13. Vocal resonance is directly controllable	5	1		5
Vocal resonance is not directly controllable	8			8
14. The voice should be consciously focussed	41	4	2	39
The voice should not be consciously focussed	19	2	2	17
15. Humming is a useful device	25	1		25
Humming is not a useful device	5		1	4
TABLE FIVE				
16. The singing voice has one register	11	3		11
The singing voice has two registers	16		6	10
The singing voice has three registers	7		1	6
17. Falsetto tones are legitimate	2		2	
Falsetto tones are not legitimate	2		1	1
18. Use the entire vocal range in beginning practice	2			2
Use only middle range in beginning practice	30	6	1	29

TABLE ELEVEN (continued)

	total number of statements	statements by prof. singers	documented statements	undocumented statements
TABLE SIX				
19. Loud tones should be used when practicing	18		4	14
Loud tones should not be used when practicing	38	12	1	37
TABLE SEVEN				
20. Self-listening is recommended	17	2		17
Self-listening is not recommended	4		1	3
21. Sensation is a reliable vocal aid	15	2		15
Sensation is not a reliable vocal aid	20	2	1	19
Sound and sensation combined are reliable aids	6	1		6
TABLE EIGHT				
22. Vowels should be altered on high pitches	15	2		15
Vowels should not be altered on high pitches	7			7
TABLE NINE				
23. Foreign language study is essential for singers	21	4		21
Foreign language study is not essential	7			7
TOTALS	662	66	50	612

book of musical and pedagogical information. These terms are also listed in the final *Index*.

III. *Research problems.* Numerous problem areas are defined in this study by textual references to specific needs of the teacher of singing; by unanswered questions; by the emergence of many conflicting pedagogical theories or procedures that call for scientific investigation and proof. The most important derivative problem areas have been crystallized in a list of 97 questions and suggestions for the vocal scientist. These problems present many complex variables, involving psychological, acoustical and physiological factors. They are derived from nine main areas as follows:

Main Area	Number of Problems
Vocal pedagogy	23
Breathing	9
Phonation	17
Resonance	9
Range	8
Dynamics	5
Ear training	13
Diction	7
Interpretation	6
TOTAL	97

Problem 1. By what research procedures can the minimum mental, physical, aural, aesthetic, cultural, etc. prerequisites for successful vocal training be determined? How can these requirements be tested and measured in beginning vocal students?

Problem 2. What is the average desirable length of vocal training required of prospective professional singers? Questionnaire methods could be used to interrogate singing teachers and professional singers on their judgments about this and other pertinent pedagogical problems.

Problem 3. What objective tests could be devised for predicting vocal talent or for measuring a student's aptitude for singing? Such factors as general intelligence, ability to concentrate, memory, powers of aural visualization, emotional stability, freedom from vocal inhibitions, general musicianship, capacity for learning music and languages, interpretational skill, general physical health and health of the vocal organs, hearing acuity, and other similar factors would have to be tested and measured.

Problem 4. What procedures could reliably determine optimal age levels for students (male and female) to begin a systematic course of training in singing? Physiological and mental factors would have to be considered.

Problem 5. By what objective criteria can the minimum prescribed training and vocal accomplishments of known successful professional singers be determined and compared? Such factors as years of vocal training, educational background, musicianship, public appearances, physique, general health, etc., could be considered.

Problem 6. What are the general and specific objectives of vocal training now most commonly endorsed by singing teachers? A questionnaire could be used to elicit these opinions from the vocal teaching profession.

Problem 7. How can contributions to the knowledge of the functioning of the singing voice, thus far made in the field of psychology, be explored and evaluated? Research data would have to be compiled, compared, evaluated and classified for ready reference by teachers of singing, with a view to formulating a basic psychology of the singing voice.

Problem 8. What procedures can be used for exploring and evaluating the contributions to vocal pedagogy of such sciences as physics, physiology, anthropology, neurology, speech, acoustics, etc.?

Problem 9. How can vocal reflexes be tested and measured so as to determine the controllability of certain vocal actions by the singer (e.g., in breathing, phonation, resonance, etc.)? It would also be helpful to know to what extent the habitual practicing of conscious vocal controls and voluntary vocal techniques introduces abnormal inhibitory factors into the nervous response of the vocal organs.

Problem 10. a) How can the effects upon the singing voice of the muscle *tonus* of a healthy body be measured? Physiological and acoustical objective comparisons made between voices produced in superior, normal and pathological states of health would reveal the importance of stressing health factors when training the singing voice. b) Do singers tend to build an immunity toward certain types of disease, e.g., pulmonary disorders?

Problem 11. What is known about the condition called "stage fright" (or extreme self-consciousness) and its effects upon the singing voice? A thorough-going psychological and physiological investigation of this problem would be revealing and useful to the teacher of singing.

Problem 12. Can an objective analysis of spontaneous, vocal utterances, produced in off-guard and unpremeditated situations, reveal the fundamental characteristics of the natural singing voice? An acoustical and physiological comparison of spontaneous vocal tones and consciously controlled tones would produce valuable conclusions for vocal teaching.

Problem 13. On what objective criteria can an accurate comparison of the vocal factors in singing and the vocal factors in speaking be made? A research study in this area might consider both static and variable vocal components of both singing and speaking; e.g., resonance, duration, pitch, intensity, vowel formant, etc.

Problem 14. How can corrective exercises be used to offset the known common vocal faults of students of singing? A system of tested exercises is needed, progressively arranged from elementary to advanced stages of training, covering every known type of vocal handicap, and applying sound pedagogical principles to remedial vocal teaching.

Problem 15. How can an objective comparison be made between whole and part methods of vocal instruction as applied to individuals (or groups) studying singing? Certain technical and aesthetic criteria might be devised that can be useful as reliable bases for comparison.

Problem 16. How can the efficacy of the song approach in vocal training be tested and evaluated? Experimental and control group methods might be applied to teaching procedures used in this area.

Problem 17. Can the effects of unsupervised vocal practice be tested by experimental means? A survey of present day opinion among professional singers and teachers regarding this factor in vocal teaching might also prove useful.

Problem 18. By what method of research can the value of unaccompanied vocal practice be determined? Is the use of piano accompaniments during the vocal lesson period an aid or a detriment to the singer? Hearing acuity measurements could be made and certain musical-vocal responses of numerous pupils could be tested both before and after each lesson, some using piano accompaniments, some unaccompanied. Results would be applicable to choral as well as to individual instruction.

Problem 19. Is it possible to devise a systematic measuring or rating scale whereby all the various known methods and techniques of training the singing voice can be listed, analyzed and evaluated for pedagogical content? It would also be necessary to determine the predictive value (validity) of such a scale of measurement.

Problem 20. Can a progressively arranged list of published songs and arias be compiled that would encompass all the technical problems of vocal training known to singing teachers? Technical exercises, derived from these songs, could be compiled as a supplementary feature. The list would have to be tested and approved by the teaching profession.

Problem 21. By testing and comparing many types of trained voices, is it possible to arrive at a fixed basis of classification for all voices? Such a testing procedure would have to employ acoustical and other scientific measuring instruments for gathering reliable data on optimal range and timbre (quality) factors in normal, inferior and superior voices.

Problem 22. Can a teacher-training program be formulated that would include every basic requirement for the preparation and training of professional teachers of singing? By what standards of selection and objective testing could the candidacy of applicants for such a course of training be determined?

Problem 23. What reliable historical evidence is there of the teaching principles and methods employed by the old bel canto masters of singing, pertaining to the various factors of vocal training outlined in this study? An authentic historical study is needed.

Problem 24. Is singing a strenuous form of physical exercise involving breathing reactions that are typical of other types of strenuous physical activities like running, lifting, etc.? Does the training of the singer's voice require superior physical development of the body as a prerequisite or corequisite? Or should physical fitness be entirely ignored? The solution of this problem might require a survey of contemporary opinion among teachers and singers as well as an experimental procedure to determine, by objective measurement, the physical fitness of singers, samplings being taken from successful, unsuccessful and non-singer groups.

Problem 25. What is the best posture for singing? Does the singing act require a high chest position, neutral chest position or stationary chest position? The resolution of this problem would require a clear understanding of the physiological nature of the respiratory process and the vocal act and the testing of the postural habits of many successful singers.

Problem 26. What is the nature of breath control in singing? Is breathing in singing a voluntary or involuntary act? Experimental data on this subject are needed.

Problem 27. Can experimental procedures be devised for measuring diaphragmatic and chest movements in singing by means of such devices as X-ray photography and the pneumograph, in order to determine the exact nature of diaphragmatic and abdominal action in singing and in strenuous exercise? The action of the ribs in relation to the diaphragm is also a controversial subject in that it involves many possibilities. There may be a dominance of rib raising over diaphragmatic movement or vice versa. The two actions may be equal or unequal in varying proportions. This problem should be thoroughly investigated.

Problem 28. What can the singing profession learn about natural breathing coordinations from other-than-normal breathing reflexes that involve the organs of respiration, e.g., coughing, yawning, sneezing, laughing, gasping-for-air and other spasmodic and unpremeditated utterances such as cries of pain, joy, surprise, etc.? Are the muscular reactions in these reflexes analogous to the coordinations required for singing? Experimental techniques for investigating these actions are not available at present and their formulation would constitute a valuable contribution.

Problem 29. What is the collective opinion of professional singers concerning the orificial control of breathing? Do they recommend mouth breathing, nose breathing or both? How can the breathing habits of singers be tested experimentally?

Problem 30. How is economy of breathing related to the physiology of phonation, to vocal intensity and volume, to abdominal and diaphragmatic controls and to spontaneous vocal utterances? What breathing exercises or physical routines can be devised to establish coordinations for economizing breath emission in singing?

Problem 31. Can a system of corrective physical exercises be prepared, that would overcome faulty breathing action, weak posture, and shallow breathing habits in singing? These would be valuable to the teaching profession.

Problem 32. Is it possible to develop breathing by means of actual singing practice? A repertoire or list of songs is needed which will have a corrective influence on beginners who need training in breath support, phrasing, endurance, posture, attack and other breathing techniques. Such a list should be inexpensive and musically palatable.

Problem 33. What is the exact physiology of glottal vibration and phonatory action for each pitch, register and vowel quality of the singing voice? For soft tones and loud tones? For initial attack and sustained singing? How are intrinsic and extrinsic muscles related to all these factors of phonation?

Problem 34. How can the true vibratory area of phonation be determined? Modern exploratory procedures should be devised for testing and measuring the vibratory activity, during phonation, of such areas as the glottis, the cartilages of the larynx, extrinsic laryngeal muscles, the spine, chest, various parts of the nose and head, the muscles and walls of the throat, in artistic singing performance and under ordinary conditions of spontaneous vocal utterance.

Problem 35. How does the mechanism of swallowing, coughing and normal respiration coordinate with the action of the various parts of the larynx during phonation at various pitch and dynamic levels? A complete physiological action chart is needed.

Problem 36. How does the force of the expiratory blast of sub-glottic air (breath) affect the raising of the larynx in low and high pitched vocal tone production? What muscular action controls the stability of the larynx during phonation?

Problem 37. Can an accurate mechanical working model of the larynx be constructed, showing all the parts of the living larynx in their exact inter-relationships? Cadaveric dissection studies and acoustical measurements of each tonal product of the larynx would be helpful.

Problem 38. How may reeducational training techniques be applied to the correction of irregularities in the vocal vibrato such as a too rapid vibrato? too slow vibrato? too wide (more than a semitone)? too narrow? too strong? too weak?

Problem 39. Can teaching and testing procedures be devised that would measure the efficacy of mental imagery and tonal anticipation in controlling the accuracy of pitch attack on single notes and in phrases; and in interval jumps at various dynamic levels?

Problem 40. Can off-pitch singing (i.e., sharping and flatting at various levels) during single note attacks and interval jumps be related to sub-glottal breath pressure and the control of respiration? How can standardized teaching techniques for correcting such faults be developed?

Problem 41. Can testing procedures be devised for compiling objective evidence of the efficacy of mouth position in improving phonation? Also for testing the influence of lips, tongue position, palatal height, and level of larynx on phonation?

Problem 42. How can the effect of teaching the "open throat" concept in singing be tested objectively under conditions of direct control and indirect control (as in yawning)?

Problem 43. How does the muscular tonus of the body affect phonation in normal health? During conditions of bodily fatigue? After rest or a refreshing sleep? Before and after a meal? During various emotional states such as stage fright, joyous enthusiasm, dejection, etc.? In various conditions of bodily health and activity?

Problem 44. Can the muscles of phonation be exercised independently of the singing act? Develop a system of simple graded exercises for silently or audibly warming-up the laryngeal and respiratory muscles before singing.

Problem 45. Can a list of simple but musically palatable songs be prepared to serve as warming-up exercise material in teaching singing? The use of slow, sustained tones within a moderate middle range of the voice should be followed by more vigorous singing at different dynamic levels. *Messa-di-voce* effects (Chapter VII) would also be helpful.

Problem 46. How could the comparative usefulness, in vocal research, of the following devices be measured; laryngoscope; laryngo-periskop; stethoscope; kymograph; phonodeik; magnetic-tape sound mirror and other recording devices; artificial larynx; high speed motion pictures and X-ray photography? Also various microphone, loud speaker and ear phone techniques for observing and analysing the operation, control and acoustical output of the phonating mechanisms during singing?

Problem 47. How may graded vocal or silent physical exercises be utilized for promoting the various phonatory conditions, skills and abilities that are essential to artistic singing? The development of suitable methods and devices for the further investigation of laryngeal action and the laryngeal muscles would be helpful.

Problem 48. How can such conditions as jaw freedom, lingual flexibility, palatal strength, open throat and other optimal conditions of the vocal tract be taught by indirect or psychological methods? A system of indirect exercises should be formulated, tested and evaluated.

Problem 49. Is it possible to arrive at accurate determinations of ideal pitch frequency variations in a vocal vibrato? Also ideal amplitude and intensity components? Further investigation of the vocal vibrato in singing is needed.

Problem 50. What is the function of the vocal sinuses in singing? Despite the convictions of many teachers favoring the usefulness of sinuses as resonators, there is strong if not positive evidence to the contrary. In surgical operations, the sinuses may even be completely eliminated by incorporating them into the nasopharynx without any noticeable effect on the laryngeal sound. [Curry 124, p. 117] Research in this area would provide valuable information for teachers of singing.

Problem 51. What is the true nature of nasal resonance? Apparently the pupil singer is in a better position to perceive the existence of nasal resonance than the teacher since sensations, in this instance, are more practical as guides than sounds. But there is a surprising lack of knowledge concerning the simplest anatomical structures of the head. Many authors advocate conscious control of nasal resonance without knowing how it is brought about, the assumption probably being that the average singer can consciously regulate the rising and falling of the velar muscle which controls the passageway into the nose, an assumption that has never been experimentally demonstrated. Although it is generally agreed that nasal resonance is an important factor in determining the quality of the singing voice, we must conclude from the evidence at hand that adequate teaching techniques in this area have not yet been developed. This area should be explored. A further investigation of the action and adjustment of all the vocal resonance cavities would also be helpful to the teaching profession.

Problem 52. How may humming be employed in vocal instruction? Statements regarding the use and value of humming are conflicting, and students of singing are caught between two antithetical admonitions? *do hum!* and *don't hum!* The preponderance of author opinion favors humming as a teaching device. The sound of *m* is proposed as a basic tonal pattern since it is characteristic of the natural or residual resonance tones of the head before articulatory movements take place. This problem needs further experimental investigation.

Problem 53. How can the physiology of "open throat" be explained? The open throat concept is still open to question. *Open throat* is apparently a misnomer for what else could a singer's throat be but open? This term is widely used to describe a teaching nostrum for all singing maladies. The technique of the open throat is intended to promote a type of relaxation or vocal release in the throat that would obviate the disastrous bottle neck constrictions that throttle the tone in poorly produced voices. The open throat theory needs scientific confirmation or refutation.

Problem 54. How may synchronous vibratory activity in various parts of the singer's body be determined and measured? Authors who declare that the entire body is a resonator base their opinions on the following concept: "The entire skeletal body consisting of some 206 bones serves as a sound vibrator and conductor either *per se* or by continuity. In other words, if there is a vibration in any portion of the bony structure of the body, there is bound to be vibration in all bones of the body but, of course, to a lesser degree. [Owsley 441, p. 11] Curry's explanation is even more explicit. With each cycle of laryngeal vibration there is an almost instantaneous propagation of initial sound waves throughout the whole volume of the vocal system. Singers falsely believe that they can selectively direct or focus vocal sound to certain areas like the skull, hard palate, chest, etc., only because they more readily perceive the sensations that are caused by the sympathetic vibration of those parts. [124, p. 49] Experimental procedures should be devised whereby these vibratory phenomena can be objectively measured.

Problem 55. Is the voluntary control of vocal focus possible? Forty-one out of sixty authors who discuss vocal focus favor voluntary control of this factor in singing. Although opinions vary as to the exact place of focus, all forty-one seem to agree that the use of some form of upward and forward imagery is good pedagogical procedure since the attention of the singer is thus directed away from the laryngeal and throat muscles where most vocal constrictions originate. This diversion of attention has the indirect effect of inducing a normal relaxation of the vocal tract during phonation and a normal functioning of the vocal reflexes results. [Bartholomew 40] Nineteen authors are opposed to voluntary control of vocal focus. Some even deny the existence of a focal point of resonance, claiming that resonance is rather evenly spread over a large area of the vocal tract. They contend that forward focus is a sensory illusion; that any portion of the vocal tract can be sensitized by continually concentrating upon that portion. In other words, the so-called vocal focus is really an attention focus which immediately heightens the singer's sensitivity to vibrational activity in that area of the vocal tract where attention is being concentrated. This controversy needs a solution.

Problem 56. How can the effects of a singer's so-called "focussing techniques" be tested? Teachers claim that the conscious directing of vocal tone to the point of focus produces two perceptible effects. First, the point of focus becomes filled with vibrational activity which the singer himself can perceive by touch sensations. Second, the tonal effect emitted when the voice is being consciously focussed becomes decidedly more agreeable to the ear than before the conscious focus was attempted. Experimental evidence is needed of the actual increase in the vibratory output of vocal tone which the so-called point of focus contributes. Such evidence would justify the emphasis now laid upon this controversial concept or it would definitely dispel any illusions regarding the efficacy of teaching methods that employ voluntary focussing techniques.

Problem 57. Is voice production in singing subject to voluntary controls? Unlike the pipe of an organ, whose tone is fixed in pitch and quality, the human voice may be varied through a wide variety of resonances which respond to the expressional intent of the singer. Scientific data would help to settle the controversy that arises as to whether the singer's vocal responses to his thoughts and moods should be voluntarily controlled or whether his vocal organs react spontaneously to the mood and meaning of his song while he remains totally oblivious of technique.

Problem 58. What are the acoustical and physiological characteristics of a natural voice. The *natural* voice is one that seems to meet every aesthetic and artistic requirement without ever having received formal training from a singing teacher. Hence this phenomenon among singers is an object of great curiosity and vocal teachers and scientists are continually striving to ferret out the mystery of the natural voice without disturbing the spontaneity of its action. The vocal profession may well be grateful that certain illustrious examples of the natural singing voice exist. These perfect voices show forth the possibilities of correct development to singers who are less fortunately endowed but who are striving to achieve a so-called natural result through systematic vocal training. In this connection Van der Veer writes: "Beware of the word 'natural' for that word often means 'habitual.' Habitual processes are often far from being natural." [714] It would be interesting and valuable to consider the characteristics of the so-called natural singing voice from the standpoint of experimental research.

Problem 59. What is the average compass of untrained and trained singing voices in each main classification of range, as obtained by objective standards of measurement? Several hundred vocal samplings in each category could be measured and an accurate table of findings prepared. The location of the central pitch, middle range and the various registers in each classification of voices might also be indicated.

Problem 60. What are the criteria of artistic performance regarding the flexibility and range of the singer's voice? By what objective standards can these criteria be determined in trained singers whose singing range is not very extensive but who nevertheless give musically satisfactory performances?

Problem 61. What is the exact physiological action of pitch controls in singing? Is pitch variation a function of intrinsic glottal muscles? Of extrinsic laryngeal muscles? Of the intensity of breath pressure during phonation? Of the size of resonance cavities? Of the size and anatomical conformations of muscular and cartilaginous laryngeal structures? Of combinations of all these factors? What coordinations are involved in making vocal pitch changes?

Problem 62. How may pitch controlling coordinations be educated by direct physical exercise? By means of musical vocalises? By means of ear training programs?

Problem 63. How may our knowledge of pitch regulating mechanisms in the singer's voice determine the correct instructional techniques for correcting register breaks? Can experimental procedures be devised that would measure the conditions under which register breaks usually occur in the singer's voice? Laryngoscopic, high speed motion picture and stroboscopic photography of glottal activity during sliding and disjunct pitch changes would be helpful.

Problem 64. What research procedures can be devised that would reveal accurate information regarding the nature of the falsetto range in all types of voices? Can such physiological data be applied to voice training procedures so that the falsetto register may be adapted to regular singing performance?

Problem 65. Can diagnostic and remedial procedures be devised that will correct the detrimental influence that habitual daily vocal behavior, as in speaking, has upon the use of the voice for singing?

Problem 66. Can a list of musically wholesome songs be prepared for all types of voices and graded according to their usefulness as teaching materials for cultivating the range of the singing voice?

Problem 67. What are the exact physiological constituents of the act of vocal intensification in singing? Which of these are related to breath pressure? To resonance? Research in this area is needed.

Problem 68. Can the physiological factors of vocal dynamics be related to specific pedagogical procedures for training or refining the control of dynamics in the singer's voice by means of technical exercises? A list of such exercises with evaluations would be helpful.

Problem 69. Is it possible to determine experimentally whether, in any program of vocal training, the emergence of the improved singing voice is accompanied by measurable improvements in dynamic vocal controls? It will also be necessary to determine whether dynamic controls are residual concomitants of the vocal act, and therefore not directly influenced by the acquisition of singing skills.

Problem 70. Can a relationship be traced between tonal imagery and dynamic vocal utterance in singing? Experimental procedures are needed whereby vocal utterance can be measured as an auditory-physical response to preconceived mental images of tonal volume. From such observations, a proper teaching approach to this subject might be derived.

Problem 71. Can a song repertoire be prepared that would be conducive to the systematic improvement of dynamic controls of the singing voice? Such factors as the exercise of forte and pianissimo attacks, swelling and diminishing of single tones and entire phrases, and the sustaining of pianissimo and forte tones and passages might be considered. Such a list should be properly graded and should include actual song literature that is inexpensive, not too difficult to sing, and musically palatable.

Problem 72. To what extent does tonal imagery influence the activity of the vocal organs? What experimental procedures can be devised to test the effects of conscious self-listening on the singing voice?

Problem 73. How can tonal memory drills, tonal visualization drills and "silent (mental) singing" drills be utilized in an ear training program? An objective evaluation of such drills would be necessary.

Problem 74. How does bone conduction during singing influence the singer's auditory awareness of his own voice? How does the subjective hearing acuity of self-listening compare with the ear's sensitivity toward tonal impressions received from an outside source through the outer ear? This area of hearing needs experimental investigation.

Problem 75. Can a method be devised whereby each acoustical attribute of the singing voice (e.g., pitch, quality, dynamics) is separately and objectively presented to the ear of a listener and studied for possible values in ear training and for improving tonal imagery?

Problem 76. Can a direct relationship be traced between the tonal input of a specific listening experience and the tonal output of the vocal performance elicited thereby? Experimental procedures are needed that would measure this cause and effect relationship for single tones, phrase passages and complete songs.

Problem 77. To what extent do subjective factors such as intellectual attitudes, emotional states, mental alertness and receptivity toward specific impressions, influence the listening experience? How can these factors be tested and measured?

Problem 78. Can intellectual and emotional responses that are deeply imbedded in the listening experience be simplified or analyzed? Listening to any piece of vocal music with the purpose of forming objective evaluations of a given performance involves complicated individual reactions that are not yet amenable to pedagogical analysis. These should be investigated.

Problem 79. How can factors of primacy, frequency, recency and intensity or vividness of the tonal experience and their effect upon listening be analyzed, tested and measured? For instance, it is possible that casual familiarity with a piece of vocal music (afforded by a recent studio lesson) can heighten the student-listener's awareness of certain of its attributes while, on the other hand, over familiarity with the same piece of music can deaden his sensitivity toward, or interest in, the details of its performance. Reliable ear training procedures should account for such variables.

Problem 80. In what way can attention-arresting devices be used to accentuate the values of self-listening? Such devices as the microphone, loud speaker, ear phones, stethoscope, megaphone, magnetic-tape "sound mirror" and other forms of sound reflection and reproduction should be explored and tested for their educational possibilities in establishing ear-training techniques for singers.

Problem 81. How can available audio-visual media such as the cinema and radio be utilized for systematic technical and aesthetic singing instruction to supplement the work of the studio and classroom? How can such techniques be evaluated?

Problem 82. Can a list of phonographic recordings by artist singers be compiled that would progressively illustrate to the student all the essentials of correct voice production and interpretation? Such recordings should preferably be solo performances of simple songs and arias with instrumental accompaniments subdued or entirely absent. This set of records would provide valuable supplementary teaching materials for either studio instruction or home practice.

Problem 83. Is it possible to prepare a series of vocalises, technical exercises and simple songs that would illustrate the technical "high-lights" of exemplary recorded vocal performances so that, in practicing, the student can continually check his own singing performance against recordings that are worthy of emulation? A self-rating chart for home practicing might be devised.

Problem 84. How can objective tests of hearing acuity be applied to the measurement or prediction of aptitude for singing?

Problem 85. How can the reflex movements and adjustments of the various organs of articulation be tested and analyzed in actual successful singing performances? Are the tongue movements of diction controlled by means of localized kinesthetic sensations in the lingual muscles themselves or by means of auditory conditioning to the sound effects of such movements, or both? Can such lingual sensations be localized for testing purposes?

Problem 86. Would it be possible to prove experimentally the assertion that lingual activity is not a primary factor of vowel formation in singing? Some means of demobilizing the tongue by anesthetic or mechanical agents might be devised in order that the lingual effect (or its absence) upon vowel production (and phonation) could be studied objectively in many subjects. The same type of experiment could be applied to the study of the action of the lips and various other parts of the oral cavity during the production of vowel and other vocal sounds.

Problem 87. Can experimental procedures be used to determine the ideal vowel frequencies and format for the perfectly used voice?

Problem 88. Are there optimum pitch levels for singing individual vowel sounds? Can the influence of pitch level upon the purity and accuracy of vowel production in the singing voice be tested experimentally? How can vowel format be related to the pitch of the singing voice?

Problem 89. What is the physiology of the mechanism used in *covering* vocal tones? How can the efficacy of *covering* techniques be tested by acoustical or other means?

Problem 90. Can the usefulness of sol-fa training as a technique for improving the singer's diction be tested objectively? An experimental control group might be used whereby two methods of instruction could be compared and evaluated. Similar experimental procedures could be devised for testing such teaching devices as speaking, whispering, chanting and exaggeration, (by whole and part methods) in training the singer's diction.

Problem 91. How can diction be taught through a graded series of songs that would provide progressively difficult diction exercises, set in music that is not too complicated or vocally difficult?

Problem 92. To what extent should the singer indulge his own emotions in the interpretation of a song? Should interpretative effects be genuine or simulated? A comparative study might be formulated that would test conditions of vocal release and the general reactions of the vocal instrument under genuine and simulated emotional effects.

Problem 93. How can the empathic response of a listener to the genuine (or simulated) emotional expression of a singer be studied and tested? (*Empathy* is defined as the "imaginative projection of one's consciousness into another being." (W) By the principle of empathic response, an audience can receive vicarious emotional experiences through listening to the interpretations of a singer.)

Problem 94. Can the learning of a song be improved or accelerated by means of "speaking-the-text" methods of analysis and study? An experimental procedure, involving the comparison of two different methods of instruction to individual vocalists might be formulated, utilizing experimental and control groups of individuals, under test conditions.

Problem 95. How can the ratios of vowel and consonant sounds in the English language be compared with those of other languages, such as Italian, for the purpose of comparing the euphony or singability of texts in each language?

Problem 96. Would it be possible to prepare and evaluate for study and voice training purposes, a list of songs that are graded according to increasing difficulties of interpretation? Such factors as melodic movement, predominant mood, simplicity and meaning of text, legato and staccato techniques, phrasing, variety and tone color requirements might be considered.

Problem 97. To what extent do the ebb and flow of the singer's emotions during the interpretation of a song induce physiological reactions in his breathing and vocal organs? How would such physiological changes condition his singing voice?

IV. *Annotated bibliography.* Since there was no exhaustive bibliography on the training of the singing voice in existence, it was necessary to compile one for the purposes of this study. A comprehensive bibliography was indispensable, inasmuch as all the concepts were derived entirely from the published statements of authors, teachers, scientists and singers. The 702 items listed hereafter include 164 books and 538 articles. There are also 72 scientific papers and experimental reports and 66 published interviews and articles by professional singers. Seven historical and musical reference books containing useful vocal information are also included. The ten asterisked items that were not used in this study include repetitions of previously listed items and commercial and nonpedagogical publications. The bibliography was annotated insofar as it was relevant to the problems of training the singing voice. Twelve supplementary references are listed separately, following the annotated bibliography.

ANNOTATED BIBLIOGRAPHY

1. Abbott, Eugenie B. "The Singing and Speaking Voice Are One." *Musician,* New York, April, 1934, Vol. 39, p. 6.
   From the very first lesson beautiful diction is impressed upon the pupil, for diction is the vehicle of tone.
2. Abney, Louise. "Singing and Speaking Voice." *School and Community,* Spokane, 1939, Vol. 25, p. 188.
   Singing and speaking are mutually beneficial, each enhancing the other.
3. Acton, Florence C. "Those Middle Tones." *Etude,* Philadelphia, 1932, Vol. 50, p. 654.
   The extremes of the vocal compass should be attempted only after songs have already been sung with the trained middle range. Humming and other vocalises are prescribed.
4. Aikin, W. A. Article on "Singing" in *Grove's Dictionary of Music.* Macmillan, New York, 1941, Vol. IV.
   A brief description of the vocal act with some notes on diction.
5. Alda, Frances. "The Girl with a Voice." *Good Housekeeping,* New York, June, 1930, Vol. 90, p. 55.
   Advice to beginners includes health, diet, finding a good singing teacher, cost of vocal training, musical background and how to live. There is little technical instruction.
6. ———— *Men, Women and Tenors.* Houghton Mifflin, Boston, 1937.
   A fictional and biographical narrative dealing in generalities of singing and historical data. Good reading. Nontechnical. Voice culture is only briefly considered.
7. Allen, Mrs. Joyce (Herman). *The Technique of Modern Singing.* Pitman, London, 1935.
   A conventional presentation with a British viewpoint. Largely theoretical.
8. Altglass, Max and Kempf, Paul, Jr. "The Problem of Voice Placement." *Musician,* New York, March, 1934, Vol. 39, p. 7.
   Qualifications for a vocal career are discussed.
9. Althouse, Paul. "Wisdom and Whim in the Study of Singing." (An interview.) *Etude,* Philadelphia, 1941, Vol. 59, p. 91.
   No matter how lavish the singer's vocal equipment, common sense is the essential guide to correct development. The suggestions offered are simple and convincing.

10. American Academy of Teachers of Singing. "Care and Development of the Human Voice." *Music Education Journal*, December, 1938, Vol. 25, p. 26.
A statement of principles by the committee on adolescent voice.

11. —— *Singing, the Well-spring of Music.* The Academy, New York, 1933.
An interesting pamphlet expressing generalized ideas on singing in nontechnical language, based on a series of radio talks sponsored by the Academy.

12. Anderson, Marian. "Some Reflections on Singing." (An interview.) *Etude,* Philadelphia, 1939, Vol. 57, p. 631.
The distinguished American contralto discusses range, natural singing, teaching methods and other helpful topics. Reminiscences of early training are added.

13. Anonymous. "Academy Offers Sound Advice to Vocal Students." *Musician,* New York, February, 1929, Vol. 34, p. 35.
A statement issued by the American Academy of Teachers of Singing discusses problems of launching a vocal career and offers seven criteria for choosing a singing teacher.

14. —— "Best Voices Vibrate 2900 a Second." *Musician,* New York, January, 1933, Vol. 38, p. 14.
A report based on the Peabody Conservatory research on voice.

15. —— "Dearth of Superior Singing Voices Now Explained." *Science Digest,* Chicago, 1940, Vol. 7, p. 54.
W. T. Bartholomew of Peabody Conservatory reports on singers' difficulties.

16. —— "The Joy of Singing." *Etude,* Philadelphia, 1939, Vol. 57, p. 427.
The joy of singing supersedes the demands of mere exhibitionism. With the song truly in his heart, the singer often stumbles upon a natural method of singing by himself.

17. —— "Opinions of Two Authorities on Voice Production." *Musician,* New York, July, 1932, Vol. 37, p. 11.
William Shakespeare and Nellie Melba discuss certain principles of breath control. Essentially, breath economy is advocated.

18. —— "Singing in a Foreign Language." *Etude,* Philadelphia, 1934, Vol. 52, p. 741.
Italian, French and German are essential languages to the modern singer. The public demands it, and that settles the matter beyond further argument.

19. —— "Variations in Pitch of the Voice." *Science n.s.,* New York, 1934, Vol. 80 supplement, p. 7.
Report given at American Psychology Association meeting, on experimental results in pitch testing of vocal artists, by Harold G. Seashore.

20. Armstrong, Felice M. "Breath Control and How to Attain It." *Etude,* Philadelphia, 1936, Vol. 54, p. 448.
Breath control is the first essential in learning to sing. Eleven short exercises are listed which the author extravagently claims "will solve practically any problem of breathing."

21. Armstrong, William G. "Building a Program." *Etude*, Philadelphia, 1935, Vol. 53, p. 741.
    Audience appeal is an important factor in choosing a repertoire. Artistry in performance is not voice alone. It is also communication.
22. ———— "The Diaphragm in Its Relation to Breathing." *Etude*, Philadelphia, 1938, Vol. 56, p. 402.
    Some breathing exercises are given and posture is discussed.
23. ———— "Is Singing a Gift or an Accomplishment?" (Two articles), *Etude*, Philadelphia, 1939, Vol. 57, pp. 532, 598.
    The so-called *gifted* voice is always the product of intensive and patient cultivation. Therefore, method is all important in learning to sing. Twelve vocalises are given.
24. ———— "On the Treatment of Vocal Registers." (Two articles), *Etude*, Philadelphia, 1939, Vol. 57, pp. 52, 196.
    The main topics discussed in these two articles are sex differences in vocal range, vowel alteration and register breaks. Seven vocalises are given.
25. ———— "Shorter Road to Fine Singing." *Etude*, Philadelphia, 1940, Vol. 58, p. 525.
    Singing demands extraordinary vocal effort, compared to speaking. Therefore, at every stage of development, extraordinary devices should be used for vocal practice. Several daily exercises are given to tone up the voice.
26. ———— "The Song in Vocal Study." *Etude*, Philadelphia, 1938, Vol. 56, p. 608.
    Well chosen songs are invaluable as vocal exercises and should be studied as soon as possible. Some fine points for interpretation are given.
27. ———— "Tone." *Etude*, Philadelphia, 1942, Vol. 60, p. 91.
    Five types of faulty vocal tone are discussed with corrective exercises. Perfect "freedom" produces ideal tone, a tone that "rests entirely on the chest."
28. Austin, Herbert Wendell. "Artistic Tones." *Etude*, Philadelphia, 1939, Vol. 57, p. 599.
    Faulty diction is bad singing, regardless of tone quality. By patient practice of vowels and syllables can such faults be overcome. The vowels are individually discussed.
29. ———— "Expression in Singing." *Etude*, Philadelphia, 1936, Vol. 54, p. 513.
    It is expression that brings the song to life and lifts the ordinary singer to the level of an artist. Some general comments on interpretation are added.
30. ———— "The Singing Tempo." *Etude*, Philadelphia, 1939, Vol. 57, p. 271.
    A song sets its own tempo by its very mood or message. When the singer really feels this message he unconsciously swings into a correct tempo.
31. Austin-Ball, Thomas. *Answers to Some Vocal Questions* (In: Eastman School of Music Publication No. 7). Eastman School of Music, Rochester, 1938.
    Twelve fundamental questions are posed, then answered, covering many interesting aspects of vocal pedagogy.

32. Bairstow, Dent and others. "Vocal and Unvocal" (articles). *Music and Letters*, London, 1929, Vol. 10, pp. 235, 346.
   A series of excellent articles in which the attributes of good singing and singable literature are discussed by ten eminent commentators. Helpful and provocative.

33. —— "Vocal and Unvocal" (articles). *Music and Letters*, London, 1930, Vol. 11, p. 50.
   Concluding series of articles on the attributes of good song writing and good singing. Helpful to composers, singers and teachers.

34. Barbareux-Parry, Mrs. Mame. *Vocal Resonance.* Christopher House, Boston, 1941.
   A philosophical treatment of singing as a form of vocalized speech. Opinionated ideas are reinforced with some drills culled from studio experience. A strong personal bias is evident throughout.

35. Barnard, Bernice. "Whither 'Singing' in Idaho Schools." *Idaho Journal of Education*, Boise, 1932, Vol. 13, p. 292.
   The value of vocal training as a curriculum subject is briefly considered.

36. Bartholomew, Wilmer T. "Definition of 'Good Voice Quality' in the Male Voice." *Acoustical Society of America Journal*, Lancaster, Pennsylvania, January, 1934, Vol. 5, p. 224.
   Abstract of symposium paper read at tenth meeting of the Acoustical Society of America.

37. —— "The Paradox of Voice Teaching." *Journal Acoustical Society of America*, Lancaster, Pennsylvania, 1940, Vol. 11, p. 446.
   The open throat principle is explained acoustically.

38. —— "The Role of Imagery in Voice Teaching." *Music Teachers National Association Proceedings for 1935*, Oberlin, Ohio, 1936, Vol. 30, p. 78.
   Circumlocution is a helpful teaching device since laryngeal control is unapproachable by direct means. Some interesting research problems are discussed.

39. —— "A Survey of Recent Voice Research." *Music Teachers National Association Proceedings for 1937*, Oberlin, Ohio, 1938, Vol. 32, p. 115.
   Emphasis is laid on the pedagogical implications of vocal research. Vocal action is described in terms of experimental findings. An attempt to reconcile conflicting pedagogies.

40. —— "Voice Research at Peabody Conservatory" (In: *Bulletin of the American Musicological Society*), August, 1942, No. 6, p. 11.
   Abstract of paper reporting objective research program launched by the Peabody Conservatory.

41. Bas, Ami. "Correcting Faulty Pitch." *Etude*, Philadelphia, 1931, Vol. 49, p. 885.
   A useful suggestion to improve listening concentration.

42. Beddoe, Dan. "Singing at Three Score and Ten." (An interview.) *Etude*, Philadelphia, 1935, Vol. 53, p. 276.
   The noted Welsh tenor gives general advice on how to practice and how to avoid strain in singing.

43. Bellporte, Claude. "Student's Repertoire." *Etude*, Philadelphia, 1939, Vol. 57, p. 666.
   Choose a song with an emotional content that lies within the natural experience of the singer. A brief comment on over-ambitious teachers.

44. Benedict, Frank J. "Making Friends of the Consonants." *Etude*, Philadelphia, 1931, Vol. 49, p. 204.

English is a singing language if properly approached by the vocalist. Problems of diction are ingeniously handled and controversial points convincingly argued.

45. Bergère, Lawrence. "Ideals of a Singing Master." *Musician*, New York, April, May, June, July, 1934, Vol. 39, pp. 14, 10, 7, 10.

A series of short articles in which the author gives his conclusions after a personal investigation of the old Italian school of bel canto. The series is not completed.

46. Berto, Lili. "Speaking of Singing." *Musician*, New York, 1940, Vol. 45, p. 112.

A conventional treatment of breathing and head resonance.

47. Bjoerling, Jussi. "Good Singing is Natural." (An interview.) *Etude*, Philadelphia, 1940, Vol. 58, p. 655.

There is no trick about singing. It is a natural function, like eating, and should be kept free from conscious controls that interfere with its spontaneous activity.

48. Blalock, R. "Proper Breath Control Simplified." *Etude*, Philadelphia, 1937, Vol. 55, p. 603.

Maintaining a high chest during voice production will solve many breathing and tonal problems.

49. *Blatherwick, Barbara. "Bel Canto." *Musician*, New York, January, 1935, Vol. 40, p. 11.

The author decries the specious use of the term *bel canto* for advertising purposes. Manuel Garcia is briefly quoted. There are no pedagogical items.

50. ———— "Expression in Singing; Principles of Manuel Garcia." *Musician*, New York, September, 1935, Vol. 40, p. 8.

Individuality of expression is essential to the proper coloration of vocal tone.

51. ———— "Function of the Glottis in Singing." *Musician*, New York, April, 1935, Vol. 40, p. 6.

A consideration of "light" and "dark" vowel timbres.

52. ———— "The Futility of Searching for 'the Great Vocal Maestro.'" *Musician*, New York, February, 1935, Vol. 40, p. 15.

A short article written in the style of an interview. Foreign languages, registers, lieder singing and the author's predilections for bel canto are briefly discussed.

53. ———— "Preparation for Emitting Vocal Tone." *Musician*, New York, July, 1935, Vol. 40, p. 10.

The mouth is the door through which the voice passes. The correct opening is essential when singing. Breathing is also discussed.

54. Bokor, Margit. "Vocal Problems and Breath Technic." (An interview.) *Etude*, Philadelphia, 1941, Vol. 59, p. 735.

A virtuoso discusses breathing principles.

55. Bonavia-Hunt, Noel A. "The Science of the Human Voice." *Musical Opinion*, London, 1942, Vol. 65, p. 268.

The vortex theory of phonation is advanced with acoustical comments.

56. Booker, Otto. "Throat and Jaw Stiffness." *The Techne Magazine,* Pittsburg, Kansas, September-October, 1939, Vol. 13, p. 10.

    The most frequent obstacle to good singing is discussed in a short article.

57. Borchers, Orville J. "The Relation between Intensity and Harmonic Structure in Voice." *Psychological Record,* Bloomington, Indiana, 1939, Vol. 3, p. 59.

    Report of an experiment in which acoustic spectra of three tones of the same artist singer and vowel were analyzed at different intensity levels, with interesting results.

58. ———— "Vocal Timbre in its Immediate and Successive Aspects." *Music Teachers National Association Proceedings for 1941,* Pittsburgh, 1942, Vol. 36, p. 346.

    Experimental findings pertaining to vocal pitch, intensity and vowel components are discussed.

59. Bowlly, Al. *Modern Style Singing.* Henri Selmer and Company, London, 1934.

    A conventional method is used for developing microphone and crooning techniques.

60. Brainard, Paul P. "Psychology Analyses Musical Appeal in Song Interpretation." *Musician,* New York, 1936, Vol. 41, p. 125.

    Words are joined to music to intensify the message imparted by the song. Hence sincerity of interpretation is always paramount in singing.

61. Braine, Robert. "Voice and Violin." *Etude,* Philadelphia, 1935, Vol. 53, p. 242.

    Ear training for the singer can best be accomplished by listening to good violin playing, since the violin most nearly resembles the human voice.

62. Brainerd, Jessie. "How to Preserve the Voice." *Etude,* Philadelphia, 1938, Vol. 56, p. 609.

    Eight suggestions are given embodying rules of vocal health and hygiene.

63. Brines, Mrs. John Francis. "Supreme Test of Singing." *Etude,* Philadelphia, 1930, Vol. 48, p. 816.

    Making the song interesting is the supreme test of good singing. All technical requirements subserve this end. Interpretation is a type of story telling.

64. Brouillet, Georges A. *Voice Manual.* Bruce Humphries, Incorporated, Boston, 1936.

    A "natural voice" method is superficially treated.

65. Brown, Hubert. *The Principles of Expression in Song.* Oxford University Press, London, 1928.

    A compact but useful reorientation for the finished singer but of little scientific value.

66. ———— *Success in Amateur Opera.* William Reeves, London, 1939.

    Instructions on auditions, rehearsals, conducting and training soloists are the main features. Superficially treated.

67. Brown, William Earl. "Achieving Vocal Action by Instinct." *Musician,* New York, August, 1932, Vol. 37, p. 6.

The singing act is a coordination of the whole organism, mind and muscle.

68. ——— "Aphorisms on Singing." *Musician,* New York, 1941, Vol. 46, pp. 25, 73, 154.

Worthwhile nuggets of learning by the author of *Vocal wisdom.*

69. ——— "Balance between Voice and Breath." *Musician,* New York, April, 1935, Vol. 40, p. 11.

Vocal maxims are discussed briefly.

70. ——— "Consummate Art of Song." *Musician,* New York, March, 1933, Vol. 38, p. 16.

A song should be seamless; that is, an integrated performance of continuous texture and unity of effect.

71. ——— "Essential Quality in the Singing Voice." *Musician,* New York, January, 1933, Vol. 38, p. 14.

A fragment of Lamperti's vocal wisdom.

72. ——— "Pure Vocal Tone." *Musician,* New York, August, 1935, Vol. 40, p. 12.

Direct manipulation cannot awaken the subtle vibrations and overtones of the singing voice; tone production involves thinking as well as muscle reflexes.

73. ——— "Sensation in Voice Production." *Musician,* New York, 1937, Vol. 42, p. 106.

The sensations in the head during voice production mirror the entire expressional output of the voice and may be used as a guide to correct singing.

74. ——— "Song Tone Evolves." *Musician,* New York, January, 1934, Vol. 39, p. 17.

The singing tone evolves from the speaking voice according to Lamperti. The author endorses this with his comments.

75. ——— "Subtle Powers of Singing." *Musician,* New York, 1937, Vol. 42, p. 25.

The illusion of beauty that singing creates is a subtle coordination of mind and body that transcends the mere union of physical factors such as breathing, phonation and pronunciation.

76. ——— "Teachers and Doers." *Musician,* New York, November, 1934, Vol. 39, p. 11.

Why great singers are rarely great instructors.

77. ——— "Train Your Ears!" *Musician,* New York, December, 1931, Vol. 36, p. 15.

Your ears only can tell you how to sing. Therefore train your ears if you would control your voice.

78. ——— *Vocal Wisdom; Maxims of Giovanni Battista Lamperti.* The author, New York, 1931.

Although the treatment is philosophical, this book is well named and is worth reading. It contains a summation of bel canto principles in succinct paragraphs and provides a useful orientation for the teacher of singing. The author writes: "This wisdom of the Golden Age of Song came down the centuries to me; I pass it on to you." Certain portions of this book are broken into fragments and reprinted, with or without comment, in the following issues of *Musician* under the following captions. These are listed here for reference only.

"Acoustical Laws of the Voice." February, 1932, Vol. 37, p. 6.

"Diction for Singers." December, 1933, Vol. 38, p. 2.

"Final Technique of Singing." July, 1932, Vol. 37, p. 18.

"Ideal Vocal Tone." April, 1932, Vol. 37, p. 15.

"Ideal Vocal Tone." September, 1934, Vol. 39, p. 7.

"Inherent Energy Sings the Song." June, 1934, Vol. 39, p. 7.

"Inhibitions that Prevent Successful Singing." April, 1934, Vol. 39, p. 6.

"Kinship of Tones." November, 1931, Vol. 36, p. 15.

"Positive and Negative Poles of Vocal Energy." March, 1934, Vol. 39, p. 9.

"Self-producing, Self-placing Voice." January, 1935, Vol. 40, p. 11.

"Sing as You Speak." December, 1934, Vol. 39, p. 10.

"Sing the Silences." April, 1933, Vol. 38, p. 10.

"Singer's Sixth Sense." July, 1934, Vol. 39, p. 7.

"Singers Urged Not to Practice Humming." August, 1933, Vol. 38, p. 10.

"Spontaneous Singing." August, 1934, Vol. 37, p. 13.

"Tactile Sense of Singing." June, 1932, Vol. 37, p. 8.

"Vocal Philosophy of Lamperti." May, 1932, Vol. 37, p. 25.

"Wherein Vocal Noises Differ from Singing." July, 1933, Vol. 38, p. 4.

79. Brownlee, John. "Style's the Thing." (An interview.) *Etude*, Philadelphia, 1939, Vol. 57, p. 561.

The operatic stylist creates more than the external attributes of a character portrayal. He also imbues it with inner meaning. The seasoning of a role is a point of training often missed by young artists.

80. Buck, Dudley. "The American Academy of Teachers of Singing." *Music Teachers National Association Proceedings for 1933*, Oberlin, Ohio, 1934, Vol. 28, p. 129.

The aims and accomplishments of the academy are briefly outlined.

81. Burke, Joanna B. (Joan O'Vark, pseudonym). *The Fundamentals of Tone Production*. Schroeder and Gunther, New York, 1928.

Extravagant claims for a few exercises based on nonsense syllables.

82. Bushell, Sidney. "Covered Tones." *Etude*, Philadelphia, 1939, Vol. 57, p. 739.

In establishing upper voice quality, baritones should learn to think *oo* while singing *ah*. Two vocalises are given.

83. ———— "Fifteen Minutes of Stimulating Vocal Practice." *Etude*, Philadelphia, 1940, Vol. 58, p. 811.

It is better to think the tone five minutes and practice one minute than the reverse. Six items for practice are offered and discussed.

84. ———— "Poise: an Essential to Good Singing." *Musician*, New York, 1939, Vol. 44, p. 217.

Correct breathing and its consequent tone production may be brought about almost automatically by a correct standing position of the singer's body.

85. Buswell, Guy T. "The Laboratory Method in Educational Psychology." *Elementary School Journal*, Chicago, Vol. 32, p. 656.

A scientific discussion of laboratory studies in the objective analysis of the singing voice.

86. Butler, Harold L. "Resonance: What It Is and How It Can Be Developed." *Etude,* Philadelphia, 1930, Vol. 48, p. 282.
     Several generalized opinions are briefly discussed.
87. ——— "Salient Changes in Voice Teaching in the Past 50 Years." *Etude,* Philadelphia, 1928, Vol. 46, p. 220.
     A short opinionated statement on modern teaching trends.
88. ——— "What the Young Vocal Graduate Should Know." *Music Teachers National Association Proceedings for 1934,* Oberlin, Ohio, 1935, Vol. 29, p. 86.
     The syllabus of a typical graduate course in vocal training is discussed.
89. Byers, Margaret C. "Sbriglia's Method of Singing." *Etude,* Philadelphia, 1942, Vol. 60, p. 307.
     An interesting synopsis that stresses breathing.

90. Cain, Noble. *Choral Music and Its Practice.* M. Witmark, New York, 1942.
     The book is essentially for choir masters. Tone quality and interpretation are treated separately. A list of books and songs is appended.
91. Campajani, Giovanni. "Sanity in Singing." In: *Guildiana—American Guild of Organists,* New York, December, 1942, Vol. II, p. 2.
     The author deplores the lack of agreement among vocal teachers.
92. Capell, Richard (as quoted). "What's Happened to Singing?" *Literary Digest,* New York, May 10, 1930, Vol. 105, p. 22.
     The British critic issues a tirade against bad vocal teaching.
93. Carson, Leon. "The Voice Teacher's Terminology." *Music Teachers National Association Proceedings for 1941.* Pittsburgh, 1942, Vol. 36, p. 301.
     An interesting and provocative review of the vocal terminology problem intended to arouse discussion and interchange of ideas on this debatable subject.
94. Castagna, Bruna. "Good Singing Must Be Natural." (An interview.) *Etude,* Philadelphia, 1939, Vol. 57, p. 159.
     The leading contralto discusses some singing fundamentals and gives advice to beginners on breathing, and interpretation.
95. Chaliapin, Feodor. "The Singer's Art." *Etude,* Philadelphia, 1936, Vol. 54, p. 7.
     The great artist discusses generalities of singing.
96. Chesnutt, Nelson A. "Automatic Breath Control." *Musician,* New York, May, 1928, Vol. 33, p. 14.
     A prominent teacher gives his ideas on basic vocal training.
97. Christy, Van Ambrose. *Glee Club and Chorus.* G. Schirmer, New York, 1940.
     A director's handbook filled with useful hints on organizing and conducting a choral group. The classified lists of recommended music are excellent.
98. Cimini, Pietro. *My Ten Commandments for Correct Voice Production.* Preeman-Matthews Company, Los Angeles, 1936.
     The ten rules are succinctly stated, but the author adds very little information about them.

99. —— "Ten Commandments for Correct Voice Production." *Etude*, Philadelphia, 1937, Vol. 55, p. 334.

The author's opinions are expressed as generalizations.

100. Clark, Charles W. "Thoughts on Breath, Poise and the Elimination of Fear." *Journal of Arkansas Education*, Little Rock, March, 1932, Vol. 10, p. 21.

An excellent article epitomizing the singer's major problems, psychologically approached. Well worth reading.

101. Clark, Mary and Leland, Robert De Camp. *Secrets of correct singing.* Four Seas Company, Boston, 1928.

A "noted soprano" writes some conventional notes on singing. Uninformative.

102. Clark, Wallace R. "Breathing." *Etude*, Philadelphia, 1930, Vol. 48, p. 506.

An intelligent but brief discussion, useful to beginners.

103. Clippinger, David Alva. "Changes in Methods of Voice Training in the Last 50 years." *Etude*, Philadelphia, 1929, Vol. 47, p. 530.

An interesting survey of psychological vocal methods with reference to historical origins.

104. —— *The Clippinger Class-method of Voice Culture.* Oliver Ditson, Boston, 1932.

This book provides tested materials and directions for systematic voice-training in groups. It is practical and direct. The teacher's approach is evident throughout.

105. —— *Fundamentals of Voice Training.* Oliver Ditson, Boston, 1929.

A constructive and philosophical viewpoint is presented. The author is a seasoned practitioner and speaks with conviction. But practical applications, though much needed, are evaded.

106. —— "How to Escape Some Vocal Pitfalls in the Day's Work." *Etude*, Philadelphia, 1936, Vol. 54, p. 316.

Practical hints on overcoming typical studio teaching problems. Useful and authoritative.

107. —— "The Human Instrument." *Etude*, Philadelphia, 1929, Vol. 47, p. 212.

In the early stages of learning, unsupervised practice may impede growth. Before the student has acquired a correct tonal concept, practice is as likely to harm as to benefit him.

108. —— "An Outline to Guide the Student's Approach to the Study of Singing." *Etude*, Philadelphia, 1936, Vol. 54, p. 109.

Nineteen precepts of vocal pedagogy are listed without comment. The mental approach is featured.

109. —— "An Outline to Guide the Vocal Student's Practice." (Part II), *Etude*, Philadelphia, 1936, Vol. 54, p. 512.

Twenty-three vocal precepts are listed without comment.

110. —— "Studio Vocal Clinic." *Etude*, Philadelphia, 1930, Vol. 48, p. 206.

A comprehensive survey of the most typical studio problems. The ear training approach is featured.

111. —— "Throaty Singing." *Etude*, Philadelphia, 1936, Vol. 54, p. 725.

Relaxation and open throat methods are prescribed as antidotes for throatiness.

112. —— "Training of a Singer." *Etude*, Philadelphia, 1931, Vol. 49, p. 810.
Conclusions drawn from a well seasoned experiential viewpoint. A comprehensive, though philosophical, discussion without exercises.

113. —— "Trend Toward Sanity in Modern Day Vocal Pedagogy." *Musician*, New York, March, 1929, Vol. 34, p. 16.
The psychological teaching approach is convincingly presented.

114. —— "Vocal Department." *School Music*, Chicago, January, 1935, p. 9; January, 1936, p. 9; March, 1936, p. 13; Vol. 35-36.
In this series of discussions presented by the author, a sound pedagogical approach to vocal problems is used. The physiological background is of uncertain value.

115. —— "Vocal Department." *School Music*, Chicago, September, 1935, Vol. 35, p. 11.
The vocal cords as vibrators of sound are discussed. Arguments for and against the various theories of phonation are also briefly considered.

116. —— and others. "Vocal Forum." *Music Teachers National Association Proceedings for 1936*, Oberlin, Ohio, 1937, Vol. 31, p. 168.
This series includes the following ten short articles on various problems of vocal training written by vocal specialists and introduced by the author. (1) "Singing as a Cultural Subject." B. Fred Wise (Chicago). (2) "Eliminating Vocal Interference." Cameron McLean (Detroit). (3) "Emphasis on Diction." Richard De Young (Chicago). (4) "Foreign Languages in Singing." Shirley Gandell (Chicago). (5) "Vibrato and Tremolo." Adolph Muhlmann (Chicago). (6) "Ear Training in Singing." John T. Read (Chicago). (7) "Preparation of Singing Teachers." Graham Reed (Chicago). (8) "Polarity in Singing." Walter A. Stults (Evanston, Ill.). (9) "Music Theory as Part of Vocal Study." May A. Strong (Evanston, Ill.). (10) Should High School Students Study Singing?" William Phillips (Chicago).

117. —— "Vocalist's ABC." *Etude*, Philadelphia, 1929, Vol. 47, p. 212.
It is not the voice that sings. It is the musical intelligence that sings. Hence, training the musical mind is at least as important as the study of vocal technique.

118. Coleman, Henry. *The Amateur Choir Trainer*. Oxford University Press, London, 1932.
A compact but thorough and practical book for the nonprofessional director. The treatment is general although the emphasis is on training young voices.

119. Combs, William Walker. *The Voice in Singing; Its Care and Development*. The author, Dallas, Texas, 1938.
A brief theoretical treatment followed by numerous graded exercises and excellent practice materials.

120. Compton, George. "American Singers Must Learn Foreign Languages." (An interview.) *Musician*, New York, January, 1935, Vol. 40, p. 9.
Perfect diction is the royal road to artistic singing and English is as good a study medium as any foreign language.

121. Conklin, Maurice. *Fundamental Vocal Technique*. Dorrance and Company, Philadelphia, 1936.
The studio teacher gives his opinions on current vocal theories.

122. Coward, Sir Henry. *"C.T.I." The Secret: "Les Nuances Bien Indiquées."* Novello and Company, London, 1938.

A supplement to the author's *Choral Technic and Interpretation.* The method of "super-breathing" described, is unusual.

123. Crist, Bainbridge. "The 'Missing Link' in Voice Production." *Emerson Quarterly,* Boston, November, 1930, Vol. 11, p. 15.

The teaching precepts of Garcia, Lamperti and Lehmann are compared and discussed.

124. Curry, Robert O. L. *The Mechanism of the Human Voice.* Longmans Green, New York, 1940.

An attempt is made to correlate some of the many diversified lines of study in the vocal field. The vocal mechanism is exhaustively treated but the book is so broad in scope that many portions of it are slighted.

125. Curtis, H. Holbrook. "Voice Building and Tone Placing." (As quoted in *Etude.*) *Etude,* Philadelphia, 1938, Vol. 56, p. 115.

The use of vibrato in singing is briefly considered.

126. Dacy, George H. "Secrets of Your Voice." *Popular Mechanics Magazine,* Chicago, April, 1930, Vol. 53, p. 594.

Dr. Russell's vocal experiments at Ohio State University are discussed.

127. Davies, Marjorie Ffrangcon. *David Ffrangcon-Davies: His Life and Book.* John Lane, London, 1938.

A linguistic approach based on the thesis that "singing is a sustained talking on a tune." Part one is biographical. The author rests on his reputation as a singer.

128. De Bar, Dorothy. "Foundation Work in Voice Development." *Etude,* Philadelphia, 1928, Vol. 46, p. 468.

A few hints for practicing are given.

129. De Bruyn, John W. "Historical Schools of Singing." *Etude,* Philadelphia, 1942, Vol. 60, p. 667.

An interesting historical synopsis of singing methods and their leading exponents. Excellent summary.

130. —— "Male Choral Voice." Manuscript copy, 1940.

The author attempts to discuss sixty-six topics, numerous exercises, historical schools of thought, solfeggi and supplementary items in a seventy-page volume. Superficial, though interesting.

131. —— "The oldest Authentic Voice Method." *Etude,* Philadelphia, 1938, Vol. 56, p. 367.

A scholarly discussion of the speech-song approach.

132. —— "Technic of the Bel Canto." *Etude,* Philadelphia, 1940, Vol. 59, p. 597.

Imitation and ear training exercises are presented and discussed.

133. —— "What Is the Matter with My Voice?" *Etude,* Philadelphia, 1940, Vol. 58, p. 453.

The author lists twenty-eight different vocal deficiencies and defines them in general terms.

134. de Gogorza, Emilio. "The Essentials of Vocal Art." (An interview.) *Etude,* Philadelphia, 1942, Vol. 60, p. 811.

Generalities of training for a singing career are discussed.

135. della Chiesa, Vivian. "Successful Singing." (An interview.) *Etude*, Philadelphia, 1942, Vol. 60, p. 583.
A few hints on training for a vocal career are given.

136. *Dennis, Regina. "Profits from Voice Training." *Etude*, Philadelphia, 1934, Vol. 52, p. 487.
How reticence was overcome in a student is told by a voice teacher. There are no pedagogical applications.

137. De Young, Richard B. "The Paradox of Voice Teaching." *Music Teachers National Association Proceedings for 1941*. Pittsburgh, 1942, Vol. 36, p. 294.
Current teaching methods are reconciled with the findings of the vocal physicists.

138. Divver, Helen Cecilia. *Teaching Notes and Treatise on Singing*. The Graphic Press, Newton, Massachusetts, 1941.
The teaching notes of the author are posthumously published. They are terse vocal statements interspersed with bits of philosophy.

139. Dodds, George and Lickley, James Dunlop. *The Control of the Breath*. Oxford University Press, London, 1935, 2nd edition.
The physiology of breathing and several vocal methods are presented with accompanying anatomical drawings. Many theoretical digressions are included.

140. Dossert, Deane (Mme.). *Sound Sense for Singers*. J. Fischer and Brothers, New York, 1932.
A veteran teacher gives some interesting opinions on teaching, but without factual support.

141. Doubleday, H. M. "Reasons for Studying Singing." *Etude*, Philadelphia, 1931, Vol. 49, p. 510.
Twelve reasons for studying singing as issued by the American Academy of Teachers of Singing are commented upon by the author.

142. Douty, Nicholas, "Developing a Beautiful Vocal Art through Balance of Tone and Diction." *Etude*, Philadelphia, 1937, Vol. 55, p. 746.
Each song presents a new problem of diction and tone production. Proper interpretation involves the resolution of conflict between the two.

143. —— "In the Beginning Was the Word: Its Significance to the Singer." *Etude*, Philadelphia, 1934, Vol. 52, p. 740.
There can be no singing without words, and the vowel is the vocal unit in each word. Hence vowel study is all important in song analysis.

144. —— "The Singer of the Present and the Future." *Etude*, Philadelphia, 1933, Vol. 51, pp. 408, 478.
In a sequence of two articles the author broadly discusses vocal theory, radio, television, diction and personality problems of the singer.

145. —— "Voice Questions Answered." *Etude*, Philadelphia, (see monthly numbers of *Etude* starting October, 1938).
Questions from readers cover many interesting problems of vocal study. The answers to these questions are informative and frequently accompanied by useful exercises.

146. Dragonette, Jessica. "The Mental Approach to Singing." (An interview.) *Etude*, Philadelphia, 1940, Vol. 58, p. 510.
Breathing and resonance are discussed from a practical viewpoint.

147. Drew, William Sydney. *Singing: The Art and the Craft*. Oxford, London, 1937.
    A scholarly philosophic discussion emphasizing British traits and mannerisms in singing.

148. ——— "Some Principles of Voice Training." *Musical Times*, London, 1937, Vol. 78, p. 406.
    Listening to good vocal models is a valuable ear training device.

149. ——— "Voice and Verse." *Musical Times*, London, 1942, Vol. 83, p. 171.
    Interesting comments on the importance of text in interpreting a song and the failings of singers who ignore the text.

150. Dunkin, Leslie E. "Acting the Song." *Etude*, Philadelphia, 1938, Vol. 56, p. 470.
    The singer's technique is compared to the actor's technique.

151. Dunkley, Ferdinand L. *The Buoyant Voice*. C. C. Birchard, Boston, 1942.
    An interesting theory with accompanying exercises, proposing that the mood of the highest pitch in each song phrase shall dominate the mood of the entire phrase.

152. Earhart, Will. *Choral Technics*. M. Witmark and Sons, New York, 1937.
    A practical study course integrating sight singing, vocal training and repertory materials.

153. ——— *Teachers' Manual for Choral Technics*. M. Witmark, New York, 1938.
    A companion work to the author's *Choral Technics*, giving instructions for using the latter.

154. Easley, Eleanor. "A Comparison of the Vibrato in Concert and Opera Singing." (In: *The vibrato*, University of Iowa Studies in the Psychology of Music.) University of Iowa Press, Iowa City, Iowa, 1932, Vol. I, p. 269.
    An abridgement of an M.A. thesis experimental study reports that opera singers employ wider and faster vibratos than concert singers.

155. Eddy, Nelson. "Success in Voice Study." (An interview.) *Etude*, Philadelphia, 1939, Vol. 57, p. 695.
    Advice to beginners on how to launch a successful singing career includes warnings against common pitfalls.

156. Edgerton, Howard H. "Nasal Tone." *Etude*, Philadelphia, 1942, Vol. 60, p. 374.
    Part of every tone must be sung through the nose. An attempt is made to dispel the nasal tone fallacy, with doubtful results.

157. ——— "Vocal Training as Music Study." *Musician*, New York, 1939, Vol. 44, p. 171.
    The teacher must handle each pupil differently and with sympathetic tact. Hence, vocal teaching methods are administered to suit the individual's attitudes and shortcomings.

158. Edwards, Fassett. "Some Secrets of Good Singing." *Etude*, Philadelphia, 1932, Vol. 50, p. 506.
    A physician discusses vocal theory. Crude concepts of vocal action.

159. Efnor, Claude Orin. *The Voicemaster Course for Self Training of the Voice*. Voicemaster Studios, Minneapolis, 1942.
    The author professes to base his infallible method on authentic

scientific information and facts, but beyond this promise there is no documentation whatever. His ideas are psychologically treated.

160. Eley, Harriette Estelle. "Singing off Pitch; Its Cure." *Etude*, Philadelphia, 1937, Vol. 55, p. 747.

Well directed thought will correct vocal pitch aberrations. Repetitive mental practice is advocated.

161. Elverson, H. Edmund. "Interpreting the Song." *Etude*, Philadelphia, 1933, Vol. 51, p. 843.

A slow, detailed analysis of the song helps in the capture of its emotional content.

162. Engstrom, Everett Albert. "Naturalness in Voice Production." *Musician*, New York, 1937, Vol. 42, p. 27.

Beautiful singing is based on natural laws. But these laws are not presented or defined. "Reaching up" for the tone is a common fault.

163. Eustis, Morton. "Players at Work." (Chapter on the Singing Actor by Lotte Lehmann.) Theatre Arts, Incorporated, New York, 1937, p. 118.

Gives some useful pointers on song and operatic interpretation.

164. Everett, Henry E. "The 'American Twang' in Song." *Etude*, Philadelphia, 1932, Vol. 50, p. 733.

The carelessness that prevails in average American speech robs the voice of its resonance and is a cause of the rarity of great American singers.

165. Everett, Mme. Miabelle. "We Sing with the Whole Physique." *Etude*, Philadelphia, 1935, Vol. 53, p. 109.

In singing, the total coordination of many parts of the body is more important than the trained activity of any single part.

166. Evetts, Edgar T. "The Mechanics of Singing and Speaking." *Musical Opinion*, London, 1938, Vol. 61, p. 601.

The behavior of the vocal cords is described as observed under transillumination and X-ray.

167. —— and Worthington, Robert A. *The Mechanics of Singing*. J. M. Dent and Sons, London, 1928.

The idea of registers is refuted but inaccurate observations lead to numerous fallacies. Some good ideas are included.

168. Farnsworth, D. W. "High Speed Motion Pictures of the Human Vocal Cords." *Music Teachers National Association Proceedings for 1939*, Pittsburgh, 1940, Vol. 34, p. 306.

An interesting description of glottal action during phonation as the camera reveals it.

169. —— "Radiation Pattern of the Human Voice." *Scientific Monthly*, Lancaster, Pennsylvania, August, 1942, Vol. 55, p. 139.

By means of carefully planned microphone tests, 5,000 readings of vocal projection characteristics were taken, with interesting results. A report of experimental observations is given.

170. Farrar, Geraldine. "Coming Back and Looking Back." (An interview.) *Saturday Evening Post*, Philadelphia, April 14, 1928, Vol. 200, p. 18.

Interesting reminiscences of a long successful operatic career.

171. —— "How Can We Best Serve Our Students." (An interview.) *Etude,* Philadelphia, 1938, Vol. 56, p. 563.

Artistic success requires natural gifts, good teaching and a receptive audience. Personal reminiscences and some vocal methods are discussed.

172. Faulds, Edward. "Think Straight in Singing." *Etude,* Philadelphia, 1931, Vol. 49, p. 510.

An argumentative discussion of several teaching fallacies, including tone placing, blending registers and resonance.

173. Felderman, Dr. Leon. *The Human Voice, Its Care and Development.* Henry Holt, New York, 1931.

Vocal pathology is the main topic discussed from a medical point of view.

174. —— "Practical Application of Voice Dynamics." *Laryngoscope,* St. Louis, 1934, Vol. 44, p. 902.

A physician discusses problems of voice production and resonance.

175. —— "Production of the Human Voice." *Hygeia,* Chicago, August, 1933, Vol. 11, p. 731.

A popularized discussion for the layman, containing brief descriptions of laryngeal action and vocal acoustics.

176. Fellows, Townsend H. "Vocal Art History Repeats Itself." *Musician,* New York, March, 1930, Vol. 35, p. 30.

The author believes there is a dearth of thoroughly trained singing teachers; also there is a lack of willingness, among young singers, to submit to serious study.

177. Fergusson, George. (Title omitted.) *Musician,* New York, June, 1934, Vol. 39, p. 7.

An item on bel canto.

178. —— "Singer's Basic Equipment." *Musician,* New York, 1940, Vol. 45, p. 5.

Posture, tone and musicianship form the bases of the singer's training. The tonal product of correct singing is always caused by the physical reaction to a mental concept.

179. Feuchtinger, Eugene. "The Open Throat and Depth of Tone in Singing." *Etude,* Philadelphia, 1933, Vol. 51, p. 339.

The physiological approach is stressed in this brief article.

180. *—— *The Voice.* Perfect Voice Institute, Chicago, 1935, 9th edition.

The book is used largely as an advertisement for the Perfect Voice Institute's mail order course of "Physical Voice Culture" given by the author. The actual methods of instruction are not revealed.

181. Finn, Rev. William J. *The Art of the Choral Conductor.* C. C. Birchard, Boston, 1939.

An excellent work written with authority and common sense from a well seasoned and practical viewpoint.

182. Flagstad, Kirsten. "Learning How to Help Yourself." (An interview.) *Etude,* Philadelphia, 1939, Vol. 57, p. 363.

Self-discipline and self-help provide the mainstays of vocal development. Tones alone will not make a resourceful singer for character training is equally important.

183. Fleming, Cecile N. "Let Nature Guide Your Singing." *Etude*, Philadelphia, 1935, Vol. 53, p. 611.

Brief comment on the need for simplicity in vocal teaching. A simple explanation of breathing is given.

184. ———— "Preserving the Young Voice." *Etude*, Philadelphia, 1935, Vol. 53, p. 542.

Psychological methods of teaching are propounded.

185. ———— "That Groove in the Tongue." *Etude*, Philadelphia, 1934, Vol. 52, p. 431.

The tongue groove is best developed by practicing vowels with a loose, inert tongue.

186. Fory, Gurdon A. "Chest Tones or Not?" *Etude*, Philadelphia, 1937, Vol. 55, p. 818.

Chest tones are an indispensable part of the woman's voice and should be cultivated. Try to open the voice downward. Yawning helps.

187. ———— "Choosing Exercises That Do Work." *Etude*, Philadelphia, 1936, Vol. 54, p. 173.

Consonants do not sing, they obstruct. The words of simple songs provide more effective practice materials than silly nonsense syllables.

188. ———— "Coloring the Tone." *Etude*, Philadelphia, 1934, Vol. 52, p. 374.

Yawning, humming, tonal concepts and the vowel *oo* are discussed as practice aids for improving vocal quality.

189. ———— "The Need of Soft Practice." *Etude*, Philadelphia, 1935, Vol. 53, p. 45.

Loud singing is a natural outgrowth of correct soft singing. The student singer must learn to wait patiently for this development to take place.

190. ———— "Old Italian Secrets." *Etude*, Philadelphia, 1933, Vol. 51, p. 545.

Simplicity and common sense are the key notes of all good vocal teaching. The old Italians knew this secret and combined it with patient practice.

191. ———— "Opening the Voice." *Etude*, Philadelphia, 1935, Vol. 53, p. 175.

Try to sing in, rather than out. This paradoxical approach helps to open the voice.

192. ———— " 'Straightening Up' the High Tones." *Etude*, Philadelphia, 1936, Vol. 54, p. 652.

"Singing forward" can become an obsession that often robs top notes of their natural color. Each tone has its own direction; some forward, some straight up.

193. ———— "Strengthening the Laryngeal Muscles." *Etude*, Philadelphia, 1939, Vol. 57, p. 196.

Gymnastics and vocalises are essential to vocal study. They are the strength-building exercises which ordinary singing does not provide. Three exercises are given.

194. ———— "What About Nasal Resonance." *Etude*, Philadelphia, 1934, Vol. 52, p. 189.

Right and wrong qualities of nasal resonance are briefly discussed and a simple testing device is described.

195. Foster, Miss Clyde E. "Vocal Music in the Public Schools." *American Schoolmaster*, Ypsilanti, Michigan, 1929, Vol. 22, p. 329.

An inspirational appeal for greater recognition of the importance of vocal music in the school curriculum.

196. Freemantel, Frederick Charles. "High Tones and How to Sing Them." *Etude*, Philadelphia, 1940, Vol. 58, p. 741.

The technique and carrying power of a spontaneous shout may be translated into proper voice production. Open throat and breath support are also helpful.

197. Galli-Curci, Mme. Amelita. "Why I Prefer Concert to Opera." *Etude*, Philadelphia, 1930, Vol. 48, p. 849.

With the voice of experience the noted prima donna candidly gives some excellent advice to singers. Ludicrous operatic situations are discussed. Natural singing is explained.

198. Garnetti-Forbes, Elena. *The Amazing Phenomenon of Voice.* Rider and Company, London, 1936.

A novel approach to singing based on metaphysical and physiological concepts. The evolution of vocal function is also treated. The assumption that all vocal effort is centered in the lumbar region is developed without proof.

199. Gescheidt, Adelaide. "In Defense of a Scientific Basis of Voice Training." *Musician*, New York, April, 1931, Vol. 36, p. 27.

Voice is a natural function and its activity should be spontaneous and joyful. Scientific teaching helps to remove vocal obstructions.

200. —— *Make Singing a Joy.* R. L. Huntzinger, New York, 1930.

The author lays claim to a new and "better" method, the reasons for which are abstractly treated.

201. Giddings, T. P. "Developing the Ensemble and Individual Singing." *Supervisors Service Bulletin*, Chicago, September, 1931, Vol. 11, p. 45.

Problems of organizing and training singing groups are discussed.

202. —— "Vocal Music." *School Music*, Chicago, May, 1929, Vol. 30, p. 16.

A discussion of correct intonation and oversinging as applied to ensemble work. Some general principles are offered.

203. Gigli, Beniamino. "The Art of Singing." (An interview.) *Etude*, Philadelphia, 1932, Vol. 50, p. 837.

Strive for naturalness and quality of tone, not quantity. The artist's vicissitudes are discussed in a reminiscent mood.

204. Glenn, Mabelle. "A New Goal in Ensemble Singing." *Music Supervisors Journal*, Chapel Hill, North Carolina, October, 1928, Vol. 15, p. 69.

Many points are discussed for improving choir singing. Vocal and musical criteria are listed.

205. —— "Singing." *National Society for the Study of Education*, Bloomington, Illinois, 1936, Vol. 35, Part II, p. 62.

A short summation of teaching principles applied to the study of singing in schools.

206. Gould, Julia Stacy. *Successful Singing, Based on the Italian Method of Singing.* Julia S. Gould, East Greenwich, Rhode Island. 1942.

An attempt is made to review and clarify the theory of singing. But clarity is often lost for want of a suitable terminology.

207. Grace, Harvey. *The Training and Conducting of Choral Societies.* Novello and Company, London, 1938.
A collection of articles appearing in the *Musical Times* presents a seasoned and practical viewpoint. The treatment is brief but complete.

208. Graveure, Louis. "New Theories of Vocalism." (An interview.) *Etude,* Philadelphia, 1931, Vol. 49, p. 128.
Muscular sensation and control regulate nearly every factor in the act of singing. A controversial issue is rationally handled.

209. Greene, Harry Plunket. *Interpretation in Song.* Macmillan, London, 1940.
An excellent, authoritative and practical treatment, simply, yet exhaustively presented. The author knows his business.

210. Green, Spencer. "Furthering the Vocal Ideal." *Educational Music Magazine,* Chicago, November, 1936, Vol. 16, p. 29.
Voice culture can be carried on in groups with an intelligent application of the fundamentals that apply to individual voice training.

211. Gregory, Herschell C. "That Elusive Voice Placement." *Etude,* Philadelphia, 1935, Vol. 53, p. 425.
Conscious voice placement usually tightens the voice. Ear training approaches are more effective.

212. ——— "Well Placed Voice the Goal of Every Singer." *Etude,* Philadelphia, 1938, Vol. 56, p. 331.
A humming approach to voice placement is described.

213. Grove, Grace Jarnagin. "Compromise Vowels." *Etude,* Philadelphia, 1936, Vol. 54, p. 172.
By the use of subtle vowel mixtures, the singer maintains correct diction without ever sacrificing purity of tone.

214. ——— "From Vocalise to Song." *Etude,* Philadelphia, 1938, Vol. 56, p. 330.
The vocalise vowel is not always adaptable to verbal utterance. Special consonant drills are therefore offered to help effect the transfer from vowel practice to word practice in singing.

215. ——— "Mend Your Speech or Mar Your Song." *Etude,* Philadelphia, 1933, Vol. 51, p. 194.
Admonitions against careless diction in daily speech are given to help singers improve their singing.

216. ——— "On the Development of the Vowel." *Etude,* Philadelphia, 1937, Vol. 55, p. 534.
A series of nine simple remedial vowel exercises is presented with a clear and concise explanation of their usefulness to the singer. A system of verbal analysis is used.

217. Gruen, Herta. "Good Singing Depends upon Flawless Diction." *Musician,* New York, 1941, Vol. 46, p. 140.
Generalities of interpretation are discussed.

218. Grundmann, John and Schumacher, Bernhard. *Manual for the Music Reader for Lutheran Schools.* Concordia Publishing House, St. Louis, 1933.
A teacher's manual containing specific instructions for training the

young singer. Some useful hints of general importance to all singers are added.

219. Hackett, Charles. "Turning the Student into an Artist." (An interview.) *Etude*, Philadelphia, 1942, Vol. 60, p. 377.

The vocal teacher is not unlike the doctor. His methods of diagnosis and treatment must vary with the individual case. Enunciation and career making are also discussed.

220. Hagara, Evelyn. *Vocal Secrets of the Ancients*. De Vorss and Company, Los Angeles, 1940.

An interesting survey of old Italian principles in modern presentation. Lacking in scientific stature.

221. Halbe, Sara. "Establishing a Routine of Practise." *Etude*, Philadelphia, 1938, Vol. 56, p. 403.

A short daily lesson is ideal for beginners. A typical home practice routine is described.

222. Hall, Bernice. "Breathing and Breath, Their Natural Acquisition and Control." *Etude*, Philadelphia, 1935, Vol. 53, p. 480.

Theory and practice are intelligibly discussed.

223. ——— "Headtones and Mixtures." *Etude*, Philadelphia, 1936, Vol. 54, p. 244.

An attempt is made to explain vocal resonance with the use of five vocalises and a colorful but confusing terminology. Empirical assumptions abound.

224. ——— "How the Head Tones Grow." *Etude*, Philadelphia, 1934, Vol. 52, p. 486.

Two exercises for developing the head register are recommended. The discussion is vague and the terminology too elusive for practical comprehension.

225. ——— "Mental Attitude a Vital Part of Vocal Teaching." *Musician*, New York, September, 1935, Vol. 40, p. 7.

The honest teacher will foster psychological as well as technical approaches to singing. Questions should not be evaded in the lesson period, for every student has a right to expect a scientific understanding of the voice as part of his training.

226. *——— "What's Wrong with Voice Teaching?" *Musician*, New York, December, 1936, Vol. 41, p. 193.

Professional teaching requirements and general teaching faults are briefly discussed. Methodology is not considered.

227. Hall, John Walter and Brown, Ralph M. *What Every Singer Should Know*. Vocal Science Publishing Company, Youngstown, Ohio, 1928.

A few teaching hints compactly presented. Merely opinions with no foundation in fact.

228. Harper, Ralph M. *The Voice Governor, Give It a Chance*. E. C. Schirmer, Boston, 1940.

A form of diaphragmatic control is the voice governor. This and several novel ideas regarding vocal resonance are the main contributions.

229. Harris, Clement Antrobus. "How to Test Forward Tone in Song and Speech." *Etude*, Philadelphia, 1938, Vol. 56, p. 470.
    The author describes a simple test and exercise for preventing nasality in tone production.

230. Harris, Roy and Evanson, Jacob. *Singing Through the Ages*. American Book Company, New York, 1940, 2 volumes.
    An excellent anthology of singing materials which depicts the evolution of song forms from prehistoric to modern times. The two volumes are divided into three sections: melody, harmony, and counterpoint.

231. Hathaway, Helen (Durham). *What Your Voice Reveals*. E. P. Dutton and Company, New York, 1931.
    The emphasis is largely upon personality and speech.

232. Hayes, Roland. "What Do They Hear in My Singing?" (An interview.) *Etude*, Philadelphia, 1939, Vol. 57, p. 125.
    The artist should keep his own individuality in the background. He is modest but sincere in conveying the song's message to his listeners.

233. Haywood, Frederick H. "Outline of Study for Singers." *Etude*, Philadelphia, 1928, Vol. 46, p. 388.
    The "scientific" and "artistic" elements of vocal song training are classified and briefly discussed, the purpose being to prevent vocal misconceptions from forming during the early period of study.

234. —— "Pedagogical Treatment of Vocal Instruction." *Music Teachers National Association Proceedings for 1930*, Oberlin, Ohio, 1931, Vol. 25, p. 167.
    Three steps in vocal training encompass the student's needs. These are: technique, style and interpretation.

235. —— "The Pedagogy of Voice Training for High School Students." *Etude*, Philadelphia, 1930, Vol. 48, p. 478.
    Three factors in teaching singing are developed. Solo singing is the ultimate object.

236. —— "The Problems of Voice Classification." *Educational Music Magazine*, Chicago, January, 1937, Vol. 16, p. 17.
    The author announces an original method of classifying voices by studying their register, quality and range over a period of time.

237. —— *Universal Song*. G. Schirmer, New York, 1933-1942, 3 volumes.
    A compact but complete vocal method. Each of three volumes in this series contains twenty lessons graded from fundamental studies to advanced exercises in agility. Each vowel is separately treated.

238. Hemery, Haydn. *The Physiological Basis of the Art of Singing*. H. K. Lewis and Company, London, 1939.
    Physiology is interspersed with philosophy. There are too many undocumented statements for which scientific claims are made.

239. Hempel, Frieda. "Sing with Your Heart!" (An interview.) *Etude*, Philadelphia, 1939, Vol. 57, p. 229.
    The true artist will not surrender to temptations of speedy success but will be content to spend a lifetime in study for art's sake. Interpretation and tone building are also treated.

240. Henderson, Mrs. Archibald M. *Speech and Song*. Macmillan, London, 1933.

The simplicity and adequacy of the author's novel approach helps solve many problems of diction and interpretation for the beginner.

241. Henderson, Charles. "Bringing a Song to Life." *Etude*, Philadelphia, 1940, Vol. 58, p. 164.

The author of *How to Sing for Money* gives practical advice on interpretation. An audience bent on amusement wants to feel, not think.

242. ———— and Palmer, Charles. *How to Sing for Money.* George Putnam, Incorporated, Hollywood, 1939.

An excellent book for layman or professional covering many practical problems of public performance. Written by one who knows. Interesting reading.

243. Henderson, William J. *The Art of Singing.* Dial Press, New York, 1938, revised edition.

A work preeminent in historical research, providing an indispensable background for teachers and students of singing. Many practical applications in voice culture. Unquestionably the work of a scholar. Stress is laid upon the historical rather than the pedagogical aspects of singing.

244. ———— "Lost Art of Singing." *Literary Digest*, New York, December 23, 1933, Vol. 116, p. 23.

Vocal art cannot compare with instrumental virtuosity in modern times. Too many mediocre singers are allowed to appear in public performances.

245. Henley, Homer. "Bouquet of Recitative." *Etude*, Philadelphia, 1930, Vol. 48, p. 359.

A few practical suggestions are given on the study of recitative singing.

246. ———— "The First Vocal Lesson." *Etude*, Philadelphia, December 1928-February, 1929, Volumes 46, 47, p. 944.

Proper breathing is the bed rock of singing. Thoughts on diction are added. A veteran teacher gives advice to young teachers on how to conduct the first vocal lesson. Some fine points of ethics and studio procedure are also considered.

247. ———— "Garcia's Second Discovery; Correcting Breath Leakage." *Etude*, Philadelphia, 1931, Vol. 49, p. 360.

A valuable developmental and corrective technique is discussed, based upon the staccato attack.

248. ———— "In Search of the Great Tone." *Etude*, Philadelphia, 1933, Vol. 51, p. 266.

The author makes extravagent claims for emotional singing. A philosophical discussion in which tone-texture, resonance, breathing and rhythm are related to the emotions.

249. ———— "The Inner Principle of the Teaching of William Shakespeare." *Etude*, Philadelphia, 1934, Vol. 52, p. 188.

Tuning the voice to exact pitch on every note is the "inner principle." A simple vocal exercise for attaining this result is described.

250. ———— "Legato Leap." *Etude*, Philadelphia, 1930, Vol. 48, p. 358.

The importance of legato singing is emphasized.

251. ———— "Lessons from Recorded Artist Singers." *Etude*, Philadelphia, 1938, Vol. 56, p. 256.
The use of phonographic recordings of singers as a teaching device is discussed.

252. ———— "Modern Vocal Methods in Comparison with Bel Canto." *Etude*, Philadelphia, 1939, Vol. 57, pp. 406, 468.
The author favors bel canto methods and discusses their essential principles in a sequence of two articles.

253. ———— "A New Key to the Head Voice." *Etude*, Philadelphia, 1930, Vol. 48, p. 358.
A brief article on extending the upper soprano range.

254. ———— "Sbriglia's Method." *Etude*, Philadelphia, 1933, Vol. 51, p. 51.
Breathing and resonance are the main subjects discussed.

255. ———— "Singing 'as Easily as You Breathe.'" *Etude*, Philadelphia, 1933, Vol. 51, p. 700.
By acquiring a correct posture the singer finds a short cut to the mastery of breath and tone.

256. ———— "Sing Out or sing In." *Etude*, Philadelphia, 1933, Vol. 51, p. 195.
The mental approach to voice projection is discussed.

257. ———— "The Technic of Vocal Intensity." *Etude*, Philadelphia, 1936, Vol. 54, p. 47.
The abdominal press in breathing is advocated and discussed.

258. ———— "Training the Male Voice." *Etude*, Philadelphia, 1936, Vol. 54, p. 46.
Register breaks and covering high tones are the topics discussed.

259. ———— "True Relation of Consonants to Singing." *Etude*, Philadelphia, 1937, Vol. 55, p. 190.
Vowels are the vehicles of voice. But consonants convey intelligibility and are essential to enjoyment. Examples are given.

260. ———— "The Truth about Nasal Tone." *Etude*, Philadelphia, 1936, Vol. 54, p. 448.
The pros and cons of placement and breathing are discussed.

261. ———— "What the Singer Should Read." *Etude*, Philadelphia, 1932, Vol. 50, p. 434.
The singer's vocal bibliography is considered and a list of recommended readings given.

262. ———— "Where Power is Beauty." *Etude*, Philadelphia, 1933, Vol. 51, p. 613.
Soft singing is less forced and therefore usually more beautiful than loud singing. A very gradual crescendo should be practiced in segments until distortions of volume are overcome.

263. ———— "Why Must I Study Singing for Five Years." *Etude*, Philadelphia, 1936, Vol. 54, p. 172.
Can vocal training be accomplished quickly? There are thousands of details that call for protracted study. Some of these are discussed.

264. ———— "Working Key to Bel Canto." *Etude*, Philadelphia, 1938, Vol. 56, p. 680.
Seven bel canto principles are propounded with appropriate references.

265. Henschel, Sir George. *How to Interpret a Song*. Theodore Presser, Philadelphia, 1929.

     A few practical hints by a veteran teacher. Worth reading for its authority.

266. —— "How to Sing Articulately." *Etude*, Philadelphia, December, 1930-January, 1931, Volumes 48-49, p. 896.

     Excerpts are quoted from the author's *Articulation in Singing*, John Church Company, 1926. Practical instructions with illustrative exercises cover many problems of diction.

267. Herbert-Caesari, Edgar F. "The Decline of Singing." (Parts I and II.) *Musical Opinion*, London, 1939, Vol. 62, p. 502.

     A useful summary of teaching fads and fancies.

268. —— "Opening the Mouth in Singing." *Etude*, Philadelphia, 1938, Vol. 56, p. 46.

     Excerpts from a symposium on this subject are quoted from the London *Music Times*.

269. —— *The Science and Sensations of Vocal Tone*. J. M. Dent and Sons, London, 1936.

     The author attempts to formulate basic principles from an empirical analysis of the singer's "sensations" of tone. The argument is unconvincing.

270. —— "Singing Instinct or Complex." *Musical Opinion*, London, 1938, Vol. 62, p. 23.

     Psychological factors in singing are considered in a unique light.

271. Hibbs, Irene. "Rameau's Inspired Thoughts on Voice Culture." *Etude*, Philadelphia, 1941, Vol. 59, p. 669.

     The principle of naturalness and unconstraint is discussed.

272. Hill, Frank. *Freedom in Song*. The Gazette and Herald, Blackpool, England, 1938.

     An excellent non-technical discussion of vocal principles and practices that lives up to its title. For teacher and student. Written by one who is apparently free from prejudice and fads.

273. Hinman, Florence Lamont. *Slogans for Singers*. G. Schirmer, New York, 1936, 2nd edition.

     A compact and useful outline of pedagogical principles tested by the author. Occasional exercises.

274. Hipsher, Edward Ellsworth. "Eliminating the Vocal 'Break.'" *Etude*, Philadelphia, 1935, Vol. 53, p. 740.

     Bridging the registers is an important and delicate process. Five exercises are suggested and briefly explained.

275. —— "Growing Top Notes." *Etude*, Philadelphia, 1939, Vol. 57, p. 406.

     The term *register* is no bugaboo to the teacher who uses corrective exercises intelligently. A single vocalise is discussed for illustration.

276. Hjortsvang, Carl, *Amateur Choir Director's Handbook*. Abingdon-Cokesbury, New York, 1941.

     A book on conducting with a few vocal hints added.

277. Hoffrek, Ada Mae. "Classifying the Voice." *Etude*, Philadelphia, 1928, Vol. 46, p. 220.

The average compass of male and female voices is briefly described, with some arbitrary comment on registers.

278. Hok, Anton. *The Art of Voice Production.* The author, New York, 1941.
Restatement of familiar, conventional vocal principles with some syllabic vocalises added. The author tries to advance himself as a teacher throughout.

279. Holl, Minna Franziska. "An Approach to Music Study through Solfege." *Musician*, New York, June, 1931, Vol. 36, p. 8.
All music pupils should be taught to use the following formula: 1. See the note. 2. Hear the note. 3. Produce the note. Vocal ear training implications are obvious.

280. Holland, Edwin. "Voice Production." *Etude*, Philadelphia, 1929, Vol. 47, p. 298.
A few brief comments on vocal fundamentals. Loose throat, jaw and breath control are stressed.

281. Holscher, Mrs. Herbert. "Singing for Recreation." *Ohio Parent Teacher*, Greenfield, Ohio, 1939, Vol. 17, p. 7.
Make good vocal music popular and popular vocal music good.

282. Homer, Mme. Louise. "The Singer's 'Half Dozen.'" *Etude*, Philadelphia, 1934, Vol. 52, p. 315.
Six general rules on how to study are listed with brief comment.

283. Hopkins, Edwin. *Secrets of Voice Production, Self Taught.* The author, New York, 1942.
Conventional ideas, unproved and vaguely expressed.

284. Howe, Albert Percy. *Practical Principles of Voice Production.* (for schools) W. Paxton and Company, Limited, London, 1940.
A few typical vocal exercises and phonetic tables supplement the brief and simple explanations of vocal theory. Not enough substance for a text.

285. Huey, Luzern Orrin. "Breathing for Voice Production." *Etude*, Philadelphia, 1931, Vol. 49, p. 284.
The control of the diaphragm is discussed. Breath control is best acquired through the practice of phonation, with automatic breathing as an objective.

286. ———. "Developing Breath Support for Voice Production." *Etude*, Philadelphia, 1929, Vol. 47, p. 602.
Two schools of thought are vaguely presented. Physical exercise is not as effective in promoting breath control as is the actual singing of tones.

287. ——— "Mental and Physical Concepts in Song." *Etude*, Philadelphia, 1937, Vol. 55, p. 818.
An argument against the supremacy of the mental concept as a controlling factor in voice production. No mere concept can change the voice. Physical exercise is necessary.

288. ——— "The Nasal Tone." *Etude*, Philadelphia, 1932, Vol. 50, p. 879.
Several fallacies of tone production are discussed. Normal voice is always a reflex response to a mental concept.

289. ——— "Registers: Their Cause and Cure." *Etude*, Philadelphia, 1935, Vol. 53, p. 674.

Old concepts of Manuel Garcia are reworded but not clarified. Explanations of falsetto and pitch action are involved and cumbersome. Three vocalises are given.

290. ——— "Studying for the Great Tone." *Etude*, Philadelphia, 1935, Vol. 53, p. 610.

Resonance, flexibility and vocal vibrato are briefly considered.

291. ——— "Taming the Diaphragm." *Etude*, Philadelphia, 1933, Vol. 51, p. 409.

The student's anxiety to develop the voice quickly causes involuntary contractions of the diaphragm and interferes with tone production.

292. ——— "Tone and Vowel Development." *Etude*, Philadelphia, 1938, Vol. 56, p. 752.

The focusing and blending of vowel tones is considered. All speech vowels should first be sustained on a monotone. Nuances may be added gradually. Three authorities are discussed.

293. Humphreys, Granville. *How to Teach Class Singing.* William Reeves, London, 1929.

Really a book on teaching music theory through sol-fa singing. Very few vocal hints are given.

294. Ireland (Eire) Department of Education. *Notes for Teachers; Music.* Stationery Office, Dublin, 1939.

Although this manual stresses choir techniques there are some interesting hints on breathing and vocalization.

295. Irvine, Diana. "Natural Singing for Cultivated Voices." *Musician*, New York, 1942, Vol. 47, p. 157.

Natural singing is not clearly defined although it is strongly advocated and discussed. Freedom from strain is the main factor.

296. ——— "Strains that Injure the Voice." *Etude*, Philadelphia, 1941, Vol. 59, p. 21.

It is important for the singer to know what not to do. To establish vocal ease, avoid undue striving for technical effects. Seven useful suggestions are given.

297. Jacobsen, O. Irving. "The Vowel Formant in Vocal Education." *Music Educators Journal*, Chicago, December, 1939, Vol. 26, p. 21.

Pitch affects the ease and clarity of certain vowel productions and should be a factor in planning exercises and songs.

298. Jacobus, Dale A. "Three R's of Singing." *Etude*, Philadelphia, 1935, Vol. 53, p. 108.

Resonance, relaxation and respiration are discussed.

299. Jacques, Reginald. *Voice Training in Schools.* Oxford University Press, London, 1934.

Simple, compact and complete. It covers all the essentials of class teaching of singing and is a useful pedagogical orientation for all singing teachers. It should be a basic text.

300. James, Mary Ingles. *Scientific Tone Production*. Boston Music Company, Boston, 1931.

Empirical observations and opinions are offered without benefit of proof or authoritative support. A generalized treatment and a few vocalises.

301. Jeffries, Arthur. "For the Untrained Singer." *Etude*, Philadelphia, 1933, Vol. 51, p. 544.

Open throat, diction, range, volume and hygiene are the topics discussed. No exercises are given.

302. ———— "The Natural Voice." *Etude*, Philadelphia, 1934, Vol. 52, p. 430.

Every gem needs polishing. And every voice, however natural and beautiful, needs training. A useful basic vocal training method is discussed.

303. Jersild, Arthur T. and Bienstock, Sylvia F. "A Study of the Development of Children's Ability to Sing." *Journal of Educational Psychology*, Baltimore, 1934, Vol. 25, p. 481.

Tests of vocal reproduction of pitch were administered to 407 children and 65 adults with significant results applicable to vocal education at various age levels.

304. Jetson-Ryder, F. "Sensation as an Index of Vocal Quality." *Musician*, New York, 1941, Vol. 46, p. 36.

Rely on sensation rather than outer hearing in voice building.

305. Johnson, Edward. "Putting a Value on Your Music Ability." *Musician*, New York, November, 1931, Vol. 36, p. 9.

Vocal study is advocated for everyone since it conveys unmistakable benefits in culture, health and happiness.

306. ———— "Styles in Singing." (In: *Be your own music critic*, lectures edited by Robert E. Simon, Jr.). Doubleday Doran, New York, 1941, p. 43.

A brief lecture on the generalities of singing. Just a glimpse into a rather conservative thought pattern.

307. Jones, William E. *A Notebook on Singers and Teachers of Singing*. College of Industrial Arts, Denton, Texas, 1930.

A short collection of sayings vaguely worded. A list of over 500 songs for practice and repertoire is included.

308. Josephson, E. M. "The Physiology of the Singing Voice." *Science n.s.*, New York, 1929, Vol. 70, p. 380.

The employment of different types of respiration for different tone ranges is favored as the result of an experimental study of this subject.

309. Judd, Percy. *Singing Technique*. Oxford University Press, London, 1931.

A concise book of rules for students, intended to supplement the practical guidance of their teachers.

310. Karapetoff, Vladimir. "The Singer's Indispensables." *Etude*, Philadelphia, 1933, Vol. 51, p. 377.

A few generalities with the customary admonitions against faulty production.

311. Kellogg, I. "Silent Singing." *Etude*, Philadelphia, 1932, Vol. 50, p. 507.

An interesting suggestion for recovering from vocal fatigue.

312. Kelly, Reverend Joseph. "Voice Training in Our Schools." *Etude*, Philadelphia, 1938, Vol. 56, p. 114.
The educational values of singing are discussed and some methods are given.

313. Kempf, Paul, Jr. "Untwisting of Chained Thoughts a Vocal Problem Today." *Musician*, New York, December, 1934, Vol. 39, p. 8.
An interview with a vocal teacher elicits some remarks on diagnosis and teaching technique.

314. Key, Pierre Van Rensselaer. *Teach Yourself to Sing*. Reader Mail, Incorporated, New York, 1941.
The author is noncommittal and echoes the ideas of conventional theorists with a few simple vocalises thrown in.

315. ———— *This Business of Singing*. Pierre Key Publishing Corporation, New York, 1937.
Singing as a career is discussed in general, non-technical language.

316. King, Chauncey B. "Is Your Voice Method Correct?" *Educational Music Magazine*, Chicago, March, 1941, Vol. 20, p. 29.
Eight usual methods of tone placement are presented and refuted.

317. Kirkpatrick, Howard. "A Talk on Singing." *Educational Music Magazine*, Chicago, November-December, 1939, Vol. 19, p. 40.
A convincing psychological approach to singing. Sane, wise and practical.

318. Kittle, J. Leslie. "Music Education and Scientific Research." *Music Supervisors Journal*, Chicago, May, 1932, Vol. 18, p. 37.
Scientific research can improve the efficiency of music instruction by introducing objective methods of investigating and evaluating the music curriculum. A typical study of terminology is presented.

319. Kling, Norman, *Norman Kling's Master Vocal Course*. The author, Chicago, 1939.
A series of conventional vocal lessons is outlined.

320. Klingstedt, Paul T. *Common Sense in Vocal Pedagogy as Prescribed by the Early Italian Masters*. Edwards Brothers, Ann Arbor, Michigan, 1941.
An excellent historical résumé of bel canto teachers and their methods. Much useful information. Lists of practice songs.

321. Kortkamp, Ivan A. "Compensation . . . for Flatting." *Educational Music Magazine*, Chicago, September-October, 1940, Vol. 20, p. 46.
Several practical hints on improving pitch control and attack.

322. ———— "Voice Training in Plain Language." *Educational Music Magazine*, Chicago, November-December, 1940, Vol. 20, p. 10.
An article for teachers, advocating the use of homespun analogies and simplified terminologies in teaching singing. Worth reading for its style.

323. Krasnoff, Gregory. *How to Improve Your Voice*. Dial Press, New York, 1936.
An abstract opinionated discussion, followed by some practical exercises.

324. Kuester, Eugene. "What the Breath Is to the Singer." *Musician*, New York, 1939, Vol. 44, p. 212.
"Natural breathing" is discussed and criticized.

325. Kwartin, Bernard. *Fundamentals of Vocal Art.* Criterion Publishing Company, New York, 1941.

A scholarly, though opinionated treatment covering fundamentals and pedagogy. The author attempts more than he can treat adequately within one volume, hence outlines frequently suffice for textual matter.

326. La Forest, Gerald Andrew. *The Master Principle.* The author, Chestnut Hill, Massachusetts, 1928.

A "new system" of vocal training is discussed but not given.

327. La Forge, Frank. "Observations on the Art of Song." *Musician,* New York, February, 1936, Vol. 41, p. 30.

A study procedure for singers that begins with the poem or text of the song.

328. —— "Sidelights on Training of Voices." *Musician,* New York, September, 1936, Vol. 41, p. 142.

A teacher is judged by her pupils.

329. —— "Your Voice is Your Fortune." *Independent Woman,* Baltimore, April, 1934, Vol. 13, p. 108.

The singing voice, like the speaking voice, is a natural endowment. Therefore anyone can learn to sing by cultivating the voice.

330. Laine, Juliette. "A Cure for Hoarseness After Singing." *Etude,* Philadelphia, 1934, Vol. 52, p. 374.

Practicing singing while standing will prevent abnormal postural strains which adversely affect tone production.

331. Lamperti, Francesco. *Vocal Studies in Bravura.* G. Schirmer, New York, 1942.

A series of musical exercises progressively graded in difficulty. Brief textual comments are added by Estelle Liebling.

332. Landt, Karl, Jack and Dan (The Landt trio). *How to Sing Songs Professionally.* Artists Music Corporation, New York, 1940.

How to audition for radio and similar problems of a singing career are discussed. Not a course in voice training, though some vocal hints are offered.

333. Lang, Paul Henry. *Music in Western Civilization.* W. W. Norton, New York, 1941.

A significant contribution to literature on the history and appreciation of music. Vast in scope. It combines scholarly thoroughness with literary skill in a subject that has always cried out for clarification.

334. Lardizabal, Felisa C. "Why Some Pupils Would Not Sing." *Philippine Journal of Education,* Manila, July, 1935, Vol. 18, p. 118.

Six reasons for encountering difficulties in learning or teaching a song are discussed.

335. Lawrence, Alice E. *Singing Lessons for Everybody.* The author, New York, 1939.

A good understanding of the psychological approach to singing. Simple and concise.

336. Lee, Ernest Markham. *A Music Course for Teacher and Student.* Banks and Son, York, England, 1932.
   A compact but complete theory book stressing fundamentals of music and sight singing. A few vocal hints are included.

337. Lehmann, Lilli. *How to Sing.* ("Meine Gesangskunst," translated from German.) Macmillan, New York, 1929, 3rd revised edition.
   A "new revised and supplemented edition" of the 1902 original. Not for beginners. Obscure wordy explanations of her own sensations in singing. The author's style is opinionated and personal. Translation difficulties are obvious.

338. Lehmann, Lotte. "Fine Art of Lieder Singing." *Australian Musical News and Digest,* Melbourne, 1941, Vol. 32, No. 2, p. 9.
   The importance of the text when interpreting a song is discussed.

339. ———— "Let Nothing Discourage You." (An interview.) *Etude,* Philadelphia, 1935, Vol. 53, p. 701.
   Six questions on vocal training are answered.

340. Lewis, Don. "Vocal Resonance." *Journal Acoustical Society of America,* Lancaster, Pennsylvania, October, 1936, Vol. 8, p. 91.
   A preliminary report on acoustical measurements being made in the Iowa Psychological Laboratory, in which the laryngeal cord tone, several vowels and vocal resonances are analyzed.

341. ———— and Lichte, William H. "Analysis of a Perceptible Series of Partials in a Vocal Sound." *Journal of Experimental Psychology,* Lancaster, Pennsylvania, 1939, Vol. 24, p. 254.
   The ability of trained vocalists and phoneticians to perceive the relative intensities of various partials in a complex vocal tone was determined by means of an ingenious experiment. Results are interesting, but inconclusive.

342. ———— and Tuthill, Curtis. "Resonant Frequencies and Damping Constants." *Journal Acoustical Society of America,* Lancaster, Pennsylvania, 1940, Vol. 11, p. 456.
   A technical discussion of resonance with some generalizations.

343. Lewis, Joseph. *Singing without Tears.* M. Keane, Incorporated, New York, 1940.
   A simple review of familiar principles and time worn ideas. The treatment is unoriginal.

344. Lewis, Leo Rich. *The Gist of Sight Singing.* Oliver Ditson, Boston, 1931.
   A compact but complete collection of sight singing exercises. Rudimentary vocal facts are included.

345. Levbarg, John J. "The Vocal Mechanism." *Medical Times and Long Island Medical Journal,* New York, 1934, Vol. 62, p. 207.
   A doctor discusses voice problems as the medical profession sees them.

346. Lindsay, George L. "Fundamental Values of Vocal Music in Modern High School." *Music Supervisors National Conference,* Chicago, 1931, Vol. 24, p. 78.
   Promoting the value of vocal instruction in the school curricula. The author's main point is that we must promote a pupil's desire to participate in satisfying musical experiences.

347. Lindsley, Charles Frederick. "Psycho-physical Determinants of Individual Differences in Voice Quality." *Psychological Bulletin*, Princeton, New Jersey, 1933, Vol. 30, p. 594.

Interesting experimental results are announced but not discussed.

348. Lissfelt, John Frederick. *Basic Principles of Artistic Singing*. E. C. Schirmer, Boston, 1938.

The author is an exponent of Lilli Lehmann's singing methods. Too broad in scope for a pamphlet volume. Ninteen vocalises are added. Historically interesting.

349. Little, Christine. "Sing with Personality."*Etude*, Philadelphia, 1934, Vol. 52, p. 315.

Facial expression and posture are briefly discussed.

350. Ljungberg, Gota. "There Is No Royal Road to Singing!" (An interview.) *Etude*, Philadelphia, 1934, Vol. 52, p. 215.

Nobody learns to sing by simply taking lessons. Acute self-awareness and self-analysis are important contributing factors.

351. Lloyd, Robert. *The Robert Lloyd Tone System*. Herr Wagner Publishing Company, San Francisco, 1929.

Some useful hints on breathing and resonance in compact form. The author advocates keeping the diaphragm tense at all times.

352. *Lombardi, Gioacchino. "About Breath Control." *Musician*, New York, January, 1932, Vol. 37, p. 15.

The importance of breath control in singing is generally discussed without pedagogical applications.

353. ———— "Equipment of the True Vocal Teacher." *Musician*, New York, 1940, Vol. 45, p. 48.

Vowel placement and full voice practice are foundational training principles. One of Caruso's former teachers gives a few pedagogical pointers.

354. ———— "Il Canto! A Word of Magic Meaning." *Musician*, New York, 1940, Vol. 45, p. 14.

Requisites for vocal success are given.

355. ———— "Is the Human Throat Made for Singing?" *Musician*, New York, 1940, Vol. 45, p. 107.

Those who claim that singing is unnatural to man are misguided. The human larynx is as naturally adapted to phonatory functions as to other reflexes in which it participates.

356. ———— "Reasons for the Scarcity of Great Singers in America." *Musician*, New York, November, 1931, Vol. 36, p. 8.

The author deplores the lack of sound teaching principles and methods and the prevalence of vocal exploitations by incompetent teachers.

357. ———— "Voice Study to Precede Repertoire." *Musician*, New York, 1939, Vol. 44, p. 198.

Tone production is the foundation of the vocal art and must be firmly established before singing a song is attempted.

358. Luckstone, Isidore. "Important Practical Helps for the Vocalist." (An interview.) *Etude*, Philadelphia, 1938, Vol. 56, p. 433.

The singer's appearance and physical mannerisms are discussed.

359. ——— "Placing Responsibility on the Ear of the Vocalist." *Musician*, New York, May, 1932, Vol. 37, p. 19.
   The singer should be made to hear rather than feel his vocalization. The author upholds this thesis.

360. ——— "Vocal Presentation." (An interview.) *Etude*, Philadelphia, 1941, Vol. 59, p. 451.
   One should study and if necessary imitate certain features in the singing of great artists. There are several comments on career making and interpretation.

361. MacBurney, Thomas N. "Keys to Vocal Freedom." *Music Teachers National Association Proceedings for 1940*, Pittsburgh, 1941, Vol. 35, p. 377.
   Basic technical concepts in their application to voice training are discussed.

362. MacCrate, James. "The Late Start." *Etude*, Philadelphia, 1928, Vol. 46, p. 691.
   Too much consciousness of the anatomy is sometimes a deterrent to song rendition. The advantages of vocal study, even with a late start, are discussed.

363. MacDonald, Jeanette. "No Royal Road to Song." *Better Homes and Gardens*, Des Moines, Iowa, September, 1941, Vol. 20, p. 27.
   An artist singer briefly summarizes the important elements of vocal training. Endless practice is necessary.

364. Mackenzie, Sir Morell. *Hygiene of the Vocal Organs*. Edgar S. Werner and Company, Belmar, New Jersey, 1928, 9th edition.
   A competent physician contributes non-technical common sense rules for the culture and management of the voice. The information in this book, although accurate and reliable, is too old to have much practical value today.

365. Macklin, C. B. "Whispering Hope." *Oklahoma Teacher*, Oklahoma City, December, 1934, Vol. 16, p. 9.
   The breathy or whispering tone, now prevalent, makes the writer despair of its eventual evolution into full voice. Vocal principles are briefly discussed.

366. Madden, George S. "The Scientific and Mental Art of Teaching Singing." *Musician*, New York, March, 1936, Vol. 41, p. 54.
   Our first concern is to locate the causes of bad singing, to alter bad habits of long standing, to eliminate the discordancies of forced and unnatural voice production.

367. ——— "What is the Singing Voice?" *Musician*, New York, December, 1936, Vol. 41, p. 157.
   An empirical definition of the cultivated singing voice is attempted.

368. Marafioti, Pasqual Mario. *Caruso's Method of Voice Production*. D. Appleton, New York, 1933.
   A radical departure from conventional pedagogical procedure, based on the principle that the singing voice follows the track of the speaking voice.

369. Marchesi, Blanche. *The Singer's Catechism and Creed.* J. M. Dent and Sons, London, 1932.
A non-technical discussion of singing and singing methods.

370. Mario, Queena. "Distinctly American Vocal Problems." (An interview.) *Etude*, Philadelphia, 1935, Vol. 53, p. 389.
Scale practice, acquiring flexibility and conservation of vocal resources are the topics discussed.

371. —— "Queena Mario Tells an Intimate Story." *Musician*, New York, 1942, Vol. 47, p. 5.
An innovation in voice training by the use of recordings is described.

372. Marsh, Ruth Sweeney. "Making the Song 'Click.'" *Etude*, Philadelphia, 1936, Vol. 54, p. 109.
Rhythm and meaning, mood and melody are the factors which form the study of interpretation.

373. Martinelli, Giovanni. "Caring for the Vocal Instrument." *Etude*, Philadelphia, 1938, Vol. 56, p. 650.
The singer is responsible for the health of his entire body. Advice on correct living, some teacher-pupil experiences and personal reminiscences are included. Natural singing is discussed.

374. Martini, Nino. "Putting Songs Across the Footlights." (An interview.) *Etude*, Philadelphia, 1941, Vol. 59, p. 608.
A distinguished tenor gives reminiscences of a brilliant operatic and concert career with a few vocal hints added.

375. Martino, Alfredo. *Today's Singing.* Lamberti Printing Company, New York, 1938.
After a tirade against bad teaching methods, the author skims through a dozen chapters of his own ideas with indifferent and unconvincing results.

376. Maurice-Jacquet, H. "Common Sense Regarding Breath Control." *Musician*, New York, 1941, Vol. 46, p. 54.
Observations on the breathing habits of great vocal artists.

377. —— "Fundamental Law Applied to Singing." *Musician*, New York, 1941, Vol. 46, p. 94.
Acoustics and elements of musicianship are discussed.

378. —— "The Human Voice and the Law of Vibration." *Musician*, New York, 1940, Vol. 45, p. 211.
The formation of the lips is an important adjunct to voice production.

379. —— "The Physical Body and the Voice." *Musician*, New York, 1941, Vol. 46, p. 13.
Bodily posture and relaxation are important factors in singing.

380. —— "Tone Visualization the Singer's Guide." *Musician*, New York, 1941, Vol. 46, p. 74.
Vocal projection and musicianship are discussed.

381. Maybee, Harper C. *Tuning Up Exercises for Ensemble singing.* Oliver Ditson, Boston, 1930, 4 volumes.
Nonsense syllables are used for singing exercises in unison and in parts. Explanations are uninformative.

382. —— *Vocal Ensemble Exercises.* G. Schirmer, New York, 1936.
    Twelve short singing exercises based on nonsense syllables. A few vocal comments are included as text.

383. McAll, Reginald Ley. *Practical Church School Music; Methods and Training.* The Abingdon Press, New York, 1932.
    Both instrumental and vocal practice are discussed with a few notes on music theory.

384. McIntyre, Ian. "Mind, the Body and the Emotion from the Singer's Standpoint." *Musician,* New York, January, 1932, Vol. 37, p. 25.
    Mind, voice and body must be trained to act in unison in any singing act. Deviations and incoordinations set up emotional conflicts.

385. —— "The Place of Psychology in Vocal Artistry." *Musician,* New York, August, 1931, Vol. 36, p. 16.
    Qualifications for success in a vocal career are discussed.

386. McLean, Cameron. "Vocal Interference and Its Elimination." *Music Teachers National Association Proceedings for 1936,* Oberlin, Ohio, 1937, Vol. 31, p. 172.
    Mental and physical controls are juxtaposed, the former being advocated. Timing in voice production is also discussed.

387. Medonis, Vincent Xavier. *Rise and Fall of the Voice.* The author, Pittsburgh, 1933.
    The title is taken literally for the author deals entirely with pitch variations and vocal inflections throughout the vocal range. There is little text.

388. Melchior, Lauritz. "The 'Heldentenor' or Heroic tenor." (An interview.) *Etude,* Philadelphia, 1937, Vol. 55, p. 429.
    Breathing and practice methods are discussed.

389. Merritt, Grace. "Vocal Secrets Found in Nature." *Musician,* New York, March, 1932, Vol. 37, p. 8.
    The "Svana" system of corrective vocal exercises is briefly endorsed but not described.

390. Metfessel, Milton. "Effects of Removal of Fundamental and Certain Overtones on Vocal Pitch and Quality." *Psychological Bulletin,* Princeton, New Jersey, 1931, Vol. 28, p. 212.
    A brief experimental report on the effect of acoustical filters applied to vocal tone.

391. —— "Emotional Values of Deviations from Exact Pitch and Rhythm." *Bulletin American Musicological Society,* New York, August, 1942, p. 34.
    An interesting experimental summary.

392. —— "The Vibrato in Artistic Voices." (In: *The Vibrato;* University of Iowa Studies in the Psychology of Music.) University of Iowa Press, Iowa City, Iowa, 1932, Vol. 1, p. 14.
    An exhaustive experimental study of the physiology, psychology and physics of the vocal vibrato in singing, in which the fact that the vibrato is an ingredient of all celebrated voices is conclusively settled.

393. —— "Vibrato in Celebrated Voices." *Scientific Monthly,* Lancaster, Pennsylvania, 1929, Vol. 28, p. 217.

Experimental findings on vibrato analysis indicate its desirability in good voices.

394. ——— "What is the Voice Vibrato?" *Psychological Monographs*, Princeton, New Jersey, 1928, Vol. 39, p. 126.
An introductory acoustical discussion describing early experimental research on this subject.

395. Metzger, Wolfgang. "Mode of Vibration of the Vocal Cords." *Psychological Monographs*, Princeton, New Jersey, 1928, Vol. 38, No. 4, p. 82.
An excellent documentary survey, including a historical review of important theories on the subject, analyses and discussion of experimental investigations by leading theorists, a bibliography and numerous illustrations. Authentic and complete up to 1928.

396. Metzger, Zerline M. "Monotones." *Educational Music Magazine*, Chicago, September-October, 1937, Vols. 17-18, p. 22.
The author discusses several classifications of vocal handicaps and their treatment.

397. Milanov, Zinka. "Vocal Training from a Famous Master." (An interview.) *Etude*, Philadelphia, 1940, Vol. 58, p. 729.
Milka Ternina's teaching method is discussed.

398. Miller, Frank Ebenezer. *The Voice, its Production, Care and Preservation.* G. Schirmer, New York, 1931, 7th edition.
An empirical discussion of vocal theory. Somewhat opinionated, although the author claims to be scientific throughout.

399. Miller, Mrs. Harry S. "A Dozen Foundation Stones of Good Singing." *Etude*, Philadelphia, 1939, Vol. 57, p. 197.
The author emphasizes musicianship rather than vocal technique and offers twelve criteria for defining the general equipment of the well trained singer.

400. Miller, Ray Starbuck. "The Pitch Vibrato in Artistic Gliding Intonations." (In: *The Vibrato*; University of Iowa Studies in the Psychology of Music.) University of Iowa Press, Iowa City, Iowa, 1932, Vol. 1, p. 250.
The author concludes from a single experimental study of one artist singer's rendition of a musical composition that the vibrato is always present during the gliding intonations of a song. Other interesting observations as to pitch and rate variability are made.

401. Mojica, Jose. "Making the Most of the Practice Hour." (An interview.) *Musician*, New York, 1940, Vol. 45, p. 171.
Some practical suggestions on light singing, memorizing and listening.

402. Montani, Nicolas A. *Essentials in Sight Singing.* C. C. Birchard, Boston, 1931, 2 vols.
The two volumes are largely composed of vocal exercises interspersed with a few essentials of music theory and some vocal hints.

403. Mowe, Homer George. "Bridging the Gap between the Vocal Teacher and the General Public." *Musician*, New York, March, 1932, Vol. 37, p. 16.
The old idea that the singing voice is the enviable possession of a few is gradually being supplanted by an "everybody can sing" attitude.

404. ——— "The Expanding Field of the Vocal Teacher." *Music Teachers Na-*

tional Association Proceedings for 1938, Oberlin, Ohio, 1939, Vol. 33, p. 46.

Teaching singing and teaching voice training are contrasting activities that need clearer definition. A plea for voice training in the schools is made.

405. ——— *Fundamentals of Voice Use in Song and Speech.* St. Anthony Guild Press, Paterson, New Jersey, 1932.

A compact and practical presentation of the author's ideas with some useful exercises. Helpful and convincing throughout.

406. ——— "New Problems Face the Vocal Teacher." *Musician,* New York, December, 1931, Vol. 36, p. 21.

A brief discussion of the growing interest in singing in this country. Good singing is now open to all who learn the proper use of the voice.

407. Muhlmann, Adolph. "Vibrato and Tremolo." *Music Teachers National Association Proceedings for 1936,* Oberlin, Ohio, 1937, Vol. 31, p. 159.

A brief comparison of vibrato, trill and tremolo.

408. Murphy, George Alphonsus. *The Voice and Singing.* A. P. Johnson Company, Grand Rapids, Michigan, 1929.

An attempt to explain singing in a rational, though simplified, style. The ideas expressed are conventional.

409. Murray, Dom Gregory. "Science and Singing." *Downside Review,* London, 1938, Vol. 56, p. 46.

A discussion and review of E. G. White's theories of sinus tone production.

410. Mursell, James L. "How to Facilitate the Acquisition of Technic." *Etude,* Philadelphia, 1942, Vol. 60, p. 448.

Four important pedagogic principles that are applicable to vocal teaching are convincingly discussed.

411. ——— *The Psychology of Music.* W. W. Norton, New York, 1937.

A consistently thorough and scholarly treatment of the psychology of tonal and rhythmic forms, musical functions and the musician. Research materials and findings are reviewed, analyzed and discussed without fear or favor. Fundamental problems of voice are treated briefly but convincingly.

412. ——— "We Need Music." *Music Supervisors Journal,* Chicago, November, 1932, Vol. 19, p. 10.

A clear-cut and vigorous denunciation of aimless teaching methods and a formulation of pedagogical principles that provides guidance and insight for the average teacher. Vocal and instrumental instruction and discriminative listening are concomitants of all musical training.

413. ——— and Glenn, Mabelle. *The Psychology of School Music Teaching.* Silver Burdett, New York, 1938.

A complete survey of the psychological processes and problems that enter into the teaching of music and voice with a practical approach. Invaluable to teacher and student. Pages 278 to 301 deal with voice.

414. Muschamp, Stanley. "The Charm of the Low Tones." *Etude,* Philadelphia, 1928, Vol. 46, p. 860.

The mastery of the lower part of the voice will add strength without sacrificing beauty of tone. The advantages of the "forward" tone are discussed.

415. Muyskens, John H. "The Emergent Voice." *Music Educators National Conference,* Chicago, 1938, Vol. 31, p. 283.

A philosophical orientation of vocal knowledge without bias or dogma. The author's only apparent interest is to think clearly.

416. Myer, Edmund John. *The Science and Art of Breathing.* Trade Printing Company, Los Angeles, 1929, 2nd edition.

A useful series of drills for silent practice. Automatic breathing is advocated.

417. Neblette, C. B. "Motion-picture Recording of the Vocal Cords." *Photo-Era Magazine,* Wolfeboro, New Hampshire, April, 1931, Vol. 66, p. 222.

A brief account of Russell's early experiments with motion pictures of vocal action.

418. Negus, V. E. *The Mechanism of the Larynx.* C. V. Mosby Company, St. Louis, 1929.

A standard source book for information on vocal physiology. Exhaustive and authentic.

419. Newport, Stone Gables. "High Tones Cannot be Placed." *Musician,* New York, 1940, Vol. 45, p. 54.

Sensations are illusory and unreliable factors in voice placing.

420. New York Singing Teachers Association. "First Steps to Training the Voice." *Musician,* New York, May, 1931, Vol. 36, p. 25.

A discussion of several problems that face the prospective student of singing.

421. —— *Its Story.* Theodore Presser, Philadelphia, 1928.

A review of twenty years. Useful as a record of teaching and standardization trends in this field.

422. —— "Why All Should Have Their Voices Trained." *Musician,* New York, April, 1931, Vol. 36, p. 19.

Copy of a broadcast over station WOR on February 18, 1931 featuring the value of singing for ungifted as well as gifted voices.

423. New York Voice Educators Committee. "Report on Voice Clinics." *Music Educators National Conference,* Chicago, 1936, Vol. 29, p. 204.

A brief summary of the series of vocal discussions that were held at the biennial meeting of the Music Educators National Conference.

424. Nichols, Edith. "Vocal Verities from the Doctrines of Lilli Lehmann." *Musician,* New York, May, 1929, Vol. 34, p. 39.

An American exponent discusses four or five working principles of her former teacher without actually imparting knowledge.

425. Nicholson, Sydney Hugo. *Choirs and Places Where They Sing.* G. Bell and Sons, London, 1932.

A seasoned choirmaster discusses problems of choir training. A historical background is given. Chapters IV and VI deal with voice production techniques.

426. Nicoll, Irene Howland and Dennis, Charles M. *Simplified Vocal Training.* Carl Fischer, New York, 1940.

Part one deals with principles, part two with song study and interpretation. Some conventional vocalises are added.

427. Noller, Rose. "Phonetics and Singing." *Etude*, Philadelphia, 1939, Vol. 57, p. 336.

This analytical description of vowels, diphthongs and consonants provides the singer with a practice chart for overcoming his diction problems.

428. Norton, William W. "Principles Involved in Vocal Tone Production." *Educational Music Magazine,* Chicago, September, 1941, Vol. 21, p. 14.

A brief but intelligent discussion of breathing, resonance and diction.

429. —— "Vowels and the Singer: English, German, French, Latin." *Educational Music Magazine,* Chicago, November, 1941, Vol. 21, p. 29.

Methods of improving English diction are discussed. A Latin pronunciation chart is included.

430. Novello-Davies, Mrs. Clara. *You Can Sing.* Selwyn and Blount, London, 1930.

A well rounded teaching experience is epitomized in this volume. Practical, interesting and valuable hints to singers abound.

431. Novotna, Jarmila. "Don't Fear Your Limitations!" (An interview.) *Etude,* Philadelphia, 1940, Vol. 58, p. 223.

The paradox of technique is that it must be perfectly controlled in order to be perfectly concealed. A prima donna gives words of encouragement to young singers.

432. Obolensky, Alexis. "Passing from Conscious to Subconscious Control in Vocal Practise." *Musician,* New York, April, 1930, Vol. 35, p. 17.

Conscious control gradually disappears as mental and physical coordinations are built into the vocal apparatus. Breathing and relaxation are discussed.

433. Ogle, Robert B. "Modern Science vs. the Art of Song." *Musician,* New York, 1940, Vol. 45, p. 154.

A comparison of contradictory opinions on vocal physiology.

434. Olden, Mme. Margarete. "A First Lesson in Singing." *Etude,* Philadelphia, 1933, Vol. 51, p. 338.

A German prima donna discusses breathing, vowels and tone placement in general terms.

435. Onegin, Sigrid. "Coloratura Contralto." (An interview.) *Etude,* Philadelphia, 1932, Vol. 50, p. 701.

The contralto voice is not subordinated to the soprano but is equally important in opera. The distinction between the two is one of timbre rather than range. Training principles are discussed.

436. —— "Singing Student's Vacation." (An interview.) *Etude,* Philadelphia, 1934, Vol. 52, p. 275.

Scale practice and musicianship should form a regular part of the singer's study diet in season and out.

437. Ortmann, Otto. "Notes on Recent Music Research." *Music Teachers National Association Proceedings for 1934*, Oberlin, Ohio, 1935, Vol. 29, p. 94.

Parts III and V give authentic summaries of experimental findings on the attributes of good voice quality and some principles of physiologic movement used in practicing.

438. —— *Problems in the Elements of Ear-dictation*. Peabody Conservatory of Music, Baltimore, 1934.

An experimental study in the causes of typical pupil errors in writing music from dictation. Pedagogical corrective procedures derived from these studies are applicable to voice training.

439. Orton, James Louis. *Voice Culture Made Easy*. Thorsons, London, 1938.

A simple but thorough treatment of fundamental principles from the teacher's viewpoint. The importance of the false vocal cords is vaguely introduced. Otherwise informative and useful.

440. Otero, Emma. "Practical Steps toward Better Singing." (An interview.) *Etude*, Philadelphia, 1942, Vol. 60, p. 151.

The distinguished Cuban soprano discusses breath support, relaxation and methods of practicing.

441. Owsley, Stella. *Helpful Hints to Singers*. Dealey and Lowe, Dallas, 1937.

Sensation and ear are the two bases of self-criticism in this theoretical discussion for beginners. A few vocal exercises are included.

442. Parrish, John. "Voice Training in the Junior College." *Junior College Journal*, Washington, D. C., November, 1933, Vol. 4, p. 87.

Initial voice teaching problems are discussed. They are generally applicable in school or studio.

443. Passe, E. R. Garnett. *The Singing Voice*. Pitman and Sons, Limited, London, 1933.

The physiology of voice is briefly discussed. Pedagogical problems are not considered.

444. Patterson, Dr. Annie. "Enunciation in Singing." *Etude*, Philadelphia, 1930, Vol. 48, p. 53.

Enunciation is too often left to chance in the singer's voice training program. Consonant study should not be subordinated to vowel study since verbal combinations include both types of sounds.

445. Patton, John A. and Rauch, Mabel T. "Returning to Vocal Fundamentals." *Etude*, Philadelphia, 1942, Vol. 60, p. 154.

A generalized consideration of bel canto methods.

446. Philip, Frank. *Philosophy of Vocal Culture*. Scribner's, New York, 1930.

A beginner's book. Every detail of voice training is considered and appropriate exercises given. But advice on breathing is misleading and many techniques of placement are obscure. The use of a pitch graph for song selection is unique.

447. Pierce, Anne Elsie. *Class Lessons in Singing*. Silver Burdett, New York, 1937.

A repertoire of thirty-two good songs with brief instructional text and vocalises relating to the technical requirements of each song. Suggestions by Estelle Liebling are included.

448. Pitts, Mrs. Carol Marhoff. *Pitts Voice Class Method for Class and Studio.* Neil A. Kjos Music Company, Chicago, 1936, 2 volumes.

    A book of conventional practical drills with brief textual interpolations.

449. Podolsky, Edward. "Sing Lustily and Keep Healthy." *Musician*, New York, 1936, Vol. 41, p. 171.

    A physician praises singing for its salutary effects upon the human body.

450. Pons, Lily. "Fame Overnight!" (An interview.) *Etude*, Philadelphia, 1931, Vol. 49, p. 394.

    Reminiscences of a self-made career. Interesting and informative. Methods of placement and self-directed practice are also discussed.

451. ———— "Girl Who Wants to Sing." (An interview.) *Etude*, Philadelphia, 1933, Vol. 51, p. 731.

    The linguistic and operatic requirements of a singer's career are discussed. Breathing efficiency affects brain efficiency as well as vocal progress.

452. Pressman, Joel J. "Physiology of the Larynx." *Laryngoscope*, St. Louis, 1939, Vol. 49, p. 245.

    A résumé and discussion of the literature on the larynx for 1938.

453. Proschowski, Frantz. "The Development of the Singing Voice." *Music Supervisors National Conference Proceedings*, Ithaca, New York, 1930, Vol. 23, p. 131.

    "Sing as you speak" is the author's premise. Tone thinking is also discussed.

454. ———— "From Speech to Song." *Etude*, Philadelphia, 1935, Vol. 53, p. 424.

    Pure vowels are found in the correctly spoken language and vowels are the foundation of singing. Hence the spoken approach is advised.

455. ———— "Tone Thinking Relative to Culture." *Etude*, Philadelphia, 1931, Vol. 49, p. 438.

    A rational treatment of the psychological approach to voice culture. Diction and breathing are featured and correct "tone-thinking" becomes a basic principle. Interesting and informative.

456. *———— "Vocal Talent." *Etude*, Philadelphia, 1931, Vol. 49, p. 884.

    Original thinking is rare among vocal students. They incline largely toward slavish imitation, since their own vocal ideas are confused and directionless. A talented singer must learn to think for himself.

457. ———— "Voice Troubles: Chest Voice." *Etude*, Philadelphia, 1931, Vol. 49, p. 583.

    Chest tones are not always agreeable tones. Correctives are briefly discussed.

458. ———— "Voice Troubles: Pianissimo." *Etude*, Philadelphia, 1931, Vol. 49, p. 439.

    Breath pressure and intensity of tone must be regulated by the ear and not by conscious control of the muscles involved.

459. *———— "What of the 'Made' Voice or the 'Phenomenal' Voice?" *Etude*, Philadelphia, 1931, Vol. 49, p. 439.

    Real vocal talent must combine beautiful voice, intelligence and innate artistic feeling. Voices are not "made." They are merely improved by guidance. Methods are not discussed.

460. Ray, Marie B. "If You Don't Like Your Voice Get a New One." *American Magazine*, New York, June, 1930, Vol. 109, p. 70.
A prominent voice teacher is interviewed and gives some hints for voice improvement. Speech is emphasized.

461. Redfield, John. "Certain Anomalies in Air Column Behavior of Wind Instruments." *Journal Acoustical Society of America*, Lancaster, Pennsylvania, 1934, Vol. 6, p. 34.
By analogy, an acoustical explanation favoring vocal chest resonance is given.

462. ——— *Music, a Science and an Art.* Tudor, New York, 1935, new edition.
The author's non-technical style makes the subject of acoustics assimilable, even by the layman. Personal opinions are freely offered. The chapter on better voice training is unique but not documented.

463. Rethberg, Elizabeth. "The Singer's Problems." (An interview.) *Etude*, Philadelphia, 1932, Vol. 50, p. 256.
Mastering a perfect scale is more important than a hundred operatic roles. The author deplores haste in building a singing career. Relaxation is discussed.

464. Rimmer, Lotti. "Breath and Tone-Charm in Singing." *Etude*, Philadelphia, 1931, Vol. 49, p. 884.
Eight short vocalises are given to illustrate breath control.

465. ——— "Breath, the Vital Spark of Song." *Etude*, Philadelphia, 1936, Vol. 54, p. 724.
Three helpful exercises are given for increasing breath capacity and endurance functionally; that is, by reciting and intoning lines of verse.

466. ——— "Cavities, the Magic Transmitters." *Etude*, Philadelphia, 1938, Vol. 56, p. 680.
An attempt is made to explain vocal resonance in this brief empirical discussion.

467. *——— "Rarity of Tenors." *Etude*, Philadelphia, 1932, Vol. 50, p. 579.
Most of the classic operas contain high notes beyond the singing range of our modern tenors, indicating a dearth of modern artists. Pedagogy is not considered.

468. ——— "Sing with Ease." *Etude*, Philadelphia, 1934, Vol. 52, p. 430.
To obtain freedom of vocal utterance, practice spontaneous attack and breath control. Two exercises are given for illustration.

469. ——— "That Elusive Resonance of Song." *Etude*, Philadelphia, 1933, Vol. 51, p. 772.
Humming "in the mask" and correct articulation are essential factors in developing resonance.

470. ——— "True Vocal Art in Singing." *Etude*, Philadelphia, 1928, Vol. 46, pp. 137, 221.
A sequence of articles covering the fundamentals of voice production and diction. Discussions are largely theoretical and opinionated. Few exercises are given.

471. —— "Vocal Placement." *Etude*, Philadelphia, 1930, Vol. 48, p. 578.
Freedom, ease and spontaneity of tone production are concomitants of relaxed singing. Tremolo and beauty of tone are discussed and three exercises are given.

472. Roach, Lynne Jennings. "Three Master Singers on Preparing for a Lyric Career." *Etude*, Philadelphia, 1929, Vol. 47, p. 181.
This symposium was translated from the French, as it appeared originally in *Le Courrier Musical* of Paris. The confusion of teaching methods and generalities of career building are discussed.

473. Robinson, George R. "Analysis of the Vowel Sounds for Singing in English." *Etude*, Philadelphia, 1935, Vol. 53, p. 301.
The vowel is classified and compared to non-vocal or consonant sounds.

474. —— "Breath Control for Voice Control." *Etude*, Philadelphia, 1932, Vol. 50, p. 878.
The reciprocal action of abdominal and diaphragmatic muscles is discussed. The abdominal press is the basis of breath control.

475. Roman, Stella. "Building Vocal Surety." (An interview.) *Etude*, Philadelphia, 1942, Vol. 60, p. 9.
The singer must try to develop his own standards. Self-criticism is more helpful than outside criticism in the long run. Voice placing and range are also discussed.

476. Ruff, Albert E. "Improve your Voice Production." *Etude*, Philadelphia, 1939, Vol. 57, p. 738.
The vocal muscular system is explained and phonation is described. But the explanations are necessarily short and hence incomplete. A background knowledge of vocal physiology is presupposed.

477. —— "Pitch and Timbre." *Etude*, Philadelphia, 1928, Vol. 46, p. 614.
The importance of nasal resonance in singing is discussed.

478. Runkel, Bernice. "Tone Superimposed upon Breath Pressure." *Musician*, New York, 1941, Vol. 46, p. 157.
Mental concepts help the singer's achievement of tonal beauty.

479. Russell, G. Oscar. "X-ray Photographs of the Tongue and Vocal Organ Positions of Madame Bori." *Music Teachers National Association Proceedings for 1932*, Oberlin, Ohio, 1933, Vol. 27, p. 137.
Interesting studies of the tongue and voice in action that seem to contradict several orthodox theories. Experimental findings of an investigation sponsored by the Carnegie Corporation and others, in which most of the outstanding opera and concert stars of the United States served as subjects.

480. Ryan, Mrs. Millie. *What Every Singer Should Know.* Carl Fischer, New York, 1937, new edition.
Hints and helps for beginners gathered through years of experience. Not a method. There is little practical information.

481. Sacerdote, Edoardo. "Is Italian Helpful to Singers?" *Etude*, Philadelphia, 1937, Vol. 55, p. 402.
Faultless pronunciation is always necessary. Italian vowels are an in-

valuable help to tone production only when correctly pronounced. Otherwise they may be detrimental to the voice.

482. Saenger, Oscar. "What Every Singing Teacher Should Know." *Musician,* New York, February, 1928, Vol. 33, p. 15.

Pitch, quality and teaching qualifications are discussed.

483. Samoiloff, Lazar S. "Progress in Music." *Etude,* Philadelphia, 1933, Vol. 51, p. 194.

Superficial vocal study methods are deplored. The singing student needs more patience and less commercial ambition in preparing a career.

484. ———— *The Singer's Handbook.* Presser, Philadelphia, 1942.

A list of songs for repertory and a few vocalises are given. The rest of the book is devoted to the author's memoirs as singer and teacher. A book for teachers rather than for singers.

485. ———— "Successful Development of a Singing Artist." (An interview.) *Etude,* Philadelphia, 1940, Vol. 58, p. 235.

Quality, not range, sells a voice. Personality and sincerity of purpose will help establish a singer in his life work more than mere technique. Having the right teacher is all important.

486. Samuel, John Owen. *Thirty-six Modern Class Lessons in How to Sing.* The author, Cleveland, 1931.

A loose-leaf booklet, stressing the psychological approach to voice culture. Written examinations are included for each lesson.

487. Samuels, T. Guthbert. *Singing and Its Mastery.* George C. Harrap, Limited, London, 1930.

A short summary of vocal principles followed by a series of vocalises built on nonsense syllables. There is nothing original in this approach and much is overlooked.

488. Sanders, Dr. Herbert. "New Field for Singing Teachers." *Etude,* Philadelphia, 1935, Vol. 53, p. 237.

Interesting comments on the singer's approach to spoken diction. The true foundation of singing is perfect speech since speech and song are twins.

489. Sands, Mollie. "The Singing Master in Eighteenth Century England." *Music and Letters,* London, 1942, Vol. 23, p. 69.

A comparison between old and new teaching methods and responsibilities. Documented historical references are given.

490. Savage, Paul. *Creative Singing.* Petros Press, New York, 1931.

A metaphysical approach to singing, stressing the importance of mental control in every phase of practice. The author states his opinions as if they were laws.

491. Sayao, Bidu. "Art Means Preparation." (An interview.) *Etude,* Philadelphia, 1938, Vol. 56, p. 427.

Problems of operatic interpretation are discussed. Voice and musicianship are the corequisites of artistic success.

492. Schatz, Harry A. "The Art of Good Tone-production with Suggestions." *Laryngoscope,* St. Louis, 1938, Vol. 48, p. 660.

Anatomic explanations are given by a physician for accepted aids in vocalization. The role of the extrinsic vocal muscles in phonation is discussed.

493. Schoen-René, Mme. Anna E. "The Traditions of Fine Singing." *Etude*, Philadelphia, 1941, Vol. 59, p. 745.

Garcia's methods are discussed.

494. Schofield, Edgar. "Higher Vocal Teaching Standards Attained by Cooperation." *Musician*, New York, November, 1931, Vol. 36, p. 10.

The American Academy of Teachers of °Singing has raised the standards of vocal education.

495. —— "Speech to Song." *Music Teachers National Association Proceedings for 1935*, Oberlin, Ohio, 1936, Vol. 30, p. 95.

The text should be uppermost in singing for singing is really an intensified form of speech.

496. Scholes, Percy A. Article on "Voice" in *Oxford Companion to Music*. Oxford University Press, New York, 1938.

Highlights of vocal theory and history of singing are presented.

497. Schorr, Friedrich. "Creating a Character in an Opera." (An interview.) *Etude*, Philadelphia, 1940, Vol. 58, p. 58.

The leading Wagnerian baritone comments on the prevalence of "get quick results" teaching methods in this country. A slow, sincere and intensive study of the role is necessary for convincing interpretation. Comments on diction are added.

498. Schumann, Elizabeth. "The Groundwork of Vocal Art." (An interview.) *Etude*, Philadelphia, 1941, Vol. 59, p. 163.

Breath support, open throat, staccato and trill, imitation and range are the main subjects discussed.

499. Schumann-Heink, Ernestine. "You Can Sing—If You Will!" (An interview.) *Etude*, Philadelphia, 1934, Vol. 52, p. 11.

A friendly message to singers which includes comments on forcing and interpretation.

500. Scott, Charles Kennedy. *Madrigal Singing*. Oxford University Press, London, 1931, 2nd edition.

Polyphonic choral technics are discussed with illustrations. A few comments on voice production are included.

501. —— *Word and Tone—I*. J. M. Dent and Sons, London, 1933, Vol. I.

Although opionated, the book on theory helps to reveal many of the technical problems involved in singing. The treatment of these problems is reserved for book II. The lack of factual evidence makes all these assumptions purely hypothetical, although interesting.

502. —— *Word and Tone—II*. J. M. Dent and Sons, London, 1933, Vol. II.

There are many vocalises and other drills for the beginning voice student. Practical problems are discussed. The drills represent a synthesis of instructional procedure without ever mentioning the finished product.

503. Seashore, Carl Emil. "A Beautiful Voice." *Music Educators Journal*, Chicago, February, 1938, Vol. 24, p. 18.

The value of early vocal training in the child accrues to the adult.

504. —— "How Do We Express Specific Emotions in Song?" *Music Educators Journal*, Chicago, September, 1940, Vol. 27, p. 38.

A brief exposition of objective methods used for measuring inflectional vocal responses to emotional stimuli in speech and song.

505. —— "New Approaches to the Science of Voice." *Scientific Monthly*, Lancaster, Pennsylvania, 1939, Vol. 49, p. 340.

A brief summary of the eighteen different fields of vocal research now open and available to the vocal scientist. An excellent orientation in vocal science.

506. —— (Editor) *Objective Analysis of Musical Performance*. (University of Iowa Studies in the Psychology of Music.) University of Iowa Press, Iowa City, Iowa, 1936, Vol. IV.

Experimental findings on three aspects of the singing tone are convincingly presented, i.e., pitch, intensity and duration. The fourth, timbre, to be treated in a later volume. Shows up the fallacy of many modern theories on voice production by implication, not direct refutation.

507. —— "Objective Factors in Tone Quality." *American Journal of Psychology*, Ithaca, New York, 1492, Vol. 55, p. 123.

A brief report of the author's objective acoustical analysis of vocal tone quality in which all verifiable experimental factors of beautiful tone production are measured and compared. Interesting definitions are given.

508. —— *Pioneering in Psychology*. (University of Iowa Studies No. 398.) University of Iowa Press, Iowa City, 1942.

A résumé of research findings and procedures in music and other fields, with philosophical comments.

508. —— *Psychology of Music*. McGraw-Hill, New York, 1938.

The purpose is to help bridge the gap between mere love of music and an intelligent conception of its technical constituents. The style is interesting and somewhat philosophical. The voice chapter is informative.

510. —— "Psychology of Music." *Music Educators Journal*, Chicago, March, 1936, Vol. 22, p. 24.

A sample of scientific findings relating to pitch intonation in singing is presented.

511. —— *Psychology of the Vibrato in Voice and Instrument*. (University of Iowa Studies in the Psychology of Music.) University of Iowa Press, Iowa City, 1936, Vol. III.

A scholarly and convincing treatise replete with scientific data. Exhaustive treatment.

512. —— (Editor) *The Vibrato*. (University of Iowa Studies in the Psychology of Music.) University of Iowa Press, Iowa City, 1932, Vol. I.

A digest of up-to-date experimental studies made in Iowa State University on the subject of the vibrato in music and especially on the vocal vibrato in singing. Technical and exhaustive treatment.

513. —— and Tiffin, Joseph. "An Objective Method of Evaluating Musical Performance." *Science n. s.*, Lancaster, Pennsylvania, November 7, 1930, Vol. 72, p. 480.

By means of fractionally analyzed stroboscopic records, the singing of an amateur is compared objectively with the vocal performance of a professional artist, with interesting results.

514. Seashore, Harold G. "Forms of Artistic Pitch Deviations in Singing." *Psychological Bulletin*, Princeton, New Jersey, 1934, Vol. 31, p. 677.

Report of an experiment presented to the American Psychological Association.

515. ——— "Variability of Pitch in Artistic Singing." *Music Teachers National Association Proceedings for 1938*, Oberlin, Ohio, 1939, Vol. 33, p. 66.

A philosophical discussion of recent experimental findings and their pedagogical interpretation.

516. Shakespeare, William. Article on "Singing" in *Encyclopedia Britannica* (14th edition). Encyclopedia Brittanica, Incorporated, Chicago, 1939, Vol. 20.

The rationale of voice culture is compactly presented.

517. ——— *Plain Words on Singing*. Putnam, London, 1938, new edition.

A sensible discussion from a reasoned viewpoint, largely theoretical. Reviews teachings of the old Italian masters.

518. Shaw, W. Warren. *Authentic Voice Production*. Lippincott, Philadelphia, 1930.

Highly theoretical treatment of vocal phenomena based almost entirely upon the author's opinions.

519. ——— "Ban the Fetish of Breath Control." *Musician*, New York, 1938, Vol. 43, p. 108.

The training of torso muscles is the correct approach to breath control.

520. ——— "The Basis of a Precise Terminology for Singers." *Musician*, New York, July, 1928, Vol. 33, p. 24.

A technical discussion of scientific terminology theories.

521. ——— "Beacon Lights for the Singer." *Etude*, Philadelphia, 1932, Vol. 50, p. 130.

Seven fundamentals of singing are discussed with clarity and conviction.

522. ——— "Breath Support and Tone Control." *Musician*, New York, 1937, Vol. 42, p. 170.

A discussion of Mme. Rethberg's ideas on singing.

523. ——— "Censorship of Terminology Needed." *Musician*, New York, December, 1937, Vol. 42, p. 212.

Vocal methods may vary with the individual student, but all methods should be in keeping with correct vocal principles that are accepted by all.

524. *——— "Conservation of Vocal Mechanism." *Musician*, New York, August, 1928, Vol. 33, p. 29.

Pathological factors and the influence of fear on the voice are briefly discussed. Non-pedagogical.

525. ——— *Educational Vocal Technique in Song and Speech*. Theodore Presser, Philadelphia, 1936.

A practical course in voice training with song materials for practice. A few brief textual remarks are included.

526. —— "Hazy Thinking Makes Loose Talking." *Musician*, New York, 1938, Vol. 43, p. 122.

It is important for vocal teachers to use terms that are of precise and definite meaning and that actually describe the processes of vocal training and control.

527. *—— "Instinctive Singing and Science." *Musician*, New York, November, 1928, Vol. 33, p. 40.

Precise knowledge and correct reasoning are essential in arriving at accurate conclusions regarding voice. The laws of human intellect are discussed.

528. —— "Interference Applied to Singing." *Musician*, New York, 1938, Vol. 43, p. 88.

The swallowing mechanism presents a constant menace of interference to vocal tone production. This interference is defined and its remedy discussed.

529. —— "Learn to Breathe Correctly." *Musician*, New York, October, 1934, Vol. 39, p. 11.

Natural breathing is enforced by correct posture.

530. —— "Modern Trends in Voice Class Instruction." *Music Educators National Conference*, Chicago, 1936, Vol. 29, p. 217.

The subjective approach in vocal teaching is advocated and discussed.

531. —— "Muscular Control in the Production of Vocal Tone." *Musician*, New York, September, 1935, Vol. 40, p. 25.

The author righteously decries the abuse of vocal methods by those who lack understanding of basic principles underlying them.

532. —— "Place of Psychology in Singing." (A series of five articles.) *Musician*, New York, February, March, April, May, June, 1928, Vol. 33.

An interesting but opinionated discussion of needed reforms in the teaching of singing and the influence of modern scientific thought in effecting these reforms.

533. —— "The Psychological Aspect of Singing." *Musician*, New York, January, 1929, Vol. 34, p. 41.

Everybody can and should learn to sing. Vocal theories are irrational and haphazard for want of comprehensive knowledge on the singing voice.

534. —— "Scientific Study of Vocal Mechanism." *Musician*, New York, 1937, Vol. 42, p. 156.

The fundamentals of phonation and some teaching fallacies are considered.

535. —— "Some Fundamentals in Voice Production." *Etude*, Philadelphia, 1929, Vol. 47, p. 928.

A brief, opinionated statement concerning the involuntary nature of the vocal processes.

536. —— "Some Secrets of Breath and Voice Development." *Etude*, Philadelphia, 1935, Vol. 53, p. 300.

A useful analysis of breathing activity.

537. —— "Stepping Stones to a Singer's Success." *Etude*, Philadelphia, 1939, Vol. 57, p. 666.

Anyone who can carry a tune can learn to sing well. Illustrative vocalises and home study hints are given.

538. ———— "A Study of Correct Breathing for Singers." *Etude*, Philadelphia, 1939, Vol. 57, p. 270.

Although involuntary breathing is requisite for good singing, the breathing muscles can be strengthened by means of preliminary exercises which help build correct habits.

539. ———— "Vibrators and Resonators." *Musician*, New York, January, 1928, Vol. 33, p. 33.

The psychological approach to singing is discussed.

540. ———— "Vocal Art in the Light of Science." *Musician*, New York, 1938, Vol. 43, p. 5.

The laws of acoustics are applied to voice production.

541. ———— "Vocal Methods and Objectives." *Musician*, New York, 1938, Vol. 43, p. 152.

The theory and practice of scientific voice culture is discussed.

542. ———— "Vocal Technic in Song and Speech." *Musician*, New York, 1937, Vol. 42, p. 189.

The fallacy of diaphragmatic control is considered.

543. ———— "Voice Training is a Specialty." *Musician*, New York, 1938, Vol. 43, p. 168.

The voice of an accomplished singer must be able and ready to meet several important demands. Until these requirements are met it is futile to attempt to develop mere singing ability.

544. ———— "What Vocal Training Entails." *Musician*, New York, 1938, Vol. 43, p. 139.

The objectives of a singer are to be able to express himself in song in the most effective manner. There are too many obscure technical requirements and teaching terms that becloud the teacher's true purposes.

545. Sheley, Nettie B. "Helps in Vocal Study." *Etude*, Philadelphia, 1942, Vol. 60, p. 594.

Several succinct quotations from eminent singers.

546. Sheppard, Ernest H. "To Sing Well, be Natural." *Etude*, Philadelphia, 1938, Vol. 56, p. 824.

The singer's ten commandments, as listed, include breath control, posture, diction and freedom from affectation as topics of discussion.

547. Sherman, Mandel. "Emotional Character of the Singing Voice." *Journal of Experimental Psychology*, Princeton, New Jersey, 1928, Vol. 11, p. 495.

Report of an experiment to determine observability of emotional traits in a sung tone.

548. Sherwood, C. *Fundamentals of Vocalization*. The St. Gregory Guild, Philadelphia, 1939.

Vocal principles are briefly discussed with appropriate exercises.

549. Sinatra, Frank (In collaboration with John Quinlan). *Tips on Popular Singing*. Embassy Music Corporation, New York, 1941.

Unimportant vocalises set to single words and phrase fragments. There is very little instruction in this.

550. Skiles, Wilbur Alonza. "Adjusting the Vocal Organs." *Etude*, Philadelphia, 1934, Vol. 52, p. 431.
Psychological control is advocated.

551. ―― "Are You Listenin'?" *Etude*, Philadelphia, 1937, Vol. 55, p. 335.
The importance of ear training is discussed briefly.

552. ―― "Baritone or Tenor." *Etude*, Philadelphia, 1934, Vol. 52, p. 117.
Quality rather than compass should denote the classification of voices. Avoid forcing throughout the scale when testing the voice.

553. ―― "Bringing the Tone to the Front." *Etude*, Philadelphia, 1928, Vol. 46, p. 860.
The sensation of yawning should accompany soft singing, thus bringing the tone forward and eliminating harshness of quality.

554. ―― "The Diphthong Vowels." *Etude*, Philadelphia, 1939, Vol. 57, p. 532.
The constituent vowel sounds of each diphthong should first be practiced separately, then in combination.

555. ―― "Enunciation and Tone Color." *Etude*, Philadelphia, 1930, Vol. 48, p. 435.
The beneficial results of training the speaking voice will transfer to the singing voice.

556. ―― "Good Diction and Good Tone Inseparable." *Etude*, Philadelphia, 1937, Vol. 55, p. 819.
The singer should study phonetics and listen to spoken radio diction for models of good speech in song.

557. ―― The *"How" of Acquiring Freedom in Voice Production*. Skiles Publications System, Freeport, Pennsylvania, 1937.
To offset conscious interference, the singer must thoroughly understand his instrument, then learn to use it automatically. The author explains this.

558. ―― "How Should the Vowel 'E' Be Sung?" *Etude*, Philadelphia, 1932, Vol. 50, p. 283.
The tone should always float on the breath, without the slightest degree of forcing. Diction and vowels are briefly discussed.

559. ―― "Learning to Rule the Unruly Tongue." *Etude*, Philadelphia, 1934, Vol. 52, p. 675.
An indirect approach through mental attitude is advised.

560. ―― "Modulating the Voice Before the Microphone." *Etude*, Philadelphia, 1932, Vol. 50, p. 507.
The psychological control of vocal action is advocated.

561. ―― "Purifying Tone and Diction." *Etude*, Philadelphia, 1936, Vol. 54, p. 652.
The singer must learn to build words from tones, not tones from words. Two silent exercises are given for mastering an unruly tongue.

562. ―― "Singing Intelligently in English." *Etude*, Philadelphia, 1931, Vol. 49, p. 360.
An advocate of the English language discusses problems of English diction. The causes of faulty diction lie within the singer not the language.

563. ——— "Some Fundamentals of Good Singing." *Etude*, Philadelphia, 1941, Vol. 59, p. 235.

Tongue exercises and diction are discussed.

564. ——— "Some Secrets of Free and Forward Tone Production." *Etude*, Philadelphia, 1936, Vol. 54, p. 108.

Ten steps for achieving freedom are discussed.

565. ——— "The Vowels in the Singer's Diction." *Etude*, Philadelphia, 1939, Vol. 57, p. 407.

Faulty vowel formations are discussed briefly.

566. Smallman, John and Wilcox, E. H. *The Art of A Capella Singing*. Oliver Ditson, Boston, 1933.

A careful analysis of choral technique, repertoire and interpretation problems is given with sixteen illustrative choral works. The individual voice is discussed briefly.

567. Smith, Sherman K. "Bel Canto Yesterday and Today." *Music Supervisors National Conference*, Chicago, 1931, Vol. 24, p. 87.

A forceful argument for improved teaching methods.

568. Snyder, Elizabeth Jacques. *Alliterations for Articulation*. Pioneer Printing Company, Seattle, 1934.

A tiny instruction book intended to accompany studio lessons in voice and diction.

569. Speetzen, Harold. "When the Vocal Teacher Becomes the Spiritual Guide." *Musician*, New York, April, 1934, Vol. 39, p. 4.

We rely largely upon subconscious faculties in the singing process which is a direct reflection of our personal character.

570. Spier, Harry R. *Vocal Art-studies for the Mastery of Consonants*. J. Fischer, New York, 1936.

Eight original songs by the author, each embodying a different problem of diction involving the consonants.

571. Spohr, Harry Norman. *The Art and Practice of Singing*. The author, Riverside, California, 1930.

After an exhaustive presentation of vocal history and vocal acoustics, the author adds very few conventional hints on vocal technique.

572. Spouse, Alfred. "Voice Training Classes." *Supervisors Service Bulletin*, Chicago, September, 1932, Vol. 12, p. 22.

Objections to class teaching methods are listed and refuted.

573. Stanley, Douglas. "All Great Voices Have One Characteristic in Common." *Etude*, Philadelphia, 1934, Vol. 52, p. 254.

The vocal vibrato in singing is discussed.

574. ——— "Classification of Voices by Range." *Musician*, New York, 1940, Vol. 45, p. 74.

Vocal registers must first be isolated, then coordinated. The result is a maximum range of approximately three octaves for all singers.

575. ——— "Science Comes to the Aid of Vocal Pedagogy." *Musician*, New York, June, 1930, Vol. 35, p. 7.

The author attacks soft singing practice on scientific grounds and argues for an objective approach to vocal study.

576. ——— *The Science of Voice*. Carl Fischer, New York, 1929.

The author vigorously denounces the ignorance of dissenting vocal theorists while extravagantly propounding his own opinionated ideas. The basic material of the section on "vocal technique" is repeated in later editions of this work.

577. ———— *The Science of Voice*. Carl Fischer, New York, 1939, 3d edition.
A strong advocate of mechanistic voice-building. Scientific facts and personal opinions are interblended and some original experimental data is given. Exhaustively treated. The book only partially lives up to its title.

578. ———— "The Science of Voice." *Journal of the Franklin Institute*, Philadelphia, 1931, Vol. 211, p. 405.
A summarizing survey of the field of vocal research including the author's experimental findings. An excellent scientific résumé of vocal physiology and its pedagogic implications.

579. ———— "A Three-octave Range for Every Voice." *Musician*, New York, 1940, Vol. 45, p. 45.
Scientific devices that measure the voice are briefly discussed.

580. ———— and Maxfield, J. P. *The Voice, Its Production and Reproduction*. Pitman Publishing Corporation, New York, 1933.
The section on "voice production" was written by Douglas Stanley and is substantially a second and slightly revised edition of the previously published section on "vocal technique" in *The science of voice* (Carl Fischer, 1929).

581. Staton, John Frederic. *Sweet Singing in the Choir*. Clarke, Irwin Company, Toronto, 1942.
A handbook of choral techniques, presenting some vocal principles. Bibliography and song materials are added.

582. Stephens, Percy Rector. "Fundamentals That Govern Singing." *Musician*, New York, January, 1934, Vol. 39, p. 5.
The importance of posture and a knowledge of vocal anatomy are considered.

583. Stevens, F. A., and Miles, W. R. "The First Vocal Vibrations in the Attack in Singing." *Psychological Monographs*, Princeton, New Jersey, 1928, Vol. 39, p. 203.
Report of an experimental study on the relation of vocal attack to pitch accuracy in singing.

584. Stock, George Chadwick. "Simplified Vocal Method for Beginning Singers." *Etude*, Philadelphia, 1940, Vol. 58, p. 91.
Begin vocal practice with speaking tones. Then use the singing tones. The system outlined includes familiar vocalises and practice materials with few explanatory hints.

585. ———— "The Singer's Tools." *Etude*, Philadelphia, 1931, Vol. 49, p. 361.
Vocal theory is effectively epitomized in this brief statement.

586. ———— "Voices Under Twenty Must Not be Overtaxed." *Etude*, Philadelphia, 1928, Vol. 46, p. 615.
It is reported that Jenny Lind injured her voice by appearing in opera at the age of eighteen. An interview between the young Lind and her teacher, Garcia, is discussed briefly.

587. —— "Wisdom Nuggets for the Vocal Student." *Etude*, Philadelphia, 1941, Vol. 59, p. 454.
     Seven pedagogic principles are discussed briefly.

588. —— "Young Voice." *Etude*, Philadelphia, 1930, Vol. 48, p. 655.
     Both young and adult voices should be trained to sing musically, not muscularly. Well chosen songs provide adequate practice materials.

589. —— "Your Voice, Your Song." *Etude*, Philadelphia, 1930, Vol. 48, p. 654.
     Each voice has a distinctive timbre whose improvement should be the purpose of all vocal instruction. Methods that achieve this result are always good methods. Fifteen exercises are given.

590. Storey, Barbara and Barnard, Elsie I. *A Key to Speech and Song*. Blackie and Son, London, 1940.
     The authors talk around their subject and very little practical information is given.

591. Strauss, Martha. *Elements of Vocal Technique*. Mills Music, Incorporated, New York, 1935.
     A collection of daily vocal drills in all keys. Very little textual matter.

592. —— *Learn to Sing*. Clarence Williams, New York, 1936.
     A book of vocal exercises for beginners. Very little text.

593. Stueckgold, Grete. "American Singers and the German Lied." (An interview.) *Etude*, Philadelphia, 1937, Vol. 55, p. 227.
     Interpretative values and repertory are discussed.

594. —— "If You Were My Pupil." (An interview.) *Etude*, Philadelphia, 1935, Vol. 53, p. 9.
     The fundamentals of singing are discussed in general terms.

595. Stults, Walter Allen. "Are Formal Vocal-eases Prerequisites for Singing Skill?" *Music Teachers National Association Proceedings for 1941*, Pittsburgh, 1942, Vol. 36, p. 314.
     The author advocates an early use of song literature for vocal training.

596. —— "Polarity: Its Relation to the Singing Voice." *Music Teachers National Association Proceedings for 1936*, Oberlin, Ohio, 1937, Vol. 31, p. 166.
     A brief, theoretical discussion of the diagnostic approach to vocal teaching.

597. —— "The Why and the How of the Staccato." *Music Teachers National Association Proceedings for 1939*, Pittsburgh, 1940, Vol. 34, p. 317.
     Vocal attack and breath action are developed by the use of these preliminary vocal drills.

598. Swain, Edwin O. "Balanced Activity as a Basis for Vocal Success." *Musician*, New York, July, 1934, Vol. 39, p. 7.
     Students' minds are usually too preoccupied with the far distant finished vocal product to give full attention to the simple details of any vocal training period. The author's own book on "balanced activity" is discussed.

599. Swarthout, Gladys. "The American Singer's Opportunities." (An interview.) *Etude*, Philadelphia, 1934, Vol. 52, p. 707.
     The American prima donna gives sound advice on starting and con-

tinuing a singing career. The discussion is general. Methods of voice training are not considered.

600. ———— "The Singer's Equipment." (An interview.) *Etude*, Philadelphia, 1937, Vol. 55, p. 788.
    Having a good natural vocal organ is only a small part of a singer's equipment. There are other essential mental, physical and musical qualifications that determine a successful career.

601. Tapper, Thomas. "High Spots in Learning to Sing." *Etude*, Philadelphia, 1942, Vol. 60, p. 593.
    The value of interpretation in learning a song is discussed.

602. Taylor, Bernard U. *Group Voice*. G. Schirmer, New York, 1936.
    Vocal teaching materials are applied to class work. Elementary drills are added that can be used for individuals or groups.

603. Ten Haff, P. A. " 'Mixing' Registers." *Etude*, Philadelphia, 1931, Vol. 49, p. 885.
    The author theorizes on overcoming register "breaks."

604. ———— "Vocal Resonance, Its Sources and Effects." *Etude*, Philadelphia, 1931, Vol. 49, p. 582.
    The violin analogy is used to describe vocal resonance.

605. Thibault, Conrad. "The Scientific Approach to Singing." (An interview.) *Etude*, Philadelphia, 1942, Vol. 60, p. 244.
    The singer is advised to forget self entirely.

606. Thomas, Clare John. "Automatic Breath Action." *Etude*, Philadelphia, 1934, Vol. 52, p. 314.
    Relaxation is considered most important in vocal control.

607. ———— "Equalizing the Vowels." *Etude*, Philadelphia, 1933, Vol. 51, p. 122.
    An attempt to classify vowel formations by the sensations involved in their production. Five vocalises are given.

608. ———— "Legato of Song." *Etude*, Philadelphia, 1930, Vol. 48, p. 736.
    There can be no legato unless beauty of tone is given strict attention. Breath repose and a sense of good cheer are contributing factors. Five vocalises are given.

609. ———— "Studies in Vocal Release." *Etude*, Philadelphia, 1935, Vol. 53, p. 366.
    The author believes that good singing is an automatic response of the voice to the inspired thoughts of the singer. Complete vocal freedom and flexibility are necessary. Eight exercises are given.

610. Thompson, Oscar. (Editor) Article on "Singing" in *The International Cyclopedia of Music and Musicians*. Dodd, Mead and Company, New York, 1939.
    A brief synopsis of vocal history and theory.

611. Thorborg, Kerstin. "The Building and Use of a Vocal Instrument." (An terview.) *Etude*, Philadelphia, 1939, Vol. 57, p. 295.
    Advice to beginners by a prima donna.

612. ———— "How to Improve Vocal Practise." (An interview.) *Etude*, Philadelphia, 1942, Vol. 60, p. 82.
    Methods of warming up and improving tone quality are discussed. All practicing should begin with work on tone.

613. Tibbett, Lawrence. "Should I Change Teachers?" (An interview.) *Etude*, Philadelphia, 1935, Vol. 53, p. 458.

Beginners are usually slaves of the big tone habit. Working with pianissimo tones produces best results. Admonitions to teachers against vocal abuses in studio practice are given.

614. ——— "There is No Open-Sesame." (An interview.) *Etude*, Philadelphia, 1940, Vol. 58, p. 820.

Vocal and dramatic technique should be studied simultaneously.

615. Tiffin, Joseph. "The Role of Pitch and Intensity in the Vocal Vibrato of Students and Artists." (In: *The Vibrato*; University of Iowa Studies in the Psychology of Music.) University of Iowa Press, Iowa City, Iowa, 1932, Vol. 1, p. 134.

The general characteristics of the vocal vibrato are studied by means of objective records of the pitch and intensity fluctuations of the voices of artist singers and students of singing.

616. Tillery, Lloyd. "Creative Singing." *Etude*, Philadelphia, 1934, Vol. 52, p. 48.

The mechanical preparation of a song can never be as effective as the interpretation of its inner meaning.

617. Tolmie, J. R. "An Analysis of the Vibrato from the Viewpoint of Frequency and Amplitude Modulation." *Journal Acoustical Society of America*, Lancaster, Pennsylvania, January, 1935, Vol. 7, p. 29.

Intensity and pitch fluctuations are mathematically analyzed and interrelated in this technical discussion of the vocal and instrumental vibrato.

618. Toren, E. Clifford. "The Relation of the Student to His Singing; the Teacher's Responsibility." *Music Teachers National Association Proceedings for 1941*, Pittsburgh, 1942, Vol. 36, p. 324.

Character traits are interwoven with technical abilities in the student's approach to singing. Ideals are discussed.

619. Vale, Walter Sidney. *Tone Production in the Human Voice*. Faith Press, London, 1934.

A short philosophical treatment of the singing voice based on the "sing as you would speak" idea. The author stresses the psychological approach—mind over muscle. There are many gaps in the treatment of his subject.

620. Valeri, Mme. Dalia. "Mastering the Italian Vowel in Voice Study." *Musician*, New York, July, 1934, Vol. 39, p. 11.

The Italian language is the best of all tongues for singing. The argument is short and unconvincing.

621. ——— "Open Tones, Covered Tones, Closed Tones." *Musician*, New York, September, 1934, Vol. 39, p. 11.

Perfect vocal control is possible only by closing the tones. This process is advocated but not described or explained.

622. ——— "Tone Attack and Blending of Registers." *Musician*, New York, August, 1934, Vol. 39, p. 8.

Registers help to locate points of resonance for each singing tone. General hints on tone placing are given.

623. —— "Question of Breathing in Singing." *Musician*, New York, May, 1934, Vol. 39, p. 13.

Breath control is fundamental to singing. When neglected, many vocal limitations appear. The reason for this is not explained.

624. Van Orden, Jr., William. "Increasing Breath Control." *Etude*, Philadelphia, 1933, Vol. 51, p. 701.

Breath control is the foundation of good singing. But it must be effortless and relaxed at all times. A simple breathing exercise is described.

625. Votaw, Lyravine. "Vocal Possibilities of Music in the Schools." *Supervisors Service Bulletin*, Chicago, January, 1931, Vol. 10, p. 9.

The qualifications of vocal teachers and problems of class teaching are discussed.

626. Wagner, Arnold Henry. "An Experimental Study in Control of the Vocal Vibrato." *Psychological Monographs*, Princeton, New Jersey, 1930, Vol. 40, p. 211.

A doctoral thesis is summarized and three conclusions given.

627. —— "Interpretation in Singing." *Music Supervisors Journal*, Chapel Hill, North Carolina, May, 1928, Vol. 14, p. 69.

The meaning of the text and the method of expressing it prescribe the essential technical components of interpretation.

628. *—— "Remedial and Artistic Development of the Vibrato." (In: University of Iowa Studies in the Psychology of Music.) *University of Iowa Press*, Iowa City, Iowa, 1932, Vol. 1, p. 166.

In its pedagogical implications, this report is a restatement of conclusions arrived at in the doctoral thesis previously listed. (cf. *Psychological Monographs*, 1930, Vol. 40.)

629. —— "Research in the Field of Voice Training." *Music Educators National Conference*, Chicago, 1939-1940, Vol. 30, p. 343.

Four research problems are briefly discussed.

630. Waller, James L. "Goin' to Town Vocally." *Rotarian*, Chicago, November, 1937, Vol. 51, p. 33.

The three stages for rebuilding the voice are: freeing it, strengthening it, and beautifying it.

631. —— "The Teacher and Her Voice." *Oklahoma Teacher*, Oklahoma City, September, 1929, Vol. 11, p. 10.

A few vocal principles are presented, largely applicable to the speaking voice.

632. Warren, Frederic. "The Control of Vocal Resonance." *Musician*, New York, August, 1934, Vol. 39, p. 8.

The distinction between nasal resonance and nasal twang is discussed. The former needs to be cultivated; the latter should be shunned.

633. —— "Extra Load Carried by American Singers." *Musician*, New York, September, 1933, Vol. 38, p. 8.

We should have our own school of opera, stressing the great and noble English language. Some notes on American and foreign vowels are added.

634. —— "Forces That Give Vitality to Singing." *Musician*, New York, May, 1935, Vol. 40, p. 13.

No one can learn vocal technique without conscious effort. The battle of the conscious and the unconscious is present at every singing lesson. Right teaching will resolve this conflict.

635. —— "How to Equalize the Voice." *Musician*, New York, November, 1934, Vol. 39, p. 4.

Vowel alteration on high notes is advocated.

636. —— "Page for Singers." *Musician*, New York, August, 1932, Vol. 37, p. 10.

Nasal resonance and breath control are discussed. No need to fear technical study. It is fundamental to vocal mastery.

637. —— "Some First Aids for the Beginner." *Musician*, New York, January, 1931, Vol. 36, p. 14.

Relaxation, economy of effort and vocal hygiene are briefly discussed.

638. —— "Warning to Singers Who Would Discard Exercises." *Musician*, New York, December, 1928, Vol. 33, p. 31.

Vocal exercises are a means to an end and must not be ignored. Technique is discussed.

639. —— "What is Meant by the Term 'Sing Naturally?'" *Musician*, New York, February, 1929, Vol. 34, p. 41.

The expression "sing naturally" is defined and upheld in a brief statement.

640. —— "What Master Singers Tell Us about Breathing." *Musician*, New York, November, 1931, Vol. 36, p. 25.

The physiology of breathing is related to high chest position. A survey of opinions on breathing.

641. Waters, Crystal. "Are You Ready to Sing in Public?" *Etude*, Philadelphia, 1940, Vol. 58, p. 593.

The analysis and mastery of a song is a detailed process calling for intensive systematic study. A self-analytical procedure is outlined for achieving artistic thoroughness in song study.

642. —— "Bridging the Voice." *Etude*, Philadelphia, 1942, Vol. 60, p. 449.

A unique treatment for blending vocal registers.

643. —— "How Expressive Is Your Singing?" *Etude*, Philadelphia, 1940, Vol. 58, p. 667.

Natural emotions tighten the throat and choke the voice. Hence the singer must simulate emotions, not feel them. Expression in art is entirely different than that of actual human experience.

644. —— "Is Your Voice Working for You?" *Musician*, New York, May, 1929, Vol. 34, p. 33.

We liberate our true selves, eliminate emotional tensions and live life more abundantly through correct vocal expression in singing.

645. —— "Let Acoustics Bring Resonance into Your Voice." *Etude*, Philadelphia, 1941, Vol. 59, p. 381.

Fundamental acoustical facts are briefly discussed. Several tongue gymnastics are given to help relax the throat.

646. ———— "Most Rapid Way to Improve Your Voice." *Etude*, Philadelphia, 1940, Vol. 58, p. 165.

Imitation is a useful device in vocal teaching. Posture, open throat, breathing, resonance, diction and interpretation are cursorily discussed.

647. ———— *Song, the Substance of Vocal Study*. Schirmer, New York, 1930.

Lists of study songs are given, exemplifying each principle of practice. Good for teaching repertory. Useful hints.

648. ———— "Your Ears and Your Voice." *Etude*, Philadelphia, 1941, Vol. 59, p. 817.

The ears are vital to vocal expression. You must hear a tone before you can sing it. Hence learn to listen consciously to your own voice at all times.

649. ———— "Your Voice." *Woman's Home Companion*, Springfield, Ohio, April, 1939, Vol. 66, p. 15.

Seven vocal rules are given, including brief comment on posture, breathing, resonance and diction.

650. Weer, Robert Lawrence. *My Views on Voice Production*. The author, Boston, 1941.

The author's views are interesting but the treatment is too generalized for practical purposes. Personal hints take the place of exercises.

651. Westerman, Kenneth N. "Dynamic Phonetics and Their Use in Voice Training Classes." *Music Educators National Conference*, Chicago, 1936, Vol. 29, p. 211.

Combinations of vowels and consonants are considered in four phonetic groups that favor voice production.

652. ———— "The Physiology of Vibrato." *Music Educators Journal*, Chicago, March, 1938, Vol. 24, p. 48.

Interesting observations on the innervation and musculature of phonation.

653. ———— "Speech and Singing." *Educational Music Magazine*, Chicago, September-October, 1939, Vol. 19, p. 18.

A comparison of these two types of vocal expression indicates that singing is an emergent growth from the natural basic functions of the speech organs involved.

654. Wettergren, Gertrud. "Care of the Voice." (An interview.) *Etude*, Philadelphia, 1937, Vol. 55, p. 293.

The teacher-pupil relationship must be one of perfect harmony and understanding for best vocal results. The best teachers can fail for want of the right approach.

655. Wharton, Florence C. *Rotary Voice Method*. Augsburg Publishing House, Minneapolis, 1937.

The book includes a résumé of vocal principles, some vocalises for group practice and a long list of songs for study and repertory. There are many false assumptions.

656. Wheeler, Francis. "The Relation of the Paranasal Sinuses to the Singing Voice." *Science n. s.*, New York, 1930, Vol. 72, p. 630.

Anatomical differences in head structures determine differences in range, volume and quality according to X-ray experimental investigations now under way.

657. White, Ernest George. *Light on the Voice Beautiful.* J. Clarke and Company, London, 1931.

The author's almost unbelievable thesis that phonation occurs in the sinuses of the head and not in the larynx is discussed exhaustively by many vocal authorities.

658. —— *Science and Singing.* J. M. Dent and Sons, London, 1938, 5th edition.

The author pursues his main argument that voice is generated in the sinuses and not in the larynx. His case is presented with infinite detail and thoroughness.

659. —— *Sinus Tone Production.* J. M. Dent and Sons, London, 1938.

This is the third book in the author's trilogy on vocal tone production in the sinuses. Photographs and diagrams are included.

660. Whitfield, Ernest O. "Baritone or Tenor? a Vital Decision for Singers." *Musician*, New York, July, 1932, Vol. 37, p. 11.

The voice will assume its natural range only by effortless singing, not by striving up or down the scale.

661. —— "Building Confidence among Voice Students." *Musician*, New York, May, 1933, Vol. 38, p. 11.

Modern teaching methods demand a truthful exchange of ideas between teacher and pupil, not martinet tactics and mystical allusions to the unknown.

662. Whittaker, William Gillies. *Class Singing.* Oxford University Press, London, 1930, 2d edition.

A helpful, though conventional teaching guide.

663. Wielich, Ludwig. "Schumann-Heink Turns to the American Girl." (An interview.) *Musician*, New York, October, 1930, Vol. 35, p. 7.

A great singer offers to teach the younger generation what she knows about singing. Few vocal ideas are discussed in this interview.

664. Wilcke, Eva. *German Diction in Singing.* (English translation.) E. P. Dutton, New York, 1930, revised edition.

A short chapter on vocal physiology yields little significant information to the singer or teacher,

665. Wilcox, John C. "Advanced Pupil; What to Study." *Etude*, Philadelphia, 1928, Vol. 46, p. 690.

The question of repertory is considered. The singer is a "vocal athlete" and needs systematic exercise to keep in condition, no matter how advanced he is.

666. —— "A Brief Outline of the Theory of Voice." *Music Teachers National Association Proceedings for 1933*, Oberlin, Ohio, 1934, Vol. 28, p. 134.

Some principles are presented and discussed briefly.

667. —— "Developing the Voice for Song and Speech; breath control." *Etude*, Philadelphia, 1928, Vol. 46, p. 304.

The intensity of the singer's emotion will automatically stimulate a corresponding intensity of the physical action which governs voice production. Psychological approaches are considered and simple physical exercises given.

668. —— "Fundamental Voice Training." *Music Teachers National Association Proceedings for 1940*, Pittsburgh, 1941, Vol. 35, p. 361.
A general teaching procedure is outlined and discussed.

669. —— *The Living Voice*. Carl Fischer, New York, 1935.
A presentation of personal opinions with some vocal exercises.

670. —— "Prescribing Perky Practise for Vocal Students." *Musician*, New York, December, 1933, Vol. 38, p. 10.
The early part of each lesson should be devoted to infusing a joyous buoyancy into the student's attitude.

671. —— "Why Do They Sing off Pitch?" *Etude*, Philadelphia, 1937, Vol. 55, p. 49.
Lapses in pitch accuracy are caused by lack of mental concentration or the presence of throat tensions during phonation.

672. Williamson, John F. "Training of the Individual Voice through Choral Singing." *Music Teachers National Association Proceedings for 1938*, Oberlin, Ohio, 1939, Vol. 33, p. 52.
Several teaching fallacies are clarified from a practical viewpoint. The comments on diction are especially helpful.

673. Wilson, Harry Robert. *Lead a Song!* Hall and McCreary, Chicago, 1942.
A practical and thorough-going treatment of the song leaders' problems. There is meaty advice on every page.

674. —— *The Solo Singer*. Carl Fischer, New York, 1941, Vols. I and II.
"Learn to sing by singing" is the author's method. Each principle of voice production is succinctly presented and illustrated with appropriate vocalises, excellent practice songs and teaching procedures.

675. Witherspoon, Herbert. "Demonstration of Visual Method of Voice Instruction." *Music Supervisors National Conference Proceedings*, Ithaca, New York, 1929, Vol. 22, p. 336.
A cursory and amusing discussion of typical teaching problems.

676. —— "Style in Singing." *Etude*, Philadelphia, 1928, Vol. 46, p. 917.
Expression and technic must go hand in hand. Even exercises should be sung with some definite mood value. The fundamentals of style are defined.

677. —— *Thirty-six Lessons in Singing for Teachers and Students*. Miessner Institute of Music, Chicago, 1930.
An excellent digest of old and new methods embodied in a practical system of instruction. The author speaks from twenty-five years of experience, not hearsay or fancy. Intelligent and informative.

678. Wodell, Frederick W., "How Listening Helps Intonation." *Etude*, Philadelphia, 1931, Vol. 49, p. 659.
The reactions of individual students differ. Hence verbal instruction is not always reliable as standard teaching procedure. Listening to models should be more often resorted to.

679. —— "The Proper Training and Use of the Voice of Persons of School Age." *Etude*, Philadelphia, 1929, Vol. 47, p. 678.
An intelligible and useful résumé of teaching principles for developing youthful voices.

680. —— "Stepping Stones to Successful Singing." *Etude*, Philadelphia, 1928, Vol. 46, p. 776.

A few workable principles are extracted from historical sources and discussed.

681. —— "Taking Some Bunk out of Vocal Teaching in the Public Schools." *Music Supervisors National Conference Yearbook*, Chicago, 1931, Vol. 24, p. 92.

The author is impatient with some of the methods of voice culture now in common use but expresses his own opinions arbitrarily. The teaching of voice should be foremost in the music curriculum.

682. —— "Thoughts about Placing." *Etude*, Philadelphia, 1929, Vol. 47, p. 126.

Voice placement means placing the sensation of tonal vibration. Indirect devices are recommended as a preventative for local effort and straining tendencies.

683. Wolf, S. K., Stanley, D., and Sette, W. J. "Quantitative Studies on the Singing Voice." *Journal Acoustical Society of America*, Lancaster, Pennsylvania, 1935, Vol. 6, p. 265.

Acoustical analyses of tones of different singers reveal interesting characteristics of good vocal quality.

684. Wolfe, Eugene. "Study of Foreign Languages a Vital Aid to Singers." *Musician*, New York, March, 1929, Vol. 34, p. 34.

The fear of foreign language study is to be overcome by using teaching methods which the author advocates.

685. Wood, Clifton Holmes. *Vocal Vigor in Speech and Song*. Clifton Wood, Worcester, Massachusetts, 1937.

Physical and vocal gymnastics are combined in a series of sixty lessons without actually singing a song. There is much philosophical advice culled from personal reminiscences of a vocal career.

686. Wood, Sir Henry Joseph. *The Gentle Art of Singing*. Oxford University Press, London, 1930.

A brief explanatory text is followed by four volumes of vocalises and exercises exhaustively treated. The practice material is incredibly thorough. Every conceivable combination of notes is listed.

687. Woods, Glenn Howard. "Developing Our Vocal Heritage." *Supervisors Service Bulletin*, Chicago, November, 1932, Vol. 12, p. 7.

The purposes and benefits of voice training in the schools are discussed.

688. —— *Ensemble Intonation*. Music Products Corporation, Chicago, 1937.

A useful conductor's guide for teaching vocal groups. Many practical hints are included.

689. —— "On Voice Range." *Educational Music Magazine*, Chicago, March, 1941, Vol. 20, p. 48.

Some general remarks on improving range by means of vocal exercises.

690. Woodside, James. *Style in Singing and Song Interpretation*. Haywood Institute, New York, 1931.

A compendium of useful hints on the artistic interpretation of songs.

691. *Wullen, Hilda H. "Inborn Qualities of the Human Voice." Eugenical News, New York, October, 1931, Vol. 16, p. 176.

There is evidence that vocal timbre and range are inherited characteristics. A brief discussion of sex factors in vocal development is given.

692. Wycoff, Eva Emmett. "Bringing Out the Singing Voice." Etude, Philadelphia, 1930, Vol. 48, p. 507.

Constant attention to forward tone production will prevent pitch deviations and distortion of vowels. Straining comes with improper breath control.

693. ———— "Essentials for the Singer." Etude, Philadelphia, 1928, Vol. 46, p. 136.

A few general remarks on open throat, breathing and musicianship for the vocalist. The less one thinks of muscles or their names, the more natural singing becomes.

694. ———— "Good and Bad Habits in Singing." Etude, Philadelphia, 1935, Vol. 53, p. 741.

Children unconsciously imitate the bad vocal habits of their elders. Correct posture and the value of physical and mental coordination in singing are briefly discussed.

695. ———— "Mind, the Strong Factor in Singing." Etude, Philadelphia, 1935, Vol. 53, p. 543.

Natural breathing and interpretation are discussed.

696. ———— "Suggestions for the Singer." Etude, Philadelphia, 1941, Vol. 59, p. 306.

Enunciation, breathing and resonance are considered with several corrective suggestions added. The author's terminology is vague.

697. Yarroll, Harold Reeves. "Some Neglected Phases of Vocal Study." Musician, New York, March, 1936, Vol. 41, p. 54.

Abstract problems of tone production have no practical value for the individual voice.

698. Young, T. Campbell. " 'Vocal Diction'—in a Nutshell." Music Supervisors Journal, Chicago, October, 1932, Vol. 19, p. 28.

An interesting and concise summation of vowel and consonant production techniques used in singing. Vocal continuity in diction is stressed.

699. Zerffi, William A. C. "Misconceptions Over Natural Singing." Musician, New York, July, 1933, Vol. 38, p. 4.

Everyone who can carry a tune can also learn to sing. The swallowing reflexes prevent so-called natural voice production. These ideas are briefly discussed.

700. ———— "Must One Sing with an Open Throat?" Musician, New York, October, 1932, Vol. 37, p. 13.

An inquiry into the meaning of teaching nostrums that emphasize the "open throat" phrase.

701. ———— "Singing Is Musical Athletics." *Musician*, New York, January, 1934, Vol. 39, p. 17.

The vocalist, like the boxer, must follow a certain routine procedure and as long as satisfactory results are forthcoming he must persist with regularity in this routine.

702. *Ziegler, Mme. Anna E. "Pioneer in the Fight on Vocal Chaos." *Musician*, New York, June, 1933, Vol. 38, p. 7.

A brief account of the work of the author in organizing the first national singing teachers association in this country.

* *The materials contained in items marked with an asterisk were not useful to this study.*

Additional Sources Cited

703. American Academy of Teachers of Singing. "Singing English." (Printed leaflet issued by the *Academy* in 1932)

704. Apel, Willi. *Harvard Dictionary of Music.* Harvard University Press, Cambridge, Mass., 1945.

705. Glenn, Mabelle and Spouse, Alfred. *Art Songs for School and Studio.* Oliver Ditson Company, Philadelphia, 1934.

706. Good, Carter V., Editor. *Dictionary of Education.* McGraw-Hill, New York, 1945.

707. *Gray's Anatomy.* Lea & Febiger, Philadelphia, 1942.

708. *Grove's Dictionary of Music and Musicians.* (Third Edition) Macmillan, New York, 1941. 5 volumes.

709. Hale, L. L. *Rush's Philosophy of Voice.* Doctoral dissertation (in manuscript). Louisiana state University, Baton Rouge, La., 1942.

710. Haydon, Glen. *Introduction to Musicology.* Prentice-Hall, New York, 1941.

711. James, William. *Principles of Psychology.* Henry Holt, New York, 1918. vol 1.

712. Russell, G. Oscar. *The Vowel.* Ohio State University Press, Columbus, Ohio, 1928.

713. *Starling's Principles of Human Physiology.* (Fifth Edition) Lea & Febiger, Philadelphia, 1930.

714. Van der Veer, Nevada. "What Are We Doing with the Individual Voice?" *Music Teachers National Association Proceedings for 1944*, Pittsburgh, Pa., 1944. vol. 38, p. 316.

INDEX

Abdominal breathing, 73; compression, 95; muscles, 73; wall, 82

Accents, 110

Accompaniment, defined, 57; dependency upon, 57, 67

Acoustics, 123, 131, 142

Adam's apple, 124

Adult vocal range, 150

Aesthetic, benefits, 61; effect, 132, 137, 141, 218, 238, 241

Ah vowel, 120, 194, 201

Air pressure, in lungs, 74, 88; tracheal, 105

Amateur singers, 68

Amplitude, 132, 101; issuing sound wave, 174; vibratory swing, 170

Analogies, acoustical, 102; bugle, 125, 174; guy wires, 127; horn player, 102; loudspeaker, 137; mouthpiece, 102, 129, 138; musical instrument, 101, 129; nozzle, 127; open tube, 138; player's lips, 138; reed instrument, 102; siren, 102; stringed instrument, 100, 102; violin, 180; wheatfield, 131; wind instrument, 89, 96, 102, 138, 170

Analysis of technical problems, 62

Annotations, 13, 266

Anticipation, defined, 112

Anxieties, mental, 165

Appogiatura, 232

Aria, rendition of, 93, 229

Arpeggios, practicing, 160-161

Articulation, 101, 190, 196, 197; defined, 190

Artist singers, 42, 110, 218, 220, 235, 237, 242; vibrato characteristics, 110

Artistic, deviations, 121, 188, 218; performance, criteria of, 28, 72, 94, 95, 127, 214, 218, 235, 236-238

Artistic rating, 168

Arytenoid, cartilages, 98, 104, 106, 107, 124; muscle, 151

Attack, 74, 85, 113, 122, 196, 241; defined, 120; evenness of, 92, 121; first vocal vibrations, 58; gliding, 121, 219; high tone, 159; improvement of, 120, 121; moment of, 83, 92, 93, 121

Audience comprehension, 78, 215, 227

Auditory sense, 178, 182

Auditory visualization defined, 180

Aural concepts, 200; visualization, 112, 196

Authorities disagree, 4, 122

Authors, complaints of, 3; diversified viewpoints, 60, 245; pretentious claims, 59; their reputations, 12, 59

Bach's songs for breathing exercises, 78

Baritone, 147

Bass, 147

Basso-profundo, 149

Beginners, 56, 68, 171, 184, 185, 227, 228, 229; advice to, 23, 61, 89; defined, 49; exercises, 78, 160; first lessons, 51, 66; handling, 49, 65

Behavior, bodily, 101

Bel canto, 9, 24, 25, 31, 44, 58, 84, 141, 173, 180, 181, 192, 200, 206, 232, 237

Bellows, 85, 86

Bibliographic, information on card, 12; period, 10

Bibliographies, reference to, 1, 2, 4, 14

Bibliography, annotated, 14, 245, 266

Bone conduction, 100, 153

Bones as resonators, 137

Breast bone, 82

Breath, 47, 72, 101; capacity, 69, 88; economy of, 47, 77, 85, 88, 89, 90, 91; endurance, 79, 94; energy, 170; experimental study, 92; focusing the, 95; gradual release, 90; in diction, 212; intake, 121, 75; renewal, 69, 88, 92; retention, 83, 86, 90, 93; supply, 76, 138, 174; support, 73, 75, 84, 88, 91, 170; suspension, 73-74; sustained, 93; quantity of, 85, 88, 89

Breath control, artistic, 236; by hearing, 180; in infancy, 75; in sleep, 75; interpretational, 75, 78; methods of cultivating,